3 —

WORSHIP

WORSHIP

A STUDY OF CORPORATE DEVOTION

by

Luther D. Reed

MUHLENBERG PRESS

PHILADELPHIA

TO
MINISTERS, ORGANISTS
AND ALL OTHERS
WHOSE PRIVILEGE
AND RESPONSIBILITY IT IS
TO ORDER THE CORPORATE WORSHIP
OF THE CHURCH

FOREWORD

The *Service Book and Hymnal* of the Lutheran Church in America provides the church in the United States and Canada with a Common Liturgy and a Common Hymnal. This book will order public worship for many years to come, and should materially unify and strengthen the church in the Western world. The appearance of this major work suggests the possible helpfulness of a discussion of the principles and forms of corporate worship, together with practical suggestions for the use of worship materials.

Worship as a subject is as old as religion. As an activity of the living church it is as new as today and tomorrow. Many arts assist in it. Architecture, sculpture, painting, wood carving, metal work, embroidery—all these bring their offerings before the service hour and stand silent in the outer court. The Liturgy and the music of the church alone, as living, vocal arts, enter the inner sanctuary. The Liturgy embodies the faith as well as the corporate devotion of the church. Music enlivens the text, and by its emotional eloquence inspires worshipers to offer their sacrifices of prayer, praise, and thanksgiving. Because of the special importance of these two related arts they are given particular attention in this volume.

Worship attains its peaks of power in the regular ministrations of the sanctuary, rather than in outbursts of evangelistic fervor or reformatory zeal. The church is strengthened for every service in every area by the regular administration and reception of the Means of Grace in the corporate worship of countless congregations throughout the world. In a very real sense it is the congregation—the church itself—that worships.

In the leadership of this corporate activity two personalities are especially important—the minister and the organist-choirmaster. Others render valuable assistance. It is the author's hope that the present volume, which seeks to uphold liturgical and musical ideals in a practical way, may quicken interest and understanding in every aspect of this subject, not only among ministers, organists, and choirmasters, but also among theological students, choir members, and other thoughtful church people.

It will be evident that the material concerns itself primarily with the Liturgy and the Hymnal of the Lutheran Church and with the special responsibility borne by ministers and organist-choirmasters in this communion. It is possible, however, that students of the Liturgy, hymnody, and church music in other communions may find some interest in this work because of its comprehensive character and the comparative method employed throughout. A broad acquaintance with the whole field is a basic requirement for successful work everywhere. Proper proportion here, as in everything else, requires wholeness, with ample dimensions of depth, breadth, and height.

Chapters 5-9, 12, and 13 may serve as a brief introduction to the new *Service Book and Hymnal.* They describe its backgrounds, history, preparation, and significance, and offer explanations of its liturgical, hymnological, and musical materials. This will not trespass upon the wider field of a *Companion to the Liturgy* and a *Handbook to the Hymnal* which the Commissions have projected. These future works will discuss text and music much more thoroughly and in greater detail.

In this volume we have condensed or expanded material which appeared in printed reports to the churches and in articles in the church press. Several chapters are based upon articles and addresses of the author, which, at various times, reached limited circles in the columns of *The Lutheran, The Lutheran Quarterly, The American Architect, The Lutheran World* (Geneva), the *Evangelisch-Lutherische Kirchenzeitung* (Berlin), and other periodicals. More than four-fifths of the material, however, has been written specially for this volume.

In the interest of the general reader, the work is not heavily weighted with footnotes or other documentary material. Some bibliographical references are incorporated in the text. Specific directions and suggestions are given, but the real purpose is informative, inspirational, and cultural in a churchly sense, and not one of emphasis upon ritual detail or musical minutia. The wholeness and the unity of corporate worship are demonstrated by discussion of principles, origins, and development, and by comparison of systems, with special study of our own. While mindful of the doctrinal requirements of the Lutheran Church, this study is sensitive to the climate of a variety of cultural backgrounds. Its one purpose is to uphold standards of liturgical and musical propriety and performance in every area of corporate worship.

The author is not a ceremonialist or an extremist. To him the Liturgy is much more than the ceremonies that may or may not accompany it, and liturgical worship is much more than pageantry. He has no desire to introduce the principles and practices of Anglo-Catholicism into Lutheran services. He has no consuming interest in mechanical multiplications of celebrations of the Sacrament, in reservation of the consecrated host, in the general reintroduction of the full round of historic vestments, in the stations of the cross, the kissing of stoles, the use of incense, the multiplication of lights, genuflections, and signings of the cross, in crucifers, torch bearers, and the like. He appreciates the historic and symbolic considerations which give some of these features appeal, and which may be advanced in explanation of their use. He believes that extreme ceremonialism emphasizes externals which, in many instances, are so definitely identified with erroneous doctrine that features such as these should not be lightly reintroduced in evangelical services. Some of them may be unobjectionable in themselves; others are of doubtful value; and still others are misleading.

With this understood, the author would also say that there is a proper amount of pure ceremonial which should be studied and performed. The Liturgy is action. The position and the bodily movements of all who conduct the services of the church are important. These should conform to established principles and forms of ceremonial procedures.

The historic and confessional position of the Lutheran Church gives the individual pastor and congregation wide liberty in these matters. The principle of liberty also is deeply rooted in American thought and life. As a Lutheran, and as an American, the author would contend for full recognition of these facts. We have every right to study, and possibly to recover, lost ceremonies that were common practice in our church in the sixteenth century. Their reintroduction in our services today is not merely a question of right, but also one of wisdom and of concern for the good of the whole church. Liberty imposes responsibility, and liberty may be denied the irresponsible. In the exercise of his liberty the minister must act selflessly. He must put the welfare of the congregation, its growth and influence in the community, and the best interests of the whole church ahead of personal preferences or historic or aesthetic considerations. The wise churchman will willingly surrender some of the liberty that is his in consideration of the rights of others and in his concern for the common good.

Perhaps one other observation should be made. There is no desire on the author's part to downgrade the sermon, or to minimize its importance by stressing liturgical proprieties, the uniqueness and power of the Sacrament, and values in more frequent celebrations. The sermon is a vital and valuable element in the Service. We would strengthen it, and thus increase the spiritual dynamic of the Service as a whole. Sermon and Sacrament are twin peaks in the mountain range of liturgical worship. Homiletics, however, is a science and an art in its own right. Cultivation of this special field must be promoted by those specially qualified to analyze its problems, demonstrate its methods, and improve its performance. We are concerned chiefly with deficiencies in the liturgical field.

No one can deny that our services are often crudely, prosaically, and incorrectly conducted. Good practice and real progress can only be expected from those who understand and love the Liturgy and its music. The author would encourage all proper efforts for enrichment and improvement. Since this particular field is a favorite for enthusiasts, extremists, and aesthetes, he would admonish all to act selflessly and ever to seek the good of the greatest number.

The author has personally lived through eras and areas when and where it was necessary to argue even for the use of a black gown by the minister, for a cross on the altar, or for an altar itself. More than half a century ago, in association with Harry G. Archer of Pittsburgh, Pennsylvania, he introduced plainsong to the Lutheran Church in America in a series of books which provided complete, historic plainsong settings to the Liturgy. These full-scale studies attracted little attention at the time. Today our ablest musicians are making generous use of many forms of plainsong in our services, and are calling for more and more of it.

Thus in these and in many other respects, we have seen conditions improve and practices prevail which but a few decades ago occasioned bitter controversy. Forms and ceremonies opposed violently today may become commonplace tomorrow. Understanding this fully, we continue to urge selflessness and moderation as we offer these pages and all possible encouragement to all who are able to read the poetry of worship; to all who would guard its purity, promote its study, and enhance its beauty; to all who would honor and glorify the God and Father of us all in the assemblies of his people.

There remains the pleasant duty of acknowledging help received from colleagues and friends. Particularly would we mention those who prepared the three musical settings of the Liturgy in the new *Service Book:* Dr. Harold W. Gilbert, choirmaster of St. Peter's Episcopal Church, Philadelphia, and principal of its famous choir school; Mrs. Regina Holmen Fryxell, organist and composer of Rock Island, Illinois; and Mr. Ernest White, distinguished recitalist and organist-choirmaster of the Episcopal Church of St. Mary the Virgin, New York City. All of these have supplied information concerning their settings and given other assistance. Also helpful was the author's friend, William T. Timmings, Mus.Doc., for more than thirty years choirmaster of St. Michael's Lutheran Church, Germantown, Philadelphia, of which congregation the author is a member. Dr. Timmings reviewed all the chapters dealing with the work of the organist-choirmaster, made helpful suggestions, and prepared a list of anthems and several sets of organ specifications for the book. Colleagues and friends on the two Joint Commissions have also been helpful in determining details—particularly Drs. Edward Traill Horn, III, George R. Seltzer, and William R. Seaman of the eastern "study group"; Professor Leland B. Sateren of Augsburg College, Minneapolis; Dr. E. E. Ryden, editor of the *Lutheran Companion*, Rock Island, Illinois; President Conrad Bergendoff of Augustana College, Rock Island; and Dr. Ulrich S. Leupold of the Lutheran Theological Seminary, Waterloo, Canada. Dr. Edgar S. Brown, Jr., director of the Department of Worship of the United Lutheran Church in America, also read several chapters of the manuscript and gave helpful suggestions.

The illustrations in the book are designed to show the fine work that has been done within the past few decades by American architects in designing church buildings in every part of the country. Monumental structures such as the cathedrals in New York and Washington, the great university chapels at Princeton and Chicago, and the impressive Mellon Memorial Presbyterian Church in Pittsburgh have not been included. Rather the effort has been to select fine parish churches of moderate size and representing all periods and styles from early Colonial to the contemporary. Whether current experiment will eventually crystallize into a definite style only the future can reveal. However, apparently uncontrollable factors such as new materials and methods, mounting costs, and professional interest in novel and personal expressions will probably continue this type of design and construction for a very long time.

We should welcome serious modern work, resourceful and reverent, if it does not break completely with the past and if it respects the unique mission and character of the church as a divinely constituted institution in human society. Individual novelties, however clever, if they are freakish, brutal, grotesque, or merely silly are entirely inappropriate for the church and unfit for the worship of Almighty God whose Holy Name we dare not take in vain in architecture or anything else. Much contemporary work in architecture, music, and art is excellent. Some is sheer blasphemy, and should never be accepted by any Christian congregation or institution.

The author has special satisfaction in the fact that with a few exceptions all the architects whose work is shown are his personal friends and associates. Mr. George I. Lovatt and the late Eliel Saarinen were personally unknown to him. Others are the author's friends. And to them, his colleagues in the work of the Church Architectural Guild of America, he would express his grateful thanks for their interest and hearty co-operation. Among them are Messrs. Arland A. Dirlam of

Boston; Edward F. Jansson of Chicago; Harry E. Warren of New York City; T. Norman Mansell, William Heyl Thompson, and Harold E. Wagoner of Philadelphia; Philip Hubert Frohman of Washington, D. C.; and J. Alfred Hamme of York, Pennsylvania.

Finally, the author is indebted for many courtesies to Miss Margaret Janvier Hort, Librarian of the Krauth Memorial Library of the Lutheran Theological Seminary at Philadelphia, and her staff; and also to Mr. James P. Berg, candidate of theology, who typed the greater portion of the manuscript prepared the index, and offered many helpful suggestions.

LUTHER D. REED

Monday in Whitsun-Week
1959

CONTENTS

Chapter 1

WORSHIP:
AN EXPERIENCE AND AN INSTITUTION

AS AN EXPERIENCE

Corporate worship is more than an experience of the individual. But it must be an individual experience. This experience is realized in that spiritual transaction in which the individual associates himself with fellow-believers in a series of worshipful thoughts, words, and acts. As this kind of an experience, regularly repeated and planned for by the entire church, public worship has become an institution.

We cannot analyze the elements of worship with precision. Certain features may be mentioned, but their deepest values vanish under analysis, even as the loveliness of a flower is lost when we pick it to pieces. Nor is it wise to emphasize the purely psychological approach to the subject. Psychology, used alone, is too subjective a principle to be a safe guide in a field traversed by ancient highways and filled with historic monuments. Keeping broad churchly considerations in mind, we venture to enumerate some aspects of the experience of corporate worship.

The Spirit of Obedience. Obedience is the foundation stone upon which the structure of corporate worship is built. God's love, mercy, and grace were first revealed to the Disciples by their Master, and ours, Jesus Christ. The Saviour's commands, as well, were first given to them. These gifts and these commands have come down together even to us in our own time through an unbroken succession of discipleship. We, too, as true disciples, must obey his commands as well as accept his gifts.

Our Lord's commands, as they relate to corporate worship, encompass the two marks and major concerns of the church in every age. These are the Word and the sacraments. Our Saviour said to the Dis-

1

ciples of old, and he says to us today, "Go ye, therefore, and teach all nations, baptizing them in the name of the Father, and of the Son, and of the Holy Ghost." He also said to them, and he says to us, "This do in remembrance of me."

Corporate Christian worship derives from these great commands. The Liturgy, and all that is involved in liturgical worship in related fields —architecture, music, hymnody, and art—are corporate expressions of the church's faith and fellowship. But first of all, they are instruments for effective administration of the divinely appointed Means of Grace.

Obedience is the way to life and salvation. Disobedience leads into the wilderness of death. Like the great Apostle, we dare not be "disobedient unto the heavenly vision."

The Spirit of Reverence. The next facet of our subject glows with the spirit of reverence. The heathen, as he worships his deity, is moved by awe and fear. The young Isaiah saw a vision of the holiness and glory of God. He came away convinced that he was sinful.

Christian worship is something more than heathen worship purified or Jewish worship intensified. It is new and different. Yet we, too, instinctively humble ourselves in the presence of our Creator. We approach the All-Holy with reverence and ascribe to him majesty, might, and supreme worth. Luther, when saying his first Mass, was so overcome at the thought of coming into the presence of the living God that he was tempted to flee from the altar.

This matter of awe and reverence in worship has been given great significance by Rudolf Otto in his *Idea of the Holy,* as well as by Von Ogden Vogt and Willard Sperry in later discussions. It is well for us to be reminded that even though we approach God in love and not in fear, we must still "so fear and love him" as not to enter his house thoughtlessly or speak his Name lightly.

The Spirit of Communion. Yet we worship no distant God. We enter the Lord's house not as strangers but as children of the household. There is a wistful desire for a touch of the Father's hand, for an assurance of his presence, for a glimpse into his heart. Our thought reaches out beyond mere aspiration or mystical contemplation. It achieves a spiritual contact and establishes a personal communion with the divine Spirit. It is a communion which involves a real exchange, and by this exchange the fabric of worship is woven.

The idea of communion roots back, through Thomas à Kempis and Bernard of Clairvaux, in patristic and Johannine thought. It has received characteristic development in Lutheran theology and worship.

2

It gives significant meaning to our doctrines of the person of Christ, of the Spirit, and of the Word. It explains our belief that in the Lord's Supper we are incorporated with Christ so that we are truly in him and he in us. It undergirds the whole fabric of our worship, with its interplay of sacramental or objective, and sacrificial or subjective, elements. The sacramental elements include all that God imparts in repeated gifts of grace, all that rests upon his revelation—the Lessons, the Declaration of Grace, the Administration of the Sacraments, the Benediction, et cetera. The sacrificial elements are our response in prayer, praise, and thanksgiving—the Confession, the Kyrie, the Gloria, the Creed, the Canticles, the Prayer of the Church, et cetera. The minister, by his position at the altar, interprets these two elements in worship. The individual worshiper has an experience of communion with God which he could not realize in equal measure at home or alone.

The Spirit of Fellowship. Corporate worship is not only reverence for God and communion with him. It is also communion with our fellow-believers, and fellowship with the saints of all ages. True and sincere thoughts of God both draw us to him and bind us to one another. We are aware of the fellowship of kindred spirits, and of the fact that we are participating in a spiritual activity whose range covers centuries and continents. This sharing of a religious experience with others gives the individual worshiper strength and inspiration. Especially so if we keep in mind that our worshiping fellowship includes the "multitudes which no man can number" and "all the company of heaven." The supreme dimension of worship is not depth or breadth, but height.

Our Lord's discourse concerning the true vine and the branches suggests communion with Christ and fellowship among Christians. St. Paul in calling the church the body of Christ emphasizes the same thought. Augustine stressed the Eucharist as the "Sacrament of Unity." By doing away with private masses and restoring the Communion to the people, the Reformation gave powerful impetus to the idea of fellowship as an important element in worship.

In such fellowship the associations of history assert themselves, and the idea of the church as the communion of saints takes on mighty power. The thought and the prayers of the church not only encompass past centuries, but reach out as well with noble breadth of petition and intercession for all sorts and conditions of men and for the needs of the whole world. These ideas are realized in corporate worship. From communion with God worshipers receive peace and power as from a great transaction. From communion with men they derive a wealth

3

of human understanding and sympathy and a heightened sense of responsibility.

The Spirit of Sacrifice. The quieter moods of reverence, communion, and fellowship are balanced in worship by more active principles. The first of these is the spirit of sacrifice. The medieval church so exaggerated the false idea of propitiatory sacrifice that Protestant worship often fails to appreciate the intrinsic values in the eucharistic sacrifice of prayer, praise, and thanksgiving. Our very understanding of worship as communion with God implies the necessity of an interchange, of a response to God's gifts. Our worship must move us to give and to do, as well as to accept. Corporate worship involves the church's self-oblation to God through Christ. The unity of the church, the mystical body of Christ, reveals itself in corporate acts of prayer, praise, and thanksgiving, and shines forth in Christian service. The innermost meaning of the New Testament terms *leiturgia, latreia, diakonia* (the service of God) comes to expression in St. Paul's definition of worship as the dedication of our "bodies as a living sacrifice, consecrated and acceptable to God; that is your cult, a spiritual rite" (Rom. 12:1, Moffatt).

The word "eucharist" (thanksgiving) was the universal name for the Lord's Supper as early as the second century. Bishop Gore tells us that "early canons suggest that the Christian eucharist in the first age must have frequently resembled a modern harvest thanksgiving." Our services today, purified of false ideas of sacrifice, are yet rich in these same elements of praise and prayer. We are exhorted to "give thanks unto the Lord our God," and we "laud and magnify" God in every act of corporate worship.

Every church service, like every cathedral or church building, is an assertion of the faith and sacrifice which has filled the world with monuments of devotion. The spirit of consecration and service which builds and maintains churches to the glory of God and fills them with works of art and wonderful music, which supports institutions of Christian learning and mercy, and which girds the globe with missions—this spirit is developed and maintained chiefly by the inspiration of the sanctuary and its worship.

The Spirit of Celebration. The festival element is a feature of all religions. We elevate certain days and occasions above the level of the ordinary and focus the devotion of many upon a common theme. The Lord's day, no less than Easter, was from the beginning a celebration of the Resurrection. Celebrations of other events built up the church

4

year. The Liturgy incorporated the ideas of particular festivals by expanding its Propers.

The idea of celebration enters every Service. Every Lord's day is a festival. Every observance of the Lord's Supper is a celebration as well as an administration. The Preface, the Sanctus, and many other parts of the Service are keyed to the thought of glorious, exalted celebration. The mere fact of celebration in itself is of small consequence. The subject matter is important. Values depend upon what is celebrated. Human and personal themes observed in some congregations—Mother's Day, Father's Day, Children's Day, and many others—are generally sentimental, subjective, and unworthy. The liturgical churches have never admitted such to their calendars. These calendars contain only themes based upon objective facts of Christian faith and history.

The Spirit of Edification.   Doctrine is the spirit of conviction. Missions are the spirit of endeavor. Worship is the spirit of edification and inspiration. The church is on lofty levels. The faithful have left the plains of earthly ambition and the daily struggle for bread, honor, power, and wealth. They have abandoned the battlefields of politics, science, and even theology. They have climbed out of the valleys of doubt and discouragement. While they worship they dwell on the heights. Here, and here alone, they hear the command from heaven, "Be still, and know that I am God." Here, line upon line and precept upon precept, they receive godly admonitions, and are edified and built up in their holy faith by the power of the living Word.

For there is not only peace, but power in this transaction. From our communion with God and with our fellow-believers there come new resources for righteousness and service. We draw from worship that inspiration for holy living which leads beyond self-examination to rededication. Holy places, seasons, services, and associations are freighted with spiritual power, with something more than formal or intellectual belief.

Such may be the experience of worshipers who recognize reality in a realm of spirit and mystery beyond the reaches of logic. Within this realm, Christian art has enabled the common consciousness of Christendom to give classical expression to its faith in three great forms. Each one of these is a demonstration of the spirit of worship as developed by the church as a whole. Each possesses the beauty and the power of great art and the universality and permanence of a great institution. These three are the church building, the church year, and the church service.

5

AS AN INSTITUTION

Private devotion and corporate worship spring from a common faith. Both express common emotions, quickened by the thought and the love of God. Private devotion is personal and relatively free. Corporate worship is congregational and, in a liturgical church, necessarily formal.

This does not mean that corporate worship is mechanical or empty of values for the individual. The spiritual life of individuals is nourished by the preaching, the services, and the sacraments of the church quite as well as by personal reading of the Scriptures, meditation, and prayer.

Corporate worship is both an experience and an institution. These cannot be separated, even though one aspect of the subject may be discussed separately or emphasized at the expense of the other.

Many regard worship only as something subjective, immediate, individual, occasional. But worship is an experience largely because it is an institution; it is an institution because it has been and is an experience. The two go together. We speak in this place particularly of worship as an institution, the foundation and background for worship as an experience. And by "institution" we mean something necessary or important which has been established and consistently maintained by the church universal.

Divinely Enjoined and Universally Observed. Worship is a primary function of the church. The validity and vitality of corporate worship develop from the divine command, "Thou shalt worship the Lord thy God. . . . Give unto the Lord the glory due unto his name." Our Saviour by his example taught his followers to pray and gave them a form of common prayer. He himself worshiped in the synagogue and the temple.

It is not too much to believe that Christian worship as such had its beginnings in the assemblies in which the risen Lord himself appeared. Thomas' exclamation, "My Lord and my God," is a clear indication of this. The New Testament has many further references to assemblies of the faithful, not only for edification and encouragement, but for worship. Cardinal Newman, in speaking of the later history of the Eucharist, likens this to a magnifying glass which shows "the various aspects which can be distinguished already in the New Testament." Divine wisdom saw to it that the gospel and the sacraments which were committed to the church corresponded to the spiritual necessities of mankind. These were to be satisfied largely in the common worship of believers.

The Psalmist's expression, "I was glad when they said unto me, Let us go into the house of the Lord," found something more than an

6

echo throughout the Christian world. The Apostles and the early church knew poverty and persecution, but they did not forsake their assembling together for worship. The Lord's day, the Lord's house, and the Lord's service developed as institutions. With freedom, wealth, and power, the liberated church gave these enormous expansion. Churches and cathedrals were erected; services multiplied and magnified; everywhere were found the monuments of worship. Today, whether in city, hamlet, or the remotest mission field, the church is not only a believing, but also a worshiping community. It adores the divine perfection, and its members accept the challenge, "Be ye holy. . . . Be not conformed to this world: but be ye transformed by the renewing of your mind." Living in a world of human imperfection and depravity, and amid contending forces of evil, the Christian community in its worship exalts truth, confesses it, and contends against falsehood in doctrine and life. It draws art into its service and enshrines truth in beauty. Its places of worship are supreme expressions of its highest powers. Many arts enrich its edifices, and poetry and music fill their walls with melody. For worship cannot long express itself in forms of ugliness and sordidness. Thus the church in its institution of corporate worship holds aloft standards of thought and life higher than those which unaided individual worshipers could sustain. Broadly speaking, the thesis of Professor Kirk may be maintained that Christian worship, rightly understood and practiced, is the finest illustration of man's pursuit of the highest good.

Relates the Gospel to Life. Worship as an institution is far more than an aggregate of personal absorptions in the abstract and the absolute. It is a function of the community, of the whole church. This corporate expression gives a united testimony to the world and provides a high spiritual development for each and all. The individual, no less than the group, is ennobled in mind and spirit by the use of the means committed to the church and administered in worship. The church establishes proper conditions. The real Means of Grace are God-given. The Word is the power unto edification. Thought upon thought, precept upon precept, it comes into our hearts and minds giving challenging conceptions of life and powerful motives for living. The Sacrament individualizes and heightens the power of the Word with its purifying experiences, its pledges of divine favor, and its impartation of divine grace.

The church, through its institution of worship, relates the Gospel to life. Its holy days, its holy themes, its services and ceremonies emphasize the essential truths of Christianity and lead young and old into the full appreciation of the whole round of the church's faith and life. The Word of God is always powerful, but embodied in forms of common devotion it is mighty. We have scarcely begun to realize the educational possibilities wrapped up in the Liturgy, the church year, the church building, and all the features of public worship.

Mighty Monuments Attest Its Power. As a universal, permanent institution of the church, worship has a wonderful history, a great literature, and a body of theory. All of this must be mastered if we are to realize the finest possibilities it holds as an experience. We recognize this principle in our study of Holy Scripture. Our best understanding of the English Bible is gained by accurate knowledge of the original languages of Scripture combined with scientific principles of exegesis. In theology, our first concern is not with current discussions and theories, but with the mastery of distinctive doctrines and systems of historical and universal significance. Thus in the matter of worship we must first study it as an institution. We must know something of the great moments and movements in Christian history which made positive contributions to the subject.

If we study the great liturgies we shall find them works of intellectual strength and refinement. The great prayer collections and hymnals of the church are not insignificant productions. The Gothic cathedrals were not built by weaklings. The Missal and the Breviary and the collections of musical literature—plainsong, chorales, and polyphonic compositions—were created by men of the mold of the cathedral builders. In fundamental strength of conception these monuments of worship are, in their own way, as massive and mighty as are contemporary systems of theology, and quite as worthy of study. Their elaboration, with its wealth of symbolism and beauty in stone, wood, canvas, glass, and metal, or its perfection of form in Collects, Canticles, motets, and cantatas, takes us into fields inhabited by some of the greatest geniuses of history. The Liturgy and the liturgical arts bulk large in the history of the church universal because the spirit of worship is the spirit of the living church. The monuments of worship attest its vitality and power.

The Spirit of Permanence. As one of the institutions of the church, corporate worship has been threatened at various times. Circumstances have occasionally impaired its activities. Restored vigor has always expressed itself in renewed devotion. We need not now fear that the auto, the radio, television, or even the hydrogen bomb will destroy it. Often the very elements which at first threaten destruction prove beneficial. The church may undergo reformation and reorganization, but the spirit of devotion and the desire for common communion with God

8

will not perish. An institution which survived in the bare chambers of the catacombs, which filled the cathedrals of Europe with beauty, and which lives in countless communities throughout the world today, has within it the vigor of eternal youth. We speak carelessly of the "recovery of worship"; but worship has not been lost. Christianity and worship are inseparable. Baron von Huegel, quoted approvingly by Troeltsch, significantly says, "Whatever the future may bring us, we cannot expect a certainty and force of the knowledge of Christ to subsist without communion and cultus."

Worship as an experience therefore rests upon worship as an institution. This must be appreciated as something more than a passing interest or phase. It must be understood as having within it the momentum of history, the assistance and inspiration of art, the power of intellect, and the strength of discipline and order. We must recognize it as a subject of universal sweep, of permanent and practical importance, involving in its fullest scope enormous expenditures of thought, effort, and wealth.

Chapter 2

THE CHURCH BUILDING

Architecture is in many respects the greatest of the arts in the service
of the church. It fashions the fabric which other arts enrich. Within
this fabric Christian assemblies worship and work.

The early historic Christian styles were the product of many factors:
racial and national, as well as ecclesiastical; aesthetic and scientific as
well as religious. Each is an expression of long cultural development.
They are not limited to the era of their conception. The persistence
of these styles and their revival at different times and in distant places
testify to their individuality, worth, and beauty.

THE FOUR CLASSICAL STYLES

1. The Early Christian or Basilican. This name is derived from the
general resemblance of its structures to the public law buildings, called
basilicas. In its first edifices, the early church probably perpetuated the
familiar arrangement of homes and private buildings, with several rooms
grouped around a central court. As these buildings increased in size
they became patterned after the law courts, which were the only monumental buildings in Rome at the time. This was natural, as some of
the first great churches in Rome were extremely large. The emperor
himself frequently aided in their erection and endowed them with rich
gifts of gold, silver, and jeweled ornaments.

The general plan of the basilica was that of a large rectangle, a central nave, bordered by side aisles, separated from the nave by two or
more rows of columns. Occasionally galleries were placed over the
aisles. A flat roof covered the nave, which terminated in an elevated
platform or bema with a semicircular apse. The altar stood at the
entrance to the bema. The clergy took their places in the apse, the
bishop's chair in the center. Over the entrance to the apse was a tri-

umphal arch. This, with the dome of the apse itself, was ornamented with rich mosaics.

This basilican style expressed much of the directness, strength, and practical genius of Roman civilization itself. It became the usual type of church building in the West. The Romanesque and Gothic styles developed from it.

2. The Eastern or Byzantine. When the Emperor Constantine removed his capital to Byzantium early in the fourth century A.D., this ancient Eastern city, thereafter named Constantinople and now called Istanbul, became the unifying center of the political, religious, social, and artistic life of the East. Here Roman energy fused occidental character and oriental culture. The result was an entirely different type of church building.

The beginnings of this style are to be seen in the early churches of Syria, Persia, and the Near East. Instead of the long rectangle of the basilican type, we find smaller edifices, usually built upon a circular, square, or octagonal base. This base was surmounted by a dome, and directly underneath the dome was the altar. This type of building thus had a central plan and a vertical axis. The chief problem involved was how to cover a large square base with a circular dome. Byzantine architects finally solved this by the use of "pendentives." These were curved triangular surfaces of masonry whose feet rested upon the piers beneath, while their tops widened to support the circle of the dome above. This structural triumph, and the decorative enrichment of wall surfaces and ceilings by the use of colored marble sheathings and mosaics, are the significant features of the Byzantine style.

3. The Romanesque. This style was largely the product of monastic zeal. The great religious orders spread throughout Europe. Not only religion, but letters and the arts as well, were cultivated in the monasteries. The architecture of abbey groups and of secular churches and cathedrals developed under monastic inspiration, encouraged especially by the zealous and capable Benedictines and Cistercians.

The Romanesque style, as its name indicates, developed from the ancient Roman type and method of building. The floor plan was basically basilican. Massive walls, with small, round-arched windows and doors, and towers in storied design were prominent features. Transepts were added and choirs (chancels) deepened. Because of poor conditions and lack of skilled workmen, early examples were simple. Decorative features, which included foliage, bird, and animal forms, were often crude and even grotesque.

Later years saw the emergence of national and provincial types, and the use of greatly refined ornament. Italy produced the free-standing campanile or bell-tower and rich exterior arcade work. France elaborated portals and façades with detail suggestive of classic forms. Germany, especially in the Rhineland, developed buildings of great size with lofty interiors, double apses, elevated choirs, and towers picturesquely grouped. England, where the style was introduced by the Conquerors and where it is still known as Norman, built noble naves expressive of dignity, solidity, and serenity. In southern Italy and France, partly due to immigration from the East, Romanesque churches were enriched by Byzantine ornament. This combination appears frequently in modern Romanesque churches.

4. The Gothic. The thirteenth century saw the Latin church united in doctrine, organization, and a uniform system of worship. Its sway extended over the whole of Europe. The wealth of monastic communities, the power of the bishops, the rise of great city-states, and the growth of the craftsmen's guilds all contributed to the great program of church building which swept across the continent and developed the new style which we call Gothic.

Gothic is essentially organic, or structural, in principle. The effort to vault wide naves with stone, and thus reduce the risk of fire, coupled with the desire to secure loftier and better lighted buildings, led to the use of the pointed arch and a system of piers and buttresses. The latter supported the nave walls and roof and made massive walls unnecessary. The immediate result was the attainment of great height and the illumination of the interior by rays of colored light admitted through stained-glass windows.

As had Romanesque before it, this new style displayed individuality in different lands. French Gothic was the most daring and original. Its naves, with polygonal apses at the east end, are the loftiest, and its sculptured ornament the richest in the world. Germany long clung to the Romanesque. Its later Gothic architects, however, contributed lofty aisles, openwork spires, and rich carving in wood and stone as typical features. Italian architects never fully adopted Gothic principles of construction. They elaborated the details of Gothic ornament in marvelous façades of colored stone and in rich portals, altars, fonts, et cetera. Because of the intensity of natural light in Italy, they employed small windows and thus contributed little to the art of stained glass.

England produced a type of its own, with naves much lower than the French, although longer and narrower. English choirs (chancels) terminate in a square east end, and are almost as deep in some cases as the nave itself, thus securing fine perspectives in the interior. Many of the great cathedrals of England, and innumerable parish churches of picturesque charm, are in Gothic. Period developments are more definitely divided than is the case in any other country. There is distinct separation of early English, Decorated, Perpendicular, and Tudor. The Perpendicular period, for example, witnessed the development of windows of enormous size with vertical tracery, and the use of lofty and elegantly proportioned towers over the crossing of nave and transepts.

By reason of the great number of churches built in the Gothic period, and because of the vigor, artistic maturity, and exuberant detail of the style itself, Gothic has stirred the imagination of churchmen for centuries. It is still a favorite style for large church buildings for collegiate and university groups. New materials and methods, however, as well as the important factor of cost, are promoting an ever greater use of modern or contemporary styles.

THE LAST FIVE CENTURIES

1. The Renaissance. In the fourteenth and fifteenth centuries the Italian states were centers of a revived interest in classical literature and art. Architects were called upon to design palaces and civic buildings as well as churches. They found inspiration in ancient classical architecture with its three fundamental orders, the Doric, Ionic, and Corinthian. Upon the basis of these forms they evolved the style we know as Renaissance. This was not a development from Gothic, as Gothic had been from Romanesque. Rather, it was a reversion to the heavy walls, semicircular openings and vaultings, and ornamental detail of the classical styles. Elaborate cornices again covered doorways and windows; balconies protruded from the walls; columns and pilasters reproduced the forms of the classic orders. Window openings were decreased in size and wall surfaces were extended. Fresco painting and mosaic decoration were revived at the expense of stained glass. The minor arts flourished; sculpture, painting, tapestries, and exquisite work in gold, silver, bronze, and iron enriched exteriors and interiors alike.

The style spread to all lands, although not with equal rapidity. Innumerable churches were built in Italy, the largest and most famous being St. Peter's in Rome. French architects eagerly adopted the new style and employed it in building chateaux for the nobility and in decorating Gothic churches previously erected. Some new Renaissance edifices were also erected, the Church of the Madeleine in Paris being a well-known example. The German development took on the heaviness and grotesqueness of the Baroque style, which Jesuit influence had cultivated in Italy, and which spread throughout Europe as a feature of the Counter Reformation. In England, Inigo Jones and Christopher Wren designed churches and college buildings in the Renaissance style. One of Wren's greatest works was St. Paul's Cathedral in London. Many new edifices were erected after the London Fire of 1666. Certain features of these buildings, particularly the spires of such churches as St. Bride's, St. Martin's-in-the-Fields, and St. Mary at the Bourne, later influenced the design of Colonial church buildings in America.

2. Colonial Styles in the New World. The earliest church building in America was in Mexico in the sixteenth century. The cathedral in Mexico City, begun in 1573 and after 1615 carried on from plans forwarded from Spain, is one of the largest church buildings on the continent. Advances westward into California in the eighteenth and nineteenth centuries produced the Spanish Colonial or Mission style. This was a simplified type of Spanish Renaissance, with plain buildings of adobe or mud brick. The walls were massive and unrelieved by ornament. Ponderous buttresses were occasionally used and towers, pierced belfry walls, and arcaded cloisters were everywhere employed. In the interior, all the ornament was concentrated on the altar. The workmen were mostly unskilled Indians. Clerical direction provided good proportions with simple lines. The Spanish Colonial style serves today as the inspiration for much modern church work in the West and Southwest.

The English Colonial style came later and was confined to the Atlantic seaboard. The Cavaliers in Virginia, the Dutch in New York, the Swedes, Germans, and Quakers in Pennsylvania, and the Puritans in Massachusetts all built churches and meeting houses which showed the unifying influence of the English Renaissance. The Bruton Parish Church, Williamsburg, Virginia, and St. Michael's, Charleston, are among the most interesting Colonial churches in the South. Typical Massachusetts examples are the Old North and Old South Churches, Boston. Christ Church, Philadelphia, is perhaps the finest of all English Colonial churches. St. Peter's in the same city and Trinity Lutheran Church in Lancaster, Pennsylvania, are also of special interest.

The Colonial style has definite association with early American history. Its openness of plan and simplicity of construction and ornament give it dignity, which its fine spires enhance. Congregations whose history extends into the Colonial period, or whose communities possess other monuments of Colonial times, may well employ the Colonial style for their buildings today, though from several points of view the style possesses limited possibilities. Where it is used it ought to be used in

14

its entirety; its parts, especially its beautiful spires, ought not to be sacrificed for the sake of a budget.

3. Contemporary Styles. There is no single, definitely determined modern style, unless we regard the current use of structural steel and concrete, instead of masonry, as having produced a definite style or system of construction. There are many experimental types, and what is contemporary in one decade, except for a few buildings of exceptional merit, is apt to be thought of as outmoded in the next decade.

Every country in Europe has important church buildings erected recently in styles variously called Modern, International, Ferro-concrete, or Contemporary. Sweden presents some of the best examples. Local characteristics are evident, particularly in the use of ornament. There is an honest effort to give logical and scientific expression to the use of new materials and methods in a wide departure from traditional forms. Design is a matter of mass and proportion rather than of line. Primitive motifs are sought and developed in compositions of dynamic power. Classic and medieval ornament is abandoned. The important' factor of cost is kept in view. Since government bureaus or professional architects are completely responsible for design, many modern European churches have little historic or churchly association and their coarse and brutal forms impress earnest Christian people unfavorably. The interest of American architects in the contemporary work of their professional brethren abroad stimulated the importation of these current European forms, both good and bad, into our own country. Other factors have contributed, as we shall see.

We must build churches, parish halls, and parsonages. At this very moment the Christian church in America is engaged in a building program of enormous proportions, a program surpassed in volume and cost only by comparable efforts in the commercial, industrial, and civic fields. The church's program next year is expected to pass the billion dollar mark. The question constantly posed for pastors, architects, and building committees is, "Must church buildings be only of traditional design, or can we conform to secular styles?" If freedom at this point is admitted, the approach to the problem immediately becomes functional and materialistic instead of historical, and we find ourselves swept into the fast-moving currents of contemporary thought and the confusion of contemporary practice.

In fact, by now the question posed above is largely academic. There were no church buildings in America in the contemporary style before the First World War. Today probably one-third of the buildings being erected, or in the planning stage, are in the contemporary style. The

15

style is in the field and many controlling factors combine to keep it there. We can no longer sneer at it and speak contemptuously of "gas station," "supermarket," or "silo" churches. So let us seek to understand the style or movement, discover its origin, come to grips with its principles, and use the best and guard against the worst of its features as they apply to the work of the church.

Dr. Stephan Hirzel, editor of the German-Protestant, Nazi-suppressed journal, *Kunst und Kirche,* in a recent article has helped us understand how the contemporary movement in church building rose in Germany from the ruins and the rubble of World War I. The nation was exhausted, the masses were in poverty, thoughtful people were convinced that civilization itself would perish with the fall of the empire. But life went on, with the strictest economy controlling all effort. With old things destroyed, new beginnings must be made. Prosperity had produced extravagant elegancies, elaborate ornament, and the like. Poverty had to return to hard realities and primitive forms and be inventive. The most primitive forms of housing were the tent (in America, the tepee) and the cave. These became the motifs for the new movement. Otto Bartning's steel church at the Cologne Exposition in 1928 was a skeleton structure of prefabricated parts that could be taken down like a tent and set up later in another city (Essen). Le Corbusier's Roman Catholic pilgrimage chapel at Ronchamp was a cave-like structure on a hillside.

Economic and other conditions everywhere in Europe after the ravages of war prompted inventiveness and bold innovation. Theologians and thinkers like Paul Tillich (then in Germany) hastened to put philosophical and theological foundations under these radical experiments, baptizing their austere forms with such names as "architectural expressions of holy emptiness." Another factor, whose actual importance it is impossible to determine, was the eager attitude of the powerful Youth Movement toward all modern art. Disillusioned, and blaming their elders for the disasters and the defeat that had overwhelmed them, the youth of the country determined to break with all tradition and build a brave new world. Sensing this attitude, and desiring to win the allegiance of the youth, the church authorities accepted even the boldest experimental forms of contemporary design.

This is not the whole story, particularly as to the situation confronting us in America today. The contemporary movement had its inspiration and its derivation from European developments mentioned above. But today American churchmen and architects are doing their own thinking and creating their own forms. They have a wealth of new materials and new methods at their command. In the secular field surrounding

16

them they are confronted with bold and confident architectural manifestations of power, with concentration upon mass and elimination of detail, with elongation of units and other significant revisions of scale, with lavish use of color and startling effects in light. These are accepted not only as natural expressions of new-found resources, but as normal expressions of a contemporary spirit in which freshness of ideas and originality in treatment of inherited forms combine to make old institutions come alive and seem more meaningful to men and women of today. Materials and methods of the past are outmoded. Structural steel makes buttresses unnecessary. Cranes, bulldozers, and electric saws perform tasks formerly required of manual labor. Machine-made products leave craftsmanship largely without opportunity or reward. Unhappily, and with old-time idealism and aesthetic sensitivity standing sorrowfully by, craftsmanship abdicates in favor of the simple requirements of functionalism and the hard facts of economic necessity. For, to use Louis Sullivan's familiar phrase, "form follows function." Of course, other factors are important. Not only must structural steel and iron be used, but cement and glass, plasters, tiles, asbestos, silk, and fiber fabrics demand study and experimentation. Insulation, problems in acoustics, air conditioning, heating, lighting, amplifying equipment, and similar matters that did not concern our fathers must be considered, to say nothing of effective uses of light and color. New requirements in the educational, social, and recreational programs of the church must be met. In projects of large dimensions architecture must seek a partnership with engineering.

This about brings us to where we are. The church is still in the world. Its programs and its possibilities are quite different from facts faced in earlier eras. To the pessimist it seems that church architecture today is not only in the world, but of the world, and that its holiest forms are being progressively secularized. Since all the important schools of architecture in the country fail to acquaint their students with the historic styles and to teach them the skills to work in them, the case for the church seems almost hopeless.

The author would not wish to be thought of as holding this opinion, or as negative in his attitude toward contemporary movements. He believes that modern architecture has very much to offer the church, and that representative and dedicated members of the profession are earnestly seeking not only to master new materials and methods, but are striving to save the church from seeming to be an anachronism in society. They wish to make it a living member of the social and spiritual order of our time by designing contemporary forms appropriate for its use. While freewheeling individualists and novelty-seekers may produce freaks and monstrosities in the name of religion, the ablest men in the profession have not forgotten that architecture, like every other art, must enter the house of the Lord on its knees, as a servant and not as master. Some, by their undisciplined desire for experimentation and self-exploitation, may blaspheme the Name of the Most High, but the whole modern movement should not be condemned because of them or their works.

It is encouraging to note that the ablest architects working in the church field are conscious of the fact that theology must play a creative and informing role in their thinking and planning. The message of the Christian faith and hope is ageless and spiritual. Church building, like all other living, must be a response to that message and must carry that message. Church buildings must do more than provide places for assembly and worship. They must witness to the world, show forth the purpose of the church, and present Christ to the passer-by. Our theology is meaningless without him, and our church buildings will fail of their function if they do not proclaim, "This is the house of God, a building that is different, a place where God and holiness may be found more readily than in any other place." Here stone and brick, steel and glass, wood and cement, silk and metal unite to produce an atmosphere of reverence, dignity, and beauty for the preaching of the Word, the administration of the sacraments, and the fellowship and work of the faithful. When we ask of a Gothic cathedral or of a Puritan meeting house, "What do these stones mean?" this is what they tell us. The contemporary church must say the same thing. In a liturgical communion particularly, with its depth of history and doctrine and its traditional rites and ceremonies, contemporary work should flower out of earlier forms. Its exterior may not reveal a mere search for novelty. Its interior may not provide, as has been done, a mere shelf "to hold ceremonial bric-a-brac" instead of an altar or communion table of dignity and propriety.

In this connection we take pleasure in quoting a statement by Professor Joseph Sittler, lately of the faculty of the Lutheran Theological Seminary of Chicago, and presently a member of the faculty of the Divinity School of the University of Chicago. Professor Sittler writes:

"The Word became flesh and dwelt among us." This statement puts one at the central place for pondering what the form of a Christian church should announce. . . . The Lutheran tradition is Christocentric through and through. God is the God who is revealed in Christ. The knowledge of God is what is offered in Christ. The worship of Christ centres in the entire Christ-deed, from birth, through death and resurrection to his Real Presence in the household of God, the church.

Therefore every effort to give this tradition palpable, declamatory force

Church of the Abiding Presence, Lutheran Theological Seminary, Gettysburg, Pennsylvania
Architects: J. Alfred Hamme and Associates, York, Pennsylvania. Seminary chapel of quiet dignity in
Colonial tradition. Tower reminiscent of important early churches in Lancaster and Philadelphia.

Trinity Episcopal Church, Takoma Park, Maryland
Architect: Philip Hubert Frohman, Washington, D. C. Small parish church showing influence of Romanesque and early English. Massive tower is typical of small English churches.

Wyoming Presbyterian Church, Millburn, New Jersey
Architects: Thomas M. Bell, Otto F. Langmann, Harry E. Warren, New York. Modern expression of style for early churches in American colonies, using same materials. Pleasing and well-proportioned detail.

Church of the Holy Child, Philadelphia (Roman Catholic)
Architect: George I. Lovatt, Philadelphia. This impressive interior with its massive columns is strongly reminiscent of Durham Cathedral, England. Great spaciousness with warmth of feeling.

Beverly Hills Methodist Church, Chicago

Architects: Edward F. Jansson and Ralph E. Stoetzel, Associates. Suburban Gothic church of strong dignity. Scale and simplicity of detail relate to random ashlar concrete block surfaces. Limestone trim.

Gideon F. Egner Memorial Chapel, Muhlenberg College, Allentown, Pennsylvania
Architects: Frank R. Watson and William Heyl Thompson. Modern treatment of English Decorated
Gothic. Academic plan with enlarged choir for upperclassmen, stalls for president, deans, faculty seats.

St. John's Lutheran Church, Allentown, Pennsylvania
Architects: Edward F. Jansson and Ralph E. Stoetzel, Associates. Same style city church. In both interiors, stone altar, carved wood, polychromed reredos, and stained-glass window form focal point.

St. Paul's English Lutheran Church, Washington, D. C.

Architect: Philip Hubert Frohman, Washington, D. C. City church reminiscent of early English Gothic with a touch of French tradition. Structural elements and detail well proportioned. Spire over intersection of nave and transept. Wide steps to entrance. Many small, pointed-arch windows. Final drawing revised.

must set forth, point to, hold up and draw to the single Christ-centre, the multitudinous details of worship. What should be celebrated in both architecture and liturgy is not general religiousness, unspecified spirituality, or a miasmic if potent mood of sheer Otherness. The Lutheran understanding of the Christian faith asserts that all of this is intrinsically unredemptive. The sole, final and absolutely redemptive fact is God's deed in Christ; Christ in his historic actuality as Jesus of Nazareth; in his Real Presence as Lord of all things known, received and adored in his church.

The late John Knox Shear, editor of the *Architectural Record,* in his comment on these words says: "This masterful statement places the burden of the formal expression of meaning squarely on the architect; proscribing only the generalized expressions so common today." [1]

This, then, is the church's building code. Contemporary design, as such, with its simplicity, clarity, strength, and economy, may be heartily accepted. New materials and methods, new uses of light and color may be welcomed, if the designers, on their part, respect certain guiding principles upon which the church must insist. The church's primary concern is with the plan, the allotment of spaces, particularly in the central edifice appointed for worship. The traditional floor plan is the functional result of centuries of experience and must be preserved. Such required spaces, each calling for specific treatment, are the sanctuary, the choir (chancel), the sacristy, the nave, the narthex, the baptistry. Proper fittings must be provided, and simple symbolism should be retained. If this is done, and if reverence for holy things and respect for historic continuity and churchly association are evident, church buildings in contemporary design may well serve God and man in this our day.

This is what pastors and building committees must say to their architects. All share in a common problem, a problem which has to do with religion quite as much as with architecture. What is required is not only an authentic building, a work of art representing its own time, but an edifice which suggests religious purpose, which speaks reverently of the stupendous fact of divine intervention in human history. Built in a definite time and place it must proclaim truths that transcend time and place. It must assert ultimate values. It fails if it does less.

The ablest and the spiritually-minded architects will understand this and be guided by principles which the church, a unique institution in society, has formulated from its long experience. Let those who cannot understand or accept these principles build factories, office buildings, department stores, supermarkets, but not churches.

---

[1] Quotation and comment in *Religious Buildings for Today,* edited by John Knox Shear (New York: F. W. Dodge Corporation, 1957), pp. 62, 63. By permission of the publishers.

The *Christian Century* and the *National Council Outlook* both carried informative articles on contemporary church architecture in their 1957 and 1958 issues. Helpful books are: *The Modern Church*, by Edward D. Mills (New York: Frederick A. Praeger, 1956); *Religious Building for Today*, by John Knox Shear (New York: F. W. Dodge Corporation, 1957); *Contemporary Church Art*, by Anton Henze and Theodore Filthaut (London: Sheed and Ward, 1956); *The Changing Church*, by Katharine Morrison McClinton (New York: Morehouse, 1957).

THE PLAN OF THE BUILDING

Good architecture grows naturally out of the particular needs of an individual congregation or institution. It must provide adequately for this in worship, education, and social activity. We may mention certain features and requirements which have developed from experience.

1. Orientation. Whenever possible, the church building may be built with the chancel and altar facing the East. This was the general custom as early as the eighth century. The East was thought of as the region of light, the place of man's early home and of paradise, and the earthly homeland of our Lord. Orientation, however, is something more than a recognition of historic symbolism. Certain practical considerations commend it. This arrangement makes certain that the sun will be on the side of the church building toward midday, at the time of the principal service. This is preferable to having it at either end of the building, since the sunlight, entering through the side windows, more fully illuminates the nave, and shines in no one's eyes. Orientation, however, is not in any sense an essential consideration. More important matters of street direction, available ground in suitable location, et cetera, generally determine the actual location and position of the building.

2. The Narthex or Vestibule. An adequate narthex, or at least a porch or tower vestibule, should be provided. This serves as a protection against the elements, permits removal of wraps outside the nave, and eliminates confusion and unnecessary noise. It also enables special groups to assemble before entering the church, as at marriages, confirmations, and celebrations, and serves other useful purposes.

3. The Nave. The nave must provide adequate room for the congregation and promote congregational worship. Its proportion and decoration should create an atmosphere of solemnity and spiritual exaltation. The worshipers must be protected against noise and secular suggestion. Windows should be kept high and the light subdued by colored glass, unless the building is of a style which demands clear or frosted windows. Worshipers, wherever they sit, should have an unobstructed view of the chancel and the altar as well as of the pulpit.

A center alley, the technical term used to distinguish this feature from the true "aisles" outside the columns in a Romanesque or Gothic nave, of good width provides a practical and dignified approach to the chancel for communions, processions, et cetera. Radiating alleys and semi-circular seats lack dignity and historic consciousness, and suggest places of secular assembly.

The traditional plan calls for a central nave, with lofty clerestory walls, separated by columns from the aisles on either side. The latter serve as passageways and as space for extra seating (in pews or chairs) when required. While this pier and clerestory type is historic and attractive, both on the exterior and the interior, it is possible to secure excellent results by building the nave without columns and clerestory in a regular parallelogram. Transepts may be used in large buildings. They are not recommended in small edifices.

The alleys should be of tile, stone, or composition flooring. They should never be covered with carpet, which suggests domestic uses rather than public requirements. Carpet is also dirt-collecting, moth-inviting, and perishable. One of the most important features in the nave is adequate and proper lighting. This, whether from windows or fixtures, should be soft and subdued so as to create a devotional atmosphere. Dazzling chandeliers, unprotected electric bulbs, and fluorescent lighting are the foe of devotion.

Pew spacing that will permit kneeling requires a minimum back-to-back measurement of two feet and ten inches, better three feet. Pew seating requires twenty inches per sitting.

4. The Chancel. Special solemnity attaches to the place as well as to the manner in which the Word and the sacraments are administered. The building should progress in architectural interest and enrichment as we proceed from the narthex through the nave and come finally to the chancel and the altar. As a portrait painter begins with the head of his subject, the latter's most expressive and dominant feature, so the architect in planning a church should begin with the chancel. This is more than a focal feature to which all lines lead. It is the place where the altar is located, where the clergy and the choir are generally found. It possesses all the features of liturgical and practical supremacy.

This importance has been fully expressed in buildings of the historic type. Great cathedrals, and even the smallest chapels, have been provided with ample chancels properly proportioned and beautifully adorned. Some communions, however, and even our own in poorer periods, have substituted a platform for the traditional chancel and made the pulpit, rather than the altar, the central feature. Many con-

21

gregations in all communions today, however, are conforming to the historic arrangement and building chancels of adequate size with a Communion table, if not an altar, centrally placed as the dominant feature.

In our use of the term "chancel" we commonly include what may more properly be termed the "choir" and the "sanctuary." The choir is the space in which stalls for singers and the organ console are generally found. The sanctuary is the space beyond the communion rail which contains the altar. All persons, whether members of the church or not, find a place in the nave. The chancel represents the deeper fellowship of the gospel, where those called to the ministry officiate, where the communicants of the church receive the Sacrament, and where others come to make their vows. It must be adequate in size and arrangement for all occasions, and architecturally impressive. Many buildings have been redeemed from the status of an auditorium of hall-like character and given churchly dignity by the simple addition of a chancel of adequate size and appointment.

Three low and broad steps across the entire front of the chancel provide an open and easy access to it. Ample space should be given the minister to conduct the services. Communicants and others should not be crowded in coming to and from the altar. If the choir is placed in the chancel, the choir stalls will be ranged on each side at right angles to the pews in the nave. The stalls should be kept low so as not to interfere with the congregation's view of the altar. They should be three feet apart, and for vested choirs two feet should be allowed for a sitting. The central area between the stalls should be at least eight feet wide to avoid any sense of crowding and to afford an easy approach to the sanctuary. Ample space should be provided at each end of the stalls, the space toward the nave permitting the minister to reach the pulpit and the lectern, and that at the other end permitting communicants to pass freely in front of the altar rail.

Gothic churches with small chancels should terminate these in a square end, the typical English plan. A polygonal end in a small church gives the effect of pinching the altar. In large buildings the continental plan of a polygonal apse may be used with fine effect. This permits the use of relatively small and high chancel windows, an arrangement generally better than a single window over the altar. Where a single window is used, the glass must be of rich, deep tone to cut down excessive and disturbing light.

The sanctuary is separated from the choir by a low and broad step and a simple altar rail. The latter is open in the center immediately in front of the altar and in line with the main axis of the building. In the

Lutheran Church the Lord's Supper is called the Sacrament of the Altar. Communicants come to the altar to receive the elements as an individual pledge of forgiveness and gift of grace. This requires ample space provisions.

The sanctuary must be of sufficient depth to provide properly for the altar and its reredos and for the spaces required in front of the altar. In small churches at least one broad step or foot-pace (often called a predella) not less than two feet deep, nor generally more than four, is necessary for the minister immediately in front of the altar. A space of at least three feet must be provided between this and the altar rail to allow the minister to pass freely when administering the Holy Communion. In large churches there should be three low and broad steps in front of the altar, the top step being deeper than the other two. This completes the traditional number of seven steps from the nave to the altar. Churches of moderate size, however, will not require more than five—three at the entrance to the chancel, one at the altar rail, and one before the altar.

A practical feature of importance is provision for side exits at each end of the altar rail. Communicants may then come to the altar through the center of the chancel and, after communing, retire through the side exits, returning to the nave through the sacristy or other rooms on either or both sides. Circulation at this point becomes an important consideration, and one often overlooked.

The chancel and sanctuary floors should be covered with stone, tile, or other substantial and sanitary material. Carpets, we repeat, are a domestic furnishing and out of place in any public building, particularly so in the alleys and chancels of churches. Stone, marble, or ecclesiastical tile are best. This last is made especially for church use, and has nothing in common with popular asphalt tiles, which, though better than carpet, are again associated with the domestic. When ecclesiastical tiles are properly laid, their soft colors and varied patterns are rich and pleasing. If stone or tile is not used, a good hardwood flooring finished without gloss will be satisfactory. Massive wainscoting or paneling of stone, brick, or wood around the walls of the chancel adds dignity and character. The lighting should be ample, yet soft and well distributed. Radiators and other heating devices should be concealed within the walls and the heat conveyed through inconspicuous registers or screens.

THE FITTINGS OF THE CHURCH

1. *The Altar.* This feature should dominate the interior. Here communion between God and men reaches its highest peaks in the outpouring of divine gifts of grace and in the thanksgiving and renewed

consecration of the believer. Here man's communion with man reaches its most spiritual expression in the realization of the communion of saints. The altar is the table of the Lord and the place of benediction. These are its sacramental connections. It is also the place where vows of fidelity and consecration are spoken and where the united prayer of the congregation is offered. These are its sacrificial or subjective features. Communions which regard the Lord's Supper as a mere memorial and a mark of Christian fellowship may be satisfied with a communion table, with the elements on the level of the congregation. Historic and liturgical Christianity provides an elevated altar which crowns the main axis and becomes the architectural and liturgical focus of the building.

The altar, even in a small church, should never seem insignificant. It should be at least seven or eight feet in length, and longer still in larger churches. The mensa, or table, should be thirty-nine or forty inches high, no more and certainly not much less, measured from the foot-pace, and about twenty-four inches deep. If there is a ten- to twelve-inch retable the mensa may be reduced to twenty inches in depth. Whether of stone or of wood, it should have five Greek crosses, symbolic of the wounds of Christ, engraved upon it—one in each corner and a slightly larger one in the center. Back of the mensa rises the retable, a late fifteenth century feature which has demonstrated practical utility. It is usually eight or ten inches high and twelve inches deep. This provides for candlesticks and flower vases.

Vases and potted plants should never be placed on the mensa nor should the altar itself ever be used for storage of candles, vases, or linens. The central portion of the retable is elevated slightly to form a throne for the cross. If, as is the case with some more recent altars, no retable is provided—a proper procedure only in the case of the open or table style altar—the mensa will be thirty-six inches deep and the cross and candlesticks of necessity placed at the rear, on the mensa itself.

The altar should be substantial, permanent, and monumental if possible. Stone, either Caen stone or a fine Indiana limestone, is the best material. Oak of massive and thorough construction and simple carving may be used.

A reredos behind the altar or a fine dossal of rich material adds architectural dignity and impressiveness. The dossal is of some other than one of the regular seasonal colors. Crimson, or a deep powder blue, set off by rich orphreys of vertical bands in gold or another contrasting color, are effective. Much depends, of course, upon the surroundings, the color of the walls and woodwork. Sometimes a quiet neutral tone will be best. The dossal is usually suspended from a wrought-iron rod, and may or may not be surmounted by a tester. It should hang flat and not in folds suggestive of upholstery.

2. *Altar Paraments and Ornaments.* The altar, whether of stone or wood, is covered first with a heavy linen cloth the exact size of the mensa. With a stone altar, this cerecloth will be impregnated with wax, and must be separated from the fair linen by yet another linen cloth the size of the mensa. This second cloth may be that to which the superfrontal is attached (see below). If no superfrontal is provided, a separate cloth must be used.

Over this is placed the fair linen, a cloth of fine material, the exact depth of the mensa and long enough to fall over the ends of the altar two-thirds of the distance to the floor on both sides. The fair linen lies on the altar at all times, whether there be a Communion or not, and marks it as the table of the Lord. The ends of the fair linen have a plain hem or may be finished with narrow white linen fringe. Five small Greek crosses are embroidered in white on the part of the linen which covers the mensa.

The colored altar paraments are of rich fabric—brocaded silk or broadcloth—in the colors of the seasons. They are embroidered with appropriate designs. The richest and most complete vestments are the frontal and superfrontal used in combination. The frontal is the exact length of the altar and hangs from a metal rod under the front edge of the mensa so as to cover the entire front of the altar. Its lower edge may be finished with silk fringe reaching almost to the floor.

The superfrontal is a strip of silk damask, tapestry, or other rich material as long as the mensa and seven or eight inches deep. This hangs from the front edge of the mensa only, and is generally attached to a linen cloth the size of the mensa which is placed under the fair linen. The weight of the superfrontal is counterbalanced by a flat metal rod sewn into this supporting linen at the back of the mensa. The superfrontal may also be finished with silk fringe. Frequently, particularly in the case of finely carved altars, the superfrontal is used alone without the frontal.

The frontal and superfrontal are found in all liturgical communions, Roman, Anglican, and Lutheran. A different vestment, peculiar to areas of the Lutheran communion is the antependium. This is also of rich fabric, employing embroidered designs in the center, and finished at the bottom with silk fringe. It covers the center front of the altar, and is usually twenty-eight or thirty inches wide, though the width must have some reference to the width of the altar. It falls within a few inches of the floor. This is a none too satisfactory substitute for the frontal or superfrontal, and is not to be recommended where the traditional altar vestments can be used.

The embroidered ornament on all altar paraments should be in a broad style with strong color compositions, so as to produce an architectural effect and carry to the end of the building.

The sacramental linens proper consist of the corporal, the pall, the veil, and purificators, which when not in use are kept in an envelope called a burse. These are described in the General Rubrics of the *Service Book*.

A missal stand or altar desk, usually of brass, is placed on the mensa to receive the Altar Service Book, bound in red morocco and provided with ribbon markers. Both should be removed when not in use.

The cross or crucifix stands upon the retable back of the center of the altar. The crucifix is universal in European Lutheran lands except Sweden, where only the cross is found. The latter is more general in American Lutheranism, though the use of the crucifix is increasing.

The crucifix suggests most powerfully the sacrificial death of our Lord and the central importance of the doctrine of the Atonement. The "empty" cross suggests the triumphant thought of the victorious, risen Christ. If the crucifix is used, it should be restrained and symbolic in character and not overly realistic. It should have a small and refined corpus. Whether cross or crucifix is used, it should in any case be high enough to rise above the base of the candlesticks on either side.

Two Eucharistic lights are placed on the mensa and lighted at every celebration of the Holy Communion. They may also be lighted for the Service even when there is no Communion.

In addition, six tall candlesticks may be placed along the retable of a relatively long altar, three on each side of the cross. On very small altars this will give a crowded effect. These candlesticks may also be lighted for the Service regularly. When there is a Communion, however, two Eucharistic lights should be lighted whether there are other lights or not.

Separate Office lights (Vesper lights), in three- or seven-branched candlesticks, may be used at Matins, Vespers, weddings, and special services. It is to be noted that these Office lights are not sufficient for the Holy Communion, at which time, we repeat, the two Eucharistic lights should be used.

The candlesticks are generally of fine brass. Spun brass is to be avoided. The candlesticks for the two Eucharistic lights, however, may be of oak finished in gold leaf. Other materials can sometimes be effectively used, but extreme caution is in order lest the altar be made to look cheap. The simplest arrangement, and often the best for small churches, provides only a cross and two candlesticks. As indicated above, additional lights may be used, but good taste will avoid the use of too many.

Everything connected with the altar must bear the stamp of reality and sincerity. The lights must be real candles (preferably beeswax) and not electric substitutes. The altar is no place for sham. Imitation and artificial candles are no better than artificial flowers. Real candles give not only a sense of genuineness, but also an emotional warmth which artificial lights cannot produce.

Candles are lighted just before the Service begins by an acolyte or a choirman vested in cassock and cotta. He uses a taper designed for altar use which also has a cone-shaped extinguisher. The candles on the right or Epistle side are lighted first, beginning with the one nearest the cross; then those on the left or Gospel side are lighted, beginning with the one nearest the cross. After the Service the lights are extinguished in reverse order, beginning with the candle farthest from the cross on the left. The light nearest the cross on the Epistle side is the last to be extinguished. When Eucharistic lights are used in combination with Office lights, the former are lighted last and extinguished last.

The sacramental vessels should be of silver and of good quality, however simple in design. With the exception of the paten, they should be lined with gold. Wine cruets of glass are often used at small Communions instead of large silver flagons. The advice of a good house should be taken when these vessels are purchased, and no attempt should be made to economize at the expense of quality.

3. The Pulpit. In the early church the bishop addressed the congregation from his chair. Other clergy spoke from the ambo or platform from which the deacon read the Lessons. This ambo eventually became the pulpit. The medieval church saw pulpits of great size and elaborate ornament erected in the nave, and even outside the church buildings in public squares. The Reformation, with its renewed emphasis on preaching, introduced pulpits into even the smallest churches. In the Reformed communions these became the central and most important architectural feature, the communion table being given a subordinate location beneath the pulpit. The Lutheran Church—except during the period of Rationalism—and the Episcopal Church preserved the altar in its traditional location, at the rear of the chancel, and gave the pulpit a commanding position on one side of the chancel near the congregation.

Medieval churches generally had the pulpit on the north or Gospel

27

side. This symbolically expressed the idea of the time that the Prince of Darkness reigned in the cold and barren north, and that the gospel must be preached to him. The Reformation generally brought the pulpit well forward of the chancel arch on the Epistle side. This seems to have been due to practical considerations, as this location permitted the preacher greater freedom of gesture. Historic and symbolic considerations are less important today than such matters as adequate light, noise outside the building, proper entrances and exits, et cetera. Either side of the chancel is a proper location.

Representing the preaching of the Word, the pulpit should be of permanent construction, possessing dignity and beauty of design. It should be elevated, but not too greatly above the chancel level. It should not obstruct the view of the altar. The traditional Gothic octagonal design with closed or well-covered front, concealing the lower portion of the preacher's body, is the best type that has been developed. Stone may be used if the other appointments are of similar construction. Wood of fine design and thorough construction is satisfactory. Brass work must be exceptionally good to be acceptable.

The purchase of a pulpit or other chancel furniture from a manufacturer's catalog is hazardous. The best results will be obtained if the architects of the building design the pulpit and other furniture and thus secure proportion and harmony of design.

A lantern suspended above the pulpit, or some other lighting fixture, should cast an adequate light on the pulpit Bible or manuscript. It should not shine in the face of the preacher or the eyes of the congregation. Spotlights are theatrical and should be avoided.

Pulpit falls should be provided in the proper color of the day or season. These must not be too large, but well-proportioned to the size of the desk on which the Bible rests, and to the pulpit itself. Needless to say, a bookmark, though pretty, will not take the place of a good pulpit fall.

4. The Lectern. In many Lutheran churches abroad, and in some here, the custom still obtains of reading the liturgical Lessons—the Epistle and the Gospel—from the horns (ends) of the altar. American churches generally provide a lectern, and this in large buildings allows the reader to be better heard by the congregation. The lectern stands in the chancel opposite the pulpit. Bearing the Holy Scriptures, as it does, it should give the impression of permanence and stability. The lectern may take several shapes. A double desk with triangular head is sometimes found. Frequently lecterns are designed in the form of an eagle. This in medieval symbolism represented the Apostle John, who in his writings soared to loftier heights than did any of the other Evangelists. In a single desk design, the lectern is usually covered with a vestment or fall in the color of the season and harmonizing with the fall on the pulpit.

Care should be taken not to hide the reader behind the lectern. If necessary, a step should be provided for him so that his body will rise above the lectern and his voice carry over it to the distant parts of the building. By the same token, it ought not be necessary for a man of average height to lean over and throw his voice to the floor in an effort to read from a lectern of inadequate height.

The Bible on the pulpit and the lectern should be of ample size and bound in red morocco.

5. Clergy Seats. These, technically called "sedilia," should be provided in sufficient numbers for normal use and for special occasions. In the early church these were always on the south side of the chancel. The medieval church generally recessed them in the wall so as to keep them inconspicuous. In our use today, stalls of solid construction and churchly design should be placed back of the pier on either side of the chancel arch. They should be located in the chancel proper—the so-called choir—and not in the sanctuary. They should not face the congregation—the minister is not in view—but should be at right angles to the seats in the nave. If the choir is placed in the chancel, the clergy seats may be located in the row of stalls nearest the wall or in individual seats at the end of the stalls nearest the congregation. Sometimes both methods are employed, one stall on each side being separate, and additional stalls for special occasions forming a part of the back row of choir stalls on the south side. In any case, they should receive separate architectural treatment and thus be distinguished from the choir stalls. On the other hand, they should be unostentatious; upholstered chairs with high, ornate backs are out of place in the chancel. *Prie-dieux* may be provided if there is sufficient space.

6. The Font or Baptistery. The early church grew by the accession of adult converts. These were required to be publicly baptized. The church gave the Sacrament of Baptism special recognition by providing separate buildings called baptisteries. Later the font was introduced into the church building proper. The high theological importance which the church accords the Sacrament of Baptism calls for worthier architectural expressions than are often found today.

The font should have monumental character in form and material. It should be placed conveniently for all who participate in the Service

29

of Baptism. It should be reserved and respected and not used for other than sacramental purposes.

The Reformation generally drew the font forward from its medieval location near the entrance of the church building, where it had been placed to symbolize the significance of Baptism as the means of entrance to membership in the church. This change was an expression of the theological emphasis upon the sacraments as Means of Grace. The font should not, however, be placed at the foot of the center alley in front of the chancel steps. In this position it obstructs the view of the altar, introduces an additional focal feature, and impedes the approach of communicants to the chancel. It may well be elevated and placed to one side of the chancel, in one of the transepts, or in a corner of the nave just outside of the chancel. If the choir be placed not in the chancel but to one side of it, the font may be placed in a baptistery balancing the composition on the other side. Distinctive treatment by means of columns, arches, et cetera, will give it appropriate dignity. When the font is raised above the floor, the top step should be extended to form a platform for the minister.

The font, wherever placed, should be solidly fixed, and should have a drain connecting with clean soil beneath the building. It should be kept scrupulously clean, the bowl being lined with metal or other sanitary material. Font covers are decorative, promote cleanliness, and preserve the font from improper uses. When properly executed, they add impressively to the monumental character of the font.

ADDITIONAL CONSIDERATIONS

1. Choir and Organ Console. In Lutheran churches abroad the organ is placed in the west or rear gallery. This is simply a survival of pre-Reformation custom, and is the usual location in Roman Catholic churches everywhere today. The great development of organ music and choir music of concert character in the Lutheran Church in Europe in the eighteenth century—Bach's cantatas, large-scale motets, et cetera —fastened the gallery location upon our churches abroad. The gallery location was also the usual one in England for three centuries after the Reformation. It is a good location for securing fine choral effects from a large group of singers. It permits artistic antiphonal effects when the minister's parts of the Liturgy are intoned, as they regularly are in our churches abroad and in many churches here. It is difficult, however, to get a proper sense of unity between congregation, minister, and choir throughout the Service with the organ and choir in this location. The choir seems independent of the congregation, and is apt to regard the singing of anthems and other special numbers as its chief function.

The confessional and liturgical movement of the past hundred years has given our American Lutheran churches a richer Liturgy than any of our state churches in Europe possess, and quite a different type of worship. Our choirs are vested and brought forward. The leadership of worship is thus strengthened and unified. Everyone present—minister, choir, and congregation—takes part in every portion of the Service. All sing the responses of the Liturgy as heartily as the hymns. The minister remains in the chancel throughout, as do all the choir members. The entire Service is a "common service" of united and worshipful character. This forward location of the choir, in organic connection with the chancel if not actually within it, imposes greater responsibility upon the choir, and demands better discipline and the very highest standards of musical effort.

The best forward location is in the chancel itself, the stalls facing each other with a wide center area between the two sections. The universal priesthood of believers is better expressed by admitting the choir, representing the special ministry of a part of the congregation, into the chancel than by excluding it. This location, furthermore, preserves the balance and beauty of the building and meets all liturgical requirements. Any other location establishes a secondary focus and distracts attention from the altar. With this arrangement, too, organ, choir, and minister are brought together in a practical way which assures responsibility, leadership, prompt response, and other desirable features. The chancel location necessarily requires that the choir be vested. This makes a proper choir room for assembling and for care of vestments imperative.

The next best location is on either side of the chancel, just outside of it. The choir stalls face the chancel and are at right angles to the pews of the nave. Good architectural treatment will keep the choir stalls, organ console, et cetera, subordinated to the general treatment of the chancel itself and the altar. Lofty arches and open spaces will lead into the chancel and into the nave in order to give freedom to the musical tone. If placed in this location, the choir may be balanced by a baptistery on the other side of the chancel, as has been suggested.

A location in one of the transepts, or in a chamber built out from one side of the nave, is far less satisfactory. A location in a corner of the nave to one side of the chancel must be regarded as definitely poor. From this position the organist and a large portion of the choir are unable to see the altar or much of the chancel, and proper rapport between minister, choir, and congregation is made exceedingly difficult. If the choir is placed here, the organ console should be brought forward near the chancel. Whatever the position of the console, it should be kept as inconspicuous as possible without endangering the

31

teamwork of organist and choir. When it is in the nave, however, extreme caution must be taken to keep it low and prevent its interfering with the congregation's view of the chancel.

2. The Organ. Churchly qualities of tonal depth and devotional power are essential in an organ. The requirement of sufficient space is frequently overlooked in planning the building. It is bad judgment and poor economy to install an expensive instrument and then lose much of its effectiveness by crowding it into inadequate quarters. Even in the case of a small organ, sufficient height must be allowed for the largest pipes to speak freely, and comfortable room must be arranged for the repairer and tuner to work. It should not be necessary to miter the larger pipes and thus impair distinctiveness of tone.

A single organ chamber for an instrument of two manuals and twenty ranks of pipes, with a sixteen-foot open diapason in the pedal, might well be at least fourteen feet long, eleven feet deep, and twenty-two feet high. With a different arrangement of the swell and great organs it might be twenty-two feet long, eleven feet deep, and eighteen feet high. Sufficient grill space must also be provided, and ready means of access. It may well pay a congregation to consult an organ builder before plans for a new building are completed. A few changes in the drawings may save the later expense of rebuilding to provide a proper loft, or the embarrassment of owning a fine organ which produces only mediocre music.

3. Sacristies. The clergy sacristy should be in immediate connection with the chancel and, if possible, readily accessible from the nave. It should be of ample size, well lighted and heated, and provided with a table, chests for clerical vestments, lavatory, and toilet. It must assure the minister and his clerical assistants freedom from interruption. Subdued lights, a good religious picture or two on the walls, and a prayer desk will create a proper atmosphere and aid the minister in his personal preparation for his public ministrations. The sacristy should never seem like an office or a committee room. It is the place of the minister's private devotion, and he ought not have to share it with those who arrange the flowers or count the offering.

A separate working-sacristy should be provided in close connection with the chancel. This is important. Here altar vestments and sacramental vessels may be cared for, flowers arranged, et cetera. In addition to vestment cases, storage closets for linens, candles, vases, et cetera, this room should have a table and a sink of ample size.

A choir vestry for men and another for women are necessary. These should be large enough not only for regular occasions, but for special requirements. They should be easily accessible from outside the building and should connect by wide passageways with the church at the narthex, the nave, or the chancel, and preferably more than one of these. Lockers for vestments, shelves for hymnals and music, mirrors, and lavatories must be provided.

Chapter 3

THE CHURCH YEAR

The Christian Church does not reckon time according to the civil year. It goes by its own system, called the church year, and its calendar differs in many respects from the civil one. It is not determined by scientific exactness, but by spiritual experience. In the civil year, days and seasons are determined by the revolution of the earth about the sun. In the church year, however, the formative principle is the life and teaching of the Sun of Righteousness.

The church year is not the device of any one man or any single group. It is the gradual outgrowth of the experience and needs of Christian men and women throughout the centuries. Its outstanding features are the weekly Lord's day and annual festivals and seasons. The latter are frequently irregular in length, depending as they do upon the relation of Easter, a movable festival, to the other fixed festivals.

The days and seasons of the church year have an essentially religious and spiritual significance. The system as a whole has exerted a profound influence upon Christian life and thought.

ITS SIGNIFICANCE

Patriotism, if it is to be sound, requires a background of historic depth and consciousness. Similarly, Christian faith is strengthened and deepened by its appreciation of historic facts and personalities. The theology and church life of many recent religious groups are shallow because they lack this sense of historic depth. The church year in its historic perspective takes us back through many centuries and countries to the springs of Christianity itself. It enables us to discover the very foundations of the church in the life and teachings of our Lord. It commemorates the Apostles, the first Christian martyr, and St. John the Baptist. It impresses us with the developing consciousness of the communion of saints and the growth of the church. It places the Reformation and other great movements clearly before us.

One of its most valuable features is that its observance assures a definitely Christian character in worship. Its festivals and seasons specially commemorate biblical events and Christian doctrine. It protects the church's worship from the intrusion of social, secular, and unimportant themes such as New Year Sunday, Lincoln Sunday, George Washington Sunday, Mothers' Sunday, Peace Sunday, Children's Sunday, Labor Sunday, Prison Sunday, Tuberculosis Sunday, Arbor Day, Flag Day, Old Home Day, and Tin Can Day. This sort of thing has cheapened and spiritually weakened large parts of Protestantism. The church year lifts the local congregation into consideration of universally significant themes. The local, the temporary, the ephemeral give way to considerations of breadth and consequence. The great fundamentals of the Christian faith are regularly and universally brought under review. Each worshiping congregation is conscious of its participation in a transaction of deep and wide significance.

The complete and repeated presentation of important doctrines, ethical teachings, et cetera, in the cycle of the church year is in line with good pedagogical method. There is no better way of instructing the young, or believers of any age, than by definite and repeated study of important facts. As in the natural year the revolving seasons bring us their special gifts, so in the church year there is an unfolding of the spiritual seasons bringing wholesome truths home to us. In the Christian calendar the life of our Lord constantly repeats itself before our eyes. He passes among his people again as he once walked in Judaea. We may learn of him as his disciples did of old.

The church year and the Liturgy are intimately related. Order and beauty characterize both. The church year gives unity to the Liturgy by providing themes for each Sunday and festival. The details of each Service are built up harmoniously on the themes suggested by the Lessons of the day or season. The result is a Service of dignity and reverence, with rich, appropriate, and harmonious detail. The total effect is one of beauty, balance, and spiritual impressiveness.

The Liturgy provides a form which guides the local congregation in its corporate devotions. By incorporating the themes of the church year, this same Liturgy establishes a definite mood or consciousness throughout the Christian world. Church people live in the mood of its seasons. Not only during the church service, but at all times, they are conscious of the peculiar moods of Advent, Lent, or the Eastertide. Because of this, and as a result of the effort to enrich individual services throughout the different seasons, there has been a great development of music and church art. Back of church architecture and all church art is the Christian Liturgy. Back of the Liturgy is the church year.

35

Fundamental to both are the life of our Lord and the history of his church.

Observed by the greater part of Christendom, including Greek, Roman, Lutheran, Anglican, Moravian, and Reformed, the church year anchors the church to the cross. It keeps it from wandering into merely intellectual, ethical, or social fields. It is essential to a liturgical church. It underlies the order of the Liturgy and the hymnal.

ITS HISTORICAL DEVELOPMENT

The church's growth and development have spanned centuries. There were early commemorations of certain facts in the life of our Lord. The weekly celebration of the Lord's day and the annual celebration of his death and Resurrection were the two foci from which subsequent developments proceeded. Beginning with Easter as the center, and working forward and backward from this point, the church gradually fashioned the complete cycle.

Jewish elements as well as Christian are found here. The movable festivals are derived from Jewish sources; the immovable from Christian history. The weekly sabbath and the cycle of seven days underlie the entire system. Pentecost was originally a Jewish feast, the Feast of Weeks, a harvest festival held a "week of weeks" after the Passover. On the same day that the Jews celebrated the first-fruits of the harvest, the church received the first-fruits of the Spirit; and even today the church celebrates Pentecost seven-times-seven days after the Festival of the Resurrection. It was the church year, too, which occasioned the first great controversy in the Christian Church—the dispute over the date of Easter.

Pagan influences contributed to the determination of dates for the celebration of the Festival of the Nativity, December 25, the Festival of the Epiphany, January 6, et cetera. Both of the dates mentioned were observed by pagan nations as festivals of the sun. Gregory the Great instructed Christian missionaries to Britain to "transform heathen temples into churches and pagan days into Christian festivals, that hard minds may be reduced gradually, not violently." In line with this idea, the church at various times and places has taken a day observed by the pagan world and converted it into a Christian festival. Nor has this process ceased. It was after the war in Korea that Pope Pius XII set for May 1 a Feast of St. Joseph, commemorating him as a worker, in answer to the May Day celebrations of the Communist party.

The determining factor from the first was the commemoration and proclamation of Christian truth. The Lord's day was not a mere transference of the Jewish sabbath to another day. It was a new institution

36

commemorating the Resurrection, and many of the early Jewish Christians kept both days. Easter was the first great festival. Good Friday developed in close connection with it.

A. Alan McArthur in a scholarly work[1] urges his Scottish brethren to recover lost treasures in the church year. He shows how the end of the fourth century witnessed the division of each of the three primary and unitive festivals into double observances. Thus Easter, at first the one great day and season, gave birth to Good Friday; Epiphany to Christmas; and Pentecost to Ascension Day. The season of Lent only gradually assumed its present proportions as a time of preparation. Advent was later established in the West in the sixth century.

The medieval period, largely under the influence of monastic devotions, introduced many new festivals and days. The early church, indeed, observed days in honor of the Apostles and some of the earliest Christian martyrs. But the medieval church filled the calendar with commemorations of obscure saints, festivals of the Virgin, and many other features which expressed medieval doctrine, such as Corpus Christi Day. The recent papal addition of St. Joseph to May 1, which we mentioned earlier, falls also into this category. In the Middle Ages secular work was prohibited, legal proceedings interrupted, and grave social, moral, and economic abuses developed as a result of this over-elaboration and the legalistic requirements imposed by the church with regard to the keeping of such feasts.

Lutheran reform of the church year was conservative and scriptural, as was its reform of doctrine and worship in general. Radical Reformers, acting on the principle that all days should be alike to the Christian, destroyed the entire structure of the Christian calendar. They recognized the Lord's day, transferred to it the sabbath law, and observed the Jewish requirements with great severity. They lost the objective or sacramental conception of worship, and regarded it chiefly as an expression of the piety of the worshipers. Thus the Reformed churches generally developed a multitude of penitential days and days of prayer.

The Lutheran Church, with its sacramental emphasis upon worship, appreciated the value of historic days and seasons. The church regarded them as relating all time to sacred history. It also held the view that a day is rendered holy not by our preaching or praying, so much as by a word and work of God. Recognizing the grave abuses in the over-elaboration of the medieval church, it restored the Christian year to its early simplicity by the application of a scriptural and churchly

---

[1] McArthur, *The Evolution of the Christian Year* (London: SCM Press, 1953).

principle. This was that all customs contrary to the Scripture should be changed, and that only those festivals and days should be observed which were based upon and separated from common days by a Gospel fact. Luther himself said, "The festivals have been so arranged because all parts of the Gospel cannot be heard at once, and therefore its doctrine must be distributed throughout the year." [2] The main outlines were kept. Minor days and festivals of unscriptural origin were rejected. Only the festivals of our Lord and the Apostles, together with certain great days of the church, were retained.

ITS CYCLES AND SEASONS

Jewish converts continued to observe the weekly sabbath (Saturday) at first. But the Lord's day was something new. The early Christians began the day at sunset, reckoning as the Jews did, "night and day." St. Matthew and St. Paul speak of this. Then when Rome, instead of Jerusalem and Antioch, became the center of Christian development, the Roman civil day was adopted. This began at midnight. We have evidences of this in St. John's Gospel and the book of Revelation. The transference of the Christian Service from Saturday night to early Sunday morning was thus aided.

The early church regarded every Lord's day as a little Easter to be kept with rejoicing. The faithful stood in prayer in their assemblies. The Lord's Supper was regularly administered. Offerings were laid aside for the work of the church and the needs of the brethren, and efforts were made to abstain from secular labor.

As the church year developed, two parallel ideas ran throughout different national types: the celebration of the life of our Lord and the history of the church. These fundamental conceptions came to final expression in the *Semester Domini,* or the half-year of the Lord, and the *Semester Ecclesiae,* or the half-year of the church. The first or more objective division included three cycles which roughly corresponded to three related Jewish feasts.

First is the Christmas cycle, corresponding to the Jewish Feast of Tabernacles at the end of the year. This cycle contains three seasons: Advent (Preparation), Christmas (Nativity), and Epiphany (Manifestation).

The second is that of Easter, corresponding in point of time to the Jewish Passover. It begins with Septuagesima and includes Ash Wednesday, Lent, and Easter proper.

The third is the Pentecost or Whitsuntide cycle, corresponding to

[2] Quoted in *The Christian Year* by Edward T. Horn (Philadelphia: Lutheran Book Store, 1876), p. 53.

the Jewish Pentecost in early summer. It includes the Ascension, Pentecost, and Trinity Sunday, this last originally an octave of Pentecost.

Certain lesser festivals were gradually inserted in the calendar, usually on fixed dates corresponding to historic events in the lives of the Apostles, Evangelists and martyrs, the Virgin, and the history of the church.

1. Advent. This first season of the Christmas cycle originated in Gaul in the latter part of the sixth century or earlier. It is an expression of the natural principle of preparing the mind for any great event. The length of the season varied in different places from two to six weeks. The Greek Church, and the Mozarabic and Ambrosian Rites as well, prescribe forty days, beginning November 15, or a period analogous to that of Lent. Gregory the Great is supposed to have established the present period of four Sundays generally observed in the Western church.

In the early centuries Advent was not considered a penitential season. From the twelfth century onward medieval gloom began to settle upon it. The Lutheran Church regards it as a time of sober penitence mixed with holy joy. It serves not only as a preparation for Christmas, but as an introduction to the entire church year. Early Lutheran writers said that the church in Advent celebrates the lowly coming of Christ in the flesh, his spiritual and daily coming in the hearts of the faithful, and his glorious return to judge. The Lessons, Collects, and other Propers stress the importance of spiritual preparation, sober living, and faithful witnessing.

Advent, like Lent, is one of the closed times (*tempora clausa*), during which the church discourages weddings, at least public ceremonies. The thought is that the gaiety naturally associated with these occasions is not in keeping with the spiritual discipline and self-forgetfulness which the church emphasizes in this season.

Advent has appealed strongly to the Lutheran Church in all lands. This is evidenced by the number of hymns and prayers which the season has called forth, a veritable treasury. The color of the season is violet.

2. Christmas. The Festival of our Lord's Nativity, as we have said, was first observed by the Eastern church on January 6. The Western church appointed December 25. This latter date may have been chosen because of the general tradition that our Lord's death occurred March 25, A.D. 29, and that his life completed a perfect cycle of years. The date of the Annunciation would therefore have been March 25, and the date of the Nativity, December 25. The pagans celebrated the day as the birthday of the sun god (*Natalis solis invicti*). At this precise time the sun, after sinking to the lowest point on the horizon, began to ascend and bring light and life to the world. The Christians transformed this day into a celebration of the birth of the Sun of Righteousness, who comes with healing in his wings.

The festival early gained wide observance and evoked an enormous amount of hymns and appropriate music. It was the only festival upon which three services (masses) were held, each with its proper appointments. The first of these was at midnight, the second at dawn (the Aurora Mass), and the third later in the morning. The Propers in our present use are taken from two of these ancient services. The proper color for Christmas, as for all festivals of our Lord, is white.

3. New Year's Day, the Circumcision. In the early centuries this day was observed as the octave of Christmas (*Octava Domini*). It coincided with the beginning of the new year in the pagan calendars, but only by chance. The faithful were, however, urged to attend services instead of engaging in the dissipations of those around them, an admonition which has a peculiarly modern relevance. Much later, in the ninth century, the day was given an especial ecclesiastical character by the celebration of the circumcision of our Lord and the giving of his name.

4. Epiphany, January 6. This is one of the most ancient festivals in the calendar. Recent researches[3] reveal its observance in Asia Minor and Egypt as early as the second century. Here it commemorated both the birth and the Baptism of Jesus. The Baptism was supposed to have been upon the thirtieth birthday of our Lord, which explains the double celebration.

For centuries January 6 had been observed in the East as a solstice festival and as the birthday of the pagan deity Aeon. Now the faithful gave this day Christian meaning. Two centuries later, when communication between East and West became possible, the Eastern Christians accepted the Western preference for December 25 as commemorating the Nativity. January 6, however, remains to this day in the calendar of the Eastern churches as the Festival of our Lord's Baptism, while the church in the West centered its thought on this day upon the story of the star and the magi. The festival then became one of the manifestations of Christ to the gentiles, a meaning which the word "epiphany" itself suggests. The entire period of twelve days between Christmas and Epiphany was given an especial festival character in the medieval church, and the night before Epiphany received special recognition as Twelfth Night.

The Propers (Epistle, Gospel, Collect, et cetera) for the Sundays of this season refer to the manifestation of the glory of Christ in the

---

[3] McArthur, *op. cit.*, p. 30ff.

areas of nature and of grace. One of the distinctive features of the Lutheran calendar is the permissive use of the Lessons for the Festival of the Transfiguration (August 6) on the Last Sunday in Epiphany. This activates the suggestion of Luther that this would be an appropriate climax and conclusion to the season's thought. The Lutheran reformers Bugenhagen and Veit Dietrich appointed these Lessons for the Sixth Sunday. The new *Service Book* continues this provision, but, adhering to the earlier American Lutheran precedent in the *Church Book* and the *Common Service Book,* permits (without requirement) the use of these Propers on the Last Sunday after the Epiphany in every year "except when there is only one Sunday after the Epiphany."

The season has its peculiar importance in the scheme of the church year, coming as it does between the Festival of the Nativity and the season of Lent. It marks the crest of the hill before we descend into the valley of suffering. The length of the season is from one to six weeks, depending upon the date of Easter. The liturgical color is white.

5. Septuagesima to the day before Ash Wednesday. Sometimes called pre-Lent, this is an extension of the Lenten fast. It probably dates from the eighth century. The Sundays, Septuagesima, Sexagesima, Quinquagesima, indicate in round numbers respectively seventy, sixty, and fifty days before Easter. In the Roman Church Septuagesima marks the beginning of the priests' fast. Both the Alleluia and the Gloria in Excelsis are omitted from their Liturgy, and the color is violet, the same as for Lent. Fasting also begins at this time in the Eastern church.

The Lutheran Church does not recognize an extension of the Lenten fast as such, but regards this brief period as one of transition from the thought of Epiphany to that of Lent. It prescribes green as the proper color. It omits all Alleluias in the Psalm texts of its Introits and Graduals. The Epistles for these Sundays remind us of St. Paul's zeal, self-denial, and suffering for Christ and the gospel. The Gospels are parables of the kingdom and the account of Jesus' going up to Jerusalem.

6. Ash Wednesday. Since the seventh century or earlier, Ash Wednesday has been observed as the first day of Lent. It receives its name from the medieval and Roman ceremony of blessing ashes made from palms given out on the preceding Palm Sunday and marking the foreheads of worshipers with these ashes as an expression of penitence. In the early centuries the penitents were blessed, but not the ashes. Other ceremonies arose in different lands. Curtains called Lenten veils were hung between the nave and the choir. Altars were constructed with panels or wings elaborately carved and painted, and extending beyond the central panel. During Lent these outer wings were closed, and remained

41

so until Easter. The ornaments of the altar were reduced to the utmost simplicity. The prayers of the day recall the ancient emphasis upon fasting, but in our use they generally receive a spiritual interpretation. The Collect for the day, like that for Palm Sunday, is among our finest historic Collects. The color for Ash Wednesday and for Lent is violet.

7. Lent. The word is derived either from an Anglo-Saxon term meaning spring or from a German original which refers to the lengthening days. The outstanding feature of the season is that of a fast preparatory to a feast. The idea took root in the early church. Irenaeus and Tertullian both refer to it. At first the fast continued forty hours, then a week. By the time of the Council of Nicaea, A.D. 325, a period of forty days is mentioned. This included Sundays, which are never fast days. The remaining thirty-six days, one-tenth of the entire year, found general acceptance on the principle of the tithe. By the seventh century, however, the general desire to bring the period of fast in agreement with the forty days of our Lord in the wilderness, the forty hours of his entombment, the forty years of Moses, the forty days of Elijah's journey, et cetera, led to the extension of the fast and its beginning on Ash Wednesday.

In the early church Lent was the particular time for the preparation of catechumens for Baptism. The medieval and the modern Roman emphasis is entirely upon fasting and the preparation of the faithful for the worthy keeping of Easter through discipline, penitence, and abstinence. Gregory the Great wrote, "We abstain from fleshly meat and all things that come from flesh, as milk, cheese, and eggs." This became the general usage.

The civil as well as the ecclesiastical law in the Middle Ages vigilantly enforced the fast. Fish took the place of meat as the principal Lenten food. So strictly was the fast observed that garrisons and armies in the field were sometimes reduced to starvation, as in the siege of Orleans in 1429, because they lacked Lenten food, although they had plenty of meat and other supplies. Only one meal was allowed on specific fast days during Lent, and this was not permitted until after the hour of None in the monasteries. This hour was generally recited at three o'clock, but was frequently pushed back as early as midday. From this observance, incidentally, comes our word "afternoon."

Dispensations from fasting were given on condition of making gifts to the church. This was in line with the general principle of indulgences. Sufficient sums were thus amassed to build churches and accomplish other good works. One of the great towers of the Rouen Cathedral was built in this manner, and is known to this day as the

Butter Tower. The Roman Church still regards fasting as of extreme importance and rigorously prescribes the diet of its members during Lent by pronouncement of the bishop. Although in many cases today Roman bishops interpret the fast extremely liberally, the Greek and other Orthodox churches maintain a universally strict fast during Lent.

The Lutheran observance of Lent has reacted from this strong sub-jective emphasis to the objective contemplation of the Word of God. Meditations upon the sufferings and death of the Saviour, which might well be restricted to Holy Week, are still too frequently, and quite in Roman fashion, extended through the entire Lenten season. By the time Holy Week arrives the mind is saturated with morbid details and can absorb but little more of the same. The general use of Bugenhagen's *History of the Passion* throughout the entire period is largely respon-sible for this state of affairs.

We hasten to add, however, that the general Lutheran effort here, as in every other season, is to remove superstition and work-righteous-ness, and to develop a deeper devotion to Christ by the study of the meaning of his victorious humiliation. When all is said and done, how-ever, our church is still under the heavy weight of medieval conceptions of Lent. The season has become for us a time of greater and more general observance than the post-Easter season which gripped the imagination of the early Christians with its notes of joy and triumph.

8. Palm Sunday. The first celebration of this was at Jerusalem at the end of the fourth century. There the people went in the afternoon to the Mount of Olives, heard lessons from Scripture, sang hymns, and returned to the city in slow procession carrying branches of palm and olive, singing, "Blessed is he that cometh in the name of the Lord." Observance of the day became general in the West after the seventh century. Palms were blessed and distributed, first to the clergy and then to the laity. Then there was a procession around the church and a solemn hymn.

Many abuses developed in connection with the popular observance of the procession, and the Reformation discontinued it. It has come back into use in only a few scattered parishes. The Lutheran use, how-ever, retains the ancient Gospel for the blessing of the palms. The prayers in general combine the elements of joy and sorrow.

The general observance of Confirmation on Palm Sunday is in line with the early church custom of adult Baptism as preparatory to the first Communion at Easter. When observed on this day, however, Con-firmation should not suppress the thought of the day's Gospel. The day should be thought of as Palm Sunday and the entrance to Holy

Week, not as Confirmation Sunday. To this end, the Rite of Confirmation may well be observed at an afternoon service.

9. Holy Week. In the Eastern churches this is called the Great Week. In the West its days have the value of Sundays. The reading of the accounts of the Passion as recorded in the different Gospels has always been a feature. Dramatic representation of different characters by division of the accounts among a number of priests eventually developed into musical "Passions." Solo voices sang different parts, and a chorus represented the people, the mob, et cetera. A Reformation development, inaugurated by the reformer Bugenhagen in 1530, was the use of a Passion history based upon a harmony of the Gospels. This is widely used in Lutheran churches today instead of lengthy lessons from the different Gospels themselves, although the latter are retained for those who wish to use them.

10. Maundy Thursday. The name is derived from the Latin word *mandatum,* meaning a command and referring to John 13:34, "A new commandment I give unto you." In the early church the day commemorated the institution of the Lord's Supper, and in Gaul it was known as the *natalis calicis,* or birthday of the cup. In the Lutheran Church Order of Hamburg, 1529, the day is called Holy Thursday. The German *Gründonnerstag* probably refers to the early use in German lands of green vestments on this day. While Rome uses white, the Lutheran use prescribes violet, the Lenten color. The Collect is a beautiful one built about the thought of the Sacrament. During the Middle Ages the Eucharist was celebrated after Vespers. Generally, however, the medieval observance stressed our Lord's command in connection with the feet-washing at the Last Supper. A symbolic ceremony developed, and it became the custom for the pope, kings, and ecclesiastics of high degree to wash the feet of poor men and give them alms. This practice has received considerable attention in the Roman Church of late, and has been re-enforced and expanded in the 1956 changes in the Holy Week observance issued by the Congregation of Sacred Rites and Pope Pius XII.

Edward Traill Horn, III, in his book *The Christian Year* (Philadelphia: Muhlenberg Press, 1957), p. 122, gives an interesting account of the custom in the Roman Church of reading papal bulls *in Coena Domini.* These bulls contained a general excommunication of all heretics. Of this Luther remarked in his *Table Talk:* "At Rome they wait all year for Maundy Thursday, when Christ instituted the Holy Supper, to damn the heretics, of whom I, Martin Luther, am first and foremost. . . . I have been in hell for twenty-eight years—since 1518—and I'm still quite hearty in spite of it." [4]

[4] From the Latin text quoted by Heinrich Alt in *Das Kirchenjahr* (Berlin, 1860), p. 357ff.

11. Good Friday. "God's Friday" may have been the original of this name. The German *Karfreitag* emphasizes the thought of suffering and sorrow. In the early church this day was kept as a feast in which the note of solemn joy was stressed. "Christ our Passover is sacrificed for us, therefore let us keep the feast." The Western church early reacted from this and stressed the sufferings and death of the Lord, prohibiting even the usual celebration of the Eucharist on this day and the day following. During the medieval period many extravagant features were introduced in connection with the adoration of the cross and the Mass of the Presanctified.

Lutheran use has always provided services for this day. The Collects in the Bidding Prayer are taken from the ancient Good Friday services. The observance of the Three-Hour Devotion first introduced in the Roman Church in the seventeenth century and later in the Anglican communion, is now quite general in the Lutheran Church. The vestments are plain and the color is black. Holy Communion ought not to be celebrated though in some German areas where Calvinistic influence was strong this became a Lutheran custom. The altar is generally stripped and washed on Thursday evening and left bare of ornament until Saturday evening. In European churches the organ is generally silent, the Service and the hymns being sung without its aid.

12. Easter. The word is derived from old Teutonic mythology and means spring. In languages other than the German and English, the names for the festival are related to the thought of the Passover. As we have indicated, the dating of Easter occasioned the first great Christian controversy, the Jewish Christians observing the fourteenth day of Nisan, no matter what day of the week. The gentile Christians wished to keep the first day of the week, no matter what the day of the month. The latter preference was finally followed, though the Asian churches observed the other arrangement until the Council of Nicaea, A.D. 325, agreed that Easter should be observed on the first Sunday after the full moon following the spring equinox. The Gregorian reform of the calendar in 1582 resulted again in the observance of different dates in East and West, as the Eastern churches did not accept the new calendar. They now celebrate the festival about two weeks later, on an average, than the Western churches.

Easter has always been regarded as the queen of Christian festivals. The period of fifty days between Easter and Pentecost was a time of special rejoicing. There were no fast days during this time. The entire season was a continuous festival. The Council of Nicaea decreed that on Sundays during this period all should stand during prayers to commemorate the Resurrection. The Lutheran Church continues to observe this universal practice of the ancient church. The Alleluia, omitted from the Liturgy since Septuagesima, again appears in the Psalm texts of the Introits and Graduals.

From the earliest period Easter has been the especial time for the baptism of catechumens and for the Communion of the faithful. There is something impressive in the deep-rooted custom of all believers making their Easter Communion. It exhibits the solidarity and strength of individual congregations and of the entire church. But it is highly desirable that believers should also seek the privilege of more frequent Communions throughout the year, and the church should make this possible.

The liturgical color, as on all festivals of our Lord, is white. The Gospels in the Eastertide record his appearances after the Resurrection.

13. The Festival of the Ascension. The Pentecost cycle is more or less an arbitrary arrangement. The Ascensiontide is not especially a period of preparation, as in other great cycles; and the Festival of the Trinity is also a separate and historically much later observance.

Ascension Day, the fortieth day after Easter, was observed at least from the fourth century with processional pilgrimages outside the cities. This recalled our Lord's leading the disciples out to the Mount of Olives, where he lifted up his hands and blessed them. Thus processions with banners and candles, symbolic of Christ's triumphant entry into heaven, became general. The paschal candle, which had been lighted at Easter and had burned for forty days, and which represented the presence of the Lord with his Disciples, was extinguished after the Gospel. Frequently prayers for the blessing of the fruits of the earth were incorporated in the Service. In England these included the blessing of wells. In the Lutheran use the Propers refer to the historic events commemorated by the festival, the Epistle being unusual in that it is taken from the book of Acts. The liturgical color is white. The alternate Collect is unusual in being addressed to Christ.

The Ascension of our Lord and the Epiphany are major festivals of the church which generally receive minor consideration, chiefly because the one certainly, and the other usually, falls upon a weekday.

14. Pentecost or Whitsunday. This festival takes equal rank with Easter and Christmas, though this is not always appreciated. Its Jewish prototype was the Feast of Weeks, a harvest festival connected with the giving of the law. The word "pentecost" refers to the fifty days after Easter which were observed universally as a period of rejoicing, during which time even ascetics were not required to fast. In the Jewish use, of course, the name referred to the fifty days between the Feast of Unleavened Bread and the Feast of Weeks. The early church often observed Pentecost as a time of Baptism, commemorating the Baptism of three thousand by the Apostles, a kind of spiritual "first-fruits" of the Christian Church. Houses and churches were decorated with branches and flowers. In many lands roses were scattered from the roofs of the churches.

The name Whitsunday is peculiar to English-speaking peoples. It possibly refers to the wearing of white robes by the candidates for Baptism. The key thought of the day is the outpouring of the Holy Spirit and the birthday of the church.

We might expect the liturgical color to be white as on other festivals of the Godhead. The church, however, has always used red. This is probably in commemoration of the early martyrs and in remembrance of the idea that "the blood of the martyrs is the seed of the church." Another reason for red is found in the symbols of the tongues of fire mentioned in the historic account.

15. The Festival of the Holy Trinity. This is a comparatively late festival. The first observance of the day was doubtless merely as the octave of Whitsunday. In the tenth century the church in Gaul made of it a festival in honor of the Holy Trinity. The custom, under the influence of the monasteries, spread throughout the Netherlands, England, Germany, and France. The Roman authorities for a time declined to accept it, but officially approved it in 1334.

The Eastern church has no festival in honor of the Trinity. It observes the Sunday after Pentecost as All Saints' Day. Both oriental and Roman churches count the following Sundays as after Pentecost and not after Trinity Sunday. The Lutheran and the Episcopal liturgies follow the medieval uses in northern Europe and reckon these Sundays after Trinity Sunday. This is the only instance when a season is named after a doctrine, and the practice is difficult to defend. The new Common Liturgy retains this deeply rooted system, but also indicates the much to be preferred "Sundays after Pentecost." Certainly the usual title, "The Tenth Sunday after Trinity," is absurd, and should be completed to read "after Trinity Sunday."

The Trinity festival sums up the entire teaching of the Scriptures as a revelation of the Father, the Son, and the Holy Ghost, stating at once and explicitly what the church year has unfolded in its seasons from Advent to Whitsunday. The Trinity season crowns the festival half of the church year. The Preface and the Collect for the day are extremely theological in form and indicate the late origin of the festival. The color for the day and its octave is white.

47

ITS MINOR FESTIVALS

In addition to the great festivals of our Lord and the church seasons, the church year includes a number of minor festivals and days, and in the case of the Lutheran Church at least, an important festival of the church.

The Roman Church in the late sixteenth century adopted a new calendar in which an attempt was made to reform the abuses and confusion resulting from divergences in the different provincial and diocesan uses of the Middle Ages. In some countries there were nearly fifty festivals, in addition to Sundays, on which the people were required to abstain from manual labor and to attend Mass. The present Roman calendar contains eighteen such "holy days of obligation." But in addition to these there are hundreds of "feasts of devotion," which occupy nearly every weekday throughout the year, and for which special Lessons and prayers are provided. Many new saints' days have been added since the Reformation. Some of these were eliminated or suppressed by Pope Pius X, but the number has since increased again, now including one in his honor. The feasts entered in the *Roman Breviary of Pius V* in 1568 numbered less than 150; the present *Roman Breviary* (1946) includes about 280 such days, many of them in honor of two or more distinct and unconnected saints.

The Lutheran and the Anglican churches practically agreed in their reform of the church year. Luther led the way by a pronouncement as early as 1523 that only such days should be retained as were based upon a Gospel fact. This in general became the determining principle in both churches, though their respective calendars now differ in a few particulars.

The days of the Apostles and of the Evangelists and of St. Stephen, the first martyr, find a place in both systems. Both retain the Conversion of St. Paul, the Annunciation, the Nativity of St. John the Baptist, and All Saints' Day. The Common Liturgy has reintroduced the Festival of the Holy Innocents, December 28, thus completing the historic triduum of St. Stephen's Day, St. John's Day, and Holy Innocents. The Lutheran Church observes February 2 as the Presentation of our Lord; the Episcopal Church as the Purification of the Virgin Mary. They are, of course, both the same, though with different emphasis. The Lutheran Church retains the commemoration of the Visitation, July 2.

These so-called minor days generally receive but limited observance, chiefly because they usually fall upon weekdays. Theological seminaries and other church schools read the appointed Lessons and prayers in their chapel services, and occasionally individual ministers call the attention of their congregations to the lessons which may be learned from the events which these days celebrate. But practical considerations make general observance difficult. And indeed, not all of the Apostles are worthy of equal commemoration, to say nothing of the relative importance of the other days involved. Much of spiritual value, however, may be found in an appropriate observance of some of these days as opportunity affords.

The Lutheran Church also observes the Festival of the Reformation. So far as official calendars go, this is the unique property of Lutherans. This developed from an observance originally instituted by the German reformer Bugenhagen in honor of the translation of the Bible into the language of the people. It soon became an annual thanksgiving for the introduction of the Reformation into particular provinces and districts, though it was observed in different localities on different dates. In 1667 the Elector of Saxony appointed it for October 31, the date of the *Ninety-five Theses*. Since that time it has gained general recognition throughout the Lutheran Church as a festival of the church to be celebrated on or near this date. It has also spread to other Protestant communions. The establishment in recent years by Pope Pius XI of the Feast of the Kingship of Christ to be observed on this very day is probably a papal answer to this increasing Protestant recognition of Reformation Day.

Those who desire fuller information than this condensed chapter affords will find interesting and valuable material in two excellent recent works: *The Christian Year,* by Edward T. Horn, III; and *The Evolution of the Christian Year,* by A. Allan McArthur.

Chapter 4

THE CHURCH SERVICE

As we have seen, the formal expression of the spirit of worship, in so far as it has to do with the church's ordering of time, is found in the church year. Its mature product with respect to the place of worship is the church building. The instrument providing its material and method for public devotion is the church Service or Liturgy. This, like the church year and the church building, has its immediate practical values for the individual congregation. But it is also representative of the thought and life of the entire church. It is one of the historic institutions of Christianity, a fact fully appreciated in the liturgical churches.

Time is greater than any single year or century, and life is longer than any single generation. No truer test of any institution can be made than to think of it in terms of life in its longest and largest aspects. We may well ask concerning the Christian Liturgy: Is it a truthful and wholesome expression of life at its best? Has it a quickening, life-giving power? Or is it merely a lifeless relic of the past?

ITS VITALITY

Let us, then, consider the vital values in the Liturgy. Its severest critics will acknowledge the large place it has had in Christian history. They probably feel that this fact helps to discredit it in the present. Nor is this a modern point of view. It is at least as old as the sixteenth century. The radical Reformers of that day failed to distinguish between the good and the bad, between the living trees and the dead wood of the forest. They started a conflagration that destroyed both and left their worship an almost barren wilderness.

We say nothing in behalf of the dead wood. We are thankful that the conservative Reformers cleared their forest by dragging out the rubbish and burning it. We are no less thankful that they saved the living trees. These had shared and sheltered the best life of the past;

50

their fruit had sustained the race; their leaves were for the healing of the nations.

Growth is the surest indication of life. Let us recall how the Liturgy grew to meet and to express the living needs of the worshiping church. Two great ideas nourished it from the beginning: the communion of men with each other and their God; and the administration of divine gifts. Phrases of the Psalms and other Old Testament passages formed the nucleus. Some of these ancient Hebrew elements found a permanent place in the Christian Service—large portions of the Psalms; single expressions like Amen, Hallelujah, Hosanna, et cetera. Then as it grew, the New Testament began to take the most prominent place. Other expressions of faith and devotion were tested in the fluid rites of the early centuries, until finally the most fitting, the most beautiful, the most adequate gained general currency and became fixed in the parent rites of Antioch, Alexandria, Rome, and the Gallican West.

The vital process continued. Each age contributed to the growing forms. Gentile Christian influences made Sunday the day for worship and largely developed the Christian year. The reading of the Scriptures, the homily, and the administration of the sacraments were the foci from which all development proceeded. The Lord's Prayer, the Kyrie, the Agnus Dei, the Words of Institution, the various Canticles, et cetera, found a place not only in the New Testament, but also in the Liturgy. Our present Service shows this well, containing as it does items from no less than sixteen New Testament books. The Eastern church formed the noble Preface in the Communion Office, the Sanctus, and the Gloria in Excelsis. From it also came the first fragmentary types of a General Prayer. The Western church contributed the Te Deum and many fine hymns, the Confiteor, and the great series of Propers which gave the developing thought of the church year consistent expression—the Introits, Graduals, Collects, Scripture Lessons, and Proper Prefaces.

Nor did growth stop with the Reformation. The Lutheran and Anglican Reformations were constructive. The Lutheran Church restated the fundamental principles of all worship. It was the first to produce a purified and simplified text of the Liturgy in the vernacular and to procure the active participation of the congregation. It restored the sermon, gave birth to the church hymn, and produced many beautiful Collects and prayers. Later centuries contributed elements of value, not only in the matter of translation, but in original Collects and prayers and hymns in the German and Scandinavian churches. The Lutheran Church in America has demonstrated scholarship, taste, and practical ability in mastering the sources, editing a large body of material, and completing an exceptional collection of forms in English which preserve the best in the Christian tradition while fully meeting the requirements of congregations in our own land and time.

The persistence and permanence of the Liturgy challenge our admiration. Dramatic features in the Greek Mysteries threatened to choke it in the early centuries; the mysticism of the East dissipated its vital energies; the mechanical requirements of the medieval West at times quenched its spirit and checked its natural development. There were those in the Reformation who sought its life or neglected it entirely. Its strength was sapped by translation, revision, and refinement no less than by vain repetition and unspiritual performance. Subjective Pietism ignored it. Cold, calculating Rationalism mutilated it and substituted grandiloquent rhetoric for its majestic thought. The American church in the first half of the last century thought it dead, when it thought of it at all. But the vital, essential, wonderful thing in it lived. In spite of all, it revived; and it bears its fruit among us today. Who can say that the Liturgy, by its power of growth, its adaptability to environment, and its persistence in Christian use, has not demonstrated an amazing vitality?

But what of the present? Many admit the power of the Liturgy in the past and admire its creations in Christian art, yet question its value for the present. They think it cold, lifeless, inadequate to the demands of faith and feeling in worship today. They would discard its majestic forms for ill-considered phrases of the moment, products of the "existential" environment. Instead of drawing nigh to God with reverence, they would rush into his presence with a shout. The devotional inheritance of the ages, with its sincerity, depth, and power, is forgotten in the disorderly movement of a modern meeting. The communion of saints fades from view, and in its stead we have "group experience." Impatience with inherited things, the restlessness of the times, the self-sufficiency of a minority of experimenters, and, in some instances, the consciousness of waning pulpit power, encourage some to wonder. They ask whether the historical devotional order of the church is not too rigid, and whether the ancient forms still express truthfully what the modern man feels when he worships with his fellows.

The Liturgy has come to us from the past, as have the greatest and best of our possessions, alive. Like the literature of the past, like the art of the past, like the Holy Scriptures themselves, which God "in times past" caused to be written for our learning, the Liturgy lives. And like them it has power to quicken and nourish the life of the present.

The church is not a new institution in society, a mushroom growth.

Back of its present life are generations of Christian intelligence, experience, and culture. Usages and traditions, forms and ceremonies, gradually developed in the church as elsewhere. And the best of them have come down to us. These are more than mere traditions of the elders. They are media of devotional expression, means of churchly association, instruments of practical efficiency in our own day. The church of the present is united in conscious fellowship and in desirable uniformity of life by the regular and intelligent use of common forms and the consideration of common themes and tasks. Close and continued familiarity with these forms and ceremonies, as with fine models in art and literature, elevates standards of appreciation and taste and gives sincerity and depth to worship and to life. No other single feature compares with the Liturgy in promoting churchliness and conscious fellowship with the communion of saints. The Common Liturgy, common hymns, and a common order are expressions of a common faith which the common man can understand. They have an immeasurable practical value in making the individual a living member of the group, and in bringing the local congregation into vital relationship with the church as a whole.

Of course, the Liturgy is more than a collection of forms. It is a form filled with fire, the fire of the Holy Spirit. It is more than a lovely legacy whose beauty stirs the imagination of a few. It is a living instrument for the many. It is a bell, whose metal assumed enduring form centuries ago, but whose clear tones have undiminished power and purity today. Were there more of the human in it and less of the divine, it might rust or decay. But the large proportion of Scripture embedded in its several parts is one assurance of its eternal youth and power.

As the Liturgy grew in the past, we may expect to see its vitality demonstrated by growth in the present. Our services today are not exact translations or mere adaptations of other services. Our Liturgy is not the apostolic Liturgy, or the medieval Liturgy, or the Liturgy of the Roman Church, or the Liturgy of any of our Reformers, or exactly the Service of Lutheran churches anywhere in Europe today. Much of it has been built upon a "consensus of pure Lutheran liturgies of the sixteenth century." This consensus was obtained by constructive criticism of historic material. The whole has been condensed, adapted, arranged, and extended where necessary to meet the requirements and possibilities of American congregations of today and tomorrow. The day after tomorrow—this may mean many decades—will probably see further adaptations, additions, and subtractions in minor details as the life of the church continues to flow through these forms.

The communion of saints has a future as truly as a past and a present.

The power of the Liturgy reaches forward as well as backward and upward. One of the great tasks of the church today is to conserve its best and to transmit these things unimpaired to the coming generation. Next to Holy Scripture and Christian doctrine, the Christian Liturgy is the church's most valuable tradition. If we would be fair to our children's children, we must pass it on, richer if we can than it was when we first received it.

The church dare not neglect its youth or it will have no age. It must educate and train our youth in forms and acts of devotion as well as instruct them in points of doctrine. It is not enough for children to be born into a home, as we learn to our sorrow in current ravages of juvenile delinquency. They must be nourished and bred, taught and trained, inspired with tradition and principles, and given the best cultivation of gifts and character that the family and the community afford. The same responsibility for her children rests upon the church. We derive the great part of our knowledge, our great principles and our ideals from the past experience of the race. The classics in literature and art—and not the newspapers, the paperbacks, and the technical journals—nourish the real life and preserve the ideals of a people. There is no more certain road to Christian culture and churchly consciousness than the careful and constant endeavor to acquaint the youth of the church with the classics of devotion. Or maybe it would be better stated the other way around: there is no more certain road away from these great values than the failure to acquaint the youth of the church with their heritage.

The test of life is a test which the Liturgy can meet, and which it should welcome. By its persistence, adaptation to environment, and growth it has given ample proof of vitality. It is an inheritance, our birthright, and we should not despise it or barter it for a mess of pottage when we are weary. It is more than an inheritance. It is a living instrument which, in forms of greater or lesser fulness, serves the majority of Christian communions today. Many who in former times rejected it now see its value; they are reaching for it with eager hands.

It is a wise, patient, and able teacher of youth. It must, of course, be used intelligently and in a fresh and living way. And it will never be a substitute for personal conviction in the pew or for vital preaching in the pulpit. It can, however, increase the powers of both. It has its own important place in the Christian system. In filling this, it fills the temple of worship with the power of Word and Sacrament, the beauty of holiness, and the glory of common prayer and sacrifice.

SPIRITUAL DIMENSIONS

We have discussed vital values in the Liturgy. We next consider its perfection of form. As an enduring expression in noble form of great religious emotion, the Liturgy is a work of art.

Greek sculpture, which caught the stirring movement of horses and men at just the right moment and holds them forever in perfect poise for the admiration of mankind, is an example of the power of art to gather the subtle elements of a complex civilization and give them enduring expression. The Christian Liturgy is such an art form. It is not a museum case containing antique specimens of devotion for examination by anthropologists. It is a work of art in itself—complete, possessing unity, scale, purpose. It is an instrument—spiritually keen, flexible, beautiful—fashioned by the fires of faith in the forge of experience.

In all art, proportion is a fundamental quality. Whether it be a Greek temple or a Gothic cathedral, we are conscious first of all of mass and proportion. No matter how beautiful the detail, if the proportions are bad, the total impression is bad. In the same manner, the formal expression of worship must have proper proportions. Its spiritual dimensions must be adequate and impressive.

The first of these is historic depth. Christianity has suffered much from the mushroom groups that spring up overnight in unhealthy soils and flourish just long enough to draw away many from the historic churches. These movements are of many kinds: intellectual, emotional, evangelistic, socialistic. They are practically one in discarding the liturgical principle. They instinctively realize that this is inseparably connected with a dimension which their shallow institutions lack— depth of thought, length of history and experience. The radical Reformers, we have seen, generally made the same mistake. They broke sharply with the past, discarded the church year, destroyed the Liturgy, demolished beautiful church buildings, stained-glass, and organs. Their spiritual descendants generally realize the folly of this and are endeavoring to restore the lost dimension of depth as well as the lost quality of beauty to their worship.

As we have seen, twenty centuries—if not thirty—underlie the Liturgy as well as the church of today. A quick review trip across these centuries reveals the early church, freed from persecution, perfecting its public worship and investing it with a dignity and a beauty which impressed even the pagan world; the medieval centuries elaborating externals and overweighting the Liturgy as well as the cathedrals with ornament; the destructions and devastations of the radical Reformers; and the discriminating principles of the conservative Lutheran Reformation which retained significant historical usages, unless they were positively unevangelical, and also permitted freedom in nonessentials.

We see that because of these principles of the Reformation a full ceremonial persisted in Germany in many places. In conservative Lutheran districts such as Saxony, Nürnberg, and Mecklenburg, many of the ancient observances, including vestments, lights, colors, plainsong, and ministerial intonations survived well into the eighteenth and even the beginning of the nineteenth century. By this time Rationalism had effectively destroyed all liturgical life and feeling.

Poverty and simplicity naturally attended the beginnings of church life in America. The strongest Lutheran settlements were made in soil thoroughly uncongenial to liturgical worship—among the Quakers and Pietistic sectarians of Pennsylvania and the Dutch Reformed of New York. Later the first definite program of Anglicization was colored by Calvinistic and other nonliturgical influences emanating from the dominant English-speaking Protestant groups which also occupied the field. All of these factors helped dilute the liturgical tradition and confuse the church.

The liturgical revival in Europe was concerned primarily with restoring the Liturgy, with more or less complete text, the congregational hymn, and music of churchly type for the choir. The Common Service in this country (1888) was entirely a literary work. The Joint Committee which prepared it left it entirely devoid of musical settings. Relative completeness was attained in the text. Rubrical directions were of the simplest.

The *Common Service Book* of the United Lutheran Church took a long and helpful step forward in 1918. It added a fine hymnal and a series of Occasional Services. It also provided musical settings for both Liturgy and hymns. It supplied an important body of General Rubrics with detailed directions concerning simple ceremony, altar vestments, the use of colors, et cetera. It made no pronouncements on architectural appointments.

This quick trip should be a healthful corrective of the mistaken idea, rather common among us, that the sixteenth century was the beginning of all things, and that the Reformers should be glorified as Founders and given an apostolic halo which they would be the first to reject. It should help us see how the pure devotion of the developing church and the inspiration of the Spirit of God in every century have made the Liturgy a veritable chalice of salvation from which we may drink in our day and be satisfied. As we grasp these forms, the perfecting of which devout men of every nation and every century have contributed to, we

56

must be impressed with the depth of Christian thought and feeling, the length of Christian history and experience, they represent.

The second dimension is breadth. All public and corporate worship implies fellowship—common prayer and a congregational service. The individual realizes that he is but one in a congregation; the congregation feels that it is part of the church, not all of it; and the church realizes that it is but a part of the communion of saints of all time—past, present, and future.

Yet the worshiper *is* a member of the congregation; the congregation *is* a part of the church; and the church *is* the present representation of the communion of saints in space and time. The Liturgy, with its breadth of sympathy and understanding, sounds in the local congregation the note of universality. The ideals, the standards of the whole church assert themselves. The voice of universal faith and experience sounds over the limited and cruder expression of individuals. The church speaks to the congregation in liturgical worship, and develops a church consciousness which is corrective of individualism, congregationalism, localism, and intolerance.

The third dimension is height. Few indeed are the groups which have entirely discarded the written Word, the sacraments, and all forms of worship. Even among those who attempt this in theory, public worship develops a formality all its own. In the nonliturgical churches, only the gifted few are really able to sustain public worship upon the highest levels of solemnity, dignity, and spirituality.

Consider again the familiar but majestic forms of the Preface, one of the oldest parts of the historic Liturgy:

> Lift up your hearts.
>> We lift them up unto the Lord.
> Let us give thanks unto the Lord our God.
>> It is meet and right so to do.
> It is truly meet, right, and salutary, that we should at all times, and in all places give thanks unto thee, O Lord, Holy Father, Almighty, Everlasting God:
> Therefore with Angels and Archangels, and with all the company of heaven, we laud and magnify thy glorious Name; evermore praising thee, and saying:
> Holy, holy, holy, Lord God of Sabaoth; Heaven and earth are full of thy glory; Hosanna in the highest. Blessed is he that cometh in the Name of the Lord; Hosanna in the highest.

Could any individual minister, priest, or bishop, however gifted, however inspired by a particular occasion, hope to secure such a sublime sense of height by words so few, and to sustain the effect service after service, year after year, by any utterance of his own? Many other passages of equal beauty and power might be cited in illustration of this point.

The exalted character, the elevating, lifting power in this, and in similar portions of the Liturgy, comes from the fact that it is not a personal product, but the utterance of the church itself. Not the genius of a Shakespeare or a Milton, but the universal feeling of the church has carried these expressions to the heights and given them a significance which makes them a fitting medium for the expression of the many. The individual utterance is too concrete, too hard, too heavy, too unimaginative, too close to earth. The conventionalized form—the Liturgy, the ceremony, the symbol—lifts us to levels on which we can stand together and together say things we could not and would not say if we had to say them alone.

The Liturgy, as the guide and guardian of the common worship of Christendom, has preserved the essentials of the faith among the lowly when the learned lost their way among the subtleties of philosophy. It has helped to level barriers of time and place, of class and condition. It has united the church in one conscious endeavor—the effort to worship the adorable Trinity and to receive divine gifts of grace. The Liturgy achieved these results by constructive and constant search for significant form. It thus developed into a great art work itself, perfect in proportion and lovely in detail, and became at the same time the mother of all the arts. We cannot believe that anything so precious and so fair could be the work of man alone. No, "this is the Lord's doing; it is marvellous in our eyes." Wilhelm Loehe, the eminent German liturgical scholar, said of it:

I know nothing that is higher or more fair than the worship of my Lord; there all men's arts combine in the service of adoration; there is his countenance transfigured, his very form and voice made new; there he giveth God the glory; yea, the holy Liturgy of the church surpasseth all the poetry of the world.

A word from one of our esteemed contemporaries may be in place. Bishop Bo Giertz in his first pastoral letter after assuming his office as Bishop of Gothenburg, Sweden, in 1949 discussed two things which often seem to be in conflict: spiritual awakening and the Liturgy. He pleads for both. The following is an excerpt from his remarks on the significance of the Liturgy.

There can be no normal church life without Liturgy. Sacraments need form, the order of worship must have some definite pattern. It is possible to live for a short time on improvisations and on forms that are constantly changing and being made over. One may use only free prayers and yet create a new ritual for every worship situation. But the possibilities are soon exhausted. One will have to repeat, and with that the making of rituals is in full swing.

Liturgy in the church is a foretaste of the eternal song of praise, an earthly expression of that which is the content of eternity and the basic melody of creation, a never ending thanksgiving to the Creator and Father of all things. Within its earthly poverty Liturgy contains something of the beauty of the heavenly, the blessed sense of the nearness of the Eternal, and the joy of being privileged to sacrifice everything in order to be one with Christ.[1]

[1] Bo Giertz, *Liturgy and Spiritual Awakening,* English translation by Clifford Ansgar Nelson (Rock Island, Illinois: Augustana Book Concern, 1956), pp. 17, 32.

Chapter 5

THE SERVICE BOOK AND HYMNAL

Before discussing the Common Liturgy and Hymnal in detail, it may be well to review more closely the development of Lutheran worship in America and to discover, if we may, the formative factors which led to the preparation of this latest work.

The church in America is a blend of many strains and cultures. Lutheran ministers have served in our land for a full three centuries. Worship has been conducted in many languages.

The earliest settlers on the Atlantic seaboard were Hollanders and Swedes. The first Lutheran minister ordained in America, Justus Falckner, was a German ordained in Philadelphia according to the Swedish rite to minister to Dutch congregations in New York State. This unique service on November 24, 1703, witnessed by Indians and Wissahickon hermits, revealed a major problem with which the church has had to deal ever since—the diversity of its linguistic and cultural backgrounds. Those early Lutherans were but the forerunners of the German, Swedish, Norwegian, Danish, Finnish, Slovak, Hungarian, and other European Lutherans who later came in great numbers to settle in Pennsylvania and New York and, even in greater numbers, in the midwestern and northwestern states. Each of these linguistic groups organized synods, colleges, and seminaries, and worshiped in the language of the fathers. Only very gradually were services provided in the language of the land.

The first native Lutheran Liturgy in America was the Muhlenberg Liturgy of 1748. In that year six pastors, including the Swedish provost, Sandin, along with twenty-four lay delegates, organized the Ministerium of Pennsylvania. Muhlenberg's German Order for the Service and the Holy Communion, together with English forms for Baptism and Marriage, was officially adopted by the new synod, and manuscript copies of it continued in use for nearly forty years. The first printed Liturgy and hymnal, to which Muhlenberg contributed the preface, was published in 1786.

Muhlenberg himself, with prophetic vision just before his death, proclaimed the ideal of "one Church, one Book." A century and a half passed before the church could attempt to put this vision into practice. The reasons for this are the same ones which prevented the Lutheran churches of Europe from having a common Liturgy—nationalism, linguistic diversity, self-sufficiency, the isolationism of provincial churches (Saxony, Bavaria, Hannover, Mecklenburg, et cetera), and the failure to realize the practical values in a common rite and in co-operative endeavor.

Early Lutherans in America redrew the map of Europe on American soil. They established separate linguistic synods and general bodies, founded institutions, and published separate liturgies and hymnals, each after its kind. For many long years congregations continued to use liturgies and hymnals authorized by the state churches in Germany, Sweden, Denmark, Norway, Finland, Slovakia, Hungary, et cetera, or English translations of the same. While breathing a common spirit, and containing many common forms, these services were quite diverse in character.

The first permanent English Lutheran congregation in America was St. John's, in Philadelphia. This was organized under the forceful leadership of General Peter Muhlenberg in 1806. It was not until 1868, however, that a really satisfactory English Liturgy appeared. This was the *Church Book,* actually prepared by the Ministerium of Pennsylvania, but officially adopted by the General Council at its organizational meeting in 1867, and printed in time for use at its second convention in 1868. The chief authors of this Liturgy were Drs. Beale M. Schmucker, Charles Porterfield Krauth, Joseph Augustus Seiss, and the Rev. A. T. Geissenhainer. The Rev. Frederick Mayer Bird contributed materially to the preparation of the hymnal. Drs. Henry E. Jacobs and Adolf Spaeth were later added to the committee and aided in work on the Occasional Services (Ministerial Acts) which were incorporated into the *Church Book* in 1892. Years before this, Drs. Schmucker, Spaeth, and S. Fritschel had prepared a German counterpart of the *Church Book,* the *Kirchenbuch* of 1877. This book was the first to restore the full use of Matins and Vespers to the church in this country.

The *Church Book* was significant as a scholarly and native American Liturgy and hymnal in the language of the land. Its strength lay not only in its definitely confessional character, but equally in the depth of its historic foundations and the breadth of its ecumenical sympathies.

Its Liturgy owed much to the scholarly researches of Loehe, Kliefoth, Schoeberlein, and others in Germany during the two decades preceding its appearance, and also to contemporary studies by John Keble, William Palmer, Philip Freeman, Charles Wheatley, and others in England. The excellence of its hymnal was due to the fact that its compilers were in touch with current developments in England and were able to insert in the collection many of the finest fresh translations of classic hymns from the Greek, Latin, and German languages, as well as many original English hymns by Bishop Heber, William Walsham How, Christopher Wordsworth, and many others, all of which had appeared for the first time in the epoch-making *Hymns Ancient and Modern* of 1861. The one great weakness of both the Liturgy and the hymnal of the *Church Book* was the fact that its editors made no provisions for musical rendition of the texts. This lack had to be supplied by the often uneven efforts of private individuals.

THE COMMON SERVICE

The *Church Book* blazed the way for a work of larger significance and influence which appeared from the press twenty years later. This was the Common Service of 1888, a co-operative endeavor by representatives of the General Council, the General Synod, and the United Synod of the South, three general bodies which thirty years later united to form the United Lutheran Church in America. This was a Liturgy only, without a hymnal and without musical settings. The sound principles which underlay this Liturgy, and the excellence of its literary form, commended it to other groups. Within a few years it was included in the official service books of practically all Lutheran churches in the country.

The chief architects of the Common Service were Drs. Beale M. Schmucker, Edward Traill Horn, and George U. Wenner. Other more or less active members of the joint committee were Drs. E. J. Wolf, Joseph A. Seiss, Henry E. Jacobs, Adolph Spaeth, and F. W. Conrad. Dr. Horn at thirty-four years of age was the youngest member of the committee and, as events developed, the most influential. A graduate of the Philadelphia Seminary, he was pastor of historic St. John's Church in Charleston, South Carolina. His initiative, taste, and judgment gave him the balance of power in the entire enterprise.

The Common Service was something more than a projection of earlier principles and forms. Its authors stood on the foundations laid in the *Church Book* and the early American Liturgy of Muhlenberg. They leaped over these earlier works, however, and over the various contemporary recovered forms of the Lutheran state churches in Germany and Scandinavia. They set up a rule which stated their guiding principle as follows: "The common consent of the pure Lutheran liturgies of the sixteenth century, and when there is not an entire agreement among them, the consent of the largest number of those of greatest weight."

This study of the purified liturgies of the classic Reformation century placed the project upon an objective, historical basis of depth and breadth. The assertions of personal taste and preference were minimized. The Common Service, in the order and great body of its material, presented the pure Service of the Christian Church of the West in the earliest times, as simplified in some respects and in others given new emphases in the classic period of the Reformation. Dr. Beale M. Schmucker in his scholarly preface to the Common Service describes the liturgical reconstructions of the early Lutheran Reformers. This preface deserves careful study. It reveals principles and forms which underlie the fuller Common Liturgy of today.

Luther's *Formula Missae,* an evangelical revision of the Latin Mass, appeared in 1523. This stated principles and suggested forms. In 1524 the *Teutsch Kirchenambt* was introduced at Strassburg and in 1525 the Doeber *Evangelical Mass* at Nürnberg. In the same year, Conrad Rupff, the Chapel Master of the Duke of Saxony, and Johann Walther, his assistant and successor, aided Luther in arranging music for his German Mass (*Deutsche Messe*), which appeared in print early in 1526. Bugenhagen's order for Brunswick was completed in 1528; that for Hamburg in 1529; and his Danish order in 1537. In Sweden, Olavus Petri published his *Manual,* which provided evangelical forms for Baptism, Marriage, visitation of the sick, and burial, early in 1529. This was the first Protestant work of its kind. Petri followed it with his important and relatively complete Swedish Mass in 1531. Two years later, 1533, two influential Orders were authorized in Germany—the Brandenburg-Nürnberg Order prepared by Brenz and Osiander for the prosperous and art-loving city of Nürnberg; and the Order for the city and jurisdiction of Wittenberg, which superseded the personal orders of Luther and Bugenhagen, and thereafter was used by them. During the next few years many cities and provinces in Germany issued similar Orders. Many of these retained portions of the Service in Latin, but all sought to provide acceptable forms in the vernacular.

These Orders differed considerably from each other. But after a time there appeared in Saxony, northern Germany, and Scandinavia particularly, a definite and generally accepted type of Liturgy. The Order of government and worship which Justus Jonas and his associates Spalatin, Cruciger, and Myconius prepared in 1539 for the Duchy of Saxony provided a typical standard Lutheran Service with which the liturgies of Mecklenburg, Lüneburg, Calenberg, and other north German cities and states in their successive editions are in close agreement.

It is interesting to trace the relationship of many of these Orders to each other through political and ecclesiastical connections and the use of identical liturgical material. We look for such similarities as the order of parts, identical exhortations, Collects, prayers, Versicles, et cetera.

The sixteenth century services were primarily translations and revisions of the medieval Latin liturgies, with a few new features. Purity of doctrine was carefully guarded; the sermon was given increased importance; the calendar was simplified; church song took a new flight; the ancient musical intonations of the minister and the finest music of the choir were carefully preserved. An Order of Public Confession, the Prayer of the Church, an exhortation to communicants and a few new Lessons and prayers were introduced. In general, however, the whole outline and structure of the Service of the Western church for a thousand years was preserved. Only that which was contrary to Holy Scripture or otherwise objectionable was removed.

The whole series of Introits, Collects, Epistles, and Gospels, which for the most part had been completed in the reign of Charlemagne, was continued with slight changes in the German and Scandinavian liturgies of the sixteenth century. This series came into the Common Service of 1888, and it now constitutes the basic liturgical Proper of the Common Liturgy. There are but few of the Sunday Collects which have not been in continuous use for more than twelve hundred years. With some differences in the days for which they are appointed, most of these beautiful prayers are now in use in all Roman Catholic churches, though only in Latin; in the Lutheran churches of Germany, Denmark, Norway, Sweden, the United States, and wherever scattered throughout the world; in the Church of England throughout the Commonwealth of Nations, and in the Protestant Episcopal Church in this country; and in other groups besides. Here in the field of Christian worship is a notable example of ecumenicity and unity.

In the providence of God, the Lutheran Church, first of all, revised and purified the services of the church and translated them into the vernacular. The Lutheran edition of the Communion Service had been issued in many editions, had been tested by more than twenty years of continuous use, and, at Luther's own instigation, had been provided with varied musical settings for Sundays and festivals in the superb folio volume edited by Johann Spangenberg before the English revision of the old Service was made by the Church of England in the first Prayer Book of Edward VI in 1549.

The close agreement between this first Prayer Book of the Church of England and earlier Lutheran liturgies on the Continent is explained by the fact that the Sarum and other Anglican missals, from which the English revision was made, agreed almost entirely with the Bamberg, Mainz, and other German missals, and with the Swedish and Danish missals, differing, as did they, in important respects from the Roman Missal. It is important to note that these two daughter churches of the Reformation, the Lutheran Church on the Continent and the Church of England, pursued parallel paths in preserving the services of the church of the olden time, and that each, according to its genius, has further enriched the worship of succeeding generations.

Religious wars and the devastations of Pietism and Rationalism in the centuries following the Reformation practically ruined church life and worship in Germany and England alike. The confessional and liturgical movement of the nineteenth century revived the church, restored its Liturgy and produced a wealth of hymnody and music in both countries. The Common Service was definitely a product of this fruitful movement. It, however, contained only the Service with its Propers, Matins and Vespers, the Litany, the Suffrages, and a collection of Collects and prayers. It provided no forms for Baptism, Confirmation, Marriage, et cetera. There was no hymnal, and no musical settings were given.

The three bodies which had originally prepared this Service, and had issued it with variations in three separate editions, later eliminated these differences and filled out some of the outlines with proper Introits, Collects, and a complete series of Graduals. With the addition of General Rubrics, a series of Occasional Services, the Passion History, a hymnal, and complete musical settings, this work appeared in 1917 as the *Common Service Book,* and was adopted in 1918 under the same title by the newly-formed United Lutheran Church. This work considerably expanded the Common Service as such, and promptly won distinction and influence on its own account.

The Common Service contributed greatly to the development of church consciousness and unity throughout the church, in spite of the fact that numerous changes in text were separately made by all the churches which accepted it. Not a single church today uses the Common Service precisely as it was adopted in 1888. We have already noted the additions of the *Common Service Book.* Other churches—the American, Augustana, Evangelical Lutheran, Missouri Synod, et cetera —omitted certain parts of the original text and expanded other sections with alternate Collects, Lessons, Graduals, et cetera. Some of these changes are minor; others are important. These variations in a professedly "common service" called for reconciliation.

Other considerations, equally important, were the incorporation of all Lutheran groups within the fabric of American life, the restriction of immigration and the rapid process of Anglicization, the leveling influence of the public schools, and the experience of two World Wars we have already mentioned. These, together with the success of many co-operative endeavors and the acceptance of common confessional standards, made it clear that the Lutheran churches in America are one in faith and destiny. Knit together of many strains and appreciative of heritages from other centuries and lands, they seek to bear united testimony to Christian truth in this our own country and time. The use of common liturgical forms and a common hymnal will accelerate this historical process and help produce a united church of distinctive character.

THE JOINT COMMISSIONS

Occasional prophetic voices had been heard in the American Lutheran Conference, the United Lutheran Church, and the Augustana Church, suggesting the possibility of at least a common hymnal. It remained, however, for Dr. Oscar Blackwelder, of Washington, D.C., to spark the movement which produced the Common Liturgy and Hymnal. At a meeting of the United Lutheran Church in Minneapolis, October, 1944, he moved that in accepting the final report of its *Common Service Book* Committee completing the revision of the church's hymnal, the church instruct the committee "to seek the fullest possible co-operation with other Lutheran bodies, in the hope of producing, as nearly as proves feasible, a common Lutheran hymnal in America."

This proposal was enthusiastically adopted, and events proved that the churches were more nearly ready for such an endeavor than had been realized. Drs. Luther D. Reed and Harvey D. Hoover, chairman and secretary respectively of the committee, formally extended the invitation which had been authorized. Every Lutheran church body, except those in the Synodical Conference and several very small bodies, eventually accepted it.

The Joint Commission on the Hymnal was organized in Pittsburgh, at the First English Lutheran Church, June 19-21, 1945. The following representatives of the co-operating churches served throughout the full decade of the Commission's work, or for a shorter period:

The American Lutheran Church: the Rev. Drs. L. O. Burry, Albert Jagnow, Lawrence S. Price, and Hans Knauer. From the Augustana Church: the Rev. Drs. Clifford A. Nelson, E. E. Ryden, E. W. Olson, C. J. Sodergren, and C. A. Wendell. From the Evangelical Lutheran Church: the Rev. Drs. Selmer A. Berge, Lawrence N. Field, Hermann A. Preus, and Gabriel Tweet. From the Lutheran Free Church: the Rev. Dr. T. O. Burntvedt and Prof. Leland B. Sateren. From the United Evangelical Lutheran Church: the Rev. Drs. Fred C. M. Hansen and C. M. Videbeck, the Rev. C. C. Kloth, and the Rev. C. Scriver Kloth. From the Suomi Synod: the Rev. Drs. Alvar Rautalahti and Raymond Wargelin. From the United Lutheran Church: the Rev. Drs. Harvey D. Hoover, Edward Traill Horn, III, Ulrich Leupold, Luther D. Reed, William R. Seaman, George R. Seltzer, and Paul Z. Strodach. During the decade the Commission lost the valued services of Drs. Burry, Jagnow, Sodergren, Strodach, and Wendell by death.

The almost immediate promise of success by this commission led the representatives of the Augustana Church to propose a Joint Commission on the Liturgy. All concerned realized that this might present much greater difficulties than would arise in the case of hymnal preparation. The presidents of the churches, however, authorized a small exploratory conference which met in Chicago, February 25, 1946. The following were present: Professor H. C. Leupold, the American Lutheran

Church; President Conrad Bergendoff, the Augustana Church; the Rev. C. M. Videbeck, the United Evangelical Lutheran Church; Professor Luther D. Reed and Dr. Paul Z. Strodach, the United Lutheran Church.

Discussion brought these points into the clear: (1) Lutheran services in all bodies are now conducted almost entirely in the English language; (2) several bodies publish English translations and adaptations of liturgies used in Europe; (3) the Common Service was also officially recognized and appeared in all service books and hymnals; (4) the great majority of Lutherans in this country were using only the Common Service, though in slightly variant forms; (5) each general body had its own hymnal.

The following resolutions were adopted:

1. We agree unanimously that a Common Liturgy for our church in America is desirable and possible.
2. We agree that the Common Service shall be the basis and that other current uses in our church shall be considered.
3. We request each of the presidents of our General Bodies to appoint not more than three or four representatives to form a Joint Commission which shall seek to achieve this goal.
4. We believe that it is highly desirable that all Lutheran bodies in this country co-operate in this undertaking and we therefore ask authority to issue the necessary invitations.

This program was approved by the co-operating presidents, who authorized the five conferees to request the presidents of all Lutheran bodies in the country to appoint representatives to attend a conference in Pittsburgh, June 26-28, 1946. At this meeting the Joint Commission on the Liturgy, consisting of eighteen members, was organized with Dr. Luther D. Reed, chairman, and Dr. H. C. Leupold, secretary.

The president of the Missouri Synod, Dr. J. W. Behnken, D.D., stated in his reply of August 17, 1946, to a repeated invitation, "Our Synod recently published a new Hymnal. . . . This contains the Liturgy which is now used quite extensively in our circles and is being introduced in many places where very little Liturgy formerly was in use. Our Synod would not be interested now in effecting another change."

The personnel of the Commission changed somewhat as the work proceeded. The following participated in part or all of the work:

The American Lutheran Church: the Rev. Drs. H. C. Leupold and Samuel F. Salzmann. The Augustana Synod: the Rev. Drs. Conrad Bergendoff, Otto H. Bostrom, and Oscar N. Olson. The Evangelical Lutheran Church: the Rev. Drs. Selmer A. Berge, Lawrence N. Field, H. A. Preus, and Gabriel Tweet. The Suomi Synod: the Rev. Dr. Alvar Rautalahti. The United Evangelical Lutheran Church: the Rev. Drs. F. C. M. Hansen and C. M. Videbeck, the Rev. C. C. Kloth, and the Rev. C. Scriver Kloth. The United Lutheran

Church: the Rev. Drs. Emil E. Fischer, Harvey D. Hoover, Edward Traill Horn, III, Luther D. Reed, George R. Seltzer, and Paul Z. Strodach. The Commission mourned the loss of Drs. Strodach and Bostrom by death during the progress of the work.

Many meetings of both commissions were held in Chicago and Philadelphia. Several joint sessions were also held. The commissions included representative groups of scholars and church musicians. The Hymnal Commission numbered twenty-three; the Liturgical Commission eighteen. In seven instances individuals were members of both commissions. The group, thirty-four in all, included ten persons who were or had been presidents of or professors in theological seminaries or colleges of the church. Others were presidents of synods, editors, musicians, and prominent pastors.

The commissions appointed subcommittees for study of assigned subjects. The general officers elected were: Dr. Reed, chairman of both commissions; Dr. E. E. Ryden, secretary of the Commission on the Hymnal; Dr. H. C. Leupold, secretary of the Commission on the Liturgy; Dr. George R. Seltzer, chairman of the subcommittee on text, and Dr. Edward Traill Horn, III, chairman of the subcommittee on music of both commissions; and Dr. Albert Jagnow, secretary of the music committee of the Hymnal Commission. The important Joint Editorial Committee consisted of Dr. Seltzer, chairman; Dr. William R. Seaman, secretary; the other above-mentioned officers of both commissions; and the following additional members: Drs. Conrad Bergendoff (Augustana), Lawrence W. Field (Evangelical Lutheran), and F. C. M. Hansen (United Evangelical Lutheran Church).

THE WORK OF THE COMMISSIONS

All major decisions concerning texts, tunes, music, et cetera, for the Common Liturgy and Hymnal were made by majority action of the respective commissions. Reconciliation of the forms of approved texts, rubrics, and musical settings; the securing of permissions for the use of copyrighted material; capitalization, punctuation, and styling of the book; proofreading; and other similar matters became the responsibility of the Editorial Committee. This committee also acted for the commissions in necessary and important arrangements with the publishers.

From the beginning the commissioners were deeply conscious of the hope of all the churches that agreement might be reached. Initial study uncovered a substantial core of common material in both hymnody and Liturgy, though there were many differences. Each group had special items which it desired to place in the common book. Some of these were not of special merit but were suggested because of traditional or sentimental attachments. It soon became evident that compromise and uncritical deference to individual taste would produce an inferior and unbalanced book. Constructive effort of high order was required. Lutheran uses everywhere must be studied, heritages conserved, everything must be conformed to the church's doctrine. At the same time the entire liturgical and hymnological field in various communions and countries, especially in the English-speaking world, must be reviewed. The requirements and possibilities of the church in America today, and in the foreseeable future, must govern the content and balance of the whole. In addition, the entire work must be distinguished by scholarship and high standards of English literary form.

The commissioners themselves grew in appreciation and understanding as they kept these considerations in view during a decade of endeavor. Their chief thought was to produce a representative service book, in full agreement with Lutheran doctrine, with text and music of superior quality, and in all respects suitable for the public services of congregations. The final appraisal of the work will have to do with this essential character and quality, rather than with any usefulness the book may have as an instrument of church unity.

THE HYMNAL

The problems confronting the two commissions were different, yet in some respects quite similar. The Hymnal Commission promptly found that only 153 hymns were in all four of the larger Lutheran hymnals in current use. Many of these differed in details of text and tune. *Ein' feste Burg* appeared in six different English translations and four different forms of the melody in the various Lutheran hymnals then in use in the United States and Canada, a fact which highlights the whole problem. After considering all factors, the commission adopted a set of principles which, in summary, included the following ideas:

1. The hymnal must be a new book, built upon existing collections, but possessing a character of its own.
2. It must be a true companion to the Liturgy.
3. It must be suitable for congregational rather than choral use.
4. The character of its content should be devotional rather than catechetical or homiletical.
5. It must express the continuity and catholicity of the church's life, with adequate representation of classic Greek and Latin hymns, the finest examples of our heritage hymns and of hymnody in general throughout the English-speaking world.
6. It must give increased recognition to hymns by American authors.

7. It must meet high requirements, both of doctrinal purity and of excellence of literary expression.
8. It must shun mediocrity, triviality, and sentimentality, and seek nobility of thought and expression.
9. It must provide tunes of quality comparable with that of its texts, with examples of all periods and places—plainsong, German and Scandinavian chorales, religious folk songs, French church tunes, British and American hymn tunes, et cetera.

All of this meant a new and standard work. The Commission wisely resolved not to prepare a pool of hymn texts in current Lutheran hymnals, or an anthology of hymns by Lutheran authors. The special problem was that of including and balancing acceptable translations of heritage hymns from Lutheran lands in Europe and the equally rich heritage of hymns and tunes of English origin which help to form and color our church life.

The Hymnal as finally adopted contains 602 hymns and more than an equal number of tunes. The following rubrics have been materially strengthened: Worship; Holy Communion; the Inner Life; Service; City, Nation, World. A number of translated hymns of merit, new to most of our collections, have been introduced. Many poems and translations of excellent literary quality were not included because the texts were not in fullest harmony with the teachings of the church. The search for acceptable material, however, brought into the collection many notable items from earlier English sources, nineteenth century English churchmen and scholars, modern English poets and men of letters. In a strong corrective effort, the collection includes more than fifty hymns by American authors, many of whom were not represented in previous Lutheran collections.

The music of the Hymnal is especially varied and of high order. There are sixteen plainsong melodies, approximately eighty German chorales (with fifteen Bach harmonizations), twelve Swedish chorales and melodies, twelve Norwegian tunes and folk songs, and ten folk songs from the Danish. Early English, and nineteenth century English, Scottish, and Welsh composers, as well as modern composers such as Vaughan Williams, Martin Shaw, Graham George, Gustav Holst, are well represented. A tune competition conducted by the Commission resulted in approximately four hundred entries. Of these, twenty original tunes were accepted. These included compositions by Arnold F. Keller, Giuseppe Moschetti, Rob Roy Peery, Gordon C. Ruud, Ralph Lewars, Roger C. Wilson, Catherine Deisher Baxter, Ralph Alvin Strom, and L. David Miller.

THE LITURGY

The problems confronting the Commission on the Liturgy can be understood only on the basis of conditions within the co-operating churches and of special factors of time and place. Earlier liturgical confusion in the Lutheran churches in America had been greatly reduced by the general adoption of the Common Service of 1888. But in spite of the importance of this work, we have noted that it was incomplete. Major items—musical settings, Orders for Occasional Services, et cetera—had to be provided independently by the different churches in their own service books, with resulting variety of form. Older nationalistic Orders, too, were held over, and had to be weighed and reckoned with.

The Commission knew very well that the Common Service could not have been prepared or adopted without the acceptance of an objective, historical principle or rule. This rule gave primary importance, the power of final decision in disputed cases, to the Church Orders of the sixteenth century. The commissioners, who now had to deal with the whole major problem once again, realized that these Orders were local or provincial reforms of the Roman Rite prepared for a single kingdom, duchy, or city like Nürnberg, Strassburg, Cologne, or even a town like Wittenberg or Goettingen. The theologians and jurists who edited them had very limited knowledge of the worship of the early Christian Church, or of any other than local liturgical forms. The authors of the Common Service seventy years ago were compelled to accept and to work under a rule which greatly limited their freedom.

We of this generation are not living in the sixteenth century, or the nineteenth. Pioneer conditions no longer obtain, and sectional differences are rapidly disappearing. All Lutheran groups are conscious of maturity and solidarity in our Western world and are contributing to its culture as well as to its political and economic development. The Confessions which witness to our unity in faith give us a greater freedom than the framers of the Common Service felt they could exercise. The Apology to the Augsburg Confession (VIII:15:38) says, ". . . we cheerfully maintain the old traditions . . . made in the Church for the sake of usefulness and tranquillity." But the Formula of Concord (I:10:4) adds, "We believe, teach and confess that the Church of God of every place and every time has the power, according to its circumstances, to change such ceremonies (instituted by men), in such manner as may be most useful and edifying to the Church of God."

These basic principles provided a broader platform for the Commission than the rule which had determined the preparation of the Common Service, though important values in that rule for the present day were recognized. The Common Liturgy as finally fashioned and adopted exemplifies these principles. Historical relevance finds expression in the fundamental structure of the Liturgy with its proper appointments for the church year. The principle of freedom and timeliness is well expressed by the new material which has been introduced, and which, though proportionately small in volume, is important in content and character. Four distinct ideas, taken together and held in balance, justify these new features: (1) the decision to make changes suggested by practical experience in the use of the Common Service over the past seventy years; (2) an awareness of contemporary conditions and needs which should be met on the liturgical level; (3) an ecumenical outlook which appreciates values in special features of the formal worship of other communions; and (4) a willingness to profit by the achievements of modern scholarship in recovering pertinent liturgical gems from the life of the early church.

The final result, therefore, has been shaped by the conviction that the Commission's task was not merely to preserve and refine our present Service as a witness to the faith of the past, but on the basis of this inheritance, to express the faith and life of the church in our own time in the finest and best liturgical forms that it could produce. The Common Liturgy, basically, has the structure suggested by Luther in his classic *Formula Missae* of 1523. Its component parts represent a blend of historic German, Scandinavian, and American Lutheran uses of the sixteenth and twentieth centuries, with the addition of several features which express its contemporary and ecumenical spirit. Variations in the text of the Common Service have all been reconciled. All new features have been introduced by common agreement. These features, particularly, because of their number and significance, will mark the new Common Liturgy as a distinctive American use. The Liturgy and its music will be discussed in greater detail in chapters 6, 7, and 12, but material revisions and new features are briefly listed here.

Material revisions:
> In the Liturgical Lessons—three new Epistles, four new Gospels, and several optional, alternate Gospels.
> In the calendar—insertion of the Festival of the Holy Innocents, Martyrs and August 6, Transfiguration.
> A few changes in archaic expressions in the Authorized Version of the Scriptures.
> A simplified formula for Distribution of the Sacrament.
> The Prayer of the Church (General Prayer) has a new text.
> In the collection of Collects—sixty-five new Collects and prayers.

New features:
> A Brief Order for Public Confession.
> An alternate Declaration of Grace, based upon a Compline text.

Additional historic Propers—Introits, Collects, and Graduals.

A new and expanded text of the Kyrie, a restoration of a historic form of the early church.

A complete series of Old Testament Lessons, for optional use before the Epistle.

Musical settings for ten Season Graduals.

Propers for an early service on Easter Day.

A new order of the parts following the sermon.

Permissive use of the historic word "catholic" instead of "Christian" in the Creeds.

Restoration of the ancient Prayer of Thanksgiving (Eucharistic Prayer).

Proper Prefaces for Advent and All Saints' Day.

Additional Post-Communion collects.

A new series of Lessons for Matins and Vespers.

Three complete musical settings for the Liturgy, Matins, Vespers, and the Litany, all with ministerial intonations.

A new system of pointing ("speech-rhythm") for all chants.

A modern free type of harmonization for the plainsong setting.

The Occasional Services:

Twenty-five Occasional Services—some material revisions, others entirely new—Baptism, Confirmation, Marriage, Burial, et cetera, have been adopted by the Joint Commission and approved by the churches. The following in this important group are entirely new items: Setting Apart of a Deaconess, Sending Forth of a Missionary, Induction of Office Bearers, and Blessing of a Dwelling.

WHAT OF THE FUTURE?

The evident purpose of this joint enterprise was the promotion of church unity. It was an attempt to do something of major importance for the common good, and to do it jointly. When the commissioners began their task, probably none of them believed that complete agreement could be reached. The number and variety of linguistic backgrounds, cultural strains, and traditional uses; the different levels achieved in different places in emergence from pioneer conditions; unequal progress in Anglicization and assimilation within the fabric of American life in general—all these made the problem seem insoluble. Could the Commissions hope to provide a single service book and hymnal, with complete musical settings, that would displace the eight separate liturgies and hymnals in current use? When absolute agreement was reached and ratified by formal action of the churches, no one was more astonished than the commissioners themselves.

This agreement signifies maturity and solidarity. More than two-thirds of all the Lutherans in the United States and Canada have acted concertedly and constructively. Practical and psychological values are immediately evident. One book will give the whole church a sense of oneness in faith and new life, a heightened church consciousness, especially significant in our day of restless movement. Families torn from familiar moorings and relocated in distant cities or towns easily drift aimlessly. One book, in use in all the continent, will enable many to feel at home in new environments, and thus give spiritual anchorage and help. In corporate worship, in education, and in other fields, the common book will be, next to the Bible and the catechism, the church's most important single book of devotion and instruction. The new book also definitely inspires the hope that eventually the Lutheran churches in America will indeed become the Lutheran Church in America.

In completing this work, the commissioners do not imagine that they have said the final word. As long as the church lives, there will be growth and development of its powers and activities. The church, in appointing commissions and committees to study matters of organization, education, or missions, expects these agencies to produce programs which will lift the church to higher levels of achievement, and not leave it *in statu quo*. The new *Service Book and Hymnal* points to higher levels. It is a venture in faith. It is issued in the belief that our congregations, and our people in general, share fully in the cultural developments of our times, with ever-increasing opportunities for cultivation of music and the arts, literary form, public procedure, et cetera. Congregations may at first be surprised at unfamiliar features in the book, but study of this material will reward their efforts. Ever-advancing standards of musical appreciation and instruction in our high schools and colleges, and the church's normal appreciation of quality in liturgical music and congregational song will justify the standards which have been upheld. The new items in the Liturgy, drawn from ancient and modern sources alike, give the *Service Book* strong individuality and mark it as a representative American and contemporary work.

Chapter 6

THE COMMON LITURGY:
THE INVOCATION TO THE SERMON [1]

The Service of the Lutheran Church is the counterpart of the Divine Liturgy of the Eastern churches and the Mass of the Roman Catholic Church. It developed directly from the example and direction of our Lord himself. He commanded his Disciples to preach his gospel and to celebrate together the Holy Communion he instituted in remembrance of himself. The sequence of liturgical parts preserves and presents the Word and the Sacrament in the regular assemblies of believers, as it has done throughout the centuries. This is the normal order of worship on the Lord's day.

The Liturgy is a work of the whole church which grew naturally, even as did the Creeds, the Confessions, and the Scriptures. The Reformers rediscovered the purpose of the Liturgy when they rediscovered the gospel and the Sacrament. For it is simply a corporate expression of the church's faith and fellowship, and an instrument for the effective administration of divinely appointed Means of Grace.

In its complete form, the Common Liturgy of the Lutheran Church in America (1958) has certain invariable parts (the Ordinary) and other variable parts (the Propers). The latter correspond to the changing Sundays and festivals of the church year. In its complete form the Service constitutes the Lutheran Rite, or Liturgy, which every congregation should use every Lord's day, as well as at services of Ordination, synodical conventions, et cetera.

In accordance with its purpose it consists of two main divisions which anciently were clearly marked. The Office of the Word is the ancient Service of the Catechumens (*missa catechumenorum*), which cate-

---

[1] Extended comment and discussion of individual parts of the Liturgy, fully documented, may be found in the author's *The Lutheran Liturgy* (Philadelphia: Muhlenberg Press, 1947), 692 pp.

chumens and unbaptized persons generally were permitted to attend. The Office of the Eucharist is the ancient Service of the Faithful (*missa fidelium*), to which only baptized persons were admitted. Congregations of normal size should seek to realize the ideal of the early church, and recover the practice of the Lutheran Church in the Reformation century, and use the complete Service every Lord's day, thus offering not only the Word but also the Eucharist for all who may desire it on any particular day.

In presenting an outline of the Service we call attention not only to the two main divisions of which we have been speaking, but also to a suggestive analogy between the church Service and the church building. The form of the Liturgy determines the plan of the church building. There is progression in both forms from a simple beginning to a liturgical climax. The preliminary Office of Confession and Absolution in the Liturgy has its counterpart in the narthex (vestibule) of the building. The Office of the Word in the Liturgy is represented by the nave or part of the building where the congregation hears the Lessons and the sermon and offers its response in song. We progress in the Liturgy to the Preface, and then to the Prayer of Thanksgiving and the Administration of the Sacrament. Similarly, in the church building we step up from the nave to the chancel (choir) and go to the communion rail at the entrance to the sanctuary.

OUTLINE OF THE SERVICE

Preliminary Office of Confession
    Invocation
    Confession of Sins
        Invitation
        Versicles
        Confession
        Declaration of Grace

Office of the Word (missa catechumenorum)
    Introit for the Day with Gloria Patri
    Kyrie
    Gloria in Excelsis
    Collect wtih Salutation and Oremus
    (Old Testament Lesson)
    (Hymn)
    Epistle for the Day
    Gradual for the Day (or Alleluia or Gradual for the Season)
    Gospel for the Day with Gloria Tibi and Laus Tibi
    Creed
    The Hymn
    Sermon

Office of the Eucharist (missa fidelium)
    Offering
    Offertory
    Prayer of the Church
    (Hymn)
    (Benediction, if Holy Communion is not celebrated)
    The Thanksgiving
        Hymn
        Preface
            Sursum Corda
            Vere Dignum
            Proper Preface
            Sanctus
        Prayer of Thanksgiving (or simply The Words of Institution)
        Pax
        Agnus Dei
    The Communion with Distribution and Blessing
    The Post-Communion
        Nunc Dimittis
        Prayer with Versicle and Collect
        Salutation and Benedicamus
    Benediction

THE INVOCATION

¶ *The Congregation shall rise. The Minister shall sing or say:*
In the Name of the Father, and of the Son, and of the Holy Ghost.
¶ *The Congregation shall sing or say:*
Amen.

The Invocation is a brief Scriptural phrase used in liturgical acts. In this place it is an act of corporate devotion addressed to God and not to the congregation. Even as in the Lord's Prayer we begin with the address, "Our Father," so here we begin our worship with an act of faith, acknowledging our awareness of the presence of God, and beseeching his blessing.

Historically this phrase accompanied the sign of the cross which was made in all acts of devotion, including the Confession of Sins. Its spirit is that of prayerful purification and preparation as well as reverent recognition of the Holy Trinity. The Lutheran Liturgy, in retaining this formula at this place, even though the sign of the cross has generally been dropped, has given the Invocation unusual prominence. It is not found in this place in the Roman or the Anglican liturgies.

As a sacrificial act the Invocation is said by the minister facing the altar.

THE CONFESSION OF SINS

¶ *The Minister shall say:*
Beloved in the Lord! Let us draw near with a true heart, and confess our

77

sins unto God our Father, beseeching him, in the Name of our Lord Jesus Christ, to grant us forgiveness.

¶ *The Minister and Congregation may kneel.*
¶ *They shall sing or say:*

Our help is in the Name of the Lord.
Response. Who made heaven and earth.
I said, I will confess my transgressions unto the Lord.
℟. And Thou forgavest the iniquity of my sin.

¶ *Then shall the Minister say:*

Almighty God, our Maker and Redeemer, we poor sinners confess unto thee, that we are by nature sinful and unclean, and that we have sinned against thee by thought, word, and deed. Wherefore we flee for refuge to thine infinite mercy, seeking and imploring thy grace, for the sake of our Lord Jesus Christ.

¶ *The Congregation shall say with the Minister:*

O most Merciful God, who hast given thine only-begotten Son to die for us, have mercy upon us, and for his sake grant us remission of all our sins; and by thy Holy Spirit increase in us true knowledge of thee and of thy will, and true obedience to thy Word, that by thy grace we may come to everlasting life; through Jesus Christ our Lord. Amen.

¶ *Then the Minister, standing, and facing the Congregation, shall say:*

Almighty God, our heavenly Father, hath had mercy upon us, and hath given his only Son to die for us, and for his sake forgiveth us all our sins. To them that believe on his Name, he giveth power to become the sons of God, and bestoweth upon them his Holy Spirit. He that believeth, and is baptized, shall be saved. Grant this, O Lord, unto us all.

¶ *Or, he may say:*

The Almighty and Merciful God grant unto you, being penitent, pardon and remission of all your sins, time for amendment of life, and the grace and comfort of his Holy Spirit.

¶ *The Congregation shall sing or say:*
Amen.

The Service proper actually begins with the Introit. The Confession of Sins, however, provides an appropriate and spiritually helpful introductory preparation. This is a brief, invariable form, adapted for congregational use from the ancient Confiteor ("I confess"), originally said by the minister as he vested in the sacristy. The *Didache,* one of the earliest known Christian writings, says: "Assemble on the Day of the Lord, break bread and celebrate the Eucharist, but first confess your sins."

The text of the Roman Confiteor dates from the year 1314 and reflects the doctrinal impurity of that period. The Reformation, recognizing the priesthood of all believers, made this Confession a congregational act, addressed to God alone, with all reference to the Virgin and saints omitted, and with a thoroughly Scriptural text. This text acknowledged our sinful nature as well as our many transgressions. The clause, "we are by nature sinful and unclean," is found only in Lutheran liturgies. The Anglican Prayer Book has the less positive, "there is no health in us." The text in the Common Liturgy is from Melanchthon's Order for Mecklenburg, 1552, and the later Order for Wittenberg, 1559.

Versicles and their Responses introduce the Confession. These brief passages from the Psalms occur frequently throughout the Liturgy. Their pertinent thought focuses attention upon the Collect, Canticle, or other item which immediately follows. Their responsive form strengthens the congregational and social character of the Liturgy.

The Declaration of Grace is a sacramental act and is said by the minister facing the congregation throughout, even though the final sentence, "Grant this, O Lord, unto us all," is in form a prayer—a prayer, however, which contains an element of admonition applicable to all.

The alternate Declaration, "The Almighty and Merciful God grant unto you," is based upon a form in the Office of Compline, the final Service in the series of Canonical Hours.

The essentially preparatory character of the Office of Confession is indicated by the short line or rule which follows the Office and separates it from the actual Service of the Day which now begins. Other pertinent suggestions are given in the General Rubrics, and it would be well if these were more generally followed. These state that the minister may conduct the Office of Confession from the chancel level; that the congregation may kneel before the Versicles; and that the Responses may be said instead of sung. These suggestions, if observed, will interpret the character of the Service of Confession as essentially invariable and preparatory, and will emphasize the fact that the Service proper begins with the Introit for the Day, at which point the minister ascends the altar steps, the congregation stands, and the Responses are sung.

THE INTROIT

¶ *The Congregation shall stand until the close of the Collect.*

¶ *The Introit for the Day with the Gloria Patri shall be sung or said.*[2]

Unto us a Child is born, unto us a Son is given: and the government shall be upon his shoulder.

And his Name shall be called Wonderful, Counsellor, The Mighty God: The everlasting Father, The Prince of Peace.

Ps. O sing unto the Lord a new song: for he hath done marvellous things.

Gloria Patri

Glory be to the Father, and to the Son, and to the Holy Ghost: as it was in the beginning, is now, and ever shall be, world without end. Amen.

[2] The Propers used in this chapter by way of illustration are for Christmas Day, the Nativity of our Lord—For the Later Service.

The word "introit" means entrance or beginning. These brief Psalm verses with the Gloria Patri fittingly begin the Service of the day by announcing, more or less definitely, the theme or mood of the particular Service which follows. The use of Propers such as Introits, Collects, and Graduals is a feature of the Western liturgies.

The Introit was originally an entrance Psalm sung antiphonally by a double choir as the clergy came from the sacristy. Later an especially appropriate Psalm verse was appointed and sung as an antiphon before and after the Psalm. Gregory the Great abbreviated the Psalm and established the present form. There are approximately twenty "irregular" Introits which have texts from Isaiah or the New Testament instead of from the Book of Psalms. The Introit for Christmas Day is a case in point, the antiphon being taken from Isa. 9:6.

The first words in the Latin texts of Introits for Sundays in Lent and after Easter supply the names of these days—Invocabit, Judica, Jubilate, et cetera.

The Church Orders retained the Gregorian series of Introits, usually with the Latin texts. When vernacular services became general, the problem of translation and adaptation of music was frequently solved by the choice of one Introit for a season. In towns and villages without adequate choirs, vernacular hymns were sung in place of the Introit. Thus by taking the easiest way out, the historic series of Introits retained in the sixteenth century Orders was generally dropped from Lutheran use in Germany and Scandinavia, along with the historic Graduals and many of the Collects. Similarly, though for different reasons, the historic Introits and Graduals were omitted from the Prayer Book of the Church of England, though this book retained the complete series of Collects. The entire series of historic Introits and Collects was restored in English translation in the Common Service of 1888, and the series of Graduals in the *Common Service Book* of 1918.

The Introit, like the Gradual in the Service and the Responsory in Matins and Vespers, is a choral element. The choir sings it and the congregation may join in the Gloria Patri. As a makeshift the Introit may be said by the minister, which is as inspiring as if he read the hymns. It should never be read responsively by the minister and the congregation. The antiphon should be repeated after the Psalm and before the Gloria Patri.

The Gloria Patri distinguishes the Christian use of the Psalter or other Old Testament passages to which it is appended. It affirms the orthodox belief in the divinity, equality, and eternity of the three Persons in the Holy Trinity.

As the Introit is sung by the choir, the minister steps up from the chancel level and stands before the altar. He faces the altar, since the Introit, as an entrance Psalm, is devotional in character and thus a sacrificial element in the Liturgy.

The simplest way of rendering the Introits, and the most ancient way, is by chanting them to the Psalm Tones. More elaborate anthem-like settings are also available.

THE KYRIE

¶ Then shall be sung or said the Kyrie.

In peace let us pray to the Lord.
    ℞. Lord, have mercy.
For the peace that is from above, and for the salvation of our souls, let us pray to the Lord.
    ℞. Lord, have mercy.
For the peace of the whole world, for the well-being of the churches of God, and for the unity of all, let us pray to the Lord.
    ℞. Lord, have mercy.
For this holy house, and for them that in faith, piety and fear of God offer here their worship and praise, let us pray to the Lord.
    ℞. Lord, have mercy.
Help, save, pity, and defend us, O God, by thy grace.
    ℞. Amen.

The text of the Kyrie is a new feature in a Lutheran Liturgy, but an ancient one in Christian worship. It is a restoration of the original and meaningful form in the early church.

Kyrie eleison ("Lord, have mercy") is a Greek acclamation and petition which reminds us that for three centuries or more the Christians, even in Rome, used the Greek language in worship. This was the language of culture in all the Mediterranean area. We might suppose this brief phrase to be a survival in our Liturgy of a feature in the earliest services of the church. This, however, is not the case. There is no trace of the Kyrie in the Liturgy proper in either the East or the West for the first three hundred and fifty years. Nor is there any mention of it by the church fathers of the second, third, or early fourth centuries.

The petition, "have mercy upon me," or "upon us," is found repeatedly in the Psalms—25:16; 26:11; 41:4; 51:1; 123:3—and in the Gospels according to Matthew (9:27; 15:22) and Luke (17:13; 18:38, 39). In every case, except Psalms 41 and 51, the petition is a cry for help in need—blindness, leprosy, sickness—and not a plea for forgiveness. The Kyrie, as we know it, did not enter the Christian Liturgy from these biblical sources, though the two words which comprise it were known to Greek scholars in the texts of the New Testament and the Septuagint translation of the Old Testament.

Modern research has disclosed the pre-Christian origin and use of the phrase. We now know that it was an acclamation and petition in common use throughout the Greek-speaking world, especially in Asia Minor, Egypt, and Constantinople. As an acclamation or shout of praise it had much the same meaning as the Hebrew *Hosanna!* It was also, at the same time, a plea for help or favor, not for forgiveness. It was found in different connections and forms, and apparently was used upon secular and religious occasions alike. Dölger, in his *Sol Salutis, Gebet und Gesang im Christlichen Altertum* (pp. 60-105), gives many examples of this and similar acclamations and petitions commonly found in secular and religious use in the early Christian centuries.

The phrase as we have it came into Christian use in Asia Minor. Etheria, a Spanish abbess, in describing her *Pilgrimage* to holy places in the East, states that she heard it in Jerusalem as a people's response to petitions in a litany-type prayer said at close of Vespers.

Pope Gregory in his revision of the Mass of the Western church at the end of the sixth century, transferred some of these intercessions to a later place in the Service, keeping only the people's responses in nine-fold form at this place. He also changed the middle three responses to *Christe eleison,* "Christ, have mercy." The Kyrie thus came to have the character of an invocation of the Holy Trinity, and, particularly, of an acclaim by the congregation of their Lord coming now to meet them as they worship in his temple. Thus the Kyrie of the Western church became a liturgical remnant. Its early litany form and its broad objective petitions were completely forgotten and it came to have the character of a cry for forgiveness. In this later mutilated and penitential form it received an exceedingly rich development in the lengthened melodies of the medieval tropes and in elaborate choral compositions by many masters, the greatest of whom was Bach.

The best summary discussions of this topic are in Dölger's *Sol Salutis, Leiturgia,* J. A. Jungmann's *The Mass of the Roman Rite,* and Bishop's *Liturgica Historica.*

Following immediately upon the Introit Psalm—originally a processional Psalm—the Kyrie is the first prayer of the Service proper. Its restored content lifts the Service to lofty levels at its very beginning. The simple responses, "Lord, have mercy upon us. Christ, have mercy . . ." which alone remained in the Western liturgies after the time of Gregory were exceedingly subjective, self-centered, and penitential in character. The ancient text, now happily restored, has an objective and unselfish outreach in its petitions for the church as a whole and for the state of the world in its need. In every dimension of breadth, depth, and height it is superior to the empty, fragmentary form to which the church has been so long accustomed. We stand upon high ground as we use the petitions of the restored form at the beginning of our corporate worship.

There is no known precedent in any other Lutheran Liturgy for the restoration of the original and fuller form of the Kyrie at this historic place in the Service. The 1948 Liturgy for Rhineland and Westphalia gives this material in a litany form of the General Prayer. There are similar uses of it in other Lutheran and in Anglican service books. As given here in the Common Liturgy it is a restoration of a valid form which should be a corrective of the wrong notion that the Kyrie is another confession of sins. We have made our confession and received the assurance of divine forgiveness. The worshiping church now greets its Lord and invokes his help and favor, not only for itself, but for mankind, in every time and circumstance of need.

For those who prefer to continue the old form and use of the Kyrie, the following provision has been made:

¶ *In place of the foregoing, the following Kyrie may be sung or said:*

> Lord, have mercy upon us.
> ℟. Lord, have mercy upon us.
> Christ, have mercy upon us.
> ℟. Christ, have mercy upon us.
> Lord, have mercy upon us.
> ℟. Lord, have mercy upon us.

THE GLORIA IN EXCELSIS

¶ *Then shall be sung or said the Gloria in Excelsis.*

¶ *The Minister shall sing or say:*

> Glory be to God on high!

¶ *The Congregation shall sing or say:*

And on earth peace, good will toward men. We praise thee, we bless thee, we worship thee, we glorify thee, we give thanks to thee for thy great glory, O Lord God, heavenly King, God the Father Almighty.

O Lord, the only-begotten Son, Jesus Christ; O Lord God, Lamb of God, Son of the Father, that takest away the sin of the world, have mercy upon us. Thou that takest away the sin of the world, receive our prayer. Thou that sittest at the right hand of God the Father, have mercy upon us.

For thou only art holy; thou only art the Lord; thou only, O Christ, with the Holy Ghost, art most high in the glory of God the Father. Amen.

This hymn of praise follows the Kyrie immediately. It is, in a sense, a response to the Kyrie itself, as it voices the joy of the whole church in the merciful goodness of God in the sending of his Son into the world to be its Saviour and Lord. It is more than a hymn of praise to the Father, being, rather, a "jubilant anthem of redemption." In it our worship grounds itself in the Incarnation, the Atonement, and the thought of the perpetual intercession of our Lord. For a brief moment it stoops to invoke mercy and help, but then soars to the gates of heaven in its Trinitarian ascription of worship and praise to Christ and the Holy Ghost as "most high in the glory of God the Father."

Luther thought highly of the Gloria. He said it "did not grow, nor was it made on earth, but it came down from heaven." Difficulties of translation and adaptation of music led to metrical vernacular versions, or the substitution of a hymn, in many Church Orders. The Common Service restored the full text and prescribed its use on festivals and whenever there is a Communion.

Originally the Gloria in Excelsis was a "private Psalm" sung in Greek in the fourth century, and possibly earlier, in the Morning Office but not at Mass. It was thus an Eastern counterpart to the great Western Te Deum sung at Matins. It came into the Eucharistic Service in the West in connection with the Christmas Vigil, its reference to the Song of the Angels giving it special appropriateness.

This concludes the first section of the Service of the Word, which has been largely sacrificial in character. With the Salutation and Collect a new and prevailingly sacramental division begins.

THE SALUTATION AND THE COLLECT

¶ Then shall the Minister sing or say:
The Lord be with you.
℞. And with thy spirit.

¶ The Minister shall say:
Let us pray.
¶ Then shall the Minister say the Collect for the Day.

Grant, we beseech thee, Almighty God, that the new birth of thine only-begotten Son in the flesh may set us free who are held in the old bondage under the yoke of sin; through the same Jesus Christ, thy Son, our Lord, who liveth and reigneth with thee and the Holy Ghost, one God, world without end. *Amen.*

¶ The Collect ended, the Congregation shall sing or say:
Amen.

The Salutation is a Hebrew form of greeting and response (Ruth 2:4; Judg. 6:12; and the Archangel Gabriel's greeting to Mary in Luke 1:28). The phrase came into the Christian liturgies as a responsive introduction to new and different parts of the Service, and particularly before sacramental acts.

The Salutation and its Response are not addressed to God. They are a reciprocal prayer of the minister for his people and of the people for him before they unitedly offer their petitions to God. As Loehe says, "The bonds of love and unity between pastor and people are tied anew."

The Collect is the second proper or variable part of the Liturgy. It is a brief but significant prayer usually related in thought to the Gospel or the Epistle. It provides a devotional preparation for the liturgical Lessons. Occasionally the text relates itself to the season.

There are two explanations of the origin of the name. It may be derived from the ancient custom in Rome according to which an early gathering for worship was held (*ecclesia collecta*) at which a prayer of this nature was used. At the later Service at the stational church this prayer was repeated. Or the name may refer to the monastic use of the Gallican churches according to which, after the Psalms and the Lessons, the officiant called upon all to pray in silence. This ended, the officiant offered a spoken prayer (*collectio*) which summed up the common thought.

The Collects have a prose pattern which has persisted through the centuries. Normally there are five parts: an invocation; a basis for the petition; the petition itself; the purpose or benefit desired; and the concluding doxology. Frequently the second or the fourth parts may be missing. The prayer of the Disciples after the Ascension (Acts 1:24) serves as a model for the first three parts. The second part, the "antecedent reason," recalls a divine promise or command and contributes the sacramental quality which makes the Collect "a word of man to God based upon a word of God to man" (Goulburn). Analysis of the Collect for Christmas Day reveals a transition of parts. It begins at once with the petition, then comes the address or invocation, an oblique reference to parts two and four, and the doxology.

The Collects are an important part of the church's liturgical inheritance. Their brevity of form is balanced by their breadth of thought; their humility of spirit, by their certainty of faith and their feeling for the communion of saints. As a whole, they are unique in form, in age, in universality, in excellence, and in beauty. The same historic series of Collects is used throughout the Roman, Anglican, and Lutheran churches in all the world today. These particular Collects for the Day are mostly Roman in origin, as is evinced by their crisp antithetical form. Similar prayers originating later in Gallican (Western) areas were more diffuse and ornate.

Archbishop Cranmer and his associates provided a matchless series of English translations of many of the historic Collects in the *Book of Common Prayer* (1549) of the Church of England. Cranmer added some new compositions of his own, as did Bishop Cosin in his revision of the Prayer Book in 1662. Many of the Collects in the Common Liturgy are in the classic English forms of the Prayer Book, as the King James version of the Scriptures is used throughout the *Service Book*.

85

Beginning with the Fourth Sunday after Trinity, the Anglican Collects fall one Sunday behind the Lutheran series.

A much more extended discussion of the Collect, with the sources and original texts of the Collects for the Day and others will be found in *The Lutheran Liturgy,* pp. 438-557.

THE OLD TESTAMENT LESSON

¶ *Here the Minister may read the appointed Lesson from the Old Testament, saying:* The Lesson is written in the _____ Chapter of _____, beginning at the _____ Verse. *The Lesson ended, he shall say,* Here endeth the Lesson.

¶ *Then may be sung a Psalm or a hymn version of a Psalm.*

The provision of a complete series of Old Testament Lessons for optional use before the Epistle is another important restoration of a feature in all early Christian services. From Apostolic times to the present the reading of Lessons from the Scriptures has been the central feature of the Service of the Word (*Missa catechumenorum*). This, of course, was a direct inheritance from the synagogue, and no Christian rite is without it.

Justin Martyr, about A.D. 150, is the first Church Father to mention an Old Testament Lesson. The number of Lessons varied greatly at first. The A*postolic Constitutions,* probably compiled about A.D. 400, mention five: the law, prophecy, the Epistle, the Acts, and the Gospel. The Syrian, Coptic, and Abyssinian Rites still have several Lessons before the Gospel. Eventually the number of Lessons was restricted to three—one from the Old Testament, one from the New Testament (not a Gospel), and the Gospel. This threefold arrangement still prevails in the Armenian and Gallican (Ambrosian) liturgies. After the sixth century, and as part of general abbreviation in all systems, the Old Testament Lessons generally disappeared except for special days. The Roman Liturgy still provides one or more Old Testament Lessons for Ember Saturdays, Good Friday, Wednesday in Holy Week, et cetera.

With the exception of the Psalter at Matins and Vespers, the Old Testament has practically disappeared from Christian services. This has been a definite loss. In the belief that it will be an enrichment of our Service, and also a means of acquainting our people with many of the most important passages in the Old Testament, the Common Liturgy provides, for optional use, a carefully chosen series of Old Testament Lessons, closely related to the thought of the Epistle or the Gospel.

There is no liturgical response after the Old Testament Lesson, but a rubric states that at this point a Psalm, or a hymn version of a Psalm, may be sung.

THE NEW TESTAMENT LESSON

The development of the church year in the West with its observance of festivals led to the selection of "proper" material. Definite Lessons were first appointed for the three great festivals (Easter, Pentecost, and Christmas), then for their octaves, and still later for associated seasons. These were indicated by marginal signs in the manuscripts. Later indexes with full texts were provided for use at the altar. These were called a *Comes* or "companion." The Lessons themselves, as they became fixed in a series, were called Pericopes, from the Greek word meaning "cut out." By Charlemagne's time, A.D. 800, this work was completed and accepted in the West.

The Lutheran Reformation generally accepted the historic system. In fact by its emphasis upon the Gospel, and the Scriptures generally, it strengthened the importance of the Service of the Word, the first part of the Mass. The Lessons were recognized as giving out the theme or tone of the day, as giving direction to the sermon, and as inviting new creations in hymns and melodies. Luther and his associates published homilies on these historic Lessons.

The Church Orders made a few constructive changes. They appointed eschatological texts for the last three Sundays of the year and the story of the Transfiguration for the Sixth Sunday after Epiphany. The Roman Church made a number of changes in the series, but the Anglican and the Lutheran churches generally retained the older selections of the northern European missals. The Zwinglian and the Calvinistic churches abandoned the Pericopes entirely, along with the church year. Recently the Free churches have begun a reconstruction of the church year that approximates the historic scheme, thus repudiating the radicalism of their sixteenth century forefathers.

The Gospels for the first half of the year (*Semester Domini*) follow the steps of our Lord's life on earth. The second half (*Semester Ecclesiae*) presents a selection of his parables, miracles, and teachings. On the great days of the year, and on many others, there is a harmony of the Propers, at least of the Gospel and the Epistle. There have been so many dislocations and substitutions in the course of the centuries that it is futile to try to find a complete harmony in all the appointments.

An important constructive feature of the Common Liturgy is the revised series of Lessons. Liturgical scholars in Europe and America have recently given much thought to this fundamental material, examining it critically from every angle and making numerous constructive suggestions, some of which have found general acceptance. The Joint Commission was aware of the fact that certain accepted texts began or ended awkwardly, that certain passages were in dispute, and that a few additional Proper appointments must be provided. Individuals made independent studies of all the Epistles and Gospels, the results were collated, and recommendations made to the Joint Editorial Committee. The latter spent days in careful review and laid definite recommendations before the entire Commission. The latter, after lengthy discussion, made a few changes and adopted the complete series as now given in the *Service Book*.

In the course of these studies many other lectionaries were minutely examined. Among these were the Roman Missal, the Books of Common Prayer of the Anglican churches (England, America, Scotland, the Proposed Book of 1928, et cetera), recent German Lutheran lectionaries (Rhineland, VELKD [Die Vereinigte Evangelische Lutherische Kirche, Agende], et cetera), and the *Book of Common Order* of the Church of Scotland. It would be beyond the scope and purpose of this volume to record the reasons for every change that was made, though in every case a reason could be cited. Because of the central importance of the liturgical Lessons, however, a listing is here given of all changes from the lectionary of the *Common Service Book* which in itself represented an expansion of the series in the Common Service of 1888. Prefixes or additions of a verse or two are not indicated. It must be noted that in many instances the former Epistle is appointed as the Old Testament Lesson in the new series, also that many of the new appointments are alternates for optional use.

	Epistle	*Gospel*
Christmas Day (Early)	1 John 4:7-16 (alt.)	
(Later)	Heb. 1:1-12	
(Vespers)	Lesson—Luke 2:15-20	
St. Stephen, Martyr	Acts 7:54-60	
The Holy Innocents	Rev. 14:1-5	Matt. 2:13-18
Second Sunday after Christmas	Titus 3:4-7	John 1:14-18
Epiphany	Col. 1:23-27 or Eph. 3:1-12	
Third Sunday after the Epiphany		John 1:29-34 (alt.)
Ash Wednesday	1 John 1:5-9 or Phil. 3:7-12	
Palmarum		Matt. 26:1—27:66 (alt.)
Monday in Holy Week	1 Pet. 2:21-24	John 12:1-36
Tuesday in Holy Week	1 Tim. 6:12-14	John 12:37-50 or Mark 14:1—15:46
Wednesday in Holy Week	Rev. 1:5b-7	
Thursday in Holy Week		John 6:28-37 (alt.)
Good Friday	Rev. 5:1-14	

Saturday in Holy Week	1 Pet. 3:17-22	Matt. 27:57-66
Easter (Early)	1 Pet. 1:3-9	John 20:1-18
(The Service)	1 Cor. 15:20-26 (alt.)	
The Ninth Sunday after Trinity		Luke 15:11-32 (alt.)
The Presentation of Our Lord	1 Cor. 1:26-31	
The Annunciation	Phil. 4:4-9	
The Nativity of St. John, the Baptist	1 John 1:1-4	
St. Peter and St. Paul, Apostles	Gal. 1:11-20 (alt.)	
The Visitation	1 Pet. 3:1-5a	
St. James the Elder, Apostle	1 Cor. 4:9-15	
St. Bartholomew, Apostle	1 Cor. 12:27-31a	
Reformation Day	Rom. 3:21-28	
The Festival of Harvest	Acts 14:11-18	Luke 12:15-34
A Day of Humiliation and Prayer	Acts 3:12-19a	Matt. 7:6-12
A Day of General or Special Thanksgiving	Acts 14:8-18 (alt.)	Matt. 6:25-33

THE EPISTLE

❡ *Then shall the Minister announce the Epistle for the Day, saying:* **The Epistle for** (*here he shall name the Festival or Day*) **is written in the _____ Chapter of _____, beginning at the _____ Verse.**

❡ *The Epistle ended, the Minister shall say:* **Here endeth the Epistle for the Day.**

The Epistle is the word of Christian law, but law in the spirit of Christ. In the early liturgies the Epistle was called the Apostle. St. Augustine said, "We have heard the Apostle, we have heard the Psalm, we have heard the Gospel." In liturgical use the Epistle precedes the Gospel as the lesser precedes the greater, the Gospels having always been esteemed "the crown of all Holy Scriptures." The Epistles are generally from the letters of the Apostles, but occasionally from the Old Testament, the book of Acts, or the Revelation.

The Lessons may be read from the lectern or from the altar. In the latter case, the minister reads the Epistle facing the congregation and from the south (right) side of the altar. During the singing of the Gradual (or the Alleluia) he carries the Altar Book to the other side and reads the Gospel from the north end of the altar. He should move with deliberation and read impressively. The liturgical reading of the Lessons is one of the most significant features of the Liturgy. It should never be made to appear insignificant by hurried approach or too rapid reading. The text should be set apart from everything else, with a brief pause after the announcement, and again before the words, "Here endeth the Epistle for the Day."

THE GRADUAL

¶ Then may the Gradual for the Day be sung.

All the ends of the earth have seen the salvation of our God: make a joyful noise unto the Lord, all the earth.

V. The Lord hath made known his salvation: his righteousness hath he openly showed in the sight of the heathen.

Alleluia. Alleluia. *V.* O come, let us sing unto the Lord: let us worship and bow down. Alleluia.

¶ When the Gradual for the Day is omitted, the Alleuia or the Gradual for the Season may be sung.

THE ALLELUIA

Alleluia.

¶ In Lent this Sentence shall be sung instead of the Alleluia:

Christ hath humbled himself, and become obedient unto death: even the death of the Cross.

The Gradual, like the Introit, is a choral feature. It is a liturgical arrangement of Psalm verses sung by the choir as a response to the Epistle and an introduction to the Gospel. Originally the choir chanted entire Psalms from a step (*gradus*) of the altar, whence the name. When three Lessons were read, the gradual proper was sung after the Old Testament Lesson. The second part, called the Alleluia, was sung after the Epistle. In the process of shortening the Service, the Old Testament Lesson dropped out and the Gradual proper and the Alleluia were abbreviated and united in a single text.

In the synagogue a Psalm was sung between the readings. The Hour services (Matins, Vespers, et cetera) developed the Responsory. The Service has the Gradual, which is probably as ancient a feature as the Lessons themselves.

The word "Alleluia," like the other Hebrew word "Amen," came into the Christian Liturgy very early. It is found in many Psalms, especially in the section Psalms 113-118, as a shout of joy and triumph. With its meaning of "Praise ye the Lord" it is an appropriate liturgical acclaim to the hearing of the divine Word.

Luther retained the Gradual in his Latin Service. As an accommodation to local conditions in villages, he suggested a vernacular hymn for his German Mass. This suggestion, together with difficulties of translation and adaptation of music, led to the loss of the historic Gradual texts from Lutheran services in many areas. Hymns, and later elaborate choral music such as motets and cantatas took the place of the Gradual.

The Common Service of 1888 did not include Gradual texts but provided a brief series of Sentences for the Seasons which had first appeared in the *Church Book* of 1868. The *Common Service Book* of 1918 restored the entire historic series of Graduals, and various acceptable musical settings have since been prepared by individual musicians. A brief series of Season Graduals has been included in the Common Liturgy. These may be used, when necessary, as a substitute for the full series.

When it is desired to sing two anthems in the Service, one may be sung as a substitute for the Gradual immediately after the singing of the simple Alleluia by the choir and congregation. But this should not be frequent, for what better words can be sung at this point than those which belong?

THE GOSPEL

¶ *Then shall the Minister announce the Gospel for the Day, saying:* The Holy Gospel is written in the _____ Chapter of St. _____ beginning at the _____ Verse.

¶ *The Congregation shall rise and sing or say:*

Glory be to thee, O Lord.

¶ *Then shall the Minister read the Gospel for the Day.*

¶ *The Gospel ended, the Minister shall say:* Here endeth the Gospel for the Day.

¶ *The Congregation shall sing or say:*

Praise be to thee, O Christ.

The four New Testament Gospels have always been accorded special honor as the inspired records of eye-witnesses of the person of our Lord and of his teaching and actions. These are the writings that unfold for us the drama of Christ's life on earth and give us, in all fulness, the message of salvation, the commissioning of the Apostles, and the institution of the Sacrament.

The liturgical Gospel is the devotional summit of the Service of the Word. It usually presents the central, objective thought of the day, a thought which is sustained and developed by the sermon. The supremacy of the Gospel in the Liturgy led to an early development of customs and ceremonies surrounding the actual reading. In deeper theological meaning these also expressed the homage accorded the person of Christ (the Word) in the written Word. Some of these ceremonies, such as incense, tapers, and processions gradually disappeared from most Lutheran services, but the church generally retained at least three: the rising and standing of the congregation as a mark of reverence and obedience; the ascription of praise at the announcement; and (occasionally) the reading of the Scriptural text from the liturgical "north side" of the altar. In the latter case, the transfer of the Altar Book from one side of the altar to the other may be regarded as a surviving relic of the ancient procession.

The congregational responses express our recognition of the Real **Presence of Christ in our worship.**

Again, like the Epistle, the Gospel should be read distinctly and impressively, with brief pauses before and after the actual texts, thus setting the Scripture apart from everything else.

THE CREED
¶ Then shall be said or sung the Creed.

The Creed is the church's word in answer to the Word of God. It is a corporate expression of praise and thanks for the messages of salvation which have been brought before us in the preceding variable Collect, Epistle, Gradual, and Gospel. It is also a formal public profession in summary form of the essentials of Christian belief. It not only witnesses to the faith of the church; it binds Christians to one another and to the faithful of all centuries; it testifies to the unity, universality, and perpetuity of the church. It is a late feature (early eleventh century) in the Western Liturgy and represents the general emphasis upon doctrinal definition characteristic of Western Christianity.

The two creeds correspond to the two sacraments. In the earliest times individual bishops or councils framed creeds, or concise statements of belief, for use in connection with adult Baptism. The Apostles' Creed, even though it did not receive the precise form it has today until about A.D. 750, has developed from these early local creeds. The Nicene Creed gets its name from the Council of Nicea, A.D. 325, which approved its first form. This was later amplified and introduced in the Mass in the Gallican churches of western Europe, and finally accepted in Rome, in the early eleventh century. The *filioque* clause ("and the Son"), added to the article on the Holy Spirit by the Western churches, was never accepted by the churches in the East.

The Swedish, Danish, Norwegian, and French Lutheran liturgies use the historic word "catholic," meaning "universal," in the article on the church. The Common Service, following the German use (before Luther), unfortunately substituted the word "Christian" and thus brought the American Lutheran Church out of step with other Lutheran uses except the German, and with the general use of all other Christians. The Common Liturgy breaks with this unfortunate European national use and permits the original and generally accepted clause, "I believe in the holy, catholic Church," as an alternate use.

The General Rubrics direct that "the Nicene Creed shall be used on all Festivals and whenever there is a Communion." This is not only a recognition of historic usage, but also an appreciation of the more highly developed clauses concerning the nature, life, and work of Christ in the Nicene Creed.

The liturgical use of the Creed is an act of worship as well as a response to the Lessons. The minister leads the congregation in repeating it, facing the altar with joined hands. The people stand. According to ancient custom, still observed in some churches, the choir joins the minister and congregation in facing the altar (presumably in the east), a reminder of the early church's requirement that candidates for Baptism should face the East from whence the Sun of Righteousness appears. The Creed should be recited without soft organ accompaniment which is sentimental and has the effect of clouding a clear confession.

THE HYMN
¶ Then shall be sung the Hymn.

The German word "Hauptlied" for the hymn at this particular place fittingly expresses the importance historically attached to this feature. Its position following the Lessons and Creed and immediately before the sermon gives it almost the significance of an additional Proper. It must be chosen with special care.

The Reformation gave the congregational hymn to the people, and the church orders appointed hymns for the seasons. For a century and a half the hymn at this place and the sermon closely followed the church year. Melodies for these seasonal hymns constituted a special class, and church musicians used them as thematic material for elaborate "figurated chorales," cantatas, and other choral numbers. The eighteenth century, in its general process of deterioration, saw the neglect of the church year and the Liturgy, leaving the sermon in complete control of the selection of hymns and other parts of the Service.

Every hymn should be sung in its entirety. Its text should not be abbreviated or mutilated any more than should the texts of other parts of the Liturgy. By the same token, the hymn should be sung not only by the congregation, but by the minister, choir, and congregation together, thus giving full expression to the idea of a truly "common service." The custom, common in Europe, of the minister retiring to the sacristy while the congregation sings, expresses a concepton of specialization which is foreign to our ideas of corporate worship.

THE SERMON

¶ Then shall follow the Sermon.

¶ The Sermon being ended, the Congregation shall rise and the Minister shall then say:

The Peace of God, which passeth all understanding, keep your hearts and minds through Christ Jesus.

¶ The Congregation shall sing or say:

Amen.

The Reformation had restored the sermon to its historic importance in the Service. Discussion of its function will be found in chapter 17. A few observations, however, may here be made.

As we have seen, the Creed follows the Gospel as a corporate witness to our acceptance of the gospel as the "rule of faith and life." Similarly the sermon follows the Creed as a personal testimony and witness to the common faith. It has no value apart from the gospel and the common faith. These are its sacramental foundations which give it more than personal character. A good sermon is, in effect, the living voice of the living church lifted in adoration, edification, instruction, and exhortation. Special occasions may require exceptional procedure and the introduction of material not directly related to the Propers. However, the sermon will gain added force if it can be brought into reasonable harmony with the general thought of the day or season.

The minister should offer silent prayer at the altar, or the altar rail, before entering the pulpit. Immediately before the sermon he may give the apostolic greeting, "Grace be unto you, and peace, from God our Father, and from our Lord Jesus Christ." The use at this place of brief prayers of miscellaneous character and subjective content is in poor liturgical taste.

The Votum ("The Peace of God . . .") is in the nature of a Benediction (Phil. 4:7) as well as a prayer. It fittingly concludes the Office of the Word.

Chapter 7

THE COMMON LITURGY:
THE OFFERTORY TO THE BENEDICTION

The second division of the Service now begins. The Service of the Word has been prevailingly sacramental in character, with some important sacrificial features. It conforms closely to the historic structure of the pre-Reformation Liturgy. There is a sharp break in character and content as we enter upon the second part, the Service of the Supper. This is sacramental also, but with more extended sacrificial elements.

OFFERING, OFFERTORY, AND PRAYER OF THE CHURCH

The Offering, the Offertory, and the Prayer of the Church constitute a triple unit of sacrifice: the sacrifice of substance; the sacrifice of self; and the sacrifice of prayer and praise. This is all one great corporate action. The offering of gifts is placed first because this is its historic position and in order to correct the mistaken notion that the Offertory Sentence is a response to the sermon. This is only true in the sense that the entire second division of the Service is in the nature of a response to the sacramental reading and preaching of the Word in the first division. At this point we look ahead and not back. We begin a new section of the Liturgy which is strongly sacramental in character, but with extended and important sacrificial features. Looking forward now to the celebration and reception of the Sacrament we present ourselves, our gifts, and our prayers to God in an act of corporate dedication and thanksgiving.

The Offering is a survival of the custom of the primitive church according to which the people, at this point, brought food and other gifts to a table (*prothesis*) near the altar. These gifts included fruit, wool, oil, milk, honey, olives, and cheese, as well as silver and gold. They were brought forward in an Offertory procession and solemnly dedicated in a Grace or Prayer of Thanksgiving. Sufficient bread and

95

wine were taken from the offerings and consecrated later in the Service for the Administration of the Holy Communion. The other gifts were reserved for support of the clergy and distribution to the poor. During the Offertory procession the choir sang a Psalm.

These features survived in many areas until the late Middle Ages. They were finally supplanted by a series of prayers and ceremonies of very different character, the action of the people giving way to a priestly function which developed highly objectionable prayers in preparation for the consecration. These prayers came to be known as the Offertory or Little Canon. Luther and the Reformers emphatically rejected these prayers and the Roman conception of the Sacrament as a propitiatory sacrifice or offering of man to God, contending that it is a gift of God to man. The Church Orders of the sixteenth century omitted the Roman Offertory Prayers and provided various substitutes. The Common Service accepted one of these consisting of brief passages from the Psalms (Offertory Sentences), the offering of gifts for church support and benevolences, and the General Prayer, concluding with the Lord's Prayer. The Common Liturgy has rearranged the order of these parts, for reasons already stated, and has supplied one additional text ("What shall I render . . .").

¶ Then shall the Offering be received and presented at the Altar.

THE OFFERING

¶ Then shall follow the Offertory, the Congregation standing meanwhile. One of the Offertories here following, or any other suitable Offertory, may be sung or said.

¶ When there is a Communion, the Minister, after Silent Prayer, and during the singing of the Offertory, shall uncover the Vessels and reverently prepare for the Administration of the Holy Sacrament.

THE OFFERTORY

I

The sacrifices of God are a broken spirit: a broken and a contrite heart, O God, thou wilt not despise.

Do good in thy good pleasure unto Zion: build thou the walls of Jerusalem.

Then shalt thou be pleased with the sacrifices of righteousness: with burnt-offering and whole burnt-offering.

II

What shall I render unto the Lord: for all his benefits toward me?

I will offer to thee the sacrifice of thanksgiving: and will call upon the Name of the Lord.

I will take the cup of salvation: and call upon the Name of the Lord.

I will pay my vows unto the Lord now in the presence of all his people: in the courts of the Lord's house, in the midst of thee, O Jerusalem.

Create in me a clean heart, O God: and renew a right spirit within me.
Cast me not away from thy presence: and take not thy Holy Spirit from me.
Restore unto me the joy of thy salvation: and uphold me with thy free Spirit.

The Reformation restored two important features of early Christian worship—the people's offering of gifts and the people's offering of intercessions. The latter in their earliest form were known as "Prayers of the Faithful." When the combined influences of Pietism, Rationalism, and Calvinism led to the general abandonment of weekly celebrations of Holy Communion, the three items in this unit—Offering, Offertory, and Prayer—were brought forward from the second grand division of the Service and, with an appended benediction, were made the conclusion of the Service of the Word.

THE PRAYER OF THE CHURCH

¶ *Then shall follow the Prayer of the Church.*

¶ *The indented paragraphs in the Prayer of the Church may be omitted, at the discretion of the Minister.*

¶ *If special prayers are desired by or for members of the Church, the Minister may make mention of them before beginning the Prayer of the Church, as occasion may require, or as follows:*

Intercessions: The prayers of the Church are asked for the following brethren who are sick (*or,* in adversity, *or,* in suffering, *or,* in need): *N. N.*

Thanksgivings: N. N. desires to return thanks to God, for special blessings (*or,* for restoration from illness, *or,* for gifts of grace), and asks the prayers of the Church.

Commemorations: Let us remember with thanksgiving before God our brethren who have departed this life with the sign of faith: *N. N.* (*or,* our *brother N. N.,* who has departed this life).

Let us pray.

Almighty God, the Father of our Lord Jesus Christ: We give thee praise and hearty thanks for all thy goodness and tender mercies. We bless thee for the love which hath created and doth sustain us from day to day. We praise thee for the gift of thy Son, our Saviour, through whom thou hast made known thy will and grace. We thank thee for the Holy Ghost, the Comforter; for thy holy Church, for the Means of Grace, for the lives of all faithful and godly men, and for the hope of the life to come. Help us to treasure in our hearts all that our Lord hath done for us; and enable us to show our thankfulness by lives that are given wholly to thy service;

℞. We beseech thee to hear us, good Lord.

Save and defend thy Church Universal, purchased with the precious Blood of Christ. Give it pastors and ministers according to thy Spirit, and strengthen it through the Word and the holy Sacraments. Make it perfect in love and in all good works, and establish it in the faith delivered to the saints. Sanctify and unite thy people in all the world, that one holy Church may bear witness to thee, the God and Father of all;

℟. We beseech thee to hear us, good Lord.

Upon all in any holy office in thy Church bestow thy wisdom and heavenly grace, and enable them to fulfill their duties in thy fear and in purity of heart. Let thy gracious benediction rest upon our clergy and people, and upon all who are set over us in the Lord; that faith may abound, and thy kingdom increase;

℟. We beseech thee to hear us, good Lord.

Send forth thy light and thy truth into all the earth, O Lord. Raise up, we pray thee, faithful servants of Christ to labor in the Gospel at home and in distant lands;

℟. We beseech thee to hear us, good Lord.

According to thy merciful goodness, O God, extend thy saving health and strength to the younger Churches. Grant that they may rejoice in a rich harvest of souls for thy kingdom. Support them in times of trial and weakness, and make them steadfast, abounding in the work of the Lord.

℟. We beseech thee to hear us, good Lord.

Preserve our Nation in righteousness and honor, and continue thy blessings to us as a people, that we may lead a quiet and peaceable life, in all godliness and honesty. Grant health and favor to all who bear office in our land (especially to the President and the Congress, the Governor and Legislature of this State) *, and help them to acknowledge and obey thy holy will;

℟. We beseech thee to hear us, good Lord.

Give to all men the mind of Christ, and dispose our days in thy peace, O God. Take from us all hatred and prejudice, and whatever may hinder unity of spirit and concord. Prosper the labors of those who take counsel for the nations of the world, that mutual understanding and common endeavor may be increased among all peoples;

℟. We beseech thee to hear us, good Lord.

Bless, we pray thee, the schools of the Church, universities and centers of research, all institutions of learning, and those who exercise the care of souls therein. Withhold not, we pray thee, thy Word and Wisdom, but bestow it in such measure that men may serve thee in Church and State, and our common life be brought under the rule of thy truth and righteousness;

℟. We beseech thee to hear us, good Lord.

We pray thee especially, heavenly Father, to sanctify our homes with thy light and joy. Keep our children in the covenant of their baptism, and enable their parents to rear them in a life of faith and godliness. By the spirit of affection and service unite the members of all Christian families, that they may show forth thy praise in our land and in all the world;

℟. We beseech thee to hear us, good Lord.

God of mercies, we pray thee to comfort with the grace of thy Holy Spirit all who are in sorrow or need, sickness or adversity. Remember those who suffer persecution for the faith. Have mercy upon those to whom death draws near. Bring consolation to those in sorrow or mourning. And to all grant a measure of thy love, taking them into thy tender care;

℟. We beseech thee to hear us, good Lord.

Let thy blessing rest upon the seed-time and harvest, the commerce and industry, the leisure and rest, and the arts and culture of our people. Take under thy special protection those whose toil is difficult or dangerous, and

* *In Canadian Churches, the following may be said:* especially Her Gracious Majesty the Queen, the Prime Minister and the Parliament, and all Provincial Authorities.

be with all who lay their hands to any useful task. Give them just
rewards for their labor, and the knowledge that their work is good in thy
sight, who art the Maker and Sustainer of all things;

℞. We beseech thee to hear us, good Lord.

We remember with thanksgiving those who have loved and served thee
in thy Church on earth, who now rest from their labors (especially those
most dear to us, whom we name in our hearts before thee). Keep us in
fellowship with all thy saints, and bring us at length to the joy of thy
heavenly kingdom;

℞. We beseech thee to hear us, good Lord.

¶ Here special Supplications, Intercessions, and Thanksgivings may be made.

All these things, and whatever else thou seest that we need, grant us,
O Father, for his sake who died and rose again, and now liveth and
reigneth with thee in the unity of the Holy Ghost, one God, world without end.

℞. Amen.

¶ If there be no Communion the Minister and the Congregation
shall say the Lord's Prayer.

¶ A Hymn may then be sung.

¶ Then the Minister, standing at the Altar, shall sing or say the Benediction.

The Lord bless thee, and keep thee.
The Lord make his face shine upon thee, and be gracious unto thee.
The Lord lift up his countenance upon thee, and give thee peace:
In the Name of the Father, and of the Son, and of the Holy Ghost.

¶ The Congregation shall sing or say:
Amen.

The Prayer of the Church is the third part of the Offertory, in the
larger sense of that word. Following the offering of gifts and the
Offertory Psalm immediately, this is a prayer "for all sorts and conditions of men." Its scope and character make it one of the most
significant parts of the Liturgy. The Reformation in restoring this
feature made an important constructive contribution to liturgical
development in the Protestant Church. Here we have not only full
recognition of the "priesthood of all believers," but an expression of the
church's concern for the world we live in, for the church universal, for
all its institutions and operations, and for human society in all its reaches.
This prayer is like the Creeds in that it grasps the fundamentals and the
universals. It lifts the individual and the congregation out of self-concern
and parochial considerations and bids worshiping groups remember
others and seek their welfare. In it the Apostle's injunction finds ful-
filment: "I exhort therefore, that, first of all, supplications, prayers,
intercessions, and giving of thanks, be made for all men; for kings and
for all that are in authority; that we may lead a quiet and peaceable life
in all godliness and honesty" (1 Tim. 2:1-2).

It is most unfortunate that this meaning and purpose of the

99

Allgemeines Kirchengebet is so frequently not understood or observed. The congregation's prayer at this place should never be a mere repetition of the thought of the day or of the sermon, or a narrow expression of selfish needs or desires. The minister, if he offers a free prayer at this place, should not seek to touch, please, or instruct the congregation, or to give a rhapsodic form of adoration, confession, or even thanksgiving —the so-called "Long Prayer" of nonliturgical churches. The Lutheran Liturgy provides for these necessary features in other places.

The Reformation found material for a restoration of the Prayer of the Faithful in current extra-liturgical devotions known as the Prone. These were edited and amplified, following a suggestion of Luther's, and developed into the *Allgemeines Kirchengebet,* or General Prayer. The English *Book of Common Prayer,* somewhat later, provided a prayer of similar character called "The Prayer for the Whole State of Christ's Church," which it uses without variation at every Eucharistic Service. Lutheran practice, true to its Gallican affinities, and, even more generally, because of the influence of Pietism, Rationalism, and Calvinism, frequently introduces substitute texts for the appointed prayer. The rubric in the Service permits this. In all such cases, however, the type of prayer here made should conform in its unselfish outlook and intercessory character to the church's ideal. It should in every instance be a prayer of the church for all mankind and for every need of our human society.

The Common Service and the *Common Service Book* gave translations of various sixteenth century forms. The text in each case is heavy. It was also necessary to mention many needs, such as missions, education, home life, and social welfare, which found no place whatever in the thought of the sixteenth century. The Common Liturgy gives an entirely new text in idiomatic English, with provision for congregational response after each paragraph. This was a practice in the early church and in the Reformation period. It helps secure attention and meets the frequently presented objection of length. Congregations will do well to use this approved form regularly, employing other forms only when special conditions make this necessary.

When there is a Communion, or when Baptism, Confirmation, or another Occasional Service immediately follows, the Lord's Prayer is omitted at this place. When there is no Communion the Service is concluded with the Lord's Prayer, a hymn, and the Benediction.

THE THANKSGIVING
¶ A Hymn shall be sung.
¶ The Congregation shall rise at the beginning of the Preface.

THE PREFACE

¶ *The Minister and Congregation shall sing or say:*

The Lord be with you.

℟. And with thy spirit.

Lift up your hearts.

℟. We lift them up unto the Lord.

Let us give thanks unto the Lord our God.

℟. It is meet and right so to do.

¶ *Then shall the Minster turn to the Altar and sing or say:*

It is truly meet, right, and salutary, that we should at all times, and in all places, give thanks unto thee, O Lord, Holy Father, Almighty, Everlasting God:

¶ *Here shall follow the Proper Preface for the Day or Season. If there be none especially appointed, then shall follow immediately,* Therefore with angels, *etc.*

PROPER PREFACES

For Christmas

For in the mystery of the Word made flesh, thou hast given us a new revelation of thy glory; that seeing thee in the person of thy Son, we may be drawn to the love of those things which are not seen. Therefore with Angels, *etc.*

¶ *After the Preface shall follow immediately:*

Therefore with Angels and Archangels, and with all the company of heaven, we laud and magnify thy glorious Name; evermore praising thee, and saying:

¶ *Then shall be sung or said the Sanctus.*

In the exalted responsive sentences of the Preface we have, apart from the very words of Scripture, the most ancient and the least changed liturgical text of the Christian Church. In simple, majestic phrases of great dignity, reverence, and beauty, we are here led into the heart of the Communion Office. Memory recalls our Saviour's action when he took bread and wine and "gave thanks." The Proper Prefaces provide the objective, sacramental bases for our common thanksgiving. The early church stressed this note of thanksgiving and gave the name "Eucharist" to the entire Service. The Preface thus instructs the church as to one of the great meanings of the Sacrament and guards the church against mournful misconceptions. The plural forms—"you," "we"— strongly stress the "fellowship of the faithful." There is nothing homiletical or didactic about these crisp but lofty sentences. At this point the church is not endeavoring to make or instruct believers. It is unitedly pouring out its love and gratitude in reverent commemoration and praise.

The Preface in its full form includes the Sanctus, though as generally considered it ends with the Ascription ("Therefore with Angels . . ."). The variable Proper Prefaces, between the Thanksgiving and the Ascrip-

101

tion, are a feature peculiar to the Western church. They emphasize a particular phase of our Lord's redemptive work and connect each individual service with the thought of the day or season. There is poetic inspiration in the formal dignity of their stately phrases which suggests a strong resemblance to the finest Latin Collects. They are, in a sense, a substitute for the exceedingly lengthy prayers of the early and Eastern churches which recount at this point the blessings of creation, the progressive revelation of God, and the unfolding incidents and aspects of our Lord's life upon earth. The Proper Prefaces of the West provide variety with brevity at this point.

The Common Liturgy has added two Proper Prefaces to the number in the *Common Service Book*. These are the Preface for Advent, for the most part a composition by the Commission, and the Preface for All Saints' Day, taken, by permission, from the *Book of Common Order* of the Church of Scotland. The texts of the Proper Prefaces in the Lutheran Liturgy differ materially from corresponding texts in the American *Book of Common Prayer,* the Lutheran use being in closer agreement with the historic Latin originals.

The Prefatory Sentences are recited from memory by the minister, facing the congregation. He turns to the altar to say, "It is truly meet. . . ." All that follows to the Sanctus is read from the Altar Book on the missal stand to the left of the sacramental vessels. The minister may read these portions with joined hands, or he may follow the Jewish and early church practice and raise his separated hands to shoulder height and extend them straight forward, the palms facing each other.

The Preface melodies, like the text, belong to the ancient and universal tradition of the church, with an unbroken use of more than a thousand years. They were preserved in the Lutheran Church Orders and Cantionales of the sixteenth century, and are found in all liturgical uses today. As befitting their ancient origin, centuries before the invention of harmony, they are always sung in unison, with simple organ accompaniment.

THE SANCTUS

Holy, holy, holy, Lord God of Sabaoth; Heaven and earth are full of thy glory; Hosanna in the highest.

Blessed is he that cometh in the Name of the Lord; Hosanna in the highest.

The Sanctus (from the Latin word for "holy") climaxes and concludes the Preface. In a solemn song of adoration and acclamation the congregation dramatically joins with the angel throng in a hymn of praise which balances the Gloria in Excelsis in the ante-Communion. The first paragraph proclaims the glory of God the Father. The second acknowledges Christ as God. "Heaven and earth are full of thy Glory"

102

suggests the lengthy commemorations in the early Christian liturgies. Relating references to Isaiah's vision and the Hosanna to Christ unites the Old and New Testament Scriptures. "Hosanna in the highest" has the meaning of "Save now, I beseech thee in high heaven" (Ps. 118:25), which our Lord chanted with his Disciples at the Last Supper. "Blessed is he that cometh" (Ps. 118:26) anticipates the thought of the administration, though the early church gave eschatological significance to these words by placing them in a concluding prayer after the Communion which looked forward to Christ's return in glory.

The traditional Sanctus melody is a chorale-like adaptation of an ancient plainsong melody appointed for the First Sunday in Advent. This ancient melody evidently was deeply loved in Germany. It was carried over, with its Latin text, into the Lutheran Cantionales (Spangenberg, Keuchenthal, et cetera). Luther's melody for the Sanctus in his German Mass (1526) is reminiscent of the plainsong form. Johann Sebastian Bach gave this melody again in simplified, but still ornate, chorale-form, as we may see in the *Choräle für vier Singstimmen aus der Sammlung von Carl Philipp Emanuel Bach* (No. 72), or in May de Forest Payne's *Melodic Index* (New York: G. Schirmer, 1938), p. 70. Later editors further simplified this four-part form as we have it today. It is frequently "ascribed to Bach," but its original is unquestionably plainsong.

THE PRAYER OF THANKSGIVING

The Prayer of Thanksgiving (Eucharistic Prayer) is a feature universally found in all the ancient Christian liturgies, and in the use of practically every Christian Church—except the Lutheran—in the world today. Its reintroduction in the Common Liturgy, in thoroughly evangelical form, will strengthen a weak spot in our customary use.

¶ *Then may the Congregation kneel.*
¶ *The Minister standing before the Altar, and facing it, shall say the Prayer of Thanksgiving.*

THE PRAYER OF THANKSGIVING

Holy art thou, Almighty and Merciful God. Holy art thou, and great is the Majesty of thy glory.

Thou didst so love the world as to give thine only-begotten Son, that whosoever believeth in him might not perish, but have everlasting life; Who, having come into the world to fulfill for us thy holy will and to accomplish all things for our salvation, IN THE NIGHT IN WHICH HE WAS BETRAYED, ᵃTOOK BREAD; AND, WHEN HE HAD GIVEN THANKS, HE BRAKE IT AND GAVE IT TO HIS DISCIPLES, SAYING, TAKE, EAT; THIS IS MY BODY, WHICH IS GIVEN FOR YOU; THIS DO IN REMEMBRANCE OF ME.

(a) *Here he shall take the* BREAD *in his hand.*

AFTER THE SAME MANNER ALSO, HE ᵇTOOK THE CUP, WHEN HE HAD

SUPPED, AND, WHEN HE HAD GIVEN THANKS, HE GAVE IT TO THEM, SAYING, DRINK YE ALL OF IT; THIS CUP IS THE NEW TESTAMENT IN MY BLOOD, WHICH IS SHED FOR YOU, AND FOR MANY, FOR THE REMISSION OF SINS; THIS DO, AS OFT AS YE DRINK IT, IN REMEMBRANCE OF ME.

(b) Here he shall take the CUP *in his hand.*

Remembering, therefore, his salutary precept, his life-giving Passion and Death, his glorious Resurrection and Ascension and the promise of his coming again, we give thanks to thee, O Lord God Almighty, not as we ought, but as we are able; and we beseech thee mercifully to accept our praise and thanksgiving, and with thy Word and Holy Spirit to bless us, thy servants, and these thine own gifts of bread and wine, so that we and all who partake thereof may be filled with heavenly benediction and grace, and, receiving the remission of sins, be sanctified in soul and body, and have our portion with all thy saints.

And unto thee, O God, Father, Son, and Holy Spirit, be all honor and glory in thy holy Church, world without end. Amen.

This central portion of the Liturgy, known as the Canon, or Rule, has presented serious difficulties in all parts of the church and in all periods. The Roman Canon has been practically unchanged for a thousand years. It is a collection of fragmentary material which in earlier times knew many transpositions and omissions.

The early church, at this point, focused its thought upon the offering of gifts by the people in a great Prayer of Thanksgiving. With growing perception, in the post-Nicene era, of the work of the Holy Spirit, there developed particularly in the East a specific invocation (*Epiclesis*) of the Spirit's presence and power. The Roman Church, which also had the Epiclesis in the early period, dropped it in the fourth century and shifted emphasis from thanksgiving to consecration, the latter effected by recitation of the Words of Institution. The Reformation, in turn, shifted emphasis to the administration and reception. As indicated above, various attempts were made by the Reformers to revise the Roman Canon. For the most part, however, Lutheran reform accomplished nothing more than the omission of all forms of prayer, with retention only of the Words of Institution. The Verba thus came to have a mechanistic force even greater than before. Objections increasingly felt, particularly in recent years, have led to the preparation and adoption of the new text in the Common Liturgy.

Luther's reform of the Service at this point was drastic, and very unlike his usual conservative procedure. His amputation of all prayer forms—good as well as bad—surrounding the Words of Institution robbed the Liturgy of its historical and ecumenical character and fastened a strange and unique use upon subsequent Lutheran history. This has invited severe criticism from liturgical scholars of other communions. They believe that the Lutheran Church has not only broken with universal Christian practice, but in using these words as a mere formula of consecration, effects a "mechanical materialization" of the Sacrament which is "more Roman than the Romans." Dissatisfaction among Lutheran students of the Liturgy has also been general in all periods. All agree that a carefully framed Eucharistic Prayer continuing the exuberant strains of the Preface and the Sanctus, and encompassing our Saviour's life-giving words with solemn thoughts of remembrance and exalted expressions of thanksgiving is desirable.

The early church developed a definite pattern for such a prayer: a post-Sanctus, with its continuing notes of adoration; a recitation of the Words of Institution; a solemn reference to our Lord's Incarnation, sufferings and death, Resurrection and Ascension (the *Anamnesis*); an invocation of the Holy Spirit (*Epiclesis*); and petitions for the spiritual blessing of the Sacrament upon all who partake of it. Several Lutheran Church Orders of the sixteenth century attempted, though not too successfully, to surround the Verba with pure prayer forms. Thus the Kantz Order, 1522, Strassburg, 1525, Pfalz-Neuburg, 1543, Austria, 1571. The English Prayer Book, 1549, developed lengthy forms of evangelical character. In the nineteenth century, Loehe's Agende, 1844, Bavaria, 1879, and Russia, 1898, provided brief forms, as did several American liturgies—e.g., the Ministerium of Pennsylvania, 1853, and the Joint Synod of Ohio, 1863. More recent Lutheran liturgies which give a Eucharistic Prayer include an extended form in India, 1936, and a brief form in the Church of Sweden, 1942.

Since all that should be said in such a prayer has been fittingly and beautifully expressed in the historic liturgies, a prayer suitable for our use may well consist chiefly of selections and arrangements of historic material. The Prayer of Thanksgiving in the Common Liturgy is a pure text of this character which follows the order of the Creed. It is entirely pre-Roman in character. In addition to its historic and devotional features, it makes manifest, as no other single part of the Service does, the real meaning of the Sacrament we celebrate, and its relation to the Last Supper and to the entire redemptive work of Christ.

Because of the general interest in this new, yet very ancient, feature, it may be well to indicate the sources of particular clauses in the Prayer of Thanksgiving. Careful study was made of dozens of early and contemporary liturgies, and from these the most felicitous and meaningful phrases were chosen. Many of these appear in slightly variant forms in the different liturgies. Following is a listing of the earliest known sources for particular sentences or clauses.

"Thou didst so love . . ."	John 3:16; St. Chrysostom
"to fulfill for us thy holy will"	St. Chrysostom

"to accomplish all things for our salvation"	John 19:28
"In the night in which . . ."	Narrative of the Institution from the Common Service
"Remembering . . . life-giving Passion . . . his coming again"	St. James. Common **Order,** Scotland, 1940
"We give thanks . . . as we are able"	Apostolic Constitutions
"Mercifully to accept our praise and thanksgiving"	Common Order, Scotland, 1940
"With thy Word and Holy Spirit . . . **gifts of bread and wine"**	First Prayer Book of Edward VI, 1549
"So that we . . . benediction and grace"	Roman Missal
"Receiving the remission of sins . . . our portion with all thy saints."	St. Basil

THE WORDS OF INSTITUTION[1]

¶ *Or, instead of the above Prayer of Thanksgiving,* "Holy art thou, Almighty and Merciful God," *the Minister may say the Words of Institution, followed by the Lord's Prayer.*

OUR LORD JESUS CHRIST, IN THE NIGHT IN WHICH HE WAS BETRAYED, [a]TOOK BREAD; AND, WHEN HE HAD GIVEN THANKS, HE BRAKE IT AND GAVE IT TO HIS DISCIPLES, SAYING, TAKE, EAT; THIS IS MY BODY, WHICH IS GIVEN FOR YOU; THIS DO IN REMEMBRANCE OF ME.

(*a*) *Here he shall take the* BREAD *in his hand.*

AFTER THE SAME MANNER ALSO, HE [b]TOOK THE CUP, WHEN HE HAD SUPPED, AND, WHEN HE HAD GIVEN THANKS, HE GAVE IT TO THEM, SAYING, DRINK YE ALL OF IT; THIS CUP IS THE NEW TESTAMENT IN MY BLOOD, WHICH IS SHED FOR YOU, AND FOR MANY, FOR THE REMISSION OF SINS; THIS DO, AS OFT AS YE DRINK IT, IN REMEMBRANCE OF ME.

(*b*) *Here he shall take the* CUP *in his hand.*

These words, as printed in capital letters in the Prayer of Thanksgiving, are found in all liturgies, though in slightly different forms. Our text is a harmony of the four Gospel accounts with the additional phrase "which is given for you." This phrase was incorporated by Luther in his Latin Service, and before that was a part of the Mozarabic Liturgy.

These words, the so-called "Verba," are at this point more than a recital of a historic event. They are the central feature of a solemn corporate act of prayer, a reverent liturgical celebration in which the worshiping congregation vividly recalls the divine command and promises and invokes the divine blessing. They also are the warrant for the Service in which we are now engaged, for, as used by the Saviour in the Upper Room, they established the institution of Holy Communion as a Sacrament. Nor may we forget their force as immediately connected with the administration. All of these meanings are inherent as the minister, representing the congregation, solemnly repeats the Lord's

[1] Full discussion of this important and involved subject will be found in *The Lutheran Liturgy,* pp. 317-341.

106

own words and, in a measure, his actions too—actions which in Scripture have equal importance with the words.

These words, therefore, naturally find their place in the Prayer of Thanksgiving which is addressed to God, and which invokes the blessing of the Word and the Holy Spirit upon all who partake of the heavenly gifts. We solemnly set these elements apart for their sacred use. It is Christ who consecrates them. For the actual continuing power of consecration derives from the original institution of our Lord, who said not only "This do," but also "This is." We repeat his words, and his actions, as we take, bless, distribute, and receive the gifts. The consecration finds its completion in the administration and reception, apart from which there is no Sacrament.

The omission in the Lutheran Rite of one of our Lord's actions—the breaking of the bread—is due to Luther's direction in his *Formula Missae* (*nec frangatur hostia*). Luther probably feared that this practice might be regarded as expressive of the Roman doctrine of sacrifice. The Anglican, Presbyterian, and many other Protestant churches have retained the Fraction, and it would appear that Luther's fears in this matter were groundless. There is little point in our continuing to fear a shadow that has no substance, and we might as well get in step with the rest of Christendom.

The Verba are said or intoned clearly, and with solemn dignity. The paten and the chalice may be lifted to shoulder height. The Church Orders generally rejected the sign of the cross in the recitation of the Verba. European churches quite generally revived this practice in the seventeenth century. Its propriety at this place is very questionable because of possible erroneous doctrinal implications.

THE LORD'S PRAYER
¶ Then shall the Minister sing or say:

Our Father, who art in heaven, Hallowed be thy Name, Thy kingdom come, Thy will be done, on earth as it is in heaven. Give us this day our daily bread; And forgive us our trespasses, as we forgive those who trespass against us; And lead us not into temptation, But deliver us from evil.

¶ The Congregation shall sing or say:

For thine is the kingdom, and the power, and the glory, for ever and ever. Amen.

The Lord's Prayer is found in every Liturgy in connection with the Communion, though its exact location varies. It is the distinctive prayer of God's children. Conscious of their fellowship and unity as brethren in Christ, and of their part in the communion of saints, they come to the altar with this prayer upon their lips. It is a prayer of humble access and may be thought of as consecratory of believers, but not of the elements. In the early church no one was permitted to know or use the Lord's Prayer except the faithful who had been baptized. Our Liturgy might well have retained the medieval liturgical introduction found in many Church Orders: "Admonished by thy saving precepts and instructed by thy divine ordinance, we make bold to say: Our Father . . . ."

As in the case of most other prayers throughout the Liturgy (Collects, Prayer of the Church, Prayer of Thanksgiving, Litany), the minister voices the thought of the people, the congregation responding at the end with an Amen, or otherwise. The Eastern, Gallican, and Anglican churches direct the congregation to unite in the Lord's Prayer at this place. The Mozarabic Liturgy directs the priest to say the prayer alone, with the people responding with Amen after each clause. The Common Liturgy, following the pre-Reformation Latin use, gives the prayer to the minister alone, with the provision that the congregation shall sing or say the concluding doxology, "For thine is the kingdom," when the Prayer of Thanksgiving is used. This latter feature, which has its precedent in a number of German liturgies, unites the congregation with the minister in the liturgical conclusion to this solemn prayer of sonship and brotherhood.

Luther in his German Mass provided music for the minister to chant the Verba and the Lord's Prayer, both of which had previously been said silently by the priest. In many Lutheran congregations today, even when the minister does not chant any other part of the Service, the Words of Institution and the Lord's Prayer are solemnly intoned to a simple musical inflection.

THE PAX

¶ Then shall the Minister turn to the Congregation and sing or say:
The peace of the Lord be with you alway.
¶ The Congregation shall sing or say:
And with thy spirit.

This short Benediction is a surviving fragment of two observances of the early church—the solemn blessing of the people, as found in the Eastern and Gallican churches and the Kiss of Peace, a mark of fellowship and unity found in all early liturgies at the very beginning of the Mass of the Faithful. In Roman services today it is the private prayer of the priest at the time of the ceremonial Fraction of the Bread. Luther thought highly of it, not because of its early significance or its use in the Roman Service, but as a blessing, and indeed an absolution. He called it "the voice of the gospel announcing the forgiveness of sins . . . the only and most worthy preparation for the Lord's Table."

108

Archbishop Brilioth criticizes this sharply as a "violent importation by Luther of his favorite idea." Luther's insight and forthrightness, however, enabled him to seize this relatively unimportant phrase and relate it significantly to the deepest thought of the Liturgy. Some recent Prayer Books of the Anglican communion have restored the Pax, dropped in 1552. All emphasize its ancient meaning in the words, "Ye who . . . are in love and charity with your neighbors . . . draw near." The Scottish Liturgy, 1929, adds the words, "Brethren, let us love one another, for love is of God."

The Response in the Common Liturgy, "and with thy spirit," is a change from the simple "Amen" of the Common Service. It has the authority of Lutheran Church Orders, and is in agreement with the usual response to the Salutation throughout the Service.

THE AGNUS DEI

¶ *Then, the Congregation standing, shall be sung or said the Agnus Dei.*

O Christ, thou Lamb of God, that takest away the sin of the world, have mercy upon us.

O Christ, thou Lamb of God, that takest away the sin of the world, have mercy upon us.

O Christ, thou Lamb of God, that takest away the sin of the world, grant us thy peace. Amen.

This beautiful communion hymn has its source in John 1:29, "Behold the Lamb of God, which taketh away the sin of the world," and in repeated references to Christ as a lamb in the book of the Revelation. It is not in the earliest or the Gallican liturgies. Pope Sergius I, about A.D. 700, introduced it as a Eucharistic devotion sung by the choir during the Fraction, or ceremonial breaking of the Bread. In our use we connect it with the Distribution. We think of it not so much as a confession of our unworthiness but as a spiritual communion with the Christ who is directly addressed and whose Presence we sense. Its petitions embrace the blessings which his sacrificial death secured for us.

The text of the Agnus resembles the second part of the earlier Gloria in Excelsis. The "musical Masses" of Mozart, Haydn, Gounod, and other composers include it as one of their five Mass texts (Kyrie, Gloria, Creed, Sanctus, Agnus). The simple but beautiful melody in the *Service Book* is of plainsong origin, and is first found in Bugenhagen's Church Order for Brunswick, 1528, set to the German text, *Christe, du Lamm Gottes,* which in its address is, of course, an inaccurate translation of the Latin original.

The radical reform of the Anglican Prayer Book in 1552 swept out the Agnus, along with the Introit and the Gradual. In the case of the

Agnus this probably was due to fear that the use of this particular hymn at this place might foster the practice of adoration of the host. Unbroken Lutheran use of the Agnus shows how groundless was this fear.

THE COMMUNION

¶ *Then shall the Communicants present themselves before the Altar and receive the Holy Sacrament.*

¶ *When the Minister giveth the* BREAD *he shall say:*
The Body of Christ, given for thee.

¶ *When he giveth the* CUP *he shall say:*
The Blood of Christ, shed for thee.

¶ *The Communicant may say Amen after each Element has been received.*
¶ *After he hath given the* BREAD *and the* CUP, *or after all have been communicated, the Minister shall say:*

The Body of our Lord Jesus Christ and his precious Blood strengthen and preserve you unto eternal life.

Individual communicants at this point personally receive all that has been celebrated and invoked by the congregation in previous parts of the Service. At the altar they also realize, as nowhere else, their common fellowship as members of the mystical body of Christ. The officiant makes his Communion first, thus formally completing the ceremonial action. If there is an assistant minister he may administer the elements to the officiant, and then receive the same from the latter. Self-communion of the minister was favored by Luther and is defended in the Confessions as the natural completion of a liturgical action which has more than purely personal values, and which expresses the fellowship of pastor and people in a spiritual transaction. Certainly, a Communion in which the minister does not receive the elements himself is an anomaly unknown in Greek, Roman, Anglican, or other Protestant churches.

Spiritual preparation of the individual before reception is important, and is provided for in the Order of Confession. Pietism so magnified self-examination and the fear of unworthy reception that attendance at Communion greatly declined. This attitude still persists in some places. The Sacrament is greater than confession or any other preparation for it. It is a New Testament ordinance, the message of the gospel, not the lash of the law. We come to it in love and not in fear.

The Lutheran and the Anglican churches follow the ancient Gallican use and bring communicants to the altar. In the Roman Church the laity receive at the chancel rail. Presbyterian practice carries the elements into the pews, and, upon occasion, even into the vestibules!

The deacons may direct the communicants' approach, though this certainly is not necessary. If this is done, groups of proper size should

110

be brought forward promptly. While one group kneels at the altar the next group stands near or in the chancel and facing the altar. After the Blessing the group at the altar retires by side exits, or by passing through an open lane in the center of the group standing in the chancel. The second group then comes to the rail immediately. The Distribution continues without the delay so frequently found when the celebrant awaits the slow arrival of communicants brought forward belatedly from distant pews.

Communicants receive the Sacrament kneeling or standing. The latter was the practice of the early church. Kneeling became general after the twelfth century. It fittingly expresses the spirit of reverence and humility.

Liturgical churches have universally retained the use of the common chalice until quite recently when individual cups were introduced in many congregations. The common chalice is a clear symbol of the fellowship and unity of which St. Paul speaks, and which is referred to in the Order for Public Confession: "For as we are all partakers of this one Bread and drink of this one Cup, so are we all one body in him." If individual cups are used, the common chalice is retained by the minister for the consecration and for administering the wine. The chalice should be provided with a pouring lip, and the minister will fill the communicants' cups from the common chalice. Individual cups must never be filled beforehand in the sacristy, and trays must not be placed upon the altar. Communicants receive cups from racks in the pews, or from a cabinet at the entrance to the chancel. After communing the cups are deposited in the cabinet or placed in the pew racks.

The celebrant has complete charge of details at the altar. If there is an assistant minister (liturgically the "deacon"), the officiant administers the bread and the deacon the wine. The Blessing is pronounced by the celebrant.

The formula of Distribution repeats the simple words of the early church and of the Church of Sweden, "the Body of Christ" and "the Blood of Christ," with the addition of the words suggested by Luther, "given for thee" and "shed for thee." Communicants may quietly respond "Amen" after each element has been received, a custom also of the early church. The minister places the bread in the communicant's hand, the custom of the early church, or directly in the mouth, the medieval practice. If in the hand, this must be ungloved, the right hand resting upon the left, both palms open. When individual cups are used, one hand will hold the cup and the other hand will receive the bread between the thumb and forefinger.

The sacramental Blessing has been shortened by the omission of the words "true faith." The formula is an adaptation of a form used in pre-Reformation times in distributing the bread. According to ancient usage the sign of the cross may be given with the Blessing. The General Rubrics provide that the Blessing may be given but once, after the last table has been communicated.

Communicants upon returning to their pews, kneel and offer a prayer of thanksgiving and self-dedication. During the Administration the congregation may sing stanzas of appropriate hymns, a pre-Reformation custom of the Gallican churches, or the organist may play softly and discriminatingly.

THE POST-COMMUNION
NUNC DIMITTIS

¶ Then shall the Congregation rise, and the Nunc Dimittis may be sung or said.

Lord, now lettest thou thy servant depart in peace: according to thy word;
    For mine eyes have seen thy salvation: which thou hast prepared before
the face of all people;
    A light to lighten the Gentiles: and the glory of thy people Israel.
    Glory be to the Father, and to the Son, and to the Holy Ghost;
    As it was in the beginning, is now, and ever shall be, world without
end. Amen.

St. Augustine said, "When that great Sacrament has been partaken, a Thanksgiving concludes all." The liturgical Post-Communion is brief in most liturgies. The Anglican Prayer Books transfer the Gloria in Excelsis to this place from its usual position at the beginning of the Service. The Lutheran use consists of the Nunc Dimittis, which may be omitted, the choice of several thanksgiving Collects, the Salutation, Benedicamus, and Benediction.

The Nunc Dimittis is a New Testament Canticle which appropriately relates the thought of the Incarnation to the mystery of the Sacrament. As we sing it here we remember the ending of the Last Supper—"When they had sung a hymn they went out into the Mount of Olives." The words, "thy servant," give it personal application, but the phrase, "thy salvation which thou hast prepared before the face of all people," gives the moment world significance.

This Canticle is found at the conclusion of the Greek Liturgy and also in the ancient Spanish (Mozarabic) Liturgy. It is not a part of the Roman or the Anglican Communion Office. It came, first of all, into Lutheran use as a Vesper Canticle borrowed from the Office of Compline. The early Lutheran Orders of Nürnberg and Strassburg and the Liturgy of the Church of Sweden made it a part of the Post-Communion. A strict application of the Rule of the Common Service would have excluded it from the latter. There was general desire for it, however, and on the basis of good, if limited, precedent it was inserted as a permissive use.

THE PRAYER

¶ Then shall be said The Prayer.

*¶ The Minister shall say one of the following Prayers; or he
may say the Collect for Thursday in Holy Week.*

**O give thanks unto the Lord, for he is good.
℞. And his mercy endureth for ever.**

We give thanks to thee, Almighty God, that thou hast refreshed us with this thy salutary gift; and we beseech thee, of thy mercy, to strengthen us through the same gift, in faith toward thee and in fervent love toward one another; through Jesus Christ, thy dear Son, our Lord, who liveth and reigneth with thee and the Holy Ghost, one God, world without end.

Or,

Pour forth upon us, O Lord, the spirit of thy love, that by thy mercy thou mayest make of one will those whom thou hast fed with one heavenly food; through thy Son, Jesus Christ our Lord, who liveth and reigneth with thee and the Holy Ghost, one God, world without end.

Or,

Almighty God, who givest the true Bread which cometh down from heaven, even thy Son, Jesus Christ our Lord: Grant, we beseech thee, that we who have received the Sacrament of his Body and Blood may abide in him, and he in us, that we may be filled with the power of his endless life; who liveth and reigneth with thee and the Holy Ghost, one God, world without end.

Or,

Almighty God, who hast given thine only Son to be unto us both a sacrifice for sin and also an ensample of godly life: Give us grace that we may always most thankfully receive that his inestimable benefit, and also daily endeavor ourselves to follow the blessed steps of his most holy life; through the same Jesus Christ our Lord, who liveth and reigneth with thee and the Holy Ghost, one God, world without end.

¶ The Congregation shall sing or say:
Amen.

¶ Then may be sung or said the Salutation and the Benedicamus.
The Lord be with you.
℞. And with thy spirit.
Bless we the Lord.
℞. Thanks be to God.

The Service now concludes on the brighter note of a congregational thanksgiving. The Common Service provided only one Collect at this place—the fine prayer which Luther, upon the basis of a broad liturgical tradition and several earlier texts, fashioned for his German Mass (1526). With characteristic warmth, yet with almost Roman terseness, Luther's Collect expresses the great ideas of thanksgiving, the givenness of the Sacrament, its function as a Means of Grace, and the goal of stronger faith and more fervent love among Christians. It is found, in variant and expanded forms, in every Lutheran Liturgy. The English translation in the Common Liturgy first appeared in late editions of the *Church Book* of the General Council.

The Common Liturgy, following the general practice of all Western liturgies, has provided three additional appropriate Collects for optional use at this point. The first, "Pour forth upon us . . ." is from an early Roman source. The second, "Almighty God, who givest the true Bread . . ." was prepared by the Commission on the Liturgy, but based upon a prayer in *The Kingdom, the Power and Glory* (The Grey Book, Part III, third edition, London, 1925), a book leading up to the *Proposed Book of Common Prayer,* 1928. The third, "Almighty God, who hast given . . ." is a Collect composed for the First Prayer Book of 1549 and appointed for the Second Sunday after Easter, being based upon the thought of the Epistle for that day.

Rubrical permission is also given for the use at this place of the Collect for Thursday in Holy Week, "O Lord God, who hast left unto us in a wonderful Sacrament. . . ." This fine prayer was composed by Thomas Aquinas in 1264 for the new Feast of Corpus Christi. This feast itself, with its processions and adoration of the host, was most objectionable to the Reformers, but various Lutheran Orders, appreciative of the beauty and spiritual quality of this Collect, appointed it as an alternate to Luther's Collect for the Service on Holy Thursday. (Thus Duke Henry's Order for Saxony, 1539, Spangenberg, 1545, Austria, 1571, et cetera). The address to our Lord himself is unusual, but appropriate.

The final sacramental feature of the Liturgy, the Benediction, is introduced by the Salutation and Benedicamus. The latter, "Bless we the Lord," is a doxology found at the end of each of the five books of the Psalter (Psalms 41, 72, 89, 106, 150). The response appropriately leaves the word, "Thanks," as the final expression of the congregation at every Eucharist.

THE BENEDICTION

¶ *Then the Minister, standing at the Altar, shall sing or say the Benediction.*
The Lord bless thee, and keep thee.
The Lord make his face shine upon thee, and be gracious unto thee.
The Lord lift up his countenance upon thee, and give thee peace:

In the Name of the Father, and of the Son, and of the Holy Ghost.

¶ *The Congregation shall sing or say:*
Amen.

The use of an Old Testament text to conclude a New Testament Sacrament may seem strange. It is, however, appropriate. The direction to Aaron and his sons (Num. 6:22-27) to "put my name upon the

children of Israel" is accompanied by the promise, "I will bless them."
We also recall our Saviour's action just before his Ascension. He led
his Disciples out to Bethany, and then "lifted up his hands, and blessed
them" (Luke 24:50). This is the only Benediction definitely commanded
by God. The Mozarabic Liturgy gives these words before the Reception.
Luther in his Latin Mass suggested them as the Benediction to conclude
the Service, and definitely employed them in his German Mass. The
Church Orders generally followed him in this and established a unique
Lutheran use. The Liturgy of the Church of Sweden added to this
Aaronic Benediction the New Testament form: "In the Name of the
Father, and of the Son, and of the Holy Ghost," thus concluding the
Service with the Trinitarian formula. Muhlenberg in his Liturgy for the
Ministerium of Pennsylvania, 1748, followed the Swedish use, as did
also the Augustana Church. These precedents, as well as the impressive
propriety of the form itself, led the Commission to incorporate this form
in the new *Service Book*.

Upon the final thought and word of peace—a note that has been
sounded repeatedly in the Kyrie, the Pax, the Agnus, and the Nunc
Dimittis—the entire Service of Thanksgiving and Communion comes to
a blessed conclusion. The organist modulates into the key of the final
hymn, and in louder volume gives out the opening and concluding
phrases of its tune. The choir may remain in the stalls throughout the
hymn and then retire in silent procession; or on festivals, it may sing
as it leaves the nave. The minister may go with the choir, or go directly
from the chancel to the sacristy. The congregation stands throughout,
and afterward remains standing or kneeling for several moments of
silent prayer.

Chapter 8

MATINS AND VESPERS,
THE LITANY, THE SUFFRAGES

MATINS AND VESPERS

The Orders for morning and evening worship have an ancient origin and an interesting history. The Jews observed the third, sixth, and ninth hours of the day as Hours of Prayer. In the fourth century we learn of public services held in the morning and in the evening. As monastic communities developed they increased the number and complexity of services. This finally stabilized in a series of seven Hours of Prayer, with two services combined for the first Hour (Matins and Lauds). The Rule of St. Benedict, about A.D. 530, definitely established the succeeding Hours as Prime, Terce, Sext, None, Vespers, and Compline. Each Hour had its own distinctive character, and the series of Hours came to be known as the Divine Office. Groups of clergy in cathedrals and collegiate chapels also observed them and the laity frequently attended morning and evening.

The Hour Services were simple at first, the chief features being the reading or chanting of the Psalter, Lessons from Scripture, hymns, and prayers. Monastic ingenuity eventually overloaded them with intricate detail and made the daily recitation of the entire Office a burdensome obligation. The Reformers appreciated the valuable features in them and encouraged the daily use of simplified forms of Matins and Vespers in the schools of the church and in the congregations on Sundays and festivals. The destructions of war, Pietism, and Rationalism later led to the general abandonment of these historic forms. The churchly revival of the nineteenth century restored the observance of several of the Hours to deaconess motherhouses and similar religious communities and to congregations particularly in services of Confession preparatory to reception of Holy Communion (*Beicht-Vesper*). The Prayer Book of the Church of England made a successful simplification and adaptation of some of the Orders, and Morning Prayer and Evening Prayer (Evensong) have become regular and important features of the Anglican system of public worship. The *Common Service* of 1888 restored Matins and Vespers to the Lutheran Church in America.

In the Lutheran system the Eucharistic Service retains its primacy, whether in full form with Holy Communion or in the briefer Service of the Word. Matins and Vespers are additional minor Offices of more subjective character and stressing praise and prayer. Their outlines are adaptable and, in addition to regular congregational use, they may be built up with rich liturgical and musical material into festival forms, or used in daily services of institutions or at commencements, synodical conventions, and many other special occasions. In some of the latter instances the Order may be used throughout as a corporate devotion, after which addresses and exercises of miscellaneous character may be introduced with freedom.

We may consider six features found in both these Offices. These are Psalmody, hymnody, Scripture Lessons, the Responsory, prayer, and the Canticle.

The recitation of the Psalter was a principal feature of Jewish worship and was carried over into early Christian use. The medieval church incorporated large sections of the Psalter in the Liturgy of the Mass. In its developed system of Hour Services it made the recitation of the entire Psalter every week a definite obligation. The chanting of the Psalms antiphonally by divided choirs became a noteworthy feature in cathedrals, monasteries, and collegiate churches. Nine melodies, known as the Gregorian Tones, each of which was supplied with varied "endings" or "finals," were employed. Antiphons introduced and concluded each Psalm.

The Lutheran Orders and Cantionales provided for continuance of chanting the Psalms to the Gregorian Tones, as we find in the works of Spangenberg, Lossius, Eler, and others. The development of vernacular hymnody and the discontinuance of corporate clerical worship, however, combined to lessen interest in chanting the Psalms. The Anglican churches, with strong emphasis upon Morning and Evening Prayer, and with local continuance of cathedral and college choirs, retained the chanting of the entire Psalter once every month as a general practice. This was facilitated by the introduction, after the Restoration, of hundreds of so-called "Anglican chants" which quite generally supplanted the historic Psalm Tones everywhere in the English-speaking world.

Wherever chanting of the Psalms is well done, it can be an impressive feature. Good reading, however, is to be preferred to poor chanting.

117

We may well restore to our use the ancient antiphons, texts of which are provided in the *Service Book*. This distinctive and beautiful feature is found in all Lutheran service books of the sixteenth century, though it dropped entirely from the texts and usage of the Anglican communion, except that the English anthem is an art form which developed from the ancient antiphon.

Hymnody is a very important feature. The Benedictine Rule appointed one or more hymns for every Hour in the Latin Rite, and definite association of certain texts with certain festivals and Hours resulted in a series of Office hymns, many of which we have in translation in our *Hymnal* today. German scholars have edited nearly ten thousand Latin hymn texts, though the modern *Roman Breviary* contains only 155 hymns, most of which date from the early centuries.

Calvin, Zwingli, and Knox abandoned the centuries-old use of hymns and began the manufacture of crude paraphrases of the Psalms. Luther, with his artistic appreciations and musical abilities, built his early vernacular hymns, at least fifteen of them, upon earlier Latin texts. The Church Orders kept many of the finest Latin hymns in their original form or in German translations. Thus the spirit and forms of Latin hymnody profoundly influenced the development of German and Scandinavian hymnody during the next two or three hundred years, a phenomenon of astonishing proportions and very great importance. It is one of the significant facts of liturgical history that the Lutheran Church in Europe during these centuries adapted and used this hymnological inheritance and produced a massive volume of vernacular hymnody while the Church of England, no less than the Calvinists and Zwinglians, broke with history and art and left the field of hymnody a barren waste for this length of time.

These churches, however, beginning with Watts and the Wesleys and later employing the full resources of the Oxford Movement in the Established Church, subsequently produced a flood of translations of Greek and Latin hymns and original hymns in quantity and quality quite comparable with the Lutheran developments of earlier centuries, and in a time when creative inspiration had ceased to flow on the continent. Modern standard hymnals in all communions draw heavily upon all these sources for much of their finest content.

Scripture readings were a feature of both Jewish and early Christian worship. The medieval Hour Services appointed consecutive readings from Isaiah for Advent, Genesis for Lent, the Acts of the Apostles for Eastertide, et cetera. Luther outlined a complete scheme in his German Mass. The Church Orders made similar provisions, as did Archbishop Cranmer in England. A fair criticism of the Lutheran systems in general might be that selections are often too brief. The Anglican churches provide more extended texts, a provision which acquaints their people with a broader knowledge of Scriptures, particularly the Old Testament.

The Responsory is a definite choral form anciently sung following each Lesson at Matins. Its first part, the Responsory proper, contains Psalm verses and Responses. The second part is a contrasting section called the Verse. It is followed by the first half of the Gloria Patri and the concluding part of the Verse. On a Sunday or festival with nine Lessons, the *Roman Breviary* requires eight Responsories, the Te Deum being sung after the last Lesson. The Responsories in the Office, like the Graduals in the Mass, have provided some of the finest liturgical texts and music ever produced. Bishop Frere of the Church of England laments that "the whole of this rich treasure had to be sacrificed and excluded from the Prayer Book." Again, the Lutheran Reformers revealed their conservative method and musical interest by providing for one Responsory after the last Lesson, and also introducing the Responsory in Vespers in similar fashion. The *Psalmodia* of Lucas Lossius contains texts and melodies of forty-seven Responsories. Though adequate musical settings are available for the Responsories provided in the *Service Book,* this fine feature of the ancient Hour Services has largely passed from general use. Attention may be called to the un-usually fine collection of four-part settings of sixteen Responsories by the eminent German composer Max Reger. Harry G. Archer and Luther D. Reed personally arranged for these compositions as part of their series of service books in 1914.

Canticles are hymn-like scriptural passages (not Psalms) appointed for singing at Matins and Vespers after the Responsory and address, if there is an address. The Offices prescribe the Te Deum or the Bene-dictus for Matins, and the Magnificat or the Nunc Dimittis for Vespers. Alternate Canticles are also given separately for optional use. The breviaries of the Benedictine Order and of the French dioceses are pro-vided with a large collection of Canticles. The Anglican Prayer Books have the unique provision of the four Canticles mentioned above as chant forms between Scripture Lessons, somewhat after the manner of a Responsory.

Originally Collects or prayers followed each Psalm or Canticle in the ancient Hour Services. Later the Collect for the Day was borrowed from the Mass and placed at the end of the Office. Still later other brief prayers were assembled here in the form of Versicles and Responses. Some of these, with the addition of the Kyrie, the Lord's Prayer, et cetera, eventually developed into the Suffrages as we have them today. The Anglican Prayer Book concludes Morning Prayer and Evening

Prayer in this fashion. The Lutheran use concludes its minor services with the Kyrie, Lord's Prayer, Collect for the Day, and other Collects, ending with the Collect for Grace at Matins and the Collect for Peace at Vespers.

Matins[1]

Matins ("of the morning") in its origin represents what probably was the most ancient public Service of the church apart from the Eucharist itself. It was a continuation of the vigils held on nights preceding festivals. It had its full development as a Night Office in the monasteries, where, by reason of richness of material and variety of form, it became the most important Office of the day. Luther and the Church Orders retained Matins with its historic outline, but in simplified form. Latin was used in the schools on weekdays "so that the boys may learn the language." German was usual on Sundays and festivals. On Christmas, Easter, and Pentecost the laity attended in numbers. Restored to our services today by the *Common Service* (1888), Matins is increasingly used in daily services of schools, seminaries, and in conference and synodical meetings, et cetera, as well as in the early services of congregations on festivals.

As a congregational service, Matins, like Vespers, is generally conducted from the altar. It is entirely correct, however, in recognition of its ancient character as a choir office, for the minister to read it from a prayer desk in the chancel, going to the altar for the final prayers and the Benediction. The significant quality of Matins is praise, with prayers for strength and grace for the day. The selection of hymns should be in accordance with these ideas, along with reference to morning or special days or seasons.

The Versicles ("O Lord, open thou my lips . . .") are a liturgical introduction to the Office and have retained their place here since the sixth century. The first is particularly appropriate for the day's beginning. The second anticipates the duties of the day and seeks help from above. Anciently the monks repeated the entire Psalm (Psalm 70) upon waking or while going to the chapel. The Alleluia ("Praise ye the Lord . . .") was the ancient Hebrew conclusion to Psalms of praise.

The Invitatory and Venite constitute an extended invitation to worship which is found only in Matins. The Invitatory has the character of a responsive antiphon. Scholars relate its origin to the custom of the monks who wakened their brethren for the Night Office by intoning passages of Scripture.

---

[1] Because of limitations of space, the text is not given in this volume. The reader is referred to the *Service Book and Hymnal,* pp. 129-140.

The so-called "Office hymn" separates the Venite (Psalm 95) from the other Psalms which follow. An antiphon may be sung by a solo voice before each Psalm, if the Psalms be chanted. The full choir repeats the antiphon after the Gloria Patri. The latter is a formula which provides a Christian conclusion to the Old Testament texts. Psalmody, like hymnody, is prevailingly sacrificial in character and the minister faces the altar.

Tables of appropriate Psalms are given in the *Service Book*. The Response, "Lord, have mercy upon us," concludes every Lesson. We confess our failures in keeping God's Word, but, upon second thought, thank God for his unfailing mercy and forgiveness. In reading, the text of Scripture should be separated from everything else. The reader should pause slightly before the words, "Here endeth the Lesson," and again before, "O Lord, have mercy upon us."

The Responsory has liturgical and musical interest and its use should be encouraged. The rubrics permit a hymn as a substitute. The history of worship is crowded with melancholy examples of such substitutions of hymns for choral features (Introit, Gradual, Responsory, et cetera). The final result has always been liturgical and musical impoverishment. Our choirs should master these choral elements first of all, with anthems, motets, et cetera, taking second place in every rehearsal.

A sermon or address may follow the Lesson and Responsory, though the full provisions of hymns, Psalms, Lessons, and prayers in the Office itself furnish an adequate Service of praise and prayer without a formal address. If an address is given, this may follow the Lesson, or it may come after the Benedicamus. The latter arrangement is preferable upon social occasions, commencements, musical programs, discussions, et cetera. The Office may well be read through in its entirety. After having said our common praise and prayer we can then give larger freedom to the special features of the moment.

The Canticle is an exalted response to the message of God's Word. The Te Deum and the Benedictus are appointed for Matins. The Te Deum is a Western text in general use in the early sixth century. It has three distinct parts, two principal ones and an appendix. The first part includes thirteen verses offering praise to God and the Holy Trinity. The second part (vv. 14-21) recounts Christ's redemptive work, seeks divine aid, and ends with, "in glory everlasting." The final eight verses are of miscellaneous character and represent a later addition.

Luther translated the Te Deum into German in 1529. The English translation in the *Service Book* is based upon the text in the *King's Primer* of 1545, with several features from the American *Book of Common Prayer*. The historic plainsong melody of this Canticle is closely related to the Preface melodies. The Te Deum is sung straight through, not antiphonally, and without antiphons or Gloria Patri. While definitely a Matin Canticle, there is ample authority for its use as a Hymn of Praise and Thanksgiving at the Service on special occasions, such as church anniversaries, national days, declaration of peace, et cetera. Thus it may take the place of the Gradual or the Gloria in Excelsis, if there is no Communion, or it may be sung at the very end of the Liturgy.

The Benedictus, like the other New Testament Canticles, the Magnificat and the Nunc Dimittis, commemorates the Incarnation. It was anciently appended to the Psalter. It is a Western feature. Its ancient association was with Lauds, the Dawn Office, probably because of its reference to the Light—the "Dayspring from on High." It is a proper alternate for the Te Deum, particularly in Advent and from Septuagesima to Palm Sunday.

The Prayer is a general heading for the conclusion of the Office. The Kyrie ("Lesser Litany") is a Christian form of the ancient synagogue prayer based upon Ps. 51:1. The word itself is the first part of the Greek phrase *Kyrie eleison*. The Kyrie regularly precedes the Lord's Prayer. The Kyrie in the Service is in responsive form. In Matins and in Vespers the minister says the first petition only, the congregation responding with one continuous petition. This accords with the use of the early church and of the Greek Church today. The other arrangement represents the Latin use.

The "Our Father" (*Pater Noster*) sounds the depths of our personal needs, and in its breadth encompasses the fundamental needs of humanity. The English text follows an ancient liturgical and popular use with the word "trespasses" and the concluding doxology, "For Thine is the kingdom," et cetera, which is not in the best manuscripts, though found as early as the *Didache* (*ca.* A.D. 110).

The Salutation and Response are of Hebrew extraction. Bishops of the early church used them upon entering the church building. The formula entered the Liturgy as an introduction to specific prayers such as the Collects for the Day and the Preface, and such sacramental features as the reading of the Gospel and the Benediction.

The Oremus ("Let us pray") is a fragmentary form of an earlier and longer use according to which it formed part of a specific "bid," e.g., "Let us pray for Holy Church." After this invitation to silent prayer the officiant collected and framed the petitions of all in a brief, audible prayer (*Collectio*).

The Collect for the Day is the Mass Collect, the brief prayer before the Epistle in the Service. It is repeated in Matins and Vespers throughout the week. If a festival falls within the week its proper Collect takes precedence, and the Collect for the previous Sunday is read second. This prescribed use of this Collect throughout the week links the minor offices with the preceding Sunday or festival. The Collect for the Day and the final Collect for Grace have the full liturgical termination. Instructions concerning terminations are given in the General Rubrics.

The final Collect for Grace is introduced by a very appropriate and beautiful Versicle and Response chosen from the Greek Office by the committee which prepared the *Common Service Book*. Basic elements of the Collect itself are found in the Gelasian Sacramentary. The prayer in its backward glance acknowledges divine Providence and invokes divine defense and governance for the hours ahead.

The Benedicamus ("Bless we the Lord") is a liturgical conclusion derived from the Latin Rite and found universally in Lutheran services, but not in the Anglican. When a lay reader conducted the Office this formula ended the Service in the Reformation Orders. Inspiration for the Versicle text is found in the doxologies to the first four books of the Psalter. The Response may have its basis in I Cor. 15:57.

The New Testament Benediction (II Cor. 13:14), called the Grace, introduces the Preface in the Greek Communion Office. It was not a part of the Latin Hour services. It is found at the end of the English Litany of 1559 and later came into the Prayer Book, where it is a prayer: ". . . be with us all." Lutheran use regards it a Benediction: ". . . be with you all." It is thus a sacramental act.

Vespers[2]

Vespers ("evening") is the historic name for the Evening Office of the Latin and the Lutheran rites. Sentiment and poetic feeling come to expression in this Hour. Men, no less than sun and winds and water, have done their work. There is a sense of achievement and of calm. Thankful hearts recount the mercies of the day and ask protection for the night.

The ancient Jewish evening sacrifice became a Christian Office of Lights (*Lucernarium*). Benedict's Order for the monasteries (*ca.* A.D. 530) divided this with Vespers appointed for the early evening and a new Office, Compline, to be said before retiring.

In all periods the laity have been encouraged to participate in the Order of Vespers. Luther provided lengthy readings from Scriptures for these evening services. The Church Orders and Cantionales made full provision for them, supplying German hymns in place of the Latin Office hymns, but retaining fully the ancient melodies of the Psalms,

---

[2] Because of limitations of space the text is not given in this volume. The reader is referred to the *Service Book and Hymnal*, pp. 141-148.

antiphons, Responsories, Canticles, et cetera. A special form of *Beicht-Vesper* developed, with use of the Litany instead of the Magnificat. Eventually, and chiefly because no attempt was made to translate the entire Office into the vernacular, as was successfully done in England, Vespers was supplanted by a miscellany of "free services." The nineteenth century revival of church life partially restored the ancient Office of Vespers to Lutheran schools and deaconesses' institutions, and less generally to congregations. The Common Service restored it to Lutheran use in America.

The significant quality of Vespers is contemplation, thanksgiving, and prayer. The Swedish and early English name, "Evensong," well expresses its character. It differs from Matins in having no Invitatory and Venite, in placing the Psalm immediately after the opening Versicles, and in connecting the Office hymn with the Canticle instead of the Psalm. The normal Canticles are either the Magnificat or the Nunc Dimittis, and the final Collect is the Collect for Peace.

In general congregational use Vespers is conducted at the altar, though it is proper to read it from a prayer desk in the chancel, going to the altar for the final prayers. The entire Office may be said, and not sung, by small groups without organist or choir.

The first Versicle, "O Lord, open thou my lips" (Ps. 51:15), originally was used only at Matins. The Common Service did not appoint it for Vespers. The *Common Service Book,* 1917, however, did so appoint it. The second Versicle, "Make haste to help me" (Ps. 70:1), anciently began every Hour Service except Matins. It is absent from the American *Book of Common Prayer*.

Particular attention is called to the table of Scripture Lessons (*Service Book and Hymnal,* pp. 280-281). The Lesson should be announced and concluded precisely as indicated in the General Rubrics. Miscellaneous introductions and conclusions are disturbing, and sometimes ungrammatical. The text of all Scripture readings should stand out with cameo-like clarity, being separated from everything else.

The Canticles regularly appointed for Vespers are the Magnificat and the Nunc Dimittis. The Magnificat is proper on festivals and may be used at other times. The Nunc Dimittis has been borrowed from Compline and should not be used on greater festivals. It is particularly appropriate during Advent, Lent, and the Trinity season. The appropriate Versicle which introduces the Canticle reminds us of the evening hour of sacrifice in the Jewish temple.

The Magnificat (Luke 1:46-55) is often called the Song of Mary. It contains similarities to the Song of Hannah (I Sam. 2:1-10) and to certain Psalm verses, but on the whole it has a character of its own,

124

expressing exalted thought in terms of humility of spirit. As the church uses it today it joins with the Virgin Mary in giving thanks to God for the Incarnation and for the mercy of the Lord upon "all them that fear him from generation to generation." In the Greek Church the Magnificat is a morning Canticle. In the West it has been sung at Vespers since the sixth century, and a rich ceremonial and elaborate musical settings appropriate to the Office early developed. The Lutheran Orders refer to it as "an excellent hymn of praise," and its Latin text was generally retained with the beautiful musical settings.

The Nunc Dimittis is the Song of Simeon (Luke 2:29-32). It is a hymn of parting and a prayer for peace and rest perfectly suited to the close of day. It contains allusions to the Old Testament (Isa. 52:10; Ps. 98:2). The Apostolic Constitutions of the fourth century refer to it as a Canticle in the ancient Office of Lights. Eventually it was made a part of the Roman Office of Compline. The Lutheran Church Orders appointed it as an alternate for the Magnificat in Vespers, and the First Prayer Book in England, 1549, followed this procedure.

The Prayer is a general heading for all that follows. Comments on the Kyrie, the Lord's Prayer, the Salutation, the Oremus, and the Collect for the Day will be found on pp. 84-85, 107-108.

The Collect for Peace is one of the earliest liturgical prayers. It is unequaled for beauty and spiritual appeal. It was anciently read in the Mass for Peace, and also at Lauds, Vespers, and in the Litany. Luther translated it into German in 1533. Canon Bright speaks of its composition toward the end of the fifth century "when sieges and barbaric invasions made men's hearts fail for fear, when Rome but narrowly escaped the Huns and did not escape the Vandals when the Western Empire itself passed away before Odoacer, and Odoacer was overthrown by Theodoric." [3] The "fear of our enemies" is a constant experience, whether social upheavals threaten or the temptations of body and spirit.

The introductory Versicle and Response (Ps. 29:11) lay a solid foundation for the Collect. Luther particularly appreciated the strong sacramental character of many of the ancient Latin Versicles, and he personally selected many and prefixed them to Collects of his own composition or translation. The Lutheran Church has followed him in this and its liturgies are rich with pertinent passages of Scripture introducing Collects and prayers in many Orders and Offices. This feature is not found in the Anglican Prayer Books, just as we note the omission of the Benedicamus as well from the Anglican Offices.

---

[3] *Prayer Book Commentary for Teachers and Students* (London: Society for Promoting Christian Knowledge, 1891), p. 92.

The New Testament Benediction (II Cor. 13:14), called the Grace, introduces the Sursum Corda, "Lift up your hearts," in the Greek Liturgy. It came into the English Litany of 1559. It is a sacramental act, and not a prayer.

THE LITANY[4]

The Litany ("prayer, entreaty") is a unique people's prayer, penitential in character, responsive in form, unselfish in its wide reaches, and powerful in its grip upon the goodness and mercy of God as a basis for its intercessions. The earliest liturgies, Greek and Latin, began with a Litany, of which the Kyrie is a surviving fragment. Later Eastern and Gallican liturgies have a prayer of this sort after the sermon and before the Mass of the Faithful. A Western development, independent of the Eucharist, resulted in forms associated with processions, out-of-doors and within church buildings. The chanted responses gave the people a voice in worship, and the Litany form of prayer became popular everywhere. Medieval developments incorporated objectionable features and the prayer became known as the Litany of the Saints. Fundamental values, however, were intrinsic and so important that the Lutheran and the Anglican churches sought to preserve them and made successful revisions for evangelical use.

Luther regarded the Litany as "next to the Lord's Prayer the very best that could be made, not excepting the Te Deum." He revised the Latin text and made a German translation which incorporated several characteristic original petitions. His revision found immediate acceptance in all Lutheran lands. Official liturgies, hymnals, and private Cantionales retained it with less alteration of text than in the case of his hymns and Collects, which have often suffered severely at the hands of editors and critics. Archbishop Cranmer in his stately but ornate English revision of the Litany, which also contains considerable original material, was definitely influenced by Luther's spiritual insight and warmheartedness. His Litany contains more than a dozen items taken directly from Luther's Latin Litany. The radical Reformers rejected all litany types of public prayer, and insisted upon "one long prayer to be offered by the Minister." Luther and Cranmer must be recognized as the only leaders who sensed the spiritual and popular values in this particular form and purified and preserved it.

High appreciation of the Litany has been voiced by such moderns as Wilhelm Loehe, Bishop Hooker, Bishop Gore, Professor Bayard H. Jones, Canon Percy Dearmer, and many others. Bishop Hooker regarded its form as "finished perfection." Bishop Gore characterized it

---

[4] Because of limitations of space the text is not given in this volume. The reader is referred to the *Service Book and Hymnal*, pp. 156-161.

as "among the noblest and most searching instruments of devotion in the whole range of liturgical literature." [5] Bishop Parsons and Professor Jones say the ancient faiths "contain none of the trust in the prevailing goodness of God's providence which inspires the Litany. . . . Christianity alone accepts the fact of suffering . . . lifts it up . . . and nails it to the Cross of Christ." [6] Percy Dearmer observes that the Lutheran and the Anglican litanies, "with so much in common and yet so different, stand together in a place apart from the tedious repetition of the Roman Litany . . . and from the sentimental and selfishly limited utterances of many modern devotions." The Moravians have made special use of litany forms of prayer. The past century has witnessed the appearance of many so-called Litany hymns in the hymnals of all communions. The Lutheran Church in all lands is awakening to the merit of Luther's work in purifying, preserving, and enriching the ancient "Great Litany" of the church. His omissions, rearrangements, and additions (twenty-five new petitions) made of it an effective, pure, people's prayer.

The Common Liturgy has made a few changes from the text previously given in the Common Service. It has restored at the very beginning the historic invocation of the Holy Trinity, immediately following the separate addresses to the Father, the Son, and the Holy Ghost. It has omitted the petition "give to our nation perpetual victory over all its enemies," and the final "O Christ, hear us" and Kyrie. It has also inserted the words "or air" in the petition for travelers.

Like the Lord's Prayer itself, the Litany begins in the mood of adoration. Its central portions contain four distinct types of material which have been defined as deprecations, obsecrations, supplications, and intercessions. The deprecations ("to avert by prayer") seek deliverance from all manner of evil, beginning with the words, "From all sin." This section is briefer in the Lutheran form than in the Roman and Anglican litanies. The obsecrations ("to ask on religious grounds") lead us into the mysteries of the redemptive work of Christ, beginning with, "By the mystery of thy holy Incarnation." They have the response, "Help us, good Lord." The supplications are prayers for ourselves, beginning with, "In all time of our tribulation." Their brevity reveals the essential character of the Litany as a fine general prayer expressing the concern of the people of God for the world and all human need, rather than a prayer of personal import. The intercessions are prayers in behalf of others. They constitute the largest group of petitions. They seek the

[5] Charles Gore, *Reflections on the Litany* (London: Mowbray and Company, 1932), p. 1.

[6] Edward Lambe Parsons and Bayard Hale Jones, *The American Prayer Book* (New York: Charles Scribner's Sons, 1937), p. 136.

127

welfare and protection of the church, the nation, and our fellow-men; and they have the response, "We beseech thee to hear us, good Lord."

Luther's Latin Litany refers to the church as "Thy Holy Catholic Church." The Prayer Book form is "Thy Holy Church universal." The early Christians prayed for their pagan rulers even though some of these persecuted them and destroyed the peace they sought. These petitions express our obligations as citizens. The clauses "to raise up them that fall . . ." et cetera, and the intercessions for all sufferers are Luther's own. His Litany concluded with the Lord's Prayer and six Collects, each with an introductory Versicle.

The excellence of Luther's work has preserved his Litany practically unchanged for four centuries. Altered conditions of modern life might well find recognition in new petitions for missions, for the spread of Christ's Spirit among all peoples, and for Christian unity. Broad petitions of this character would be in agreement with the Litany's grasp of the whole gospel and its deep understanding of all human need. It must never be thought of as exclusively penitential. It is a great general prayer of the church which may be used in the Service on Sundays which are not festivals and when there is no Communion. When preceded by the Invocation, a Psalm, a Lesson, and a hymn, it constitutes a Special Office which concludes with appropriate Collects and a Benediction.

THE SUFFRAGES[7]

The Suffrages ("a prayer of intercession") are objective and poetic forms of prayer, resembling the Litany but with a spirit and character all their own. These Preces, as they were anciently called, consist of Versicles and Responses, chiefly from the Psalms. They recognize the importance of congregational participation in common prayer. The Roman Rite, which at first had no such Preces, eventually accepted and abbreviated certain Gallican forms, and the practice of following the Psalms in Offices by the Preces has been in use since Charlemagne.

The Morning Prayer and the Evening Prayer of the Anglican liturgies have preserved several beautiful, though fragmentary, Preces with their Responses. Loehe's Agende, 1844, prepared for the use of German Lutheran congregations in the American Middle West, contained the Great Suffrages, the Morning Suffrages and the Evening Suffrages. The Church Book of the General Council, 1868, provided the English text of the Great Suffrages. The Common Service (1888) added texts of the Morning Suffrages and the Evening Suffrages. The Common Service Book, 1918, provided introductory material and a conclusion which

[7] Because of limitations of space the texts are not given in this volume. The reader is referred to the Service Book and Hymnal, pp. 153-156.

made possible the use of any of these forms as a Special Office. Their responsive character holds attention, and well expresses the importance of common belief, fellowship, and work.

The text of the Suffrages comes, practically unchanged, from the *Roman Breviary*. The Great Suffrages are the Preces at Lauds and Vespers, with the omission of certain petitions. The Morning Suffrages and the Evening Suffrages are from the ferial Preces of Prime and Compline respectively. The Creed finds a place in both these forms. These services conclude with "The Prayers for Morning and Evening" in Luther's Small Catechism which, in turn, are noteworthy expansions of the Collects which concluded the Offices of Prime and Compline. Here is another illustration of the fact that in all his Collects and prayers— and there are many, scattered through his works—Luther kept within the great historic tradition of the church, without striving for originality or novelty. This, in view of his great ability, is a remarkable example of liturgical restraint as well as of church consciousness.

Considerations of space permit only passing reference to the Bidding Prayer, the other General Prayers, and the fine collection of Collects and Prayers provided in the Common Liturgy.[8] The Bidding Prayer is the modern counterpart of the ancient Deacon's Litany which followed the Gospel. Many Church Orders adapted and expanded its forms. The Common Service followed the *Church Book* in the omission of features peculiar to the Roman Church and incorporating some from the Church Orders. The Lutheran Church is probably unique among Protestants in retaining this prayer. It is not in Anglican Prayer Books.

A brief word must be said concerning the fine collection of Collects and Prayers provided in the Common Liturgy. This is a major revision and extension of similar collections in the Common Service (1888) and the *Common Service Book* (1918). As now constituted there are 138 Collects in the collection, only 55 of which had appeared in the *Common Service Book*. Nineteen of the Collects have been traced to the Leonine, Gelasian and Gregorian sacramentaries of the Western church (sixth to ninth centuries A.D.); four have been translated from the early Eastern liturgies; six from the later Mozarabic, Roman, and Sarum liturgies. Twenty-seven were composed in the Reformation era, eleven first appearing in German and in the Lutheran Church Orders and ten in the Prayer Book of the Church of England. No less than eighty Collects are of relatively modern composition, fifty-seven of these dating from the twentieth century—twenty-nine from Lutheran, thirty-nine from Anglican, and ten from Presbyterian sources.

[8] For their texts see the *Service Book and Hymnal*, pp. 218-241.

Chapter 9

THE COMMON HYMNAL: CONTENT AND CHARACTER

TRANSLATED HYMNS

A previous chapter (5) has traced the early history of liturgies and hymnals in American Lutheranism, the decision to prepare a common hymnal, the principles which guided the Commission, and the Commission's organization and procedure. We also noted certain factors which influenced the preparation of the book. We now turn to a brief treatment of the new hymns, with their authors. In order to keep the work within reasonable bounds we take as the basis of determining newness the collection in the Hymnal of the *Common Service Book* of the United Lutheran Church.

Of the 230 new hymns with which this standard leaves us, eighty are translations and one hundred and fifty are original English hymns. In both of these categories, but especially in the translated group, there are a number of hymns which are not really new, but are found in the *Common Service Book* with a different first line or a different translation.

Hymns from the Greek and Eastern Church

220 O gladsome Light, O grace. Φῶς ἱλαρόν. Probably a hymn of the third century. St. Basil (*ca.* A.D. 370) referred to it as "ancient" in his day. It was part of the Vesper Office held "at the lighting of the lamps," and is still in the Greek Office for this Hour. It is often called the candle-lighting hymn. The fine translation is by Robert Bridges, late poet-laureate of England.

281 Let all mortal flesh keep silence. Σιγησάτω πᾶσα σὰρξ βροτεία. From the Cherubic hymn of the Liturgy of St. James of Jerusalem. Dating from about the fifth century, its original is not a hymn at all, but a prayer said by the deacon in the Orthodox churches, appended to the hymn which covers the action at the beginning of the Liturgy of the Faithful, as the elements are brought to the holy table in the "Great Entrance." The metrical paraphrase is by Gerard Moultrie, vicar of Southleigh, England, and author of much religious verse.

JOSEPH THE HYMNOGRAPHER (*ca* 810-83). A Sicilian, St. Joseph became a monk at Thessalonica about 830, spent much of his life in Constantinople, and some time as a slave in Crete. The most voluminous of the Greek hymn writers, he is said to have composed a thousand hymns, of which more than two hundred survive.

546 Let us now our voices raise. Τῶν ἱερῶν ἀθλοφόρων· A cento from a canon for the Festival of Martyrs observed in the Greek churches on May 3. The free translation is by John Mason Neale.

601 Praise ye the Lord, ye servants of the Lord.

Hymns from the Latin

Latin hymnody, chiefly monastic, and spanning more than a thousand years, is monumental in volume and importance. It flows in an unbroken stream from the fourth century to the Paris Breviary of 1736. More than ten thousand texts have been listed. Its best examples are unsurpassed in nobility of thought and in elegance, even grandeur, of expression. There are nineteen new hymns from the Latin, bringing the total number of hymns from this source in the Hymnal to fifty-five.

95 At the Lamb's high feast we sing. *Ad coenam Agni providi.* Appointed in the *Roman Breviary* for Vespers on Saturday in Easter week. The translation is by Robert Campbell (1814-68), a Scottish lawyer, originally a Presbyterian, later an active member of the Episcopal Church of Scotland, and finally a Roman Catholic.

245 Blessed city, heavenly Salem. *Urbs beata Jerusalem.* This probably dates from about the seventh century, and is, as its first line shows, a picture of the heavenly Jerusalem of Revelation, a favorite theme of hymn writers through the ages. The English translation is by Neale. Other hymns in the *Hymnal* on this theme are Nos. 332, 583, 584, 587, 589, 591, 595, 596.

509 Conquering kings their titles take. *Victis sibi cognomina.* A late eighteenth century French Breviary hymn for the Feast of the Name of Jesus.

AMBROSE, ST. (*ca.* 340-97). The earliest Latin hymn writer. Of noble birth, he was educated in Rome for the law and public office. He was in government service in Milan when he was seized by the Christians of the city and made their bishop in 374. He withstood both the Arians and the emperor, and made the church of Milan a power. Its Liturgy, which bears his name, is still used there. It was Ambrose who introduced the Syrian custom of hymn singing into the West, and began, if tradition is correct, the writing of metrical hymnody in Latin.

204 Father, we praise thee, now the night is over. *Nocte surgentes vigilemus omnes.* Probably dates from the time of St. Ambrose, though some ascribe it to Gregory the Great. It is a morning Office hymn.

206 O Splendor of God's glory bright. *Splendor paternae gloriae.* This is the Office hymn for Lauds on Mondays. The English version is one of six fine translations by Robert Bridges in the *Hymnal.*

94 That Easter Day with joy was bright. *Aurora lucis rutilat.* An Office hymn appointed for Lauds in the Eastertide.

133 O Trinity of blessed light. *O lux beata Trinitas.* Definitely by St. Ambrose. A Vesper hymn for Saturday and for Trinity Sunday.

PRUDENTIUS, AURELIUS CLEMENS (348-*ca.* 410). A Spanish lawyer whose religious interests developed late. Unlike his great contemporary, St. Ambrose, he did not write hymns as such, but composed sacred verse from which selections were included in the Mozarabic Rite. In this respect he may be compared with George Herbert, John Keble, and John Greenleaf Whittier of much later date.

51 Earth has many a noble city. *Quicumque Christum quaeritis.* A cento from the poem from which "Of the Father's love begotten" (No. 17) is also taken.

FORTUNATUS, VENANTIUS HONORIUS (*c.* 530-609). Born in Italy, and a contemporary of the great St. Gregory, he was the most prominent Latin poet of his age. A year before his death, he became bishop of Poitiers.

61 Sing, my tongue, the glorious battle. *Pange lingua gloriosi.* Probably this hymn was originally connected with No. 75, "The royal banners forward go." These great processional hymns may have been inspired by the historic occasion of November, 569, when the emperor, Justin II, sent the supposed relics of the True Cross, which Constantine's mother Helen had found in the fourth century, to Queen Rhadegonda, who deposited them in the monastery church at Poitiers.

ABELARD, PETER (1079-1142). A brilliant but irresponsible teacher and canon of the Cathedral of Notre Dame, Paris, he boasted that two popes, several cardinals, and fifty future archbishops and bishops had been his pupils. His romance with Heloise is well known. St. Bernard of Clairvaux had him condemned for heresy, and he died on his way to Rome to appeal this sentence.

596 O what their joy and their glory must be. *O quanta qualia.* Written to be sung on Saturday at Vespers.

THOMAS AQUINAS, ST. (*ca.* 1227-74). A Dominican, St. Thomas was the greatest theologian of the Middle Ages, and one of the most brilliant minds the world has known. In 1263, at the request of Pope Urban IV, he wrote a series of hymns for the Mass and the Office of the Feast of Corpus Christi.

272 Thee we adore, O hidden Saviour, thee. *Adorote devote.* Written for private devotion.

277 O saving Victim, opening wide. *O salutaris hostia.*

280 Very Bread, good Shepherd, tend us. *Bone pastor, panis vere.* These two hymns are excerpts, abbreviated and altered, from the Corpus Christi series of St. Thomas. No. 280 is from the sequence "Lauda Sion" in the Mass; No. 277 is from the hymn for Lauds, in a translation by Caswall.

JACOPONE DA TODI (d. 1306). A Franciscan lay brother.

84 At the Cross, her station keeping. *Stabat mater dolorosa. A sequence,* possibly by this author, and one of the five sequences now used by the Roman Church. More than sixty translations of it are known, and it is found in many Protestant hymnals.

132

THOMAS À KEMPIS (1379-1471). A member of the Brethren of the Common Life, and the reputed author of *The Imitation of Christ.*
591 Light's abode, celestial Salem. *Jerusalem luminosa.* Often, but not certainly, ascribed to this author, this is another of the many heavenly Jerusalem hymns.

TISSERAND, JEAN (d. 1494). A Franciscan friar who died in Paris.
96 O sons and daughters, let us sing. *O filii et filiae.* From a trope for Easter written by Tisserand. The lively tune *O filii et filiae* may have been composed by Tisserand himself for this hymn; or, more probably, it may have been a popular trope melody or carol sung at the time in Provençal.

---

134 Father most holy, merciful and tender. *O Pater sancte.* Office hymn for Trinity Sunday from about the tenth century.
125 Love of the Father, Love of God. *Amor Patris et Filii.* A twelfth century original, beautifully and very freely paraphrased by the late poet laureate Robert Bridges. Originally it was a hymn to the Holy Spirit.
147 O wondrous type, O vision fair. *Caelestis formam gloriae.* This is an anonymous hymn for the Festival of the Transfiguration. It was used in Salisbury Cathedral as early as the fifteenth century.

Hymns from the German

German hymnody exceeds all others in quantity (about one hundred thousand items are listed in various catalogues) and in historic importance and influence. The Lutheran Reformation in Germany and Scandinavia gave the hymn to the people, instead of only to the monks and schoolmen, and developed a massive hymological literature.

Sixty-nine hymns from the German were carried over into the Common Hymnal, and eleven new such hymns were added. The new items, as a whole, do not measure up to the earlier group. Nor do they compare favorably with the new hymns from the Latin. They were accepted because they are in general use in some of the co-operating churches.

A few German hymns in the earlier hymnals were dropped from this one, but the number of chorales was greatly increased. Thus the total German heritage was not diminished, though the emphasis has shifted from texts to music.

The word "heritage" is appropriate. Nearly all the new texts and tunes from German and Scandinavian sources were composed more than a century ago. The list contains few, if any, contemporary authors or composers.

German hymnody falls into three major divisions: the Reformation and post-Reformation epoch; the time of the Thirty Years' War; and the pietistic period of the eighteenth century. Just about the time its rich volume ceased to flow, the equally important stream of English hymnody entered upon its belated but triumphant course.

Decius, Nikolaus (d. 1541). Provost of a monastery in Brunswick, and later a Lutheran pastor in Stettin.

70 O Lamb of God most holy. *O Lamm Gottes, unschuldig.* A translation of a German paraphrase of the Agnus Dei in the Communion Office. The tune is based on a Gregorian melody for the Agnus found first in Erfurt, 1542.

Heermann, Johann (1585-1647). A Silesian pastor and author of four hundred hymns. His town of Köben was plundered four times during the Thirty Years' War.

460 O God, eternal source. *O Gott, du frommer Gott.* Composed as "A Daily Prayer" for godly living. Translation by Edward T. Horn III and Catherine Winkworth. The tune is by Ahasuerus Fritsch, chancellor of the University of Jena.

Rist, Johann (1607-67). Pastor and patriot who lived during the terrible days of the Thirty Years' War. He was a poet and dramatist as well.

29 Break forth, O beauteous heavenly light. *Ermuntre dich.* A translation of the ninth stanza of Rist's Christmas hymn. The tune is by Johann Schop, his musical editor. The harmonization is that of J. S. Bach from his *Christmas Oratorio.*

Franck, Johann (1618-77). An able lawyer and burgomeister at Guben, Brandenburg. He wrote 110 hymns, of a quality such as to rank him next to Paul Gerhardt as a hymn writer of this period.

575 Jesus, priceless Treasure. *Jesu, meine Freude.* Modeled on a love song, "Flora, meine Freude," this hymn is regarded by some as too subjective, but has been translated into many languages, including Russian.

Schmolck, Benjamin (1672-1737). A Lutheran archdeacon serving in strong Catholic communities, later an inspector. He became famous throughout Germany as a poet, though his many hymns (almost one thousand) were for that reason alone not all of highest quality. The earliest three collections are decidedly his best.

186 Light of light, enlighten me. *Licht vom Licht, erleuchte mich.* A hymn for the Lord's day, published in 1715.

Garve, Carl Bernard (1763-1841). A Moravian, he was a leading hymn writer among the Brethren.

100 Alleluia! Jesus lives. *Hallelujah! Jesus lebt.* The tune (*Easter Glory*) is by the Norwegian, Ludvig Matthias Lindeman, six of whose tunes are in the *Hymnal.* This is an Easter hymn of 1825.

Hausmann, Julia von (1825-1901). A gifted governess of Riga and St. Petersburg.

292 O take my hand, dear Father. *So nimm denn meine Hände.* A popular Confirmation hymn.

---

44 Long ago and far away. *Joseph, lieber Joseph mein.* A new text by Edward T. Horn, III (see p. 154) for this Christmas dialogue cradle song.

87 O darkest woe. *O Traurigkeit.* The Winkworth translation of this heavy hymn for the burial of our Lord found in the Roman Catholic Hymnal of Würzburg, 1628. The tune is from Mainz and of about the same date.

167 Holy God, we praise thy Name. *Grosser Gott, wir loben dich.* This

so-called German Te Deum first appeared in the hymnal of the Austrian empress, Maria Theresa, in 1774. The tune has the rhythmic feel of a folk song. It is the original of the later English tune *Hursley*.

501   O Jesu so meek, O Jesu so kind. A rather sentimental item from Cologne, 1623, with a popular lilting tune with bass part by J. S. Bach.

Scandinavian Hymns

Many hymns from the Greek, the Latin, and the German came into standard English hymnals in exceptionally fine translations. Gifted men and women, masters of language and of English style, produced translations and paraphrases that frequently surpass their originals in poetic value.

We note three contributing factors: the deepened interest in hymnology and its backgrounds awakened by the Oxford Movement in England in the mid-nineteenth century; the classical scholarship which enabled translators to capture the spirit as well as master the literary form of the originals; and the political atmosphere of the Victorian era, which was particularly friendly to everything German.

Scandinavian hymn writers have not enjoyed such advantages. Thus many of their finest hymns have not become known beyond the borders of their homelands and the covers of hymnals in bilingual congregations in America. The Common Hymnal contains more than forty hymns by Scandinavian poets, generally with chorale or folk song tunes traditionally associated with them. Many of these are translations by Drs. Hansen, Ryden, Field, and Olson of the Commission. We believe that much of this material, particularly the music, will meet with hearty acceptance and enrich our congregational song.

Danish

KINGO, THOMAS HANSEN (1634-1703). Grandson of a tapestry weaver who emigrated from Scotland to Denmark, Kingo became a Danish bishop and his country's first great hymn writer. His style combined strength and beauty. He zealously espoused the cause of original Danish hymnody instead of translations from foreign languages, and contributed 136 hymns to a hymnal of 1689.

71   Print thine image pure and holy. *Skriv dif Jesus paa mit hejrte.*

194   Praise to thee and adoration. Written as a Christmas hymn, based on John 21:19-24.

259   He that believes and is baptized. *Enhver som tror og bliver døbt.* A hymn for Holy Baptism.

284   O Jesus, blessed Lord, to thee. *O Jesus, søde Jesus, dif.* A hymn of thanksgiving after Communion. This translation, by Arthur James Mason, first appeared in the revised edition of *Hymns Ancient and Modern*, 1889.

BRORSON, HANS ADOLPH (1694-1764). A scholarly bishop and hymn writer, representing the pietistic school. Three-fourths of his hymns are translations of German hymns. At Töndern, where he had a mixed congregation, he preached in Danish, but his congregation sang in German.

49 Thy little ones, dear Lord, are we. *Her komme, Jesus, dine smaa.* A children's Christmas hymn.

599 Behold a host, like mountains bright. *Den store hvide Flok vi se.* A hymn for saints' days which has become popular in both Europe and America largely because of its association with the Norwegian folk song arranged by Edward Grieg. "The best known and most popular Scandinavian hymn in the English-speaking countries." [1]

BOYE, BIRGITTE CATHRINE (1742-1824). A gifted linguist and poet. Guldberg's large hymnal of 1778, in which she had a hand, contained 128 original hymns and 24 translations from her pen.

32 Rejoice, rejoice this happy morn. *Os er i dag en frelser født.*

101 Our Lord is risen from the dead. *Han er opstanden, store Bud.*

GRUNDTVIG, NIKOLAI F. S. (1783-1872). An honorary bishop, the nineteenth century Danish "poet of Whitsuntide" and the champion of the Christian faith in a time of Rationalism and indifference to religion in his homeland. His influence did much to achieve needed reforms in the public school systems of Scandinavia. His poems and hymns were published in five volumes.

28 The happy Christmas comes once more. *Det kimer nu til julefest.* Translation by Charles Porterfield Krauth.

57 Bright and glorious is the sky. *Dejlig er den himel blaa.*

151 Built on a rock the church doth stand. *Kirken den er et gammelt hus.* This hymn, exceedingly popular in Scandinavian circles, intertwines the themes which particularly absorbed Grundtvig's thoughts in his hymn writing—the church and the sacraments.

200 Peace to soothe our bitter woes. *Fred til Bod for bittert Savn.*

210 Golden light, serene and bright. *Morgen Stund har Guld i Mund.*

257 God's word is our great heritage. *Guds ord det er vort arvegods.* This is the fifth stanza of Grundtvig's Danish version of Luther's "A Mighty Fortress."

288 My Lord, I hear thee pleading. *Han, som paa Jorden bejler.*

---

46 Christmas brings joy to every heart. *Julen har bragt velsignet Bud.*

Norwegian

Early Norwegian hymnody was largely dependent upon Danish authors. The nineteenth century, however, saw the rise of indigenous hymn writers of quality. There are six new hymns from these Norwegian writers in the Common Hymnal. One is translated by Dr. Lawrence N. Field of the Commission.

BRUN, JOHAN NORDAHL (1745-1816). An eloquent preacher and bishop of Bergen.

[1] John Dahle, *Library of Christian Hymns* (Minneapolis: Augsburg Publishing House, 1928), Vol. III, p. 684.

253 How blest are they who hear God's word. *O saligden, Guds ord her hört.* One of Bishop Brun's early hymns, with a typical Lutheran emphasis upon the Word of God.

LANDSTAD, MAGNUS BRORSTRUP (1802-80). Born in the extreme north of Norway, he was asked to prepare a Norwegian hymnal after the separation of Norway and Denmark in the Napoleonic wars unleashed a renewed nationalism and made the Danish hymnals unpopular.

299 I know of a sleep in Jesus' Name. *Jeg veed mig en Sovn i Jesu Navn.* A hymn of the eventide of life, of death, and of the Resurrection morn.

333 Full many shall come from the east and the west. *Der mange skal komme fra ost og fra vest.* A hymn based on the Gospel for the Third Sunday after the Epiphany.

380 To thee, O Lord, the God of all. *Jeg Staar for Gud som al Ting Veed.*

KOREN, ULRIK VILHELM (1826-1910). A native of Bergen, when he was ordained in 1853 he accepted a call to minister to Norwegians in Iowa. Thus he became the first Norwegian pastor to live and work west of the Mississippi.

423 O sing, all ye lands, with a jubilant voice. *Al verlden Nu Raabe for Herren med Fryd.* A metrical version of Psalm 100.

WEXELSEN, MARIE (1832-1911).

45 I am so glad each Christmas eve. *Jeg er saa glad hver julakveld.*

---

197 O happy day when we shall stand. *O taenk Naar Engang Samles Skal.*

Icelandic

THORSTEINSSON, STEINGRIMUR BJARNSSON (1831-1913).

236 The fading day adorns the west.

BRIEM, VALDIMAR (1848-1930).

128 Lord, let thy Spirit, from earthly passion weaning.

449 How marvelous God's greatness.

Swedish

Five Swedish poets are represented by ten new hymns. There is also a Swedish folk song. Of the translations, three are by Dr. Ernst W. Olson, a member of the Commission.

PETRI, OLAVUS (1493-1552). Olavus Petri was born the year after Columbus discovered America. He and his brother Laurentius were students of Luther and Melanchthon at Wittenberg. Returning to Sweden, they became the leaders of the Swedish Reformation.

102 O Paschal Feast, what joy is thine. *Nu kommen ar var Paskafrojd.*

FRANZÉN, FRANS MIKAEL (1772-1847). A lyric poet born in Finland, he became a pastor in Stockholm, and later a bishop of the Church of Sweden. He was an early associate of Archbishop Wallin.

9 Prepare the way, O Zion. *Bereden väg för Herran.* An objective hymn for Advent, frequently the first hymn in Swedish church hymnals.

264 Thine own, O loving Saviour. *O Jesu, än de dina.* A more subjective, even poignant, Communion hymn.

WALLIN, JOHANN OLOF (1779-1839). Archbishop of Upsala, he was the greatest of the Scandinavian hymn writers. His most important work was his *Den Svenska Psalmboken* (*The Swedish Psalmbook*) of 1819, which he edited, and to which he contributed 128 original hymns, 23 translations, and nearly 200 revisions.

33 All hail to thee, O blessed morn. An exceedingly popular Christmas hymn in Sweden.

116 To realms of glory in the skies. *Till härlighetens land egen.* An Ascension hymn successfully combining objective and subjective elements.

174 We worship thee, almighty Lord. *Vi love dig, o store Gud.*

270 A voice, a heavenly voice I hear. *Vad röst, vad ljuvlig röst jag hör.* A brief Communion hymn.

462 O my soul, on wings ascending.

HEDBORN, SAMUEL JOHAN (1783-1849). A Lutheran pastor and lyric poet whose folk songs were no less popular than his hymns.

189 Glorious Majesty, before thee. *Höga Majestät, vi alla.* An exalted hymn of praise, noble in conception and worthy of its traditional association with the king of chorales, *Wachet auf*, by Philipp Nikolai.

BERG, CAROLINE V. SANDELL (1832-1903). A gifted woman who, like Charlotte Elliott and Frances Havergal in England, wrote hymns of strong appeal to her countrymen. She wrote more than six hundred hymns.

572 Children of the heavenly Father. *Tryggare kan ingen vara.*

---

35 When Christmas morn is dawning. *När juldagamorgon glimmar.* This is a German folk song which enters the *Hymnal* by way of its Swedish translation and its use as a children's hymn.

Finnish

KAHL, JOHAN (1721-46). A Swede, whose hymn was translated into Finnish.

180 Arise, my soul, arise. *Nyt ylös, sieluni.* A popular hymn, sung on great occasions in Finland. Set to a Finnish folk tune.

RUNEBERG, JOHAN LUDVIG (1804-77). A clergyman and rector of a high school, he was a national figure whose poetry has inspired Finnish patriotism.

396 I lift my eyes unto heaven above. *Mä silmät luon ylös taivaaseen.* Tune by Rudolf Lagi (1823-68), an organist in Helsinki and editor of a Finnish chorale book.

MALMIVAARA, WILHELMI (1854-1922). Dean, member of the Diet, religious leader, and poet.

536 Lord, as a pilgrim, on earth I roam. *Oi Herra, jos mä matkamies maan.*

POHJALA, JENNY (1899-   ).

383 Jesus, hear my humble pleading. *Jeesus, kuule rukoukset.* Written when the author was seventeen years of age. The tune is by Armas Maasalo (1885-   ), an organist in Helsinki and composer of tunes and cantatas.

Hymns from Other Countries

Dutch

450 We praise thee, O God, our Redeemer, Creator. *Wilt heden nu treden vor God den Heere.* This hymn, in its original form, is of unknown authorship. First published in 1626, it celebrated Dutch freedom from Spanish rule. More than two centuries later it gained wide popularity by its inclusion in a collection of Dutch folk songs by Edward Kremser (1838-1914), director of a male chorus in Vienna, whose name the tune now bears. Miss Julia Bulkley Cady Cory, an American, gave the hymn a Christian character by her paraphrase.

French

BUDRY, EDMOND (1854-1932).
566 Thine is the glory, Risen, conquering Son. *À toi la gloire, O Ressurcité.* Written in 1884, this hymn has achieved popularity in Europe through its appeal to ecumenical gatherings. The tune, *Judas Maccabaeus,* is from the oratorio of the same name by Handel, his twelfth English work in that form.
30 Angels we have heard on high. *Les anges dans nos campagnes.* A French carol text and melody of the eighteenth century, which came into American use in English form in the *New Church Hymnal* of 1937. The text is in a version by Earl Marlatt, and the music is an arrangement by Edward Shippen Barnes.

Indian

TILAK, NARAYAN VAMAN (1862-1919). An Indian Christian poet.
384 One who is all unfit to count. *Sishyahi ganaya nahim yogya zo tayala.* An unusual hymn from one of the younger churches. The translation is by a missionary in India of the Free Church of Scotland, Nicol Macnicol.

Italian

FRANCIS OF ASSISI, ST. (1182-1226). One of the favorite saints of Christendom, whose rejection of his high social station and founding of the mendicant order which bears his name are known the world over.
173 All creatures of our God and King. *Laudato sia Dio mio Signore.* This is a free rendition of the glorious *Canticle of the Sun,* made by William H. Draper for a school children's Whitsuntide festival at Leeds, England. The equally splendid tune, *Lasst uns erfreuen* (Cologne, 1623), has swept this fine nature hymn into great popularity.
BIANCO DA SIENA (d. 1434). Member of a religious order founded there.
123 Come down, O Love divine. *Discendi, Amor santo.* The translation is by Richard Frederick Littledale, a learned leader of the Oxford Movement who translated hymns from Greek, Latin, German, Italian, Danish, Swedish, and Syriac.

Syriac

286 Strengthen for service, Lord, the hands. This interesting item is from the Syriac text of the Liturgy of Malabar, an ancient Nestorian Rite used by the Church of St. Thomas in south India. The original is a prayer said

by the deacon while the people receive the Sacrament, and the hands referred to are the outstretched hands of the communicants as they receive the host.

HYMNS BY BRITISH AUTHORS

As we have seen, most German and the Scandinavian hymns were written a hundred or more years ago; many of the Greek and Latin hymns have been sung for a thousand years. The best of all these belong to the ages and to ecumenical Christianity today.

Although much later in development, English hymnody is equal in importance to older hymnody. Creative leadership in the field has been held, during the past century and longer, by the English-speaking peoples in Britain and America.

The English language enjoys acknowledged supremacy in the field of poetry. Once enlisted in the service of religion and of the church, gifted personalities have produced a wealth of sacred verse and music congenial to the spirit of the English-speaking peoples and the temper of the times in which they lived. In this they were moved by spiritual conviction and influenced by moments and movements of historic significance.

More than two-thirds of the hymns in the *Hymnal* are by English-speaking authors. Of the eighty new hymns of British origin, seventeen were written within the past twenty-five years. Of the sixty-seven new hymns by American authors, thirty-one were written by our contemporaries—men and women now living, or dead not more than thirty years. English and American hymnody is very much alive.

All periods of British post-Reformation hymnody are represented in the new material. The lines of development frequently cross, one style beginning before the preceding style has begun to decline. For our purposes we shall observe a threefold division, as follows: I. 1550-1700. Early religious verse, the Psalters. II. 1700-1800. Original English hymnody, chiefly Dissenting. III. 1800-present. General development, largely under Church of England leadership.

For two hundred years after the Reformation, the British people knew practically nothing but the dreary doggerel of metrical Psalm versions. There were one or two abortive attempts to provide English hymns by translating Latin originals. Miles Coverdale, bishop of Exeter, published English paraphrases of the Commandments, Creed, and Lord's Prayer, plus thirteen translated hymns, all based on German Lutheran originals. In 1623, George Wither published his *The Hymnes and Songs of the Church,* to which Orlando Gibbons contributed sixteen tunes. But the English people remained complacent with the Psalm paraphrases of the "Old Version" of Sternhold and Hopkins, completed in

1562. The first edition (1562), which exists in only one copy, goes under the title: *The Whole Booke of Psalmes*. The Church of England, influenced by earlier Lutheran liturgical reforms on the Continent, had produced a magnificent prose liturgy in the *Book of Common Prayer* of 1549. But in the sphere of poetry, the models of Zwingli and Calvin prevailed. There were real poets in England in the Elizabethan, the Jacobine, and the Caroline eras, but their voices were silent in the churches, where David ruled supreme.

The return of the Scottish refugees from their exile in Geneva brought a fanatical enthusiasm for the metrical Psalm versions. The slogan became "the Bible and the Bible only." More than 350 different Psalters were published, about 150 of them complete. The British people thus became Psalm singers, not hymn singers, and remained so for two hundred years. Hymn singing as such in the Protestant churches awaited the work of Isaac Watts, the Wesleys, and other Independents. The Church of England gave them no encouragement. It required the Oxford Movement and the church revival of the mid-nineteenth century to awaken this great church to the possibilities of an original English hymnody. Once awakened it has quickly come to the fore. Representatives of the Anglican communion have since been the leading contributors to the flood of congregational song which has so enriched the English-speaking world during the past century.

The First Period, 1550-1700

The fine devotional verse of George Herbert, John Donne, Robert Herrick, and Henry Vaughan is unsurpassed in the literature of any country. These were literary writers. Modern editors, however, have brought extracts from their poems into our hymnals, as they have done also with the much later works of Whittier and others in our own country.

KETHE, WILLIAM (d. 1608?). Appears to have been a Scottish minister in exile during Queen Mary's time. He is known to have written twenty-five metrical Psalms.
169 All people that on earth do well. A famous version of Psalm 100 found in all hymnals.

MILTON, JOHN (1608-74). Blind English poet and associate of Cromwell, most famous for his *Paradise Lost*. He was the author of nineteen Psalm versions.
327 The Lord will come and not be slow. A cento from a paraphrase of three Psalms (82:4; 85:1-3; 86:5-6).
405 Let us, with a gladsome mind. A paraphrase of Psalm 136 made by Milton "at fifteen years old."

MORE, HENRY (1614-87). A Fellow of Christ's College, Cambridge, who declined preferment and remained as a tutor from 1639 until his death.
34 The holy Son of God most high. A fine Christmas hymn.

BAXTER, RICHARD (1615-91). Baxter, who has since been called "a Puritan within the Anglican Church," was offered the bishopric of Hereford after the Restoration, but refused. When the Act of Conformity was passed, he resigned to become a Nonconformist minister, and thereafter suffered persecution and imprisonment.

409   Ye holy angels bright. A hymn on the communion of saints, from Baxter's *Poor Man's Family Book*, 1672.

QUARLES, JOHN (1624-65). A literary man and an ardent loyalist.

175   O King of kings, before whose throne. An adaptation from a longer poem.

CROSSMAN, SAMUEL (1624-83). Dean of Bristol Cathedral.

65   My song is love unknown. A hymn of rare beauty, one of nine in Crossman's *Sacred Poems*, 1664.

BUNYAN, JOHN (1628-88). The humble tinker who became an itinerant preacher and who wrote *Pilgrim's Progress* in 1684 while serving a twelve-year sentence in prison.

563   He who would valiant be. Altered for use as a hymn from the poem in the chapter of *Pilgrim's Progress* entitled, "Mr. Valiant for Truth."

DRYDEN, JOHN (1631-1700). A poet laureate who wrote for the stage. He became a Roman Catholic and translated several Latin hymns.

124   Creator Spirit, by whose aid. A portion of his translation of the *Veni, Creator Spiritus*.

TATE AND BRADY ("New Version" of the Psalter, 1698). This version was by two Irishmen: Nahum Tate (1652-1715), poet laureate at the time, and Nicholas Brady (1659-1726). It gradually superseded the "Old Version" of Sternhold and Hopkins (see pp. 140-141), chiefly because of its better literary values and the quality of its new tunes.

420   Through all the changing scenes of life. A portion of the eighteen-stanza version of Psalm 34.

ADDISON, JOSEPH (1672-1719). Prominent in law and politics. A writer noted for his mastery of English style.

442   The spacious firmament on high. A famous paraphrase of the first six verses of Psalm 19.

The Second Period, 1700-1800

Five authors from this century are represented among the new hymns. The great names are Watts and Charles Wesley, with Cowper not to be ignored. With the Church of England not yet aware of the values of hymnody, hymn writing was chiefly the work of Dissenters: Congregationalists, Methodists, and Baptists.

WATTS, ISAAC (1674-1748). Watts has certain claims to the title "founder of modern English hymnody." He has even been compared with St. Ambrose as an innovator who secured the triumph of hymnody as such, enriched it by his own compositions, and set the pattern for a host of followers. He began in an attempt to "renovate" Psalmody, but soon produced original verse, about six hundred items in all. Some of his work is below the level of mediocrity; yet at his best he stood on the loftiest heights. Fifteen of his hymns have been carried over from previous Lutheran hymnals. One new item has been added.

594   Give me the wings of faith to rise. Watts entitled this "The example of Christ and his saints."

WESLEY, CHARLES (1707-88). This name ranks with that of Isaac Watts as one of the two greatest in English hymnody. His older brother John was that founder and organizer of Methodism who dated his own conversion from the day in May, 1738, when he attended a meeting at which Luther's Preface to the Epistle to the Romans was read. John Wesley published hymnals and made many fine translations of German hymns, seven of which are in the Common Hymnal. His brother Charles, his constant companion and helper, was endowed with great poetic gifts. His hymns total more than sixty-five hundred. Fourteen have been carried over from earlier hymnals, and three new items have also been included in the *Hymnal*. Like his brother John, Charles visited Georgia, having been invited to accompany General Oglethorpe as his secretary and chaplain. Returning to England, he became an itinerant preacher, traveling on horseback over wide areas. He never renounced the Church of England, and he died in that communion.

274   Victim Divine, thy grace we claim.

446   Ye servants of God, your Master proclaim. An exalted hymn of praise written in a time of political tension and confusion when Methodists were charged with being Papists in disguise.

471   Come, O thou Traveler unknown. Charles Wesley's finest poem, though its intensity of passionate personal feeling has kept it out of most hymnals.

STENNETT, SAMUEL (1727-95). A Seventh-Day Baptist minister, the author of thirty-eight hymns, and a personal friend of King George III.

570   Majestic sweetness sits enthroned.

COWPER, WILLIAM (1731-1800). A gentle, sensitive spirit, endowed with great poetic gifts, but subject to spiritual despondency and despair. He collaborated with John Newton in the Olney Hymns, contributing sixty-eight hymns to the collection, which was intended for the evangelicals in the Church of England.

466   O for a closer walk with God. Written during the illness of a dear friend, and based upon the story of Enoch (Gen. 5:24).

495   Sometimes a light surprises. A hymn of comfort.

FAWCETT, JOHN (1740-1817). A Baptist minister who wrote more than 160 hymns to be sung immediately following his sermons.

543   Blest be the tie that binds. Supposedly inspired by the tears of his congregation in Yorkshire when he prepared to leave for a church in London.

The Third Period, 1800-Present

The Evangelical Awakening quickened religious fervor and broadened the horizon. The Romantic Movement related hymnody to general poetry. The Oxford Movement called forth the latent power of the Church of England, and uncovered the treasures of Greek, Latin, and

German hymnody. A new type of hymnal appeared—comprehensive in character, critically edited, with fine texts and music from all sources.

The new hymns are difficult to classify. Roughly, the Church of England authors fall into two groups: the Evangelicals and the High Church party. Representatives of other communions constitute a third broad grouping.

CROLY, GEORGE (1780-1860). An Irishman who became an Anglican clergyman. Author of poems, novels, dramas, and theological works.
129 Spirit of God, descend upon my heart.

GURNEY, JOHN HAMPDEN (1802-62). Prebendary of St. Paul's Cathedral in London. He supported the S. P. C. K. and organizations for relief of the poor. We have three hundred hymns from his pen.
455 Lord, as to thy dear Cross we flee.

HAWKER, ROBERT STEPHEN (1804-75). An eccentric clergyman of Cornwall.
335 Sing to the Lord the children's hymn.

ALFORD, HENRY (1810-71). Dean of Canterbury, and a scholar of Greek.
565 Forward! be our watchword. Based on Ex. 14:15, this was written as a processional hymn.

DARLING, THOMAS (1816-93). Anglican clergyman, author, and editor.
175 O King of kings, before whose throne. Altered by Darling.

KINGSLEY, CHARLES (1819-75). Poet and novelist, champion of the social responsibilities of the church. He was also a bitter opponent of the Tractarians.
216 From thee all skill and science flow.

WARING, ANNA LAETITIA (1823-1910). A Quaker lady who became an Anglican because of a strong desire for the sacraments.
574 In heavenly love abiding.

HENSLEY, LEWIS (1824-1905). Canon of St. Alban's Cathedral.
329 Thy kingdom come, O God. An Advent hymn.

CHARLES, ELIZABETH RUNDLE (1828-96). Writer of history and fiction, author and translator of hymns.
421 Praise ye the Father for his lovingkindness.

HATCH, EDWIN (1835-89). A Nonconformist, later an Anglican clergyman, he was an eminent scholar.
470 Breathe on me, Breath of God.

The following were more or less closely identified with the Oxford Movement.

NEWMAN, JOHN HENRY (1801-90). A highly controversial figure whose spiritual earnestness, intellectual power, and moral integrity won respect even from those who disagreed with his various positions. Preacher to the University at St. Mary's, Oxford, and an early defender of the Church of England and the *Book of Common Prayer,* he became, after bitter controversy, a convert to Roman Catholicism, and was made a cardinal. His poetry is of high order.
411 Praise to the Holiest in the height. A hymn of adoration on the mystery of the Incarnation.

523   Lead, kindly Light. A poem rather than a hymn, its strength of faith and belief in the power of prayer are often not recognized because of the gentleness of its lines.

FABER, FREDERICK WILLAM (1814-63). Of Huguenot stock, yet he became an early convert to Tractarianism and later to Catholicism. He ranks with Keble and Newman as a writer of original hymns. His emotional style suggests the fervor of Charles Wesley and the Olney Hymns. Thus his finest hymns are superb, while his poorest are marred by sentimentality.

138   Most ancient of all mysteries. A good hymn on the Holy Trinity —a most difficult subject—saved from mediocrity by the omission of some very poor stanzas.

498   Hark! hark, my soul! Overly sweet, but popular. This, too, has been improved by omissions.

516   Faith of our fathers! living still. Another popular item sung with enthusiasm by Protestants who do not know that Faber was here extolling the faith of the Roman Church.

589   O Paradise, O Paradise. Yet another item saved for general church use by the omission of some intensely personal stanzas.

BAKER, HENRY WILLIAMS (1821-77). English baron and clergyman. He was chairman of the committee that produced the epoch-making *Hymns Ancient and Modern* in 1861, to which he also contributed translations and original hymns.

239   We love the place, O God. A rewriting, with additions, of a hymn by Dean Bullock of Nova Scotia.

PLUMPTRE, EDWARD HAYES (1821-91). Dean of Wells. He was an able scholar and writer in many fields.

159   Thy hand, O God, has guided. A hymn entitled, "Church Defence."

555   Rejoice, ye pure in heart. A fine processional hymn, written for a choir festival at Peterborough Cathedral.

THRING, GODFREY (1823-1903). Prebendary of Wells Cathedral, editor of hymnals of merit, and author of seventy-five hymns.

597   I heard a sound of voices.

BRIGHT, WILLIAM (1824-1901). Professor of ecclesiastical history at Oxford. He was also a liturgical scholar and author of valuable studies in the Collects.

203   At thy feet, O Christ, we lay.

278   And now, O Father, mindful of the love. A fine Communion hymn, devoid of mawkish sentimentality. It is at once profoundly reverent, penetrating to the heart of Christ's sacrifice for us, interceding tenderly for "our dearest and our best," and finally praying that in God's own service we may be made "glad and free."

ROSSETTI, CHRISTINA GEORGINA (1830-94). Member of a gifted family of Italian background. Author of lovely poems and religious verse.

36   In the bleak midwinter. A beautiful poem carried to instant success by Gustav Holst's tune.

37   Love came down at Christmas. Significant thought in brief compass.

The following, mostly non-Anglican writers, were English authors whose hymns are not specifically literary or liturgical in character. In general, these hymns are purely devotional, or else show response to various Christian movements of the nineteenth century—missionary, social betterment, early ecumenical outlook, et cetera.

WORDSWORTH, WILLIAM (1770-1850). Poet of the Lake Country, and poet laureate of England.
218   Blest are the moments. An extract from his "The Laborer's Noonday Hymn."

MONTGOMERY, JAMES (1771-1854). Son of a Moravian missionary. Crusading editor of *The Iris*, he was an avowed enemy of the slave trade. Of his four hundred hymns, many are elegant in style but tinged with melancholy. Fourteen are in the Common Hymnal, a large number. There are three new items.
82   Come to Calvary's holy mountain.
269   Shepherd of souls, refresh and bless.
458   Prayer is the soul's sincere desire. Written for Bishop Bickersteth's *Treatise on Prayer*.

BARTON, BERNARD (1784-1849). A Quaker poet, friend of Charles Lamb, Sir Walter Scott, and Robert Southey.
474   Walk in the light: so shalt thou know.

BOWRING, JOHN (1792-1872). A brilliant linguist, editor, social reformer, and governor of Hong Kong, he was a Unitarian.
525   Watchman, tell us of the night. A dialogue hymn between traveler and watchman.

BURTON, JOHN (1803-77). A Congregationalist layman, he was the author of many children's hymns.
549   Saviour, thee my heart I tender.

NOEL, CAROLINE MARIA (1817-77). An invalid who wrote hymns for other sufferers.
430   At the Name of Jesus. A bright processional hymn for Ascension Day.

SMITH, WALTER CHALMERS (1824-1908). Moderator of the Free Church of Scotland.
172   Immortal, invisible, God only wise. Based on I Tim. 1:17.

PROCTOR, ADELAIDE ANNE (1825-64). Daughter of a poet and dramatist. She was a friend of Dickens and a worker among the poor. She eventually became a Roman Catholic.
447   My God, I thank thee, who hast made.

CLEPHANE, ELIZABETH CECILIA (1830-69). Of Scottish ancestry, she was an author of so-called "gospel hymns."
482   Beneath the Cross of Jesus.

OAKLEY, CHARLES EDWARD (1832-65). A Welshman, rector of St. Paul's, Covent Garden, London.
321   Hills of the North, rejoice. A spirited missionary hymn which is also suitable for Advent.

CHARTERIS, ARCHIBALD HAMILTON (1835-1908). Moderator of the Church of Scotland.
540   Believing fathers oft have told. Written for the Young Men's Guild of the Church of Scotland.

DIX, WILLIAM CHATTERTON (1837-98). Manager of an insurance company in Glasgow, he translated hymns from the Greek and the Ethiopic.
48 What child is this, who laid to rest. Extract from the Christmas carol, "The Manger Throne."

MATHESON, GEORGE (1842-1906). Brilliant blind Scottish Presbyterian minister and hymn writer.
508 Make me a captive, Lord. A paradoxical hymn on the theme of surrender, but with the title "Christian Freedom."

The following are twentieth-century authors.

BROOKE, STOPFORD A. (1832-1916). Chaplain to the Queen, though a liberal in theology and later of pronounced Unitarian sympathies.
414 Let the whole creation cry. An imitation of Psalm 148.

OXENHAM, JOHN (1852-1941). Pseudonym for William Arthur Dunkerley, a widely traveled English businessman, publisher of the London edition of the *Detroit Free Press*. He wrote forty novels and twenty other volumes, mostly poetry.
342 In Christ there is no east or west. A hymn of Christian brotherhood, brief but broad in its sympathies.
359 Lord God of hosts, whose mighty hand. Written in 1914, "for the men at the front," but of universal significance.

GRUBB, EDWARD (1854-1939). Of Irish extraction, he was editor of the monthly journal, *The British Friend*.
171 Our God, to whom we turn. A serious hymn, much in the style of Whittier, whom Grubb admired.

LOWRY, SOMERSET CORRY (1855-1932). An Irish Anglican.
542 Son of God, eternal Saviour. A hymn of brotherhood and service.

KIPLING, RUDYARD (1865-1936). Journalist, editor, author of tales of India and sparkling verse which earned for him the unofficial title of "poet laureate of the Empire."
347 God of our fathers, known of old. "The Recessional" was written for Queen Victoria's diamond jubilee. In style of grandeur its prophetic warning hits arrogant imperialism. It inspired a reply from G. K. Chesterton in a poem of similar meter entitled, "Post-recessional."

DEARMER, PERCY (1867-1936). Canon of Westminster and professor of ecclesiastical art at King's College, London. A high churchman in early life, he became an evangelical later. Aided by Ralph Vaughan Williams and Martin Shaw, he rejuvenated and greatly advanced English hymnody by his *English Hymnal, Songs of Praise* (with its companion volume, *Songs of Praise Discussed*), *Oxford Book of Carols*, et cetera. He was a trenchant thinker and writer.
134 Father most holy, merciful and tender. A translation.
317 Remember all the people. A bright children's hymn for missions.

PIGGOTT, WILLIAM CHARTER (1872-1943). A Congregational minister.
598 For those we love within the veil. Written for a commemoration service in 1915 (World War I).

ALINGTON, CYRIL ARGENTINE (1872-1955). Dean of Durham.
109 Good Christian men, rejoice and sing! An Easter hymn written for Dearmer's *Songs of Praise*.

MACNUTT, FREDERICK BRODIE (1873-1949). Provost of Leicester Cathedral and chaplain to the king.
113 Let all the multitudes of light. A hymn for the Festival of the Ascension.

CHESTERTON, GILBERT KEITH (1874-1936). A journalist and poet with a gift for subtle paradox. Also a critic and story-teller. He became a Roman Catholic in his later years.
344 O God of earth and altar. A national hymn.

BRIGGS, GEORGE WALLACE (1875-). Canon of Worcester Cathedral, a living hymn writer of note, and a leader in the field of religious education.
248 Our Father, by whose servants. Written for a grammar school in 1920 with the thought of "the continuity of traditions." A hymn for anniversaries.
251 The Spirit of the Lord revealed. A hymn on the Word.

ROBERTS, KATHERINE (1877-). Singer and playwright.
258 O Lord, thy people gathered here. A baptismal hymn from the parents' point of view.

MASEFIELD, JOHN (1878-). Poet laureate, succeeding Robert Bridges in 1930.
97 Sing, men and angels, sing. From his play, *Easter,* produced at Oxford in 1929.

BAX, CLIFFORD (1886-). An artist, dramatist, and author.
348 Turn back, O man, forswear thy foolish ways. Written to voice the hope, "Earth shall be fair, and all her folk be one!"

RILEY, JOHN ATHELSTAN (1858-1945). Hymn writer, translator, and co-editor, with Percy Dearmer and others, of the *English Hymnal,* 1906.
437 Ye watchers and ye holy ones. A hymn of the heavenly choirs and "all saints triumphant."

HYMNS BY AMERICAN AUTHORS

English-language hymnody in America presents a complicated picture. The English-speaking colonists were Psalm singers. They used Tate and Brady (the "New Version") or the *Bay Psalm Book,* which was issued in 1640 and reprinted in at least seventy editions. Benjamin Franklin printed the first American issue of Watts' *The Psalms Imitated* in 1729.

The early New England poets were not hymn writers, though their poetry contained some fine religious verse. Individuals, notably Congregationalists, Presbyterians, and Unitarians, began to issue privately prepared hymnals. Among these were Samuel Longfellow, Lyman Abbott, Henry Ward Beecher, Park and Phelps, and Charles S. Robinson. Publishers saw a market and invited scholars to edit hymnals. As a reaction to the constantly improving literary quality of these collections, a flood of cheap revival songs and gospel hymns spread over the country. Rather belatedly the denominations recognized their responsibility and prepared official hymnals. Editors generally were responsive to broad movements—missionary, evangelistic, liturgical, social gospel, national, ecumenical. Generally improved cultural conditions gradually lifted literary and musical standards.

The early Lutheran settlers brought their hymnals, as well as their Bibles, with them from their European homelands. As the necessity for English services arose, the various linguistic groups—German, Swedish, Norwegian, Danish, Finnish, et cetera—published hymnals containing English translations, frequently poor in quality, of foreign-language hymns, together with items from Watts, the Wesleys, and other English authors.

The earliest collection used by English-speaking Lutherans was the *Psalmodia Germanica,* edited by John Christian Jacobi, pastor of the Royal German Chapel at St. James' Palace, London. This was first published in London in 1722 with a dedication "to their Royal Highnesses the Prince of Wales and the Princess Royal." An enlarged reprint of the third edition (1732) appeared in New York in 1756. Muhlenberg, who met the language situation in New York by preaching in Dutch in the morning, German in the afternoon, and English in the evening, lined out hymns from this collection at his English services. This interesting volume of hymns contains 279 pages of translations from the "High Dutch." The English style of these translations is so deficient, indeed often so ludicrous, that it has not been possible to include a single item from this book in the Common Hymnal.

Later hymnals privately prepared by Dr. Kunze, George Strebeck, and Ralph Williston in New York, by the Henkels in Virginia, by Drs. Seiss and Passavant in Pennsylvania, failed of general acceptance. Dr. Kunze's Hymn Book of 1795 had some excellent verses, though others are not so happy, e.g., the translation of *O Haupt, voll Blut und Wunden,* which begins, "O Head, so full of bruises," or the hymn which reads:

> Jehovah, Thy wise government
> And its administration,
> Is found to be most excellent
> On due consideration.

The hymnal of the General Synod, 1828, with an appendix added in 1852, was perhaps more Calvinistic and Arminian than Lutheran in tone.

The first creditable Lutheran hymnal in English was the *Church Book* of the General Council, published in 1868. Its character and quality were due in large part to Dr. Beale M. Schmucker and the Rev. Frederick M. Bird. This volume contained 167 translations from the German, 42 from the Latin, and 11 from the Greek, with excellent representation of all periods of English hymnody. Dr. Louis F. Benson, America's foremost hymnologist, said of the *Church Book,* "There was at the time no American hymnal so fully representative of the development of hymnody, so discriminating in selection, so scholarly in treatment." For extended statement of Benson's views, see the whole section in his *The English Hymn* (New York: Doran, 1915), p. 561. Harriet Reynolds Krauth (later Mrs. Adolph Spaeth) gave this book worthy musical settings in her *Church Book with Music.*

The wider knowledge and sympathies of Dr. Schmucker and Mr. Bird led them beyond strictly Lutheran "heritage hymns." Their breadth of English culture gave them instant appreciation of that remarkable work, *Hymns Ancient and Modern,* which appeared in England in 1861. From it they brought many fine translations and original hymns into the *Church Book* of 1868. This resulted not only in the enrichment of the quality of this book, but in the assurance of ecumenical outlook and literary excellence in later English Lutheran hymnals in America.

None of the Lutheran hymnals prior to the Common Hymnal have given adequate representation to American hymn writers. The *Common Service Book* included only thirty hymns by Americans, and other books generally less. The Common Hymnal contains sixty-six new hymns by American authors.

New England Poets

WHITTIER, JOHN GREENLEAF (1807-92). Massachusetts born, of Quaker parents, sometime editor of an antislavery paper in Philadelphia, he later returned to Massachusetts. Though denied a college education, he became one of the country's most famous poets. His works made a strong appeal because of their simplicity and sincerity. Though scorn of every rite, ceremony, or symbol pervades all his poetry, other qualities of simple faith and trust have won acceptance for his hymns by editors in all communions. At least seventy different centos from his writings are found in hymnals throughout the English-speaking world.

244 All things are thine; no gift have we. Written for the opening of Plymouth Church, St. Paul, Minnesota.

371 I bow my forehead to the dust. A cento from a twenty-two-stanza poem on "The Eternal Goodness."

467 Dear Lord and Father of mankind. A cento from a prayer which concludes a lengthy poem called "The Brewing of Soma."

476 Immortal Love, forever full. A cento from a poem of thirty-eight stanzas entitled "Our Master."

539 O brother man, fold to thy heart thy brother! The final stanzas of the poem, "Worship."

593 I know not what the future hath. A portion of the poem, "Eternal Goodness."

HOLMES, OLIVER WENDELL (1809-94). Born at Cambridge, Massachusetts, he was professor of anatomy and physiology at Harvard University, and a distinguished man of letters, known best, perhaps, for his "Breakfast Table" series. Four books of his poems appeared by 1888. With a deep interest in theology, he reacted strongly against the "iron of Calvinism." He was an Episcopalian and later a Unitarian.

170 Lord of all being, throned afar. A poem which concluded his *Professor at the Breakfast Table.*

STOWE, HARRIET BEECHER (1812-96). Famous author of *Uncle Tom's Cabin.*
496 Still, still with thee, when purple morning breaketh. A mystical poem based on Ps. 139:18.

LOWELL, JAMES RUSSELL (1819-91). Lawyer, professor of modern languages at Harvard, ambassador to England and to Spain, editor, and poet.
547 Once to every man and nation. Written in protest against the war with Mexico.

LONGFELLOW, SAMUEL (1819-92). Younger brother of Henry Wadsworth Longfellow. Samuel was a Unitarian minister, sometime pastor in Germantown, Philadelphia. Author of twenty-seven hymns and editor of hymnals.
130 Holy Spirit, truth divine. A "prayer for inspiration," which enumerates the attributes of the Holy Spirit.
490 I look to thee in every need. The power of religious faith in maintaining mental and physical well-being.

HOWE, JULIA WARD (1819-1910). Poet, philanthropist, and social reformer. A Unitarian.
356 Mine eyes have seen the glory of the coming of the Lord. "Battle Hymn of the Republic," written after the outbreak of the Civil War.

Baptist

PHELPS, SYLVANUS DRYDEN (1816-95). Baptist minister, editor, and author, the father of William Lyon Phelps of Yale.
463 Saviour, thy dying love. Published, with a tune by Dr. Lowry, in *Pure Gold,* a collection of gospel hymns which sold over a million copies.

GILMORE, JOSEPH HENRY (1834-1918). Baptist minister and professor of English at the University of Rochester.
478 He leadeth me: O blessed thought. Based on Psalm 23. The hymn has been sung in many languages.

HAWKS, ANNIE SHERWOOD (1835-1918). Author of four hundred Sunday school hymns.
479 I need thee every hour. Based on John 15:5. The refrain and tune are by her pastor, Robert Lowry.

Congregational

GLADDEN, WASHINGTON (1836-1918). Pastor of First Congregational Church, Columbus, Ohio. Author of thirty-two books, he was a leading exponent of the social gospel.
537 O Master, let me walk with thee. A hymn of service, based on intimate fellowship with Christ.

BATES, KATHERINE LEE (1859-1929). Professor of English at Wellesley College.

346 O beautiful for spacious skies. "America the Beautiful," written in Colorado Springs after a trip to the summit of Pike's Peak.

SHURTLEFF, ERNEST WARBURTON (1862-1917). Congregational minister who held charges in Massachusetts, Minnesota, Germany, and France.

550 Lead on, O King eternal. Written as the graduation hymn for his class at Andover Theological Seminary, 1887.

LITTLEFIELD, MILTON SMITH (1864-1934). Congregational minister, author, and editor of hymnals.

217 O Son of Man, thou madest known. The nobility of service in the spirit of the Master.

TAYLOR, SARAH E. (1883-1954).

250 O God of Light, thy word.

Episcopal

BULLOCK, WILLIAM (1798-1874). Naval officer, missionary to Newfoundland, Dean of Halifax, Nova Scotia, he was the author of *Songs of the Church* and much devotional poetry.

239 We love the place, O God. A hymn on the sanctuary. The original text has been altered by Henry Williams Baker.

HOPKINS, JOHN HENRY, JR. (1820-91). Clergyman, son of the bishop of Vermont, author of hymns and carols.

283 Come with us, O blessed Jesus. A hymn of the Incarnation and the Holy Communion.

DOANE, WILLIAM CROSWELL (1832-1913). Bishop of Albany, he was chairman of the commission which prepared the Episcopal Hymnal of 1892.

137 Ancient of Days, who sittest throned in glory. Written for the bicentenary of Albany, New York.

DOUGLAS, CHARLES WINFRED (1867-1944). Canon of St. John's Cathedral, Denver. He was an eminent linguist, musicologist, composer, author, and editor, outstanding authority on plainsong and church music in general, and musical editor of the Episcopal hymnals of 1916 and 1940.

255 Awake, thou Spirit of the watchmen. Translated by Douglas and Arthur W. Farlander from the German hymn by K. H. von Bogatzky.

ROBBINS, HOWARD CHANDLER (1876-1952). Dean of the Cathedral of St. John the Divine, professor at General Theological Seminary, New York, author, and hymn writer.

243 Put forth, O God, thy Spirit's might. A general hymn, strong in thought, concise in form.

HODGES, LEIGH MITCHELL (1876-1954). Literary man and journalist, author of books and poems. He wrote the column, "The Optimist," in the *Philadelphia Evening Bulletin.*

287 Lord of the everlasting light. A Confirmation hymn written for the Common Hymnal at the request of his friend Dr. Paul Z. Strodach.

BURT, BATES GILBERT (1878-1948). Rector of All Saints' Church, Pontiac, Michigan.

548 O God of youth, whose Spirit. Written for a high school commencement in 1940. He also wrote the tune.

Bowie, Walter Russell (1882-). Rector of Grace Church, New York City, professor at Union Theological Seminary, lecturer, and author whose social vision has won a place for his hymns in hymnals here and abroad.
332   O holy city, seen of John. A hymn of the heavenly Jerusalem, with thought of the preparation that should be made for it here.

Stillman, Mildred Whitney (1890-). A native of San Francisco, graduate of Barnard College, novelist, essayist, poet.
382   Now once again for help that never faileth. This "Hymn in Distress" was written after returning from a church where she had gone to pray for the recovery of a friend's young son.

Farlander, Arthur W. (1898-). Born in Germany. Rector of Church of the Incarnation, Santa Rosa, Calif. Member Episcopal. Hymnal (1940) Commission.
255   Awake, thou Spirit of the watchmen. Translated by Farlander and Charles Winfred Douglas from the German hymn by K. H. von Bogatzky.

Lutheran

Schaeffer, Charles William (1813-96). Pastor of St. Michael's Church, Germantown, Philadelphia, professor in the Philadelphia Seminary (Mount Airy), and president of the General Council.
293   Lord, to thee I now surrender. Translated by Schaeffer.

Loy, Matthias (1826-1915). President of the Joint Synod of Ohio, professor and president of Capital University, Columbus, Ohio, author, and hymn writer.
260   Jesus took the babes and blessed them. A baptismal hymn.
518   Jesus, thou art mine forever. A hymn of communion with Christ.

Wendell, Claus August (1866-1950). Clergyman, author, hymnal editor. Member of Joint Commission on the Hymnal.
378   Search me, God, and know my heart. Paraphrase of Ps. 139:23, 24.

Copenhaver, Laura Scherer (1868-1940).
320   Heralds of Christ, who bear the King's command.

Olson, Ernst William (1870-). Historian, translator, poet, editor. Born in Sweden and editor of Swedish periodicals. Office editor, Augustana Book Concern, 1911-1949. Member Joint Commission on the Hymnal.
349   God of peace, in peace preserve us.

Reed, Luther Dotterer (1873-). President emeritus of the Philadelphia Seminary (Mount Airy), author, and editor. Secretary of the joint committee which prepared the *Common Service Book* in 1917, and chairman of the two Joint Commissions which prepared the *Service Book and Hymnal* (1958).
353   O God of wondrous grace and glory. A hymn of trust for the nation and the church suggested by Ps. 31:15, "My times are in thy hand." At a resort in the Adirondacks in the summer of 1950, a group gloomily discussed national, social, and religious problems of the hour. The author suggested that we might take courage if we had the faith of the Psalmist. Retiring to his room, he wrote this hymn.

Seebach, Margaret Reynolds (1875-1948).
318   Thy kingdom come! O Father, hear our prayer.

STRODACH, PAUL ZELLER (1876-1947). Clergyman, liturgical scholar, author, artist, editor. Member of the joint committee which prepared the *Common Service Book* and of the Joint Commissions on the *Service Book and Hymnal.*

103 Now let the vault of heaven resound.

209 God of our life, all-glorious Lord.

RYDEN, ERNEST EDWIN (1886-   ). Born in Kansas City, Missouri, of pioneer parents, graduate of Augustana College and Seminary, pastor of Gloria Dei Church, St. Paul, Minnesota, editor of the *Lutheran Companion.* He was chairman of the Hymnal Committee of the Augustana Synod, coeditor of the Augustana *Hymnal,* secretary of the Joint Commission which prepared the Common Hymnal, 1945-1958. Translator and author of hymns and of books about hymns.

178 Eternal God, before thy throne we bend. Written in 1941 as a hymn of invocation of the Holy Trinity, and dedicated to the class of Augustana Seminary ordained that year, of which class the author's son-in-law was a member.

233 The twilight shadows round me fall. Written at the request of Professor Peter Johnson, an organist of St. Paul, to fit a tune composed by him. The tune was subsequently named "Cecile," after Dr. Ryden's daughter, then eight years old.

241 How blessed is this place, O Lord. Written in 1924 at the request of the Augustana Hymnal Committee. Intended for church dedications, specifically of an altar. Based on Jacob's experience at Bethel.

291 With solemn joy we come, dear Lord. Written in 1923 for the Confirmation class at Gloria Dei Church, St. Paul.

295 Beyond the everlasting hills. The author's elder brother George, professor of history and political science at the University of Delaware, died in October, 1941. Speeding eastward on a train through the mountains of western Pennsylvania, in a mood of depression, Dr. Ryden composed this hymn.

KELLER, ARNOLD FREDERICK (1890-   ). Born in Cuba, pastor emeritus of the Church of the Redeemer, Utica, New York.

43 Under the feeble stable light. A Christmas carol, with both text and tune by the author.

SELTZER, GEORGE RISE (1902-   ). Pastor at Hartford, Connecticut, librarian of the Hartford Theological Seminary, then professor of liturgics and church art at the Lutheran Theological Seminary at Philadelphia. A member of both Joint Commissions which prepared the *Service Book and Hymnal,* chairman of their subcommittee on text, and chairman of the Joint Editorial Committee.

249 Come, all ye people, come away. A hymn for anniversaries.

HORN, EDWARD TRAILL, III (1909-   ). Pastor of the Lutheran Church at Ithaca, New York, then of Trinity Lutheran Church, Germantown, Philadelphia. He is the author of *Altar and Pew, The Christian Year,* et cetera. Chairman of the music committees of the two Joint Commissions which prepared the *Service Book and Hymnal.* Besides writing the text noted here, he translated five hymns for the collection.

44 Long ago and far away. An original text substituted for the text of

the medieval Christmas cradle song, "Joseph, lieber Joseph mein." Set to the fourteenth century carol melody *Resonet in Laudibus,* with the original text of the refrain retained as in the *Oxford Book of Carols.* The harmonization is that of Ralph Vaughan Williams.

JOHNSON, WILLIAM (1906-   ).

80   Deep were his wounds, and red. A poignant poem on the Passion which first appeared in the *Lutheran Companion.*

Methodist

CROSBY, FANNY JANE VAN ALSTYNE (1820-1915). Blind author of gospel songs, approximately seventy-five of which have been identified as hers. At least sixty have crossed the sea and appeared in British hymnals.

461   Pass me not, O gentle Saviour. Written in 1868 and first published in William Howard Doane's *Songs of Devotion.*

LATHBURY, MARY ARTEMISIA (1841-1913). A professional artist, editor of religious papers, and hymn writer. She was frequently called the "poet laureate of Chautauqua."

234   Day is dying in the west. Written at the suggestion of Bishop Vincent, founder of the Chautauqua Assembly.

491   Break thou the bread of life. Written as a study hymn for the Chautauqua Literary and Scientific Circle.

THOMPSON, WILL LAMARTINE (1847-1909). From East Liverpool, Ohio, he was a graduate of the Boston Conservatory of Music. An author of hymns, he also composed their tunes. An associate of Dwight L. Moody.

578   Softly and tenderly Jesus is calling. Moody said that he would rather have written this than anything he had done in his whole life.

WINCHESTER, CALEB THOMAS (1847-1920). Professor of English literature. He was a scholarly member of the commission which prepared the Methodist Hymnal in 1905.

502   The Lord our God alone is strong. Written for the dedication of the Orange Judd Hall of Natural Science at Wesleyan University, where he taught.

HARKNESS, GEORGIA ELMA (1891-   ). Professor of philosophy and religion at Mount Holyoke College, Garrett Biblical Institute, and since 1950 at Pacific School of Religion, Berkeley, California. Active in ecumenical councils. Author and hymn writer.

581   Hope of the world, thou Christ.

Presbyterian

HASTINGS, THOMAS (1784-1872). Musician, choral conductor in New York City, hymn writer, composer and associate of Lowell Mason.

319   Hail to the brightness of Zion's glad morning. Written in 1830.

MARCH, DANIEL (1816-1909). Yale graduate, minister, Presbyterian, later Congregational.

59   Hark! the voice of Jesus crying. Written to accompany the author's sermon on the text: "Here am I; send me."

PRENTISS, ELIZABETH PAYSON (1818-1878). Wife of a Presbyterian minister and professor at Union Theological Seminary. Author of books and hymns.

392   More love to thee, O Christ. A hymn which gained great popularity in the revival of 1871.

CAMPBELL, JOHN (1845-1914).
488   Unto the hills around do I lift up. Paraphrase of Psalm 121.

VAN DYKE, HENRY (1852-1933). Princeton professor, pastor of Brick Presbyterian Church, New York City, United States minister to the Netherlands, and Navy chaplain. He was chairman of the committee which prepared the Presbyterian *Book of Common Worship.*
438   Joyful, joyful, we adore thee. Written during a preaching visit at Williams College, inspired by the Berkshire Mountains. The author intended it to be sung to the "Hymn to Joy" in Beethoven's Ninth Symphony.

BENSON, LOUIS FITZGERALD (1855-1930). America's most eminent hymnologist. A lawyer who became a minister and later edited the Presbyterian Hymnal (1895 and 1911) and other hymnals. Coeditor of the *Book of Common Worship.* Author of many distinguished hymns and of books about hymns, including his well-known, *The English Hymn* of 1915.
282   For the bread which thou hast broken. A fine Post-Communion hymn.

BABCOCK, MALTBIE DAVENPORT (1858-1901). Pastor, musician, poet, magnetic personality. He held charges at the Brown Memorial Church, Baltimore, and Brick Presbyterian Church, New York.
487   This is my Father's world. A cento from a longer poem on the fatherhood and providence of God.

MERRILL, WILLIAM PIERSON (1867-1954). Pastor in Chestnut Hill, Philadelphia, Chicago, and New York City. Noted preacher, author, and leader in the ecumenical movement.
345   Not alone for mighty empire. Written after a Thanksgiving Service in Chicago.
541   Rise up, O men of God. Written on a Lake Michigan steamer for use in the Brotherhood Movement. It has gained very wide usage.

Unitarian

BURLEIGH, WILLIAM HENRY (1812-71). Journalist, poet, social reformer, and harbor master of New York City.
472   Lead us, O Father, in the paths of peace.

JOHNSON, SAMUEL (1822-82). Graduate of the Harvard Divinity School, coeditor of a hymnal in collaboration with Samuel Longfellow.
330   City of God, how broad and far. Popular in England and Scotland, this was sung at the dedication of Liverpool Cathedral in 1924.

FROTHINGHAM, OCTAVIUS BROOKS (1822-95). Minister in Salem, Massachusetts, Jersey City, and New York City.
305   Thou Lord of Hosts, whose guiding hand. Written for the commencement of the Class of 1846 at the Harvard Divinity School.

CHADWICK, JOHN WHITE (1840-1904). Minister of the Second Unitarian Church, Brooklyn, New York, for forty years. Author and hymn writer.
350   Eternal Ruler of the ceaseless round. Class hymn at his graduation from the Harvard Divinity School in 1864.

HOSMER, FREDERICK LUCIAN (1840-1929). Minister in Massachusetts,

Illinois, Ohio, Missouri, and California. Prolific writer of hymns of merit, and an editor of hymnals.

247   O Light, from age to age the same. Written for the fiftieth anniversary of the Second Congregational Church, Quincy, Illinois.

331   Thy kingdom come! on bended knee. Written for the commencement exercises of the Meadville Theological School in Pennsylvania.

535   Not always on the mount may we. A hymn on the Transfiguration.

600   O Lord of life, where'er they be. Written in 1888 for the Easter Service in his church in Cleveland, Ohio.

Chapter 10

THE THREAD OF HISTORY

Religion is the deepest concern of the human spirit. Music is the most powerful exponent of human emotion. It is natural, therefore, that music should reach its greatest heights—attain to its purest expressions —in the service of religion.

Thoughtful men—poets and philosophers in particular—have ever recognized this. Carlyle put it in these words: "Who is there, that in logical words can express the effect music has on us? A kind of inarticulate, unfathomable speech, which leads us to the edge of the infinite, and lets us for moments gaze into that." Rabindranath Tagore writes: "Song begins where words end; the inexpressible is the domain of music." And Browning: "I state it thus: there is no truer truth obtainable by man than comes by music."

The rich resources of our musical art today can only be appreciated when we know the steps by which that art has progressed from simple beginnings to maturity. We must sketch this rich history, even if only in briefest outline.

Hebrew use of music in the temple and synagogue is well known. It was the Christian Church, however, which appreciated the greatest possibilities of this form of expression and gave it its true development as an art. The church supplied the thought, the feeling, the occasion, and largely the means for music's unfolding throughout the centuries. The church, therefore, must not be thought of merely as a patron of music. It has been a mother, under whose sheltering care music grew to artistic maturity.

The full unfolding of music was late. Architecture reached its triumphs of Gothic glory in the thirteenth and fourteenth centuries. Painting and sculpture reached ultimate achievements in the period of the Renaissance. But not until the seventeenth century were our present major and minor scales fully established. And equally late was the development of harmony as we understand it today.

BEFORE THE REFORMATION

Music before the Reformation was priestly and choral. It was cultivated chiefly in the monasteries. Early developments are for the most part lost to us. The greatest of the earlier men whose work has survived was Gregory the Great (pope from 590 to 604). It was probably he who established in the West the use of the scale system, derived from Greek forms, which bears his name, codified liturgical and musical material, and permanently established a school for singers at Rome. Charlemagne two centuries later secured the services of some of these singers to conduct schools of church music in the monasteries of St. Gall, Metz, et cetera, in the Frankish kingdom, and thus secured the continuance of their art.

This early music is called Gregorian or plainsong. It consisted of melodies only, without harmony or parts. These melodies were free in form, without bars or measures, but with accents in close agreement with the quantitative stresses of the texts. Instead of our modern major and minor scales, there were eight church modes, each of which was a scale with an individual succession of intervals. The notation, evolved after centuries of experiment, used solid square and diamond shaped characters on a four line staff.

The music intoned by the priest, with brief responses by the choir and congregation, was collectively called the *accentus*. It included recitatives with simple inflections. This music was set to the invariable parts of the Mass known as the Ordinary (Kyrie, Gloria in Excelsis, Sanctus, Agnus Dei, Versicles, et cetera). Variable numbers, called the Proper of the Mass (Introit, Gradual, Communio, et cetera), were provided with musical forms collectively called the *consensus*.

Some of these variable forms were exceedingly elaborate, e.g., the Gradual, which at one time was considered the artistic climax of the Mass. A wealth of melodic invention was expended upon the Alleluia and the verse which concluded the Gradual. The celebrant, and even the pope himself, gave strict attention when these were sung.

The supreme function of this music was to clothe the text of the Liturgy with dignity and melodic beauty. Its ideals were primarily liturgical, and secondarily artistic. It provided for all parts of the Liturgy proper. The Psalms, chanted antiphonally in the Hour services, built up a similar body of musical material around themselves. In the cathedral and monastic communities, thousands of plainsong melodies, many of them of great beauty, were copied in the medieval missals, graduals, breviaries, and antiphonaries. Plainsong hymn melodies were also used in the Hours, and have been passed down to us in some number.

The melodies varied greatly in different parts of Europe. Some had only a local, or at best, provincial use. Others gained universal currency. The Council of Trent (1545-63) inaugurated reforms which resulted in the publishing of official books—the Roman Missal, Gradual, Antiphonary, et cetera—which contained approved plainsong music for the entire church. By this time, however, the rise of polyphony and the general distaste for everything medieval had obscured the ancient musical tradition. When the Medicean edition of the Roman Missal appeared in 1614, it contained many variations from the older manuscripts. The same was true of the Mecclin and Ratisbon editions. Finally, during the pontificate of Leo XIII, late in the nineteenth century, the monks of Solesmes, after half a century of labor, convinced the church of the superiority of the ancient forms, which are now given again in the authentic texts authorized by the Holy See.

This great body of plainsong supplied the foundation for all later musical development within the church and without. Later music incorporated the freer melodic and rhythmic quality of the folk song. The artistic development of polyphonic and instrumental forms advanced beyond plainsong's simplicity and liturgical objectivity. Yet because of its beauty, virile strength, and absolute churchliness, plainsong is cultivated today in many centers. Surfeited with operatic masses, sentimental anthems, and effeminate chants and hymn tunes, the ablest musicians of our own time find inspiration and strength in these ancient forms.

DEVELOPMENT, DECLINE, AND REFORM

Plainsong held unchallenged sway for a thousand years. The first crude attempts at polyphony—so-called "organum" and "descant"—were made in the tenth century. This innovation came not from Rome, but from western Europe. The troubadors and minnesingers contributed a vitalizing influence in the form of a growing body of secular and religious folk songs. By the fourteenth century, the "new art" of counterpoint appeared. It probably originated with John Dunstable of England (*ca.* 1375-1453). Relative time values were recognized, and many voice parts were developed according to set rules. Instead of the single plainsong melody declaiming the text of the Liturgy, we now have many melodies interwoven like the strands of a vocal cable, with emphasis on musical rather than liturgical values. This music was, like the plainsong, purely vocal. It was brought to its early perfection by composers of the Netherlands school—Dufay, Josquin des Prés, and others—in a series of complicated contrapuntal masses, motets, et cetera. Contrapuntal music was brought to its culmination in Italy by Palestrina (1525-94) and the composers of the Roman school, in England by Byrd, and in Spain by Vittoria. In Germany the one man who ranked with the greatest of these was Orlando di Lasso, a Netherlander whose finest work was done in Munich.

The Venetian school (Adrian Willaert, Andrea and Giovanni Gabrieli, et cetera) led in a freer treatment of the old church modes, with bolder use of dissonances and chromatics. They also introduced instrumental accompaniment, hitherto unknown. Outside of Italy important centers of the Germanic development were Vienna (Isaak, Gallus, Fux) and Munich (Orlando di Lasso, mentioned above). The Roman Chapel in Paris boasted of Arcadelt, Lejeune, and Goudimel; Spain had Morales and Vittoria. The Netherlands, which had sent many of its ablest musicians into all these lands, had Sweelinck as its shining light in the late sixteenth century. In England the Liturgy and forms of the Roman Church dominated the first half of the same century, and the royal chapel was famous throughout Europe. Some of England's composers before the Reformation were Fayrfax, Taverner, and Christopher Tye.

As the Mass was the great and important Service of the church, the new polyphonic compositions were chiefly settings of its numbers, either the texts of the Liturgy itself (especially the Kyrie, Gloria in Excelsis, Creed, Sanctus, and Agnus Dei), or texts of extra-liturgical nature such as motets. Printing, in the earlier years, had not yet been invented, and music, like literature, had to be set forth in manuscript form. Thousands of these compositions perished or were destroyed in later centuries. We know from the portions which have survived that this material was enormous in quantity, and that much of it was high in quality.

The growth of secular influences within the church produced the so-called "musical Mass," the ecclesiastical counterpart of the secular opera. Its introduction marked the triumph of the spirit of the Renaissance, which freed all arts from the restraints of the church. As Renaissance architecture was a break in the logical development of architectural style and resulted from a return to earlier secular and pagan forms, so the modern musical Mass represents a type of music which did not originate within the church itself, but was brought in from without.

Earnest musicians resisted the movement. Johann Fux and Caldara at Vienna, Allegri at Rome, Michael Haydn at Salzburg, and even Cherubini later in Paris exerted themselves to maintain a distinction between sacred and secular forms, and to preserve purity and dignity in their compositions for the church. But, generally speaking, Roman church music throughout Italy and the rest of Europe was overwhelmed by the new forms and the new spirit, which stemmed from the opera house and the concert hall. Composers who produced secular music for the courts of the nobles produced music of the same type for the services of the church. The unaccompanied contrapuntal choruses of Palestrina and his school had rested upon medieval plainsong tonality. Because of this they achieved an objective and impersonal quality not attained by later musicians. Those who came after, under the leadership of the Venetians and Neopolitans, developed solo voices, introduced duets, subordinated the other parts, and added elaborate instrumental accompaniment.

In Italy particularly, where cardinals owned boxes in the theater and priests composed and conducted operas, there was little difference in essential quality between music for the stage and music for the church. Dukes, prince-bishops, and nobles in all countries maintained ecclesiastical establishments which were conducted quite in the same spirit as their opera houses. The musical Masses, even those by great musicians like Haydn, Mozart, Weber, Schubert, and Beethoven, reveal this secular spirit. The compositions of lesser men like Rossini and Gounod are often tawdry and sentimental.

The Roman Church, as such, has never officially recognized this type of music, though it is constantly rendered in the majority of its churches. The church has repeatedly lent its influence to efforts at reform, from the days of Trent, through the famous encyclical *Motu Proprio* of 1903, to the recent pronouncements of Pope Pius XII. Carl Proske, Franz Witt, founders of the St. Cecilia Society, and F. X. Haberl of Regensburg were the leaders of a reform movement in Germany during the last century. In France, the Benedictine Congregation of St. Pierre, Solesmes (including Guéranger, Pothier, Mocquereau, et cetera), not only revived interest in plainsong, but with prodigious labor restored its authentic forms. The Schola Cantorum was established in Paris, and Guilmant, Widor, and Saint Saëns combined solid musicianship with reverent spirit in their organ compositions.

The church has given formal approval to the work of the Benedictines of Solesmes, and has sponsored the marvelous renditions of their music recorded on twenty-four discs (78 rpm) issued by the Victor Company. A more recent set on LP records is also to be noted.

The Pius X School in New York City and St. John's Abbey (Benedictine) in Collegeville, Minnesota, are important American centers of this reform movement, with the Gregorian Institute of America, in Toledo, Ohio, publishing a great deal of material in the field (mostly for popular consumption).

One further statement must be made concerning music in the Roman Church. Congregations in Italy and France frequently sing plainsong credos; German and Austrian congregations often sing hymns to chorale melodies; and attempts have been made in this country by Monsignor Hellriegel of St. Louis and other scattered clerics to introduce congregational singing of plainsong in the Mass. But generally speaking, the music of this church is still predominantly priestly and choral, not congregational in character.

For convenient summary, texts of the decrees of the Congregation of Sacred Rites, *Motu Proprio,* et cetera, see Sir Richard Runcilman Terry's *The Music of the Roman Rite,* pp. 192, 252, 288, 291, et cetera; or, in more popular style, *Catholic Church Music* by Paul Hume (New York: Dodd, Mead, 1956).

THE LUTHERAN DEVELOPMENT

The liturgical churches of Protestantism, both the Lutheran and the Anglican, succeeded in maintaining a serious and spiritual level in their musical settings to the Liturgy. This was accomplished largely by confining their themes to melodies associated with the church; by retaining the objective supremacy of the text and its spiritual mood; and, particularly in the Lutheran Church, by the development of solid contrapuntal craftsmanship in choral and organ compositions.

The Lutheran Church took the lead in the field of liturgical music, including hymnody, and maintained it for more than two centuries in a comprehensive program that was both conservative and constructive. The Reformation, with its deep notes of conviction and sincerity, cultivated plainsong and arranged settings for the Liturgy based upon it. The Reformers opened a new field in their introduction of the congregational chorale. Once established, these melodies, together with those belonging to the old plainsong system, were used as thematic material for highly artistic choral compositions. The artistic music of the choir was built, then, upon themes associated with the church, and not upon those reminiscent of the opera. So great and so original was the work of Lutheran composers of the seventeenth and early eighteenth centuries, that leadership in the field actually passed from Italy to Germany. Heinrich Schütz was the pioneer and Bach the greatest figure.

Luther himself led the way. Brian Wibberley, in a historical and philosophical work, gives an objective appraisal and discerning analysis. He says:

The music of the Continental Protestant Churches owes its distinctive character to Luther, who called forth in the art of music an impulse that finds its parallel in the Renaissance art generally, and who, in particular, created a sacred song incorporating the spirit of the folk-song—a type of music interwoven into the texture of the life of the people, and at once intelligible, natural, and welcome to the masses. Upon this foundation Protestant church music reared a superstructure possessing entirely new aspects of art, and which, when wedded to the contrapuntal art of the Middle Ages, and passing

163

through the alembic of a genius-mind like that of J. S. Bach, produced some of the greatest type-forms which still hold the artistic imagination and religious spirit of the world as by a spell.

As a church musician Luther has been described as a second Gregory; and it is abundantly evident that his desire and aim was the construction of an evangelical choral service based on the provisions and praxis of Catholic art. Hence he employed the old *cantus firmus* . . . out of which was evolved the chorale. Similarly, he adopted the old polyphony. . . . The Protestant polyphony of Isaac, Walther, and Senfell was written in precisely the same forms and style as that of the Catholic masters. . . . Luther's purpose was to bring the liturgy within the understanding of the people; hence he allocated a more prominent part to the hymns, et cetera, in the vernacular instead of Latin. . . . Other portions of the liturgy rendered in the Latin idiom, were translated and reconstructed on the same principle, until, under Luther, the whole music of the Church was democratized. . . . The secret of the popularized Lutheran chorale lay in its assimilation of the form and spirit of the folk-song.[1]

Luther's work with respect to the Liturgy was radical, and yet conservative. It was radical in the boldness and power with which he edited the sacrosanct forms, rejecting everything expressive of false doctrine, but retaining all that was pure; also in his translation of historic texts into the vernacular. It was conservative in his historical approach and his appreciation of the heritage of the past. His work was artistic in its concern for the niceties of language and the nuances of music. It was constructive and creative in the development of new forms and in the rigorous effort to promote good music of every form.

Interesting light is thrown upon this aspect of Luther's work by a letter written late in life by the musician Johann Walther, who in 1524 published one of the earliest German hymnbooks, to which Luther contributed, and who co-operated with the Reformer in preparing the musical settings for his German Mass. Walther writes:

Some forty years ago, when he would set up the German Mass at Wittenberg, he wrote to the Elector of Saxony and Duke Johannsen, of illustrious memory, begging to invite to Wittenberg the old musician Conrad Rupff and myself to consult with him as to the character and the proper notation of the Eight Tones; and he finally himself decided to appropriate the Eighth Tone to the Epistle and the Sixth Tone to the Gospel, speaking on this wise: Our Lord Christ is a good friend, and His words are full of love; so we will take the Sixth Tone for the Gospel. And since Saint Paul is a very earnest Apostle we will set the Eighth Tone to the Epistle. So he himself made the notes over the Epistles and the Gospels, and the Words of Institution of the true Body and Blood of Christ, and sang them over to me to get my judgment thereon. He kept me three weeks long at Wittenberg to write out the notes over some of the Gospels and Epistles, until the first German Mass was sung in the parish church. And I must needs stay to hear it, and take with me a copy of the Mass to Torgau and present it to His Grace the Elector from Doctor Luther.

Furthermore he gave orders to re-establish the Vespers, which in many

[1] *Music and Religion* (London: Epworth Press, 1934), pp. 109-111.

places were fallen into disuse, with short plain choral hymns for the students and the boys; withal, that the charity scholars, collecting their bread, should sing from door to door Latin hymns, anthems and responsories, appropriate to the season. It was no satisfaction to him that the scholars should sing in the streets nothing but German songs.[2]

The numerous Church Orders which appeared in the different states and cities followed Luther's lead in adapting the ancient melodies to the new services. In many districts the use of Latin for certain parts of the Liturgy was continued for a long time, even while other parts were given in German. The Latin persisted chiefly in the choir music (Introit, Gradual, antiphons, Psalms, Responsories, et cetera). Study of more than fifty of the sixteenth century Church Orders shows adaptations of the traditional music to the Kyrie, Gloria, Preface, Pax, the Litany, et cetera, always for congregational use. New melodies also were composed to suit the German text. The traditional intonations for the minister were everywhere included. In conservative areas, such as Hanover, Saxony, and Bavaria, the ancient plainsong melodies associated with the texts of the Liturgy were never completely lost, enjoying relatively unbroken use to the present day.

Lutheran composers for a time wrote new polyphonic settings to the German texts of the old Mass numbers somewhat comparable to the later "services" of the English Church. This was, however, a procedure of limited duration. The later development of the choral motet and of the cantata opened a wider field for composers, and these forms engaged their particular interest. Another and greater reason was that every effort was made to encourage congregational participation in worship. The ancient Latin texts of the Mass (Introit, Gloria, Creed, Sanctus, et cetera) were paraphrased in the form of German hymns sung by the people themselves. Later simple musical settings to direct translations of these texts were employed.

In addition to editing settings for the Liturgy, Luther encouraged musicians like Spangenberg, Lossius, Keuchenthal, and others to publish Cantionales and similar collections of musical settings for the Liturgy and chorales for hymn texts. He urged princes and civil authorities to support choir schools and societies devoted to church music. He started Protestant hymnody on its triumphant way, and himself wrote hymns and chorale melodies. In addition to *Ein feste Burg,* he composed or arranged such chorales as *Aus tiefer Noth, Von Himmel hoch, Jesus Christus unser Heiland,* and *Wohl dem der in Gottes Fürchte steht.* Able men quickly followed his leadership, and hundreds of chorale melodies appeared. Johann Crüger, Hassler, Nicolai, Franck, Teschner,

[2] Quoted from translation of Walther's letter in Leonard Woolsey Bacon's *Hymns of Martin Luther* (New York: Charles Scribner's Sons, 1883), p. 18.

Albert, and Neumark are but a few outstanding names. The strength, beauty, and dignity of their melodies made these chorales ideal for unisonous congregational singing. They also served as thematic material for motets, cantatas, and organ compositions. The German chorale thus secured for itself an importance historically and musically never attained by the Calvinistic Psalm tunes or the later English hymn tunes.

THE LUTHERAN CANTIONALES

The old Latin motet of the choir was now supplanted by the congregational chorale on the one hand and by a new development of choir music on the other.

In addition to the musical provisions in the Church Orders themselves, special books were prepared for the use of choirs. Some of these works, which are called cantionales, were of great size and importance. The *Cantiones Ecclesiasticae,* published by Johann Spangenberg in 1545, was a large folio volume of 379 pages, prepared, we are told, "at the instigation and command of Luther," with whom Spangenberg was in close touch. It contains an elaborate *de tempore* arrangement of the parts of the Liturgy in Latin and German, with the traditional melodies set to the Latin text, and adaptations of them to the German. This work is one of the weightiest historical documents of the period concerning the developments of liturgical music within the Lutheran Church. There are only a few copies of this handsome and important work in existence in Europe and America today, one of them being in the Krauth Library of the Lutheran Theological Seminary at Philadelphia, Pennsylvania.

Lucas Lossius, who had been a pupil of Luther and Melanchthon and was for fifty years professor at Lüneberg, published his *Psalmodia, hoc est, Cantica Sacra* for churches and schools in 1553. Melanchthon wrote a preface to this work, which ran through many editions. It contained a complete selection of texts and melodies from the pre-Reformation *Missale, Graduale,* and *Antiphonarium,* adapted for use in Lutheran services. Not only is it a Lutheran liturgico-musical classic of the highest rank; it must be studied by Roman scholars who seek the original form of melodies used in Germany at that period. It antedates by more than thirty years the first authoritative collection of Roman melodies prepared by Guidetti. Within a compass of more than 800 pages it provides melodies to 56 Introits, 14 Hallelujahs, 31 sequences, 206 antiphons, and 47 Responsories, as well as forms of the Kyrie, Gloria, Nicene Creed, Proper Prefaces, Sanctus, Agnus, the Litany, and full provision for Matins and Vespers. The work is not as rare today as the Spangenberg item previously noted.

In 1573 Johannes Keuchenthal, pastor of the Lutheran Church at

St. Andreasberg, published his equally important Cantionale at Wittenberg. This was entitled *Kirchen Gesänge Lateinisch und Deudsch*. A
wordy introduction states that it was compiled in response to many
requests for a comprehensive collection of music suitable for Lutheran
churches. The Cantionales and agenda and other sources employed are
listed, particular mention being made of Spangenberg's *Cantiones Ecclesiasticae* which is here again specifically said to have been prepared
jussu et impulsu Lutheri. Personal examination by the author (L. D. R.)
of a rare copy of Keuchenthal's work in the library of the British
Museum, London, shows it to be a fine folio volume, excellently printed.
It contains a rich collection of musical settings for the Liturgy throughout the year, including saints' days (among which we find St. Lawrence's
Day). Following this are 212 hymns for the congregation, set to 165
melodies; the Litany (Latin and German); Psalms to be sung after the
sermon; Canticles, antiphons, et cetera, for Matins and Vespers; and a
German Passion. This book contains a larger proportion of German
material than that of either Spangenberg or Lossius (perhaps natural,
considering its later date), and in total number of pages it exceeds both
of the earlier works.

Fifteen years later (1588) Franz Eler, a teacher and cantor in
Hamburg, published his *Cantica Sacra,* a volume of 360 pages, in octavo.
This was prepared for Lutheran congregations and schools in the
Hamburg area. Here again we have the ancient melodies adapted to
the various parts of the Holy Communion, the Litany, Psalms and
Canticles for Matins and Vespers, 253 antiphons, 71 Responsories,
et cetera.

In these four major works—there were many minor ones—we have
a remarkable exhibition of the concern and the effort of Lutheran leaders
in Germany to preserve and use the historic liturgical music of the
church and to supply fresh and vital hymns in quantity for congregational
singing. No other church, not even the Roman, has anything comparable
with this in extent and quality for the same period.

LATER LUTHERAN COMPOSERS

Luther's zeal for services in the language of the people, and his
encouragement of vernacular hymnody, did not mark the limits of his
interest and constructive endeavor in this field. In his *Encomium
Musices* he wrote:

Where natural music is improved and polished by art-contrivance, there
one sees the boundless love of God who gave to man this power. Nothing
is so strange and wonderful as a simple tune, accompanied by three, four

and five other voices, which gambol about it and ornament it in many ways. I can but liken it to a heavenly roundelay.[3]

The appearance in 1524, the year of the first collection of German hymns, of a "Sacred Song-book for three, four and five voices," a work issued under Luther's direction, is proof of his appreciation of artistic choral music as well as of congregational song.

Choral music of this sort, as developed later by Lutheran composers, included figurated chorales, unaccompanied motets set to vernacular texts, and a wealth of cantatas and Passions. Bach brought the cantata and the Passion to their greatest heights in his own unique and marvelous way. But many other names, from Johann Walther, Luther's friend, to Praetorius, Eccard, Schröter, Calvisius, Ahle, and others, and thence down to Keiser, Telemann, Karl Graun, and Hille of the eighteenth century, might well be mentioned. Composers of the Rationalistic period —Friedrich Schneider, Bernhard Klein, Louis Spohr, Karl Loewe, et cetera—gave their strength to the oratorio, though in a different way from that in which Handel worked. Mendelssohn in the nineteenth century reminded the Protestant Church in Germany of Bach's great witness to the spirit of the Reformation, and himself composed five oratorios and much church music. Eckert, Reinthaler, Rheinberger, and others were influenced by him. Some, working more in the spirit of Bach, sought to combine congregational singing with the oratorio and definitely to suggest the spirit of divine worship. Such men were F. Zimmer, Meinardus, Albert Becker, Herman Francke, R. Succo, and especially Heinrich von Herzogenberg.

DEVELOPMENTS IN SWEDEN

Liturgical and musical reforms in Sweden in the sixteenth century followed closely upon developments in Germany. From notes supplied by Mrs. Fryxell we give the following sketch of works in this field.

The Swedish Mass of Olavus Petri was published in 1531. The medieval liturgical chants for the priest and the responses of the Ordinary (Kyrie, Gloria, Sanctus, Agnus Dei) were promptly adapted to Swedish texts. Two manuscript Missals for the Cathedral of Upsala, dating from 1540, are extant and have recently been published by Arthur Adell (*Musikhandskrifter från Högs och Bjuråkers kyrkor,* 1941). Later manuscript and printed service books of the sixteenth century (Orebro, Aspö, Skara, et cetera) also give Introits for Sundays and festivals and music for the Hour Services. An Antiphonal of 1581, influenced by the liturgical efforts of King John III, has music for the

---

[3] Quoted from Brian Wibberly, *Music and Religion* (London: Epworth Press, 1934), p. 114.

Hours and a Kyriale of four series, including Introit, Gradual, Offertory, and Communio for a few festival days.

The Nicene Creed in Latin and Swedish first appeared in a pamphlet printed for the cathedral church of Stockholm in 1578. In this the lines of the staff were printed and the notes added by hand. The Church Manual of 1614 gave printed notes for the Preface, Lord's Prayer, and a closing hymn. The earliest printed missals with music are Upsala, 1620, and the *Liber Cantus Wexionensis,* 1623. Both of these contain five series of musical appointments together with services for the Hours.

The Swedish Psalm Book of 1697 gives "The Swedish Mass with Music" with four series of musical settings. From this time on a change to modern tonality (major and minor) is evident. The Swedish Mass of 1799, with four-part settings of melodies and supposed to be by O. Ahlström and J. C. F. Haeffner, is definitely largely in the minor mode. Haeffner revised this for the Swedish Mass of 1817 which became basic for the nineteenth century service books of Möller, 1841; Lindberg, 1858; Törnwall, 1861; and Humbla, 1875.

The music for the Swedish Mass of 1897 is rich in material, with eleven Kyries, nine melodies for the Sanctus, ten for the Agnus, et cetera. These are from Gregorian sources, older German settings, and individual composers. This work was primarily intended for trained choirs. The Missal of 1914 by Ullman and Morén contained four complete series of appointments with many recently composed melodies. The same editors issued a Swedish Vesperal in 1915 which contained much material of art song character. A Vesperal of 1925 reverted to more traditional musical forms.

The Missal of the Church of Sweden, 1942, rests principally upon the Missal of 1897, with rhythms brought into conformity with manuscript sources of the sixteenth century and with changes in notation conforming to the traditional manner of chanting. The ancient plainsong melodies for the Preface are given. The Introits have been supplied with plainsong melodies, and also with settings based on the melodic outline of various chorales, but given free rhythm to agree with the prose text, and harmonized rather sparingly as for unison chant.

THE LUTHERAN CHURCH TODAY

We have devoted considerable space to this topic because the extent and importance of the liturgical music of the Lutheran Church in Germany during the early period of the Reformation is not appreciated by most musical historians. It was as conservative and discriminating a project as the reform of the Liturgy itself. Compared with the rich musical provisions of these Church Orders and Cantionales, Merbecke's

English *Booke of Common Praier Noted,* with its limited number of melodies in simplest ferial form, seems almost insignificant.

If to this impressive body of Lutheran church music of the sixteenth century be added the liturgical forms in the Church Orders, and the fact that there were weekly celebrations of Holy Communion, with the use of the full historic vestments and ceremonial—all of which was the normal and general use, in the cities at least, throughout the century— we must recognize that the liturgical life of our church in this classical period of our history was lived on a higher plateau than the higher-than-average levels we occasionally discover among us today.

It may be wholesome at this point—however it may shock our self-complacency—to quote again from that scholar of another communion whose high praise of Lutheran developments in the early centuries we quoted at some length earlier in this chapter. Commenting upon music in the Lutheran Church today, Brian Wibberley gives this objective and sobering judgment:

Bach was the supreme musical gift of Lutheranism to the service of religion. Great figures have appeared since his day, but lacking the same inspiration and power. It is one of the inexplicable ironies of history, however, that the Lutheranism which produced Bach failed to appreciate the message of its greatest son. The inestimable wealth of music which Bach bequeathed to the Protestant Church was so quickly and completely neglected, that for nearly a hundred years it lay unused and forgotten. And not until its rediscovery and resuscitation under S. Wesley, Mendelssohn and Franz, were its real values disclosed to the world and appraised. The Lutheran Church which had created it, and failed to recognize and foster it, paid the penalty of its deep failure, and, as by a process of stern natural law, this talent was taken from it and given to another. The music of the Lutheran Church entered upon a period of decadence and retrogression in which scarcely a reminiscence of its earlier pristine greatness and glory remains.[4]

While it is possible that these words may have been written without complete knowledge of the latest developments in Germany and Scandinavia, the simple fact is that in our understanding and in our practice we have, at many times and in many places, fallen far below the levels of four hundred years ago. We can, however, be grateful for recoveries that have brought us in recent years out of the deepest depths of the liturgical and musical poverty into which we had fallen. And we have faith to believe that the future will see the Lutheran Church, with its depth of religious conviction, and the God-given talents of its people, again making contributions in the field of church music worthy of its proudest past.

A significant work of large dimensions is now being completed in Germany. This is the *Handbuch der evangelischen Kirchenmusik,*

[4] *Ibid.,* pp. 115-116.

edited by Christhard Mahrenholz and Konrad Ameln (Göttingen: Vandenhoeck and Ruprecht). Its four volumes cover the following material: ministerial intonations (*Altargesang*), motets, choir music, the congregational hymn, organ music.

MUSIC IN THE CHURCH OF ENGLAND

In addition to developments within the Roman and the Lutheran churches, we now consider the important contributions made by musicians in the Church of England.

The Reformation broke in England nearly a generation later than in Germany and Scandinavia. Developments in the field of church music were at first limited and uneven, but later rose to importance.

The music of the Liturgy in the English Church, like the Anglican Liturgy itself, rests on pre-Reformation foundations. The first Prayer Book of Edward VI appeared in 1549. Luther had revised the text of the Mass a quarter of a century earlier and had made this the principal congregational Service. He also provided Matins and Vespers, but as supplementary services. The Church of England, on the other hand, laid far greater stress upon the Canonical Hours, which had been observed in all the monasteries of Europe for a thousand years or more. It revised these Orders, combining material from five of them to form the two Orders of Morning Prayer and Evening Prayer. Additional provisions were made for the Holy Communion as a separate or additional Service by revision of the medieval Mass, quite in line with the earlier revision by Luther on the Continent.

Archbishop Cranmer commissioned John Merbecke, Master of St. George's Chapel, Windsor, whose sympathy for the Protestant cause had nearly cost him his life in 1544, to prepare a musical edition of the new Prayer Book. This appeared in 1550 under the title *The Booke of Common Praier Noted*. It contained settings for Morning Prayer, Evensong, the Holy Communion, and the burial office, with musical notes throughout for the minister and people. Deferring to the wish of Archbishop Cranmer that not more than a single note be placed to a syllable of the text, Merbecke brought out a setting which deprived most of the ancient plainsong melodies of their former beauty. These simple forms, which do have great dignity, were intended for unisonous singing. Thomas Tallis, however, promptly harmonized them. Merbecke's book, which was the only plainsong setting of the Anglican Liturgy to appear in the sixteenth century, was gradually introduced, though the text of the Prayer Book itself was considerably changed in less than three years. In 1844, William Pickering issued a facsimile reprint of Merbecke's book, and the latter's plainsong setting was generally revived in cathedrals and parish churches in the nineteenth century.

The old polyphonic masses and Latin motets dropped out of English use more promptly than they did in the Lutheran Church in Germany. The old choral idea of worship, however, carried over, and composers at once began to write choir settings of Morning and Evening Prayer and the Holy Communion. The collection published by John Day in 1560 was the first attempt to provide choir music in vocal parts. It is regarded as marking the beginning of the English cathedral services. These new forms may in a sense be thought of as corresponding to the old polyphonic masses, though they included choral settings to the responses and Canticles of Morning and Evening Prayer, and even an occasional anthem, in addition to the responses of the Holy Communion. A complete Service includes the Venite (often omitted), Te Deum, Benedicite, Benedictus, Jubilate (Psalm 100), the Kyrie, Nicene Creed, Sanctus (often omitted), Gloria in Excelsis, the Magnificat, Cantate Domino (Psalm 98), Nunc Dimittis, Misereatur.

Like the anthem, the Service has developed from the relatively simple sixteenth century examples to modern forms rich in harmony and orchestral coloring. The sixteenth century composers—Thomas Tallis, William Byrd, Richard Farrant, et cetera—wrote their services, motets, and anthems in the purely vocal polyphonal style, and frequently in the old church modes. Orlando Gibbons was the last of these early composers, whose works have been given an interesting and critical comparison by Sir Richard Runcilman Terry in his *The Music of the Roman Rite*.

The Puritan program was a sad chapter. Though many Puritan leaders, like Milton and Cromwell, were capable musicians, church music received cruel blows from which it took England three centuries to recover. Many cathedrals were wrecked, and the destruction of all of them was contemplated. The use of the Liturgy was forbidden, and cathedral services were abolished. Parliament ordered that organs should be "utterly defaced." Choral music books, whether in Latin or in English, were sought and burned. All choir organization was disrupted, and organists, choirmasters, and singers were driven out of the churches. For sixteen years this orgy of fanaticism went on. There can be no doubt that it deserves the label which Sir Winston Churchill has attached to it in the subject heading he assigns to this period in his *History of the English Speaking Peoples*—"the Curse of Cromwell." [5]

[5] Used as a title in the *Life* magazine edition (November 19, 1956, p. 161), from a quotation in the text of the publisher's edition, Vol. II, *The New World* (New York: Dodd, Mead, 1956), p. 292.

After the Restoration in 1660, it became necessary, because of this wholesale destruction, to import music, musicians, and organ builders from abroad. What some writers call the "French invasion" began when Charles II sent Pelham Humphrey to Paris to study with Lully. Returning, Humphrey introduced French and Italian types of music, featuring solo passages and orchestral accompaniment, into England. These were further cultivated by Henry Purcell in vigorous and original fashion. Purcell developed the anthem, which may be thought of as the English counterpart of the old Latin motet. This form afterward received high development at the hands of many other English composers. Later English musicians also produced the Anglican chant, a modification of the old Gregorian. They made another notable contribution in the nineteenth century: the English hymn tune, a form generally lighter in spirit than the German chorale, and in its most elaborate examples less suitable for congregational use. All of these developments, in fact, were of a lighter and more "cheerful" character than the music of the Lutheran composers of the same period, but they never approached the superficiality and theatricalism of some of the Roman musical masses.

Purcell was England's most gifted musician, and his greatest work was probably in dramatic rather than in church composition. His anthem, "Thou knowest, Lord, the secret of our hearts," composed in 1695 for the funeral of Queen Mary, has been sung at every choral funeral in Westminster Abbey and St. Paul's Cathedral since that occasion. Other church composers of the seventeenth century were Blow and Rogers. Important in the eighteenth century were Clarke, Croft, Greene, King, and Boyce.

Davey's *History of English Music* (London: Curwen & Sons, 1895) gives the most complete account of the early English composers. H. E. Wooldridge, *The Oxford History of Music,* Vol. 2, discusses the early English school in relation to the Netherlands and Italian schools.

Handel is in a class by himself. A German by birth, he first visited England in 1710 and became a naturalized British subject in 1726. In addition to his great oratorios, seventeen in number, he composed quite a few anthems. The German invasion of which Handel was the early prominent figure dominated English music during the latter half of the eighteenth and the first part of the nineteenth centuries. Mendelssohn, Spohr, and other Romanticists made a great appeal to English taste in the early Victorian era. The list of native nineteenth century composers and organists begins with Attwood and includes many notable names, among them Crotch, Walmisley, S. S. Wesley, Goss, Smart, Barnby, Ouseley, Hopkins, MacFarren, Sullivan, Stainer, and Stanford.

Among our contemporaries we note Williamson, Davies, Vaughan Williams, Shaw, Foster, Holst, and others.

The Oxford Movement in the mid-nineteenth century exerted a powerful influence upon modern musical development in the Church of England. Merbecke's work was revived. The Plainsong and Mediaeval Music Society (founded in 1888) made important contributions in the recovery of forgotten medieval works. The polyphonic services of the sixteenth century masters were studied again. No musician comparable in quality to a Palestrina, a Bach, or even a Purcell, has appeared in England in the last hundred years, but many composers of excellent gifts have produced innumerable modern services, anthems, and hymn tunes of merit.

Professor Edward Dickinson in his *Music in the History of the Western Church* (New York: Charles Scribner's Sons, 1908), p. 356, has this to say of English church music:

There is no other country in which religious music is so highly honored. . . . The organists and choirmasters connected with the cathedrals, universities and Royal chapels are men whose character and intellectual attainments would make them ornaments in any walk of life. The deep religious reverence which enters into the substance of English society, the healthful conservatism, the courtliness of speech, the solidarity of culture which comes from inherited wealth largely devoted to learning, and the embellishment of public and private life—have all permeated ecclesiastical art and ceremony and have imparted to them an ideal dignity which is as far from superstition as it is from vulgarity.

Other Protestant communions, apart from the Lutheran and Anglican, contributed practically nothing to the development of church music except the Psalm tunes. Calvin led the way in preparing metrical Psalters, and these soon appeared in Switzerland, France, Scotland, and England. The Protestants in these lands, as in large parts of America later, became Psalm singers instead of hymn singers. Louis Bourgeois arranged many of the melodies for the early Psalters from secular sources. Other tunes developed later, particularly in Scotland and England. These Psalm tunes formed an important contribution to Protestant congregational music. But unlike the German chorale, they had little or no influence upon compositions for choir and organ.

THE AMERICAN SCENE

American church music was at first just a feeble perpetuation of European forms. The Virginians brought with them the music they had been accustomed to in the Church of England. The Swedes and the Germans in Pennsylvania brought their hymn books and sang the chorale melodies of their respective fatherlands. The church authorities in Sweden maintained a mission in America for ninety-five years (1696-1791) and sent at least twenty-four university-trained clergymen and quantities of musical literature to the Lutheran congregations at Wilmington, Philadelphia, and other points along the Delaware. We are told that "in no other group of composite Pennsylvania musical life are the records so early or so complete as to bells and their ringers, church music and organs." The clergy, "fresh every seven years from the academic centres of the homeland, brought with them a substantial contribution from the old-world musical culture. These men, bred in the School of Luther, well understood the power of music." [6]

The Moravian settlement at Bethlehem, Pennsylvania, early became a center for the cultivation of church music. Handel's *Messiah* and Graun's *Passion* were sung there in the eighteenth century, when it would have been difficult to render them in Philadelphia, and impossible in New York. A *collegium musicum,* a guild of vocalists and instrumentalists, was organized in Bethlehem, December 13, 1744. Two years later a traveler reported that he "heard very fine music in the church." By 1789 all instruments used in European orchestras of the period were to be found in Bethlehem, and Haydn's *Creation* and *The Seasons* here received their first rendition in America.

An interesting record in a manuscript diary preserved in the archives of the Moravian Church at Bethlehem states that in the year 1782 "the choir rendered some fine music at an evening service July 25th, when, quite unexpectedly and very quietly, his Excellency General Washington, arrived here accompanied by two aides-de-camp, but without escort." For this and other interesting items, see *The Bethlehem Bach Choir* (Boston: Houghton Mifflin, 1918), by Raymond Walters, dean of Swarthmore College.

The Puritans and Pilgrims in New England used metrical Psalters brought from England and Holland until they published their *Bay Psalm Book* in 1640. The earliest American composers were William Billings, Oliver Holden, and Samuel Holyoke. Later, Lowell Mason led the movement against the exclusive use of the Psalters in New England. He published many hymn tunes and conducted great choruses in the rendition of oratorios. Other nineteenth century church musicians were Arthur Foote, J. K. Paine, and Horatio Parker.

The last half-century has seen the organization of great choirs and oratorio societies. The American Guild of Organists, organized in 1896

[6] National Society of the Colonial Dames of America. Pennsylvania. Committee on historical research, *Church Music and Musical Life in Pennsylvania in the XVIII Century* (3 Vols.) (Philadelphia: Colonial Dames of America, 1926-1938), Vol. I, pp. 214, 218.

by 145 charter members (Founders), and growing by 1952 to 12,000 members in 190 chapters, the "largest single musical organization in the world," has been one of the most potent factors in fostering music of churchly dignity and artistic excellence. Its regular examinations, services, and recitals held under the auspices of state and local chapters in every part of the country have constantly maintained high standards and encouraged serious endeavor.

The Schola Cantorum was established in New York in 1908. John Frederick Wolle founded the Bach Choir at Bethlehem in 1900. The recent establishment of schools of church music at Union Theological Seminary in New York, at Princeton, New Jersey, and at Northwestern University in Evanston, Illinois, is a development of great significance. The St. Olaf College Choir is well known as having been brought to a point of excellence which challenges the best efforts of similar organizations anywhere in Europe or America, and other schools are taking up that challenge. Able organists, composers, and directors by the score are now maintaining church services at high levels and enriching the literature of modern church music by notable compositions of their own. The wonderful development of the pipe organ and of its proper music is also to be noted.

In this country, as in England, the attitude of the nonliturgical communions has been entirely revised. Instead of the indifference and opposition which characterized the liberal groups in the first few centuries after the Reformation, and indeed down into the present century, the past generation has witnessed serious and sympathetic cultivation of church music in practically all Protestant communions. At the present time deepened religious sincerity and aesthetic preference are both leading away from the sentimentality and overelaboration of the Romantics. Simpler, more austere, and more objective types of composition are coming to the fore. Organists, choirmasters, and choirs in all churches are seriously and sympathetically studying plainsong, the fine polyphonic compositions of the sixteenth and seventeenth centuries, the cantatas, chorale preludes, and chorale harmonizations of Bach, the noble works of Brahms, and the finest *a cappella* compositions of all periods. The ablest church composers of our time are also writing in strict churchly style. For all of this we can be profoundly thankful.

Chapter 11

THE CHURCH'S POINT OF VIEW

We must begin any discussion of music in the church today by considering the church's ideals. Only as we understand these can we establish standards by which to judge the music we have and the music we should have. Church architecture is something more than pleasing design, good material, and fine workmanship. It possesses qualities of appropriateness and purpose. Church music is good or bad as it approximates within its possibilities the ideals of the church in this particular field. These ideals must be as lofty and pure as those which the church upholds in every other department. Pure doctrine, pure life, pure worship must be the goal. Nothing less will do.

In view of lengthy historical evidence, we may well ask, "Does the church have a definite point of view with regard to its music? Is it possible to formulate principles?" The Greek Church and the Scotch Covenanters forbid the use of instruments. Zwingli and Calvin permitted nothing but Psalms to be sung. The Roman Church officially sanctions only plainsong, but encourages polyphonic choral music. In many places it tolerates the most florid musical masses. Luther, with a theory of church music which satisfied every dimension of depth, height, and breadth, preserved the plainsong, established the chorale, and encouraged artistic part singing. The Anglican Church has exploited the boy choir, produced a unique form of chant, emphasized choral worship, and promoted the independent use of the organ.

In America, the Puritans reduced church music to pitiful poverty. Their spiritual descendants, after experimenting with expensive soloists, quartet choirs, and secular transcriptions, are now editing elaborate contrapuntal music and establishing schools which strive to attain the very highest standards. When in addition to this we look at the confused and complicated picture of American Protestantism in general, with its many denominations, diverse backgrounds, and lack of a great

177

and unifying tradition, and when we think of the rampant individualism and the easy satisfaction of the many with the commonplace and the unworthy, we may well wonder whether the church as such may be said to have ideals with respect to its music.

There is an answer to this question, an answer based on many facets of the church's growth, for the church has progressed and is progressing. The breakdown of material and secular values is driving it to a renewed study of its own inner spiritual resources. The current revival of worship and everything pertaining to it is drawing all parts of the church closer together on broad foundations of historic churchly achievement. Prejudices are being discarded; leaders tend to recognize spiritual and artistic values wherever found; and men in all communions are studying the great music of all periods and countries seriously and sympathetically. Out of apparent confusion certain principles are emerging which are generally recognized as indicating a worthy and possible ideal. While some may stress certain features more strongly than others, most serious and well-informed students can agree on the general outlines of a theory of music which the liturgical communions may hold aloft as a true ideal.

1. Liturgical Propriety and Vitality. Music should enter the sanctuary to serve. It fulfils its ministry by creating an atmosphere of reverence, dignity, beauty, and order. It establishes a medium in which many may unite in the common expression of exalted spiritual emotion. It unifies and binds all parts of the Service together in a consistent and harmonious whole. Our theology must rule our liturgics; our liturgics must rule our music. The decline of church music in every period has begun with the neglect of the liturgical principle. Its improvement has followed liturgical advance.

All participants—minister, choir, organist, and congregation—must realize that they are co-operating in a true common Service, a common act of worship. They must be able to recognize the essential unity and purpose of each particular Service. Proper music will vitalize the great transaction, unify the group and the material of the particular Service, and aid in establishing real communion between man and God. If it be merely academic, archaeological, or formal on the one side, or merely sentimental or entertaining on the other, it will fail. When it possesses positive spiritual vitality, it will suggest and express the things of the spirit in elevated and impressive style. Objectively and impersonally it will enshrine truth in beauty, impress the Word of God upon the worshipers, and, by association and suggestion, bring holy things to remembrance and quicken spiritual desire. Subjectively it will aid the worshipers in adoration, assist them in the devout offering of their sacrifice of prayer, praise, and thanksgiving, and lead them in the celebration of the great facts of their holy faith.

Good church music will also demonstrate spiritual vitality and liturgical awareness by helping worshipers realize that they are a part of God's people of all time and that they may enjoy a conscious fellowship with the communion of saints. The unity of the local congregation with the church universal in the act of worship is made possible by the Liturgy and the church year. These have crystallized in devotional form the consensus of Christian thought as it has focused upon God's plan of salvation and his program for the Christian life. Each Service is an organic whole. It is also a part of a universal system or plan of services. The historic church has chosen themes which shall rule the character of particular services for certain days and festivals. This molding hand of the church is seen in the Lessons, Introits, Graduals, Collects, et cetera, as well as in the choice of hymns. It appears in anthem texts no less than in sermon themes. Most of the liturgical Propers are set to music. Their use secures unity and harmony within a particular Service, and makes that Service a part of a greater plan.

2. Churchly Purity. The church's ideal cannot be "music for music's sake." It must be "church music for the church's sake." Its first consideration must be churchly propriety and purity. In its best estate, church music will not be music *in* the church, but music *of* the church.

This principle involves, first of all, the union of pure text and pure music. There is absolutely no religious quality inherent in music itself. We distinguish between sacred music and secular music, but the religious values depend almost entirely upon the alliance of the music with religious texts or upon ecclesiastical associations. Even the wordless music of the organ which establishes a mood of spiritual contemplation, rests ultimately upon the Word of God and its invitations and assurances. The liturgical churches prepare the texts of their liturgies and hymnals with greatest care. The music set to these text should be truly expressive of and in perfect agreement with them, and in every respect worthy. In the choice of anthems the same high standards should be maintained. Frequently either the text or the music is inferior. Cheap, sentimental poetry may be set to fairly good music, or texts of high merit may be allied with inferior tunes, secular in form and spirit. Or both text and music may be below the level of the Liturgy and the Hymnal. Medieval abuses in these matters invited the severe condemnation of the church. The church today, too, must endeavor to eliminate the unworthy and the inferior, maintain a parity between texts and music, and see that both are worthy of a place in the Service.

One important aspect of this principle is referred to by Professor Archibald T. Davison in his *Protestant Church Music in America*. His comments on modern preaching, at least that represented by five sermons a week for twenty-five years in the chapel of Harvard University, are devastating. He points out the growing discrepancy between the theology expressed in the sermon and that found in the anthems and hymns.

> The truth is that the greatest composers of church music have been at their best when dealing with texts which represent a type of theology not now acceptable to many Protestants ... such, for example, as those which directly or indirectly deal with the salvation of the world through the death on the cross of our Lord Jesus Christ. ... Probably no less than eighty per cent of the greatest church music centres about this theme upon which incidentally, I have not heard a sermon preached in years [sic.].[1]

Churchly purity requires rejection of music of contemporary secular association and suggestion, though not necessarily that of secular origin. A number of secular melodies, considerably changed in rhythm and other details, have won a sure place among our finest hymn tunes. No one but a specialist will recall their origin. They do not suggest any secular association to the general worshiper today. Melodies, transcriptions, and arrangements from the opera, however, or from the concert repertoire or the literature of popular song, definitely offer secular suggestion which outweighs any possible spiritual values.

Drs. H. A. Köstlin, Franz Bachmann, Paul Krutschek, and other eminent scholars, along with Professors Davison, Waldo Selden Pratt, and others in this country agree generally on this point. They tell us that church music to be authentic must differ in style and in substance from music of the world. Its integrity and its power, like that of worship itself, derive chiefly from the fact that it is different from the accustomed idiom of our daily experience. Important in service music are a super-worldly quality, a spiritual concentration, and an evident purpose not to display itself but to aid devotion. Such music builds its thematic and harmonic structure upon lines traditionally associated with the faith and life of the church. This categorization is definite and clear enough to have developed a generally recognized church style.

The crudest violation of this principle is found in organ transcriptions and choral arrangements from operas, in adaptation of secular songs for solos, choruses, hymn tunes, et cetera. But the use of strong rhythms and dissonances, or of other dynamic or sentimental effects is quite as bad. Judged by these standards, postludes in march-time, anthems with

---

[1] Davison, *Protestant Church Music in America* (Boston: E. C. Schirmer Music Company, 1933), p. 61. Copyright, 1933, by E. C. Schirmer Music Company.

syncopated choruses or crashing discords, and solos of sentimental texture are poor indeed. The fact that they may have been composed for church use does not alter the case.

We may well turn from the study of these types to serious pursual of plainsong, the chorale, the polyphonic compositions of such masters of churchly style as Palestrina, Byrd, Hassler, Praetorius, or Bach, or to modern works by men thoroughly imbued with churchly and spiritual feeling. And in its program of religious education Protestantism might well assert its independence of the cheap choir journals, trashy hymnals, and sentimental festival pamphlets. We shall reap precisely what we sow. We cannot expect proper churchly attitudes toward music on the part of our people if we do not let them come into contact with the best.

3. Congregational and Choral But Not Concertistic. Music that is not good Service music is an intruder in public worship, no matter how beautiful it may be in itself. The Liturgy is more than a psychological program, and liturgical music is more than a pleasing concourse of sweet sounds. Service music may have congregational emphasis with choral participation, as in the normal Lutheran Service; or it may have choral emphasis with congregational participation, as in the normal Anglican Service. But concertistic character it must not have. Violations of this canon are found in all too many places. Organ transcriptions which bring the literature of the orchestra into the sanctuary, florid musical masses composed in operatic style and sung dramatically, quartet choirs with ostentatious display of individual vocal powers, and excessive solo performances of whatever character—all are out of order in the church. And it is significant that Brahms, while he composed such beautiful music for solo voices, yet wrote all of his sacred music in parts for choruses.

4. Melodic But Not Strongly Rhythmic. Rhythm is probably the most obvious trait of secularism in music. The development in the sixteenth century of the folk dance and the folk song, and of instrumental music in general, heightened the use of strong rhythm in secular music and brought it, somewhat subdued, into church use as well. Church music may employ rhythmic patterns in the melody and inner structure if they are not obtrusive, but a strong regular pulse and repeated syncopation must be avoided. Henry Purcell's funeral anthem, "Thou knowest, Lord, the secrets of our hearts," has great dignity and spiritual eloquence because of the absence of strong rhythm. On the other hand, his anthem, "Rejoice in the Lord alway," has a bass solo which obscures the sense of the text to bring out a strong rhythm in the melody. This is illustrated, with other examples of secularizing rhythm in anthems by Mendelssohn, Horatio Parker, Oley Speaks, Stainer, et cetera, in Davison's *Protestant Church Music in America,* pp. 95-112.

Melody, of course, is essential, and much depends upon its having quality and character. Sensuous, sentimental, florid, or frivolous melodies have no place in the church Service. Melodic forms must be characterized by dignity and spiritual nobility, whether in the simple inflections of a Psalm tone and other chants, or in the elaborate developments of polyphonic composition. Plainsong and the chorale both developed as pure melody. These two sources supply the richest material for melodic suggestion free from secular association and relatively independent of rhythmic scaffolding. The older polyphony built up a wealth of melodic material largely because it gave equal prominence and value to each voice or part. The more elaborate unaccompanied contrapuntal music also was essentially impersonal and undramatic, maintaining melodic interest in all voices, though frequently shifting emphasis.

When this music became so complex and difficult as to make the text practically unintelligible, composers introduced the "familiar style," which was characterized by simple harmony which did not destroy part equality and which was without pronounced rhythm. Palestrina's "Adoramus Te," Praetorius' "Lo, how a rose," and Hassler's "O sing unto the Lord" illustrate this type, with simple harmonic structure and sustained melodic interest in all parts. The development of secular forms, especially the opera with its expansion of vocal technique, and instrumental music in general, heightened the melodic effect of one part, generally the upper voice, and deprived the other parts of melodic interest. Its main fault was that it called attention to itself. Good pure melody which exalts the Word and not itself is church music's most glorious possession.

5. Often Strongly Modal in Character. Practically all music before the sixteenth century was composed in the old church modes and not in our modern major and minor scales. These modes or scales differed from each other by reason of varied arrangements of intervals (whole or half) between the notes. There were eight modes in general use in the later Middle Ages, and the variety of expression and color they afforded was far greater than is possible with our two modern scales. Even after secular music abandoned the ancient modes, church music generally continued to be written in them, or at least in forms distinctly reminiscent of them. Much ultramodern music, too, in the effort to gain wider expressiveness, has abandoned our modern scales and employs some of the old modes again, as well as inventing new scales of its own. But generally speaking, the scales in which plainsong, much polyphonic music, and many of the chorales were constructed are known as the "old church modes" because of this historic association and a certain grave dignity and unusual character. The church today even in its modern compositions may well seek to recapture and restate some of the values traditionally associated with the old system. The universal craving for harmony must be satisfied, but the more frequent use of modal scales, in both melody and harmony, will give distinctive color and value.

We recognize the power of historic association in other fields, and the principle here is the same. In our private reading of Scripture we may use the latest translations to secure accurate meanings, but in the formal church service we prefer the King James Version with its quaint and even obscure expressions. The experience of many years has confirmed an opinion expressed by the author as long ago as 1901:

It is impossible to comprehend the contrapuntal scores of the great masters of the Polyphonic School except upon the basis of an intelligent grasp of the melodic, modal and rhythmic characteristics of the Gregorian Chant. It is equally impossible for any composer ignorant of these same characteristics to hope to produce anything in the larger forms of Church Music that will have the solidity, beauty, churchly feeling and artistic merit to guarantee it existence beyond his own lifetime.[2]

6. *Largely Vocal.* The great bulk of church music, historically considered, is vocal. Plainsong developed without thought of instruments, and in our use of it today organ accompaniment should be kept quite subordinate. The congregational chorale was originally accompanied by the choir; and even now the organ accompaniment should support and bring out the melody and not suppress it. The older polyphonic compositions for the choir—of whose extent and value we have said many musicians today are learning—were entirely vocal. Emil Nauman says that "the great works of the great masters of sacred music . . . would never have been called into existence had their authors been limited to an organ accompaniment."

More important than considerations of history are the qualities of purity and distinctiveness which characterize good vocal music. The organ and the orchestra produce mechanical effects. Vocal music of quality has a tonal purity that is unique. Even Richard Wagner, who appreciated and developed the modern orchestra in connection with his great musical dramas, said, "The human voice is the immediate organ for delivering the sacred text. . . . If church music is ever to be restored to its original purity, vocal music must oust the instrumental and occupy the place this has usurped."

[2] Harry G. Archer and Luther D. Reed, *Choral Service Book* (Philadelphia: General Council Board of Publication, 1901).

7. Artistic Excellence. The church strives to establish the essential unity of the true and the beautiful in worship. It welcomes art in the service of religion. Much modern art has renounced beauty. It seeks rather to express dynamically a sordid realism and emotionalism. The church upholds a spiritual idealism which, while not unrealistic, recognizes eternal qualities and harmonious facts of the divine.

Music in the service of the church must satisfy the canons of beauty as well as of liturgical propriety and churchly purity. More is required than sincerity and devotion. There must be technical training adequate for artistic execution, and excellence in tone and interpretation.

Church music is not an emasculated or imperfect form of art. It has its own proper canons and standards, but it is true art and must be cultivated as such. In church art, as in secular art, the artist expresses his own individuality and his own gifts. These, however, must be brought into harmony with the mind of the church, whose message the individual proclaims. Individuality will not be destroyed, but individualism will be restrained by a personal conviction and consecration which will recognize the essential purpose of worship. Great ideas ultimately find great expression in art in conventional and universal forms. Thus we have the Greek temple, the Gothic cathedral, the symphony, and the Christian Liturgy. In church music, as in all art forms of the church, we recognize and respect conventions imposed by the faith and the devotional requirements of the Christian community. These conventions become an important part of the church's distinctive atmosphere and life. Within their limits, every effort must be made to attain artistic excellence.

Local conditions may limit our technical attainments. Yet simplicity is, after all, of the very essence of good art. However simple, the music of the church can be pure and beautiful. If well rendered, it will be artistically and spiritually satisfying. The difficulty with much church music, from the artistic point of view, is not its simplicity but its cheap, commonplace, and often frivolous character. Tawdry music cannot qualify for the church service simply because it has been set to a sacred text. It must, first and foremost, be good music.

8. A Balanced Program from Both Ancient and Modern Sources. We should give particular attention in the selection of music to the permanent musical achievements of the universal church. Especially should we keep in mind the history of our own communion and the contributions which it has made to musical literature. We quite naturally expect to find Roman forms and compositions featured in Roman churches, Lutheran forms and the work of Lutheran composers in Lutheran

184

churches, and Anglican forms and composers represented in Episcopal churches. The universality of music as an art and the essential unity of fundamental Christian belief, however, require that ecclesiastical boundaries should not be too rigidly observed. Palestrina, Bach, and Purcell have a universal message, just as the best hymnals include hymns by representatives of all communions. The great music of the church, no matter by whom composed, may well be used in all parts of the church. This is the music which should be studied first of all, mastered, and presented in our services today.

In addition to knowing the classics and reproducing the great music of the past, we should recognize and promote creative effort. We have the classics because in every age the church has encouraged the composition of works of spiritual beauty for the glory of God, the honor of the Christian faith, and the edification of believers. In our own time it should foster the development of individual and collective musical talents among its people and in its communities. We may adapt and use much of the past, but the music of the church must be enriched by new compositions growing out of the life of our own day and land and thus expresssing our distinctive liturgical, national, and linguistic culture. This cannot be forced. We have as yet few able composers in our midst. Much of our effort must be devoted to mastery of the great music of the past and its adequate presentation. But life requires growth, development, and self-expression. We must recognize this principle, only insisting that the music of today and tomorrow which aspires to service in the sanctuary shall breathe the spirit of the gospel and respect the traditions of the church.

Practical and comprehensive methods must be found for the cultivation and development of such a program. The chief factors will be the authority of the church itself and the labors of individual pastors, organists, and choirmasters striving to co-ordinate their work and to approximate the church's ideals.

The church must as truly seek to realize its ideals in music as it does in theology and ethics. It should provide systematic instruction in seminaries, colleges, and schools under its control. The lack of attention given historical and practical aspects of church music in most theological seminaries is deplorable. The church should also seek to uphold proper standards by conferences, convocations, summer schools, and similar efforts, and by striving to have synodical and other official services of worship truly be representative of the church's ideal. It cannot expect its sons to be taught by the world how to conduct church services, or what music to use. Like any other family, it must teach its own children the elements of refinement and culture and family history and traditions.

185

As things stand, the church is quite generally at the mercy of secular composers, mercenary publishers, and unqualified organists and choirmasters. Its most obvious and pressing need is a first-class school of church music for the training of church musicians—one adequately staffed and operating in close connection with one or another of its seminaries.

In this connection we pay tribute to the organists and choirmasters who have long upheld high ideals, and pleaded their cause consistently. The church is more deeply indebted than it realizes to its architects and musicians who, often with little understanding or encouragement from the church itself, have lifted the general standards of appreciation and practice immeasurably within the present century. We have finer church buildings and better church music than our fathers had, largely because of the earnest endeavors of these artists and churchmen.

What could be finer than this "Declaration of the Religious Principles of the American Guild of Organists," as printed in every yearbook of the Guild:

For the greater glory of God, and for the good of His Holy Church in this land, we, being severally members of the American Guild of Organists, do declare our mind and intention in the things following:

We believe that the Office of Music in Christian Worship is a Sacred Obligation before the Most High.

We believe that they who are set as Choir Masters and as Organists in the House of God ought themselves to be persons of devout conduct, teaching the ways of earnestness to the Choirs committed to their charge.

We believe that the unity of purpose and fellowship of life between Ministers and Choirs should be everywhere established and maintained.

We believe that at all times and at all places it is meet, right, and our bounden duty to work and to pray for the advancement of Christian worship in the holy gifts of strength and nobleness; to the end that the Church may be purged of her blemishes, that the minds of men may be instructed, that the honor of God's House may be guarded in our time, and in the times to come.

Wherefore we do give ourselves with reverence and humility to these endeavors, offering up our works and our persons in the Name of Him, without Whom nothing is strong, nothing is holy. Amen.

Thus individual pastors, organists, and choirmasters should work together as churchmen and strive to realize the church's ideals in the music of the Liturgy, the hymn, the choir, and the organ.

Chapter 12

MUSIC OF THE LITURGY

Modern German and Scandinavian liturgies are provided with musical settings of traditional character. There is no lack of capable composers in these countries who might produce modern settings of merit. The regard of the church for the ancient tonal forms, however, has preserved the historic melodies and provided proper harmonizations. The modern liturgies of Saxony, Bavaria, Hanover, Mecklenberg, and Sweden are fully provided with this historic material, as is the new (1955) *Agende für Evangelisch-Lutherische Kirchen und Gemeinden* (Berlin: Lutherisches Verlagshaus).

In America, as elsewhere, the influence of language is potent. Experience has demonstrated that in the text of the Liturgy, and of the Scriptures themselves, it is best to use the forms established centuries ago and recognized as classic throughout the English-speaking world. Similarly, in the music of the church—both for the Liturgy and the hymns—chants and melodies long associated with English texts are most readily learned and most heartily sung by congregations. The new *Service Book* provides three complete musical settings to the Liturgy proper.

Further comment on the three settings in the *Service Book* may be of interest. Identification of composers of chants and other items may be helpful. We should have some acquaintance with the distinguished musicians who have bequeathed beautiful and worshipful forms to the church, whose music we constantly sing, but of whom, perhaps, we know little.

THE FIRST OR ANGLICAN SETTING

This setting is called Anglican, though it is really mixed. It contains plainsong numbers (Versicles, Pax, Preface melodies, Agnus Dei, et cetera) and four-part original compositions (Healey Willan Sanctus) as well as chorale-like numbers (Freylinghausen Offertory, Bach Sanc-

187

tus, et cetera). All other numbers, however, are English and American chants with reciting notes and inflections. It should be noted, however, that the first part of the Service may be sung completely to Anglican chants and the Office of Holy Communion to plainsong, or adaptations of plainsong.

This setting has been prepared for the Commission by Harold Wells Gilbert, organist and choirmaster of St. Peter's Episcopal Church, Philadelphia, and headmaster of its famous Choir School since 1919. Born in Philadelphia in 1893, Dr. Gilbert studied piano with Constantin von Sternberg, organ with Charles M. Courboin, and theory with Hugh A. Clarke, receiving his Bachelor of Music degree from the University of Pennsylvania in 1917. He later studied church music and choir training with Sir Charles MacPherson of St. Paul's Cathedral and with Sir Sydney H. Nicholson of the School of English Church Music, London, England. His studies with the latter led to his later advocacy of speech-rhythm chanting. His study of plainsong was with J. H. Arnold, also of London. He served in France with the U.S. Army (52d Pioneer Infantry) 1918-19. Dr. Gilbert's entire professional career has been spent in Philadelphia. He has been musical director of the Mendelssohn Club since 1939 and at different times has been head of the Music Department of the Philadelphia Divinity School (Episcopal) and of the Overbrook School for the Blind, conductor of the Fortnightly Club, music editor of *Church News,* author of many articles, and member of the Joint Commission on Revision of the Episcopal Hymnal, 1940. His alma mater conferred the degree Doctor of Music upon him in 1958.

The Setting in Detail

INVOCATION. A simple monotone.

VERSICLES. Plainsong versicle form, with drop of a minor third and final monosyllable half a tone lower than the reciting note. This is the traditional English cathedral use.

INTROIT. The Gloria Patri is set to a chant by Henry Thomas Smart (1813-1879), organist of several parish churches in London, designer of important organs in England, Scotland, and Ireland, and musical editor of the Presbyterian Hymnal, 1876, and of the earlier *Chorale Book,* 1856, a work which set standards for all later hymn tune harmonizations. He was blind for the last fifteen years of his life, but composed many services, anthems, and organ works. The Hymnal contains ten of his tunes.

The alternate Gloria Patri is by Harold W. Gilbert, musical editor of the Anglican setting.

KYRIE. The first four responses have a haunting melody by Arnold Richardson, arranged by Harold W. Gilbert. The four-part harmonies provide a fine choral effect. The Amen is a long descending phrase which seems a perfect conclusion to the petitions as a whole.

A simpler response and Amen are in the key of C minor.

GLORIA IN EXCELSIS. The final note of the minister's intonation lifts the word "high" a full tone above the reciting note. The Canticle itself is set, first of all, to the Old Scottish Chant, whose origin is unknown though it is in general use throughout the English-speaking world. It appears to be an adaptation of an earlier plainchant form with modern harmonies and tonality.

The alternate setting is an unusual and arresting number by Dr. Leo Sowerby (1895-   ), distinguished American organist, composer, and teacher, at present serving St. James' Episcopal Cathedral, Chicago, and member of commission which prepared the Episcopal Hymnal, 1940. Enlisting in the U.S. Army during the First World War, Dr. Sowerby served as bandmaster. He later became a professor of theory and composition in the American Conservatory of Music, Chicago. His compositions include symphonies for orchestra, concertos, sonatas, and distinguished organ pieces and choral works, the latter gaining him a Pulitzer award.

The chant is in free form with unusual intervals in the melody and startling harmonies in the accompaniment. The threefold character of the Canticle is carefully observed. The chant as a whole, though unconventional, is deserving of study and use.

SALUTATION AND RESPONSE. The traditional inflection of a minor third.

ALLELUIA. The triple Alleluia is by William Henry Monk (1823-89), musical editor of *Hymns Ancient and Modern,* to the first edition of which he contributed more than fifty tunes. He was organist in several London churches and professor of music in King's College and two other London institutions. He edited the *Parish Choir,* a hymnal, and a Psalter for the Scottish Church and several other hymnals, in addition to composing many anthems. He is represented in the *Hymnal* by nine tunes.

The terse form of the Alleluia gives the feeling of a musical shout which steps up to a fine climax.

RESPONSES AT THE GOSPEL. Traditional form, the recitation dropping half a tone on the final syllable of the text.

OFFERTORY. The first chant is by William Crotch (1775-1847), first principal of the Royal Academy of Music established in 1822.

The downward scale-like progression of the first half of the chant is arrested and lifted to a confident conclusion in the second half.

The second chant is by John Alcock (1715-1806), organist of Litch-field Cathedral. It is a flowing melody effectively harmonized in contrary motion.

The first chorale-like setting of "Create in me a clean heart, O God" is an unusual but beautiful harmonization by Harold Gilbert of a melody by Freylinghausen (1670-1739), poet and hymn writer of the Pietistic era in Germany. This melody was first set to English text by Harriet Reynolds Krauth (1845-1925) in her *Church Book with Music,* 1869. Dr. Gilbert's harmonization has abandoned the simple chorale-like form usually associated with this number. The congregation is expected to carry the well-known melody while the choir, supported softly by the organ, sings an independent accompaniment which, with its interesting suspensions, is chorally effective.

(BENEDICTION.) See p. 191.

(AMEN.) See p. 192.

THE PREFACE. This melody, with its simple inflections for the Proper Prefaces, and consisting of only four notes, is one of the most ancient, most beautiful, and most widely known forms in the entire treasury of church music. Its origin is unknown, but it unquestionably dates from the early Christian centuries. It is given, in slightly variant forms, in practically all the Lutheran Cantionales and Church Orders of the sixteenth century. The critical studies of Palestrina and Guidetti established the authentic form universally accepted ever since. Mozart was so impressed by its beauty that he declared that it surpassed any of his own creations. All modern German and Scandinavian service books give it, as do all Anglican authorities. It was first recovered and introduced to American Lutheran churches by Archer and Reed in their *Choral Service Book* of 1901.

SANCTUS. The first setting is an arrangement of the well-known chorale-like form commonly "ascribed to J. S. Bach" and found in Steinau, 1726, and in practically every other German Lutheran service book since that time, and in all Swedish missals from 1623 to 1942. The melody is of plainsong origin, being a simplification of the eleventh century Latin *Sanctus minus summum* for Sundays in Advent and Lent found in Spangenberg, Keuchenthal, and other Lutheran Cantionales of the sixteenth century. It is barely possible that Luther knew this melody and used it, much simplified, for his clumsy metrical translation of the Sanctus in his German Mass.

The popularity of this melody among the German people probably led Bach to treat it as a chorale and surround it with rich four-part harmonies (Bach Gesellschaft edition, Vol. 59, p. 212). Regina H. Fryxell adapted the melody to the English text as it appears in the first and second settings of the Service. Thus we trace an illustrious line of descent from ancient plainsong, through Luther and Bach, to our own *Service Book*.

The second setting is an impressively beautiful original composition by Healey Willan (1880-), distinguished Canadian church musician, organist, composer, and chairman of the department of theory at the Conservatory of Music, Toronto, later professor at the University of Toronto. He was organist of the Church of St. Mary Magdalene, Toronto, for more than forty years. The melody of his setting moves in stately, free rhythmic form to a conclusion which retains its feeling of solemnity and reverence to the end.

THE LORD'S PRAYER. The melody set to the doxology as a congregational response derives from the earliest musical tradition of the church. It is thought to have its origin in even earlier Jewish worship. It was anciently used for the Gloria in Excelsis and the Te Deum as well as for the Lord's Prayer. It is found in the Mozarabic Missal of fifteenth century Spain. Merbecke employed it in England in his Prayer Book of 1550. It was given in variant forms in many Lutheran Church Orders. The "Amen," with its characteristic rise of a whole step, is the solemn form traditionally associated with the conclusion of the Lord's Prayer in the Communion Office.

THE PAX. The traditional plainsong form found in the Erfurt *Kirchenampt,* 1528, and other early Church Orders, as well as in the Swedish use.

AGNUS DEI. This beautiful melody is clearly derived from one of the Gregorian Psalm Tones. It was first set to the unique German translation (insertion of the word "Christ") in the Brunswick Church Order of 1528. Regina Fryxell has harmonized it in free rhythm. The harmony records the change from church modes to major and minor tonalities.

The alternate setting is a haunting plainsong melody of the thirteenth century as given in the Swedish Mass of 1942. Mrs. Fryxell has adapted it in a warm and sensitive manner which makes this ancient item very acceptable to modern ears.

NUNC DIMITTIS. The Anglican chant appointed for this is by George J. Elvey (1816-93), organist of St. George's Chapel, Windsor, for nearly fifty years. He contributed tunes to *Hymns Ancient and Modern,* five of which are in the *Hymnal.*

BENEDICTION. The Salutation and the Benedicamus have traditional Versicle forms which lead to the simple but strong inflection of the

Benediction and the Amen. The Old Testament text is set to monotone; the New Testament conclusion has a simple inflection traditionally associated with choral reading.

AMEN. In addition to several simple, traditional forms there is an elaborate triple Amen which concludes the Service in a reverent but triumphant mood. This is by Thomas Tertius Noble (1867-1953), organist and choirmaster at Ely and York cathedrals, England, and later, and for thirty years, at St. Thomas' Church, New York. While at York he founded a symphony orchestra, directed the York Music Society, and revived the York Music Festival. At St. Thomas' he organized a choir school and developed a famous boy choir. He composed many services, anthems, et cetera.

MATINS

VERSICLES AND GLORIA PATRI. Merbecke's simple inflections (tenor part) were set in four-part harmonies by Thomas Tallis (d. 1585), frequently called the "father of English church music." He lived in difficult times, and so discreetly as to suffer no persecution from either Catholic or Protestant queens of his time. He and his associate William Byrd enjoyed a monopoly on all music printing in England. Together they published many original Latin motets. His *Spem in alium* in forty parts has always been regarded as a masterpiece. He contributed nine four-part tunes (melody in the tenor) to Archbishop Parker's *Psalter* of 1568. After the Reformation he endeavored to compose for the English services, but his sympathies were clearly with the old order.

INVITATORY. A traditional congregational response.

VENITE EXULTEMUS. The first chant is by William Henry Walter (1825-93), an American musician born in Newark, New Jersey. He was organist of Episcopal churches and of Columbia University in New York City. He composed services and anthems and edited hymnals and Psalters. His tune, *Festal Song,* is in the *Hymnal.*

The second chant is by William Savage. The third chant is by William Russell (1777-1813), organist of the Foundlings' Hospital, London, and for several years composer to the Sadler's Wells Ballet Company. His compositions for the church include choral works, Psalms, hymns, and anthems.

GLORIA PATRI. The first chant is by Henry Smart (see p. 228). The second chant is by George Alexander MacFarren (1813-87), son of an English dramatist, principal of the Royal Academy of Music, professor of music at Cambridge, composer of cantatas, oratorios, and many services and chants for the church. Poor eyesight terminated in total blindness, but his creative work and inspiring instruction continued unabated under severe handicaps. He was knighted in 1863.

The third chant is by Harold W. Gilbert, editor of the First Setting (see p. 188).

TE DEUM. The two fine settings of the Te Deum, both of which carefully observe the triple form of the text, are by Sydney Hugo Nicholson (1875-1947) who, together with Vaughan Williams, exerted a powerful influence upon modern English hymnody—Williams chiefly through the *English Hymnal* and *Songs of Praise,* and Nicholson chiefly through *Hymns Ancient and Modern,* for the later editions of which he was musical editor. Educated at Oxford, he was successively organist of Carlisle and Manchester cathedrals and Westminster Abbey. In 1927 he founded the St. Nicholas College of English Church Music, later incorporated under royal charter and located in Canterbury as the Royal School of Church Music. He was knighted in 1938 for distinguished service to English church music.

Dr. Nicholson resigned as organist of Westminster Abbey to give time and effort to the promotion of the speech-rhythm method of chanting which Harold W. Gilbert, a pupil of Dr. Nicholson's, has employed in his pointing of chants in the First Setting of the *Service Book*. This system is now generally recognized in Europe and America as somewhat more difficult to master than earlier systems, but certainly as the best yet devised. Dr. Nicholson's anthems and services were of high order, and his books, *A Manual of English Church Music* and *Quires and Places Where They Sing,* exerted a wide influence. Speech-rhythm chanting is discussed in Chapter 23, "Chanting," pp. 353-363.

BENEDICTUS. Two free-moving double chants are appointed for the Benedictus. The first is by James Turle (1802-82), who was born in Taunton, Somerset, England. He was organist and choirmaster of Westminster Abbey, and a noted teacher, composer, and choral conductor. He edited and composed many services, anthems, and chants. The second chant is by H. Skeats.

KYRIE. The melody is from John Merbecke's (Marbeck) setting in the *Booke of Common Praier Noted* of 1550. Merbecke's dates are approximately 1510-85. He was organist at St. George's, Windsor, and in 1544 was imprisoned and condemned to death for heresy. His life was spared by the personal intervention of Bishop Gardiner of Winchester. He later published several anti-Catholic books. He composed several Latin masses and motets. Archbishop Cranmer commissioned him to set the English text of the *Book of Common Prayer* to plainsong, instructing him not to give more than one note to a syllable of the text. In spite of this severe limitation Merbecke successfully met the problem of chanting an accented language to melodies associated with the quantitative Latin. His work is standard throughout the Anglican communion everywhere today.

VESPERS

VERSICLES. See pp. 192, 355.

GLORIA PATRI. The first chant is by Samuel Arnold (1740-1802), graduated at the University of Oxford with the degree of Doctor of Music. He was the organist of the Chapel Royal, and later of Westminster Abbey. At the request of King George III he edited the works of Handel in thirty-six volumes. In addition to much church music he composed a number of successful operas. The second chant is by Vincent Novello (1781-1861) who was organist of the Portuguese Embassy Chapel, conductor of the Philharmonic Society, examiner of musical manuscripts at Cambridge, and founder of the great publication house which bears his name. He edited a four-volume collection of hymns. The chant to be used during Lent is by H. W. Gilbert (see p. 188).

MAGNIFICAT. The first chant is by Samuel Sebastian Wesley (1810-76), grandson of Charles Wesley the hymn writer and grandnephew of John Wesley the founder of Methodism. He was named after his father and the great Johann Sebastian Bach, whose music his father, a distinguished organist, helped introduce into England. S. S. Wesley was organist successively of Hereford, Exeter, Winchester, and Gloucester cathedrals and a leader in the reform of English cathedral music. He was the outstanding English organist of his day and is generally regarded as the greatest church musician between Purcell and Stanford. Most of his fine hymn tunes were composed while at Winchester. One hundred and thirty of them were included in his *European Psalmist,* 1872. The *Hymnal* contains eight of his tunes.

The second chant is by Stephen Elvey (1805-60), elder brother of the better-known Sir George Job Elvey. Stephen Elvey was born in Canterbury, was a chorister of the cathedral and later was organist of New College, Oxford. He composed many services and chants. As the result of a gun accident he lost a leg, but continued to astonish his associates by his ability to play the pedal organ with the aid of a wooden substitute.

NUNC DIMITTIS. Sir John Goss (1800-80), son of an organist, was a chorister of the Chapel Royal and a pupil of Attwood, whom he succeeded as organist of St. Paul's Cathedral. He was professor of harmony in the Royal Academy of Music for forty-seven years. Many of his compositions are prefixed by the initials INDA, an abbreviation of *In Nomine Domini, Amen.* He has been ranked as "second to S. S.

Wesley among nineteenth century church musicians." He composed fifty anthems, edited Psalters and a collection of *Chants, Ancient and Modern.* He was knighted by Queen Victoria.

Charles Hylton Stewart (1884-1932) was organist at Rochester and Chester cathedrals and at St. George's, Windsor. He composed several services, anthems, and chants.

THE SECOND OR CONTINENTAL SETTING

The Second Setting represents a different liturgical and musical tradition. On the Continent at the time of the Reformation and to the present day, Lutheran musicians everywhere sought to retain the form and flavor of the ancient plainsong, with its modal character and churchly associations, in their adaptations and original compositions for the text of the Liturgy. The strong influence of the chorale was increasingly felt in such matters as measured rhythm, harmonizations, et cetera. Interest centered primarily upon the Service, including the Holy Communion, and only secondarily upon Matins and Vespers. Great importance was given the sermon, and a new and vital element was introduced in the form of the congregational chorale. The chorale, particularly, adapting much from the ancient plainsong as well as from the religious folk song, and adding many fresh and original melodies of its own, became a popular and powerful feature of Lutheran worship in Germany and Scandinavia. Hundreds of hymn texts were set to these melodies, and texts of the Liturgy (Gloria in Excelsis, Sanctus, et cetera) were paraphrased in meter and sung like chorales, quite as the Calvinists dealt with the Psalter. In fact, in the poorest periods and places, the Liturgy practically became part of the Hymnal, instead of the Hymnal being part of the Liturgy. With less and less attention paid to Matins and Vespers, the chanting of the Psalms, and in fact the use of chant forms anywhere, these gradually disappeared before the ever-growing power and popular appeal of the chorale. The latter, as a body of congregational song, was much more deeply rooted in the traditional plainsong than was the later English hymn tune, which owed more to the Calvinistic Psalm tune than to plainsong.

In summary we may say that Lutheran liturgical music on the continent of Europe from the beginning to the present has been characterized by melodic forms sometimes modal in character, sometimes not, but always possessing special dignity and a certain majestic character. Its forms combine plainsong and chorale features, and scarcely a trace remains of the ancient chant form as such, with its reciting notes, mediations, and cadences, so characteristic of Gregorian Psalm Tones and of the later Anglican chant. These facts of history have suggested the name "Continental" as attached to the Second Setting in the *Service Book*.

The music of the second setting was prepared for the Commission by Regina Holmen (Mrs. F. M.) Fryxell, who is a graduate of Augustana College, Rock Island, Illinois, and of the Juilliard School of Music in New York City. She later continued the study of composition with Leo Sowerby in Chicago. She has taught organ and piano, given recitals, and been church organist in various parts of the country, including New York City, Washington, D. C., Berkeley, California, Moline and Rock Island, Illinois, and Davenport, Iowa. Her compositions include both choral and instrumental works. European travel gave her an opportunity to study the status of church music in England, France, Denmark, Sweden, and Norway.

Mrs. Fryxell has kindly placed at our disposal extended notes of her studies in connection with the preparation of this setting, and from these notes much of the following comment has been derived.

The preparation of this setting involved the problem of selecting items from the mass of materials in the many national and linguistic Lutheran backgrounds, and of adapting these melodies from whatever source to English texts. Agreement of verbal and musical accents was important. Attention had to be given to rhythmic groupings and the varying dynamics of underlying harmonies, all in the interest of clear exposition of the meaning of the text itself. Study of recent work in the service books of other communions and of trends in editorial practice led to the elimination of bar lines, the omission of time signatures, and the return to the simplicity of unisonal singing by phrases, that is, by thoughts instead of by beats.

The Setting in Detail

INVOCATION. A simple monotone set a whole tone lower than the Invocation in First Setting.

VERSICLES. The same form as the First Setting, but in the key of F instead of G.

KYRIE. The first chant is adapted from the tenth century plainsong Mass, *Orbis Factor,* which is given in full in the Third Setting. The responses of the congregation are based upon a form of melody in the Missal of the Church of Sweden, 1942. This melody is found in all Swedish missals. The chant for the minister is framed out of material in the Responses, and is designed with these to form a complete musical dialogue. The same is true of the Kyrie for Lent, from the Swedish Missal, 1942, where the source is given as Bohemian Brethren, 1544. This melody was also given in the Swedish Mass, 1897. The opening notes are a characteristic plainsong fragment found also in Kyries, Glorias, Agnus Deis, and Sanctuses of masses (II, VIII, XV) from the eleventh to the fourteenth centuries. The notes of the second phrase may be a simplified *Christe* from the Kyrie of Mass XIII.

GLORIA IN EXCELSIS. The original source of this melody is the tenth century Easter Gloria in the Mass *Lux et origo*. The present form is based in large part on the Decius chorale, "Allein Gott in der Höh' sei Ehr," of 1539. Nikolaus Decius made a German hymn out of the Latin Gloria. A chorale melody was provided for it by condensing certain key phrases of the well-known plainsong melody for the Gloria. This hymn with its chorale melody came into the Swedish Psalm Book in 1697. For the Gloria in the Second Setting the melody of the well-known chorale was expanded to fit the English prose text. This was accomplished with the use of only one additional characteristic figure culled from the original plainsong and fitted to approximately the same burden of syllables.

ALLELUIA. The first Alleluia is from the Prussian Church Order, 1525, the Swedish Mass, 1897, and the Swedish Missal, 1942. There is a related Agnus Dei in Mass IX of the tenth century. The second is adapted from fragments of the Sanctus in the eleventh century Mass, *De angelis*. A similar Alleluia melody is found in the *English Gradual*.

OFFERTORY. The first offertory, "The sacrifices of God," is adapted from a Swedish Litany in the Phrygian Mode, as given in the Swedish Missal of 1942, a revision of that in the Swedish Mass, 1897.

The third offertory, "Create in me a clean heart, O God," is adapted from a melody by J. G. Winer (1583-1651) in Gotha Cantionale, 1648.

THE PREFACE. The melodies are the same as those in the First Setting.

SANCTUS. From the tenth century Mass, *Dominator Deus*, for Simple Feasts. In early Swedish manuscript missals and later printed missals. Greatly simplified by Haeffner, 1817. Adapted from Church of Sweden, 1942.

AGNUS DEI. The first chant is adapted in free rhythm from the Brunswick Church Order, 1528. Origin uncertain but undoubtedly from plainsong sources.

The source of the second is a thirteenth century Mass for Sundays in Advent and Lent. Found in Swedish manuscript missals 1540, and in later Swedish missals to the present. Adapted from Church of Sweden, 1942.

NUNC DIMITTIS AND GLORIA PATRI. Adapted from Soest, 1532, and Pfalz, 1557. Source, Psalm Tone V and probably other plainsong motives, particularly an Agnus Dei of the thirteenth century, a Sanctus

197

of the fourteenth, and a Kyrie of the fifteenth and sixteenth centuries (masses VII, IX, XVII).

THREEFOLD AMEN. Adapted from Swedish Mass, 1897, and Church of Sweden, 1942.

THE THIRD OR PLAINSONG SETTING[1]

The Third Setting was prepared, at the request of the Commission, by Ernest White, musical director of the Church of St. Mary the Virgin (Episcopal), New York City, distinguished teacher, organist, editor, and authority on Gregorian music. Mr. White studied with Healey Willan and Sir Ernest MacMillan at the University of Toronto, later was a pupil of the organist Lynwood Farnum in New York. Starting his musical career as a violinist, Mr. White eventually became an eminent organ recitalist, playing more than one thousand organ programs in all parts of the country. He served at various times as head of the music department of Bard College (Columbia University), on the staff of Swarthmore College, and of the Pius X School of Liturgical Music, New York. He has had extensive experience with radio and recording, with many broadcasts from his own studio. In addition to his many other activities, he serves as consultant on tonal design and research for the M. P. Möller Organ Company.

For the plainsong setting of the Service, Mr. White adapted melodies of the popular *Missa Orbis Factor* (Mass XI in the Roman Kyriale). His comments on the chanting of plainsong will be found in the chapter on chanting (p. 361). The author's friend and colleague in the work of the Hymn Society of America, Mr. J. Vincent Higginson, musicologist, editor, and organist in New York City, has supplied the following notes on this Mass.

KYRIE. In this form the Kyrie dates from the fourteenth and sixteenth centuries. An earlier form is found in the *Liber Usualis*, a tenth century version. Each melody is repeated three times, except the melody of the last *Kyrie*, which is a synthesis of the whole. The final *Kyrie* has the part of the *Christe* melody a fifth lower. The melody of the *Christe* is one of the finest phrases in the Mass chants. A polyphonic Mass, once thought to be by Vittoria and found in his complete works, is based on these motives.

GLORIA IN EXCELSIS. This is likewise a simple melodic form. It dates from the tenth century. While not strictly based on a Psalm Tone formula, it has a freely used Psalmodic-like line. Note the similarity of the melody of the opening of the Gloria and such later sections as *Domine Deus, Rex caelestis,* and following phrases.

SANCTUS AND BENEDICTUS. These are united by the use of the same Hosanna melody and a slight similarity in the *qui venit* and *Gloria* of the Sanctus.

AGNUS DEI. This is of the fourteenth century. The melodic line shows less unity, each repetition being independent of the other. The use of similar endings in each section helps to bind them.

ITE MISSA EST (BENEDICAMUS DOMINO). This is the melody assigned for the Proper Prefaces.

---

[1] The Commission regrets that considerations of space, size of the volume, contractual agreements with the publishers, et cetera, made it necessary to omit the Plainsong Setting from the *Service Book* itself and to publish it separately.

Chapter 13

MUSIC OF THE HYMN

The ecumenical character of the new hymn texts is well matched by the variety of new tunes. These have been selected from the broad range of Christian use throughout the centuries. Among the number are some of the finest melodies known in each of these well-defined groups: plainsong; folk songs, carols, traditionals; German chorales; Scandinavian chorales; Psalm tunes; French church tunes; and British and American hymn tunes.

We shall endeavor to identify the composers and list the new tunes, that is, tunes not found in the *Common Service Book*. It may also be helpful to preface each group with a brief historical introduction.

PLAINSONG OR GREGORIAN CHANT

Plainsong is the name given to the unisonous liturgical music of the church after the invention of harmony about the beginning of the twelfth century. The "parts" in later harmonized music became elaborate, "figurated," and in contrast the ancient church melodies were simple melodies called *cantus firmus,* and the whole body of melodic form, *cantus planus* or plainsong.

The name "Gregorian chant" derives from the tradition that Pope Gregory the Great, about A.D. 600, compiled and arranged the music of his day according to principles which he developed and which have prevailed to the present time.

The earliest liturgical music developed in Milan after the cessation of persecution (A.D. 312). This "Ambrosian" music probably had its affinities with earlier Greek modes. It was, in turn, codified, modified, and systematized by Pope Gregory. The Emperor Charlemagne introduced the chant as part of his program of liturgical unification in Germany and France. Important schools of instruction were at St. Gall and Metz. For a thousand years, until approximately A.D. 1600, plainsong flourished everywhere in Europe, as may be seen in the missals of episcopal dioceses and the breviaries of monastic orders. The next three centuries witnessed a period of decadence in the overelaboration of melodies and altered methods of singing. This, in turn, was followed by the vigorous revival of interest and study begun in the mid-nineteenth century and continuing in full force today.

The Benedictine monks of Solesmes, in France, were the pioneers in the revival and reform of the chant, the recovery of which was powerfully promoted in the Roman Church by the encyclical on Sacred Music (*Motu Proprio*) issued by Pope Pius X in 1903. A few years before this Harry G. Archer and Luther D. Reed in their full-scale works, *The Psalter and Canticles Pointed for Chanting to the Gregorian Psalm Tones* and their *Choral Service Book,* had restored the historic plainsong melodies to the Liturgy of the Lutheran Church in America. Important items from these works (Preface melodies, Agnus Dei, Psalm Tones, Versicle forms, et cetera) passed into general use in the musical settings in the *Common Service Book* and the new *Service Book.*

The world lauds Luther and his followers for the invention and development of the congregational chorale. It generally fails to recognize the equally important accomplishment of Luther and of the Lutheran Church Orders and Cantionales of the sixteenth century in preserving and arranging for Lutheran services the historic liturgical plainsong of the Western church. These service books contained hundreds of plainsong Introits, Kyries, Graduals, Glorias, Preface melodies, settings for the Sanctus, the Agnus Dei, et cetera for the Service of Holy Communion, and hundreds of plainsong antiphons, Psalm Tones, Responsories, et cetera for Matins and Vespers, to say nothing of hymns for all services. Most of these melodies were still set to their historic Latin texts. Luther himself, however, in his German Mass (1526) arranged many of them to German texts. His complete familiarity with the modal character of plainsong and his skill in adapting it to the requirements of a new language are interestingly revealed in the account given by Johann Walther (see pp. 164-165).

Therefore in these two areas—the invention and development of the congregational chorale and the preservation and adaptation of plainsong melodies to contemporary needs—the Lutheran Church of the sixteenth century deserves credit for a remarkable liturgical and musical achievement. The Church of England, during the same period, produced nothing in this field beyond the very simple adaptation of the ancient plainsong by Merbecke in his *Booke of Common Praier Noted.* In the field of hymnody there was nothing. The Calvinistic wing of Protestantism produced the Psalm tunes and nothing else. The last hundred years have seen a complete reversal of this situation. Leadership in the revival of plainsong and in massive original and creative accomplishments in hymnody has definitely been taken and held by the Church of England, in whose debt we all stand.

Today there are many schools, societies, and other organizations in the Protestant churches of England, Germany, Scandinavia, and America devoting themselves to the study and cultivation of plainsong. Similar institutions of even greater strength and influence are conducted by the Roman Church in many lands. Hymnals of every communion give some of the fine old melodies. Our ablest church musicians and composers find themes for choral and organ works in the same treasure house. Plainsong is coming into its own again.

It will not be possible at this point to discuss the particular features which distinguish plainsong from modern music. Among these are the twelve (or fourteen) scale system of the ancient Church modes, the Gregorian chant forms with their cadences and finals, the free and unbarred rhythm of the melodies and their strict accommodation to the accents and rhythms of the texts, methods of expression and interpretation, and notation. We can only stress the historic character, melodic beauty, and absolute churchliness of plainsong. Like the chorale, which developed from it, and even more definitely than the chorale, plainsong is music *of* the church and not simply music *in* the church. It has none but churchly associations. These facts, together with other intrinsic values, challenge the sympathetic interest and study of earnest churchmen everywhere. The musical settings to the Liturgy in the new *Service Book* are strongly impregnated with plainsong. The new *Hymnal* contains fourteen authentic Gregorian hymn tunes.

20   *A solis ortus cardine* (Mode III). From east to west.

483   *Christe Redemptor* (Mode I). Jesus, thou Joy of loving hearts. Vesper hymn, Christmas Eve.

94   *Claro paschali gaudio* (Mode VIII). That Easter Day with joy was bright.

147   *Conditor alme siderum* (Mode IV). O wondrous type.

17   *Divinum mysterium* (Mode V). Of the Father's love begotten. A Sanctus trope in German Mass.

155   *Jesu, dulcedo cordium* (Mode II). Lord, keep us steadfast in thy word.

133   *O lux beata Trinitas* (Mode VIII). O Trinity of blessed light. Traditional association.

61   *Pange lingua* (Mode III). Sing, my tongue, the glorious battle. Traditional association.

206   *Splendor paternae* (Mode I). O splendor of God's glory bright. Traditional association.

245   *Urbs beata* (Mode II). Blessed city, heavenly Salem. Traditional association.

117 *Veni, Creator Spiritus* (Mode VIII). Come, Holy Ghost, our souls inspire. Ambrosian melody, later traditional with this text.

2 *Veni, Emmanuel* (Mode I). O come, O come, Emmanuel. Cento of Kyrie melodies in a medieval French missal.

277 *Verbum supernum* (Mode VIII). O saving Victim, opening wide. Traditional association.

75 *Vexilla regis prodeunt* (Mode I). The royal banners forward go. Traditional association.

FOLK SONGS, CAROLS, TRADITIONALS

This is music of communal origin without known composers. It generally has strong national or racial characteristics. It is, however, to be distinguished from purely national and popular songs, and also from widely sung melodies by an individual composer, for example Stephen Foster. It is music of the countryside and not of the city. It springs spontaneously from the desire and the necessity for group self-entertainment or expression. Its secular forms consist of ballads, songs, and folk dances. Its religious forms include carols, folk hymns, and spirituals.

The researches of Sabine Baring-Gould, Ralph Vaughan Williams, Cecil J. Sharp, and others in England, and of George Pullen Jackson, Mrs. Annabel Buchanan, and others in America disclosed and recorded (often by phonograph) thousands of these melodies. One of Sharp's collections contained five hundred of these unpublished melodies from the southern Appalachian highlands in America. The excellent *Oxford Book of Carols* edited by Percy Dearmer, Vaughan Williams, and Martin Shaw contains more than two hundred items, chiefly British. There are close affinities between folk songs and the ancient plainsong, particularly in such matters as scale (or mode) systems, free rhythm determined by the words, and use of melody alone without necessity of instrumental accompaniment. The earliest forms of sacred folk song in Europe developed from the mystery plays which were popular features of the great church festivals.

Great composers found thematic material in melodies of this kind. Haydn employed Croatian forms; Dvorak, Bohemian melodies; Rimsky-Korsakoff, Russian; Liszt, Hungarian, as also Brahms; Grieg, Norwegian; Vaughan Williams, English; et cetera. Long before this, Luther had adapted certain sacred folk song melodies for his German hymns. Many chorales by later German and Scandinavian composers were based upon similar material.

Current Lutheran hymnals in America contain some tunes derived from these sources. *Schönster Herr Jesu* is a Silesian folk song brought into church hymnals not much more than a hundred years ago. *Sweet*

Story ("I think when I read that sweet story of old") was arranged from a Greek melody by William Bradbury in 1859.

English folk songs, generally speaking, are tuneful, cheerful, and strongly rhythmic. Irish songs, like the American Negro spirituals, are more mystical. Welsh songs often are rugged and powerful; German songs, contemplative and introspective. The Scandinavian countries, perhaps above others, produced many hymn tunes which had their inspiration in their native folk songs.

Religious folk songs in America are of two sorts—imported (chiefly English and Scotch) and native. Scotch, English, and Irish songs are common in the southern highlands—Virginia, Kentucky, Tennessee; French songs in Canada; Negro spirituals and Creole songs in the deep South. Negro spirituals, with their profound religious fervor and intense subjectivity, are in a class by themselves. Folk hymns of more general type—*Land of Rest, Kedron, Amazing Grace,* and the like—are more widely distributed. Some of these native songs developed, with many variations, from the practice of "lining out" the hymns and metrical Psalms in New England and elsewhere. Other songs owe their inspiration to camp meetings, revival services, and similar occasions under primitive conditions.

The article "Folk Music" in Thompson's *International Cyclopedia of Music and Musicians* gives a comprehensive, yet concise, treatment of this subject.

The new *Hymnal* has considerably enlarged the number of tunes of this character, with approximately thirty new items representing various national origins.

American

WERE YOU THERE. An American traditional melody, probably by an unknown Negro slave.

500 Were you there. First published in William E. Barton's *Old Plantation Hymns,* 1899. A notable American contribution to Christian hymnody. A white spiritual of similar character has been found among the mountain folk of Tennessee.

LAND OF REST.

587 Jerusalem, my happy home. Possibly of Scottish or north England origin, but widely sung throughout the Appalachian region of North America. First published in Annabel Morris Buchanan's *Folk Hymns of America,* 1938. She thinks that the Negro spiritual, "Swing Low, Sweet Chariot," may have been derived from it.

Danish

RELEASE. A Danish folk melody.

60 How blessed from the bonds of sin.

254 Thy word, O Lord, like gentle dews.

CELESTIA. A Danish folk melody.
57 Bright and glorious is the sky.

Dutch

IN BABILONE. A Dutch melody of the seventeenth century.
542 Son of God, eternal Saviour. Appeared with English text in the *English Hymnal*, 1906.

KREMSER.
450 We praise thee, O God, our Redeemer, Creator. A folk song first published in 1626 by Valerius, and popularized by Edward Kremser (1838-1914), director of a male chorus in Vienna. It appeared in his German collection of six Dutch folk songs at the end of the nineteenth century.

English

GREENSLEEVES.
48 What Child is this, who laid to rest. A popular, secular English ballad. Twice mentioned by Shakespeare in his *Merry Wives of Windsor*.

KING'S LYNN.
344 O God of earth and altar. Arranged for this text by Ralph Vaughan Williams in the *English Hymnal*, 1906. The name is that of a town in Norfolk. A robust tune for a robust hymn.

ST. HUGH.
335 Sing to the Lord the children's hymn. An arrangement of an air sung to a ballad dealing with the legend of St. Hugh of Lincoln.

MONKS GATE.
563 He who would valiant be. A Sussex folk song adapted by Ralph Vaughan Williams for Percy Dearmer's imitation of Bunyan's text in *Pilgrim's Progress*. Odd syncopation and cross rhythm well adapted to the text.

THE FIRST NOWELL (Noel).
40 The first Noel the angel did say. An especially popular carol in the northern part of England. First appeared in print in 1833. The word "Noel" is probably derived, through the Provençal "Nadal," from the Latin "Natalis," or "birthday."

Finnish

NYLAND.
574 In heavenly love abiding. A Finnish folk melody, adapted by David Evans for this hymn in the *Church Hymnary* (Scotland, 1927). Named from the Finnish province of Nyland.

SUOMI.
180 Arise, my soul, arise.

French

GLORIA (IRIS).
30 Angels we have heard on high. A French carol, probably of the eighteenth century. Popular in Lorraine and in the Province of Quebec. This arrangement made by Edward Shippen Barnes, sometime organist and choirmaster of St. Stephen's Episcopal Church, Philadelphia.

O FILII ET FILIAE.
96   O sons and daughters, let us sing. A French melody of the fifteenth century. First printed in Paris, 1623.

ORIENTIS PARTIBUS.
509   Conquering kings their titles take. First appeared in the *Office de la Circoncision*, Sens, about A.D. 1210.

German

RESONET IN LAUDIBUS.
44   Long ago, and far away. A carol of the fourteenth century. Sung in medieval times to Latin and German texts at mystery plays in church at Christmas time. The German dialogue hymn, "Joseph Lieber, Joseph Mein," traditionally sung with this melody, was deemed inappropriate for the *Hymnal.* Dr. Edward T. Horn, III, wrote a new text for the hymn proper. The traditional refrain was retained.

CHRISTMAS DAWN.
35   When Christmas morn is dawning. A German folk song, first published 1823.

FREIBURG (ES LIEGT EIN SCHLOSS).
63   Sweet the moments, rich in blessing. A folk song of the sixteenth century.

KOMMT HER ZU MIR.
156   Fear not, thou faithful Christian flock. A German melody of the fifteenth century.

IN DULCI JUBILO.
39   Good Christian men, rejoice. A popular German melody of the fourteenth century.

Irish

GARTAN.
37   Love came down at Christmas. A popular tune in Donegal.

ST. COLUMBA.
530   The King of love my shepherd is. From the *Irish Church Hymnal,* 1873, where it is called "a hymn of the ancient Irish Church." Traditional in County Londonderry.

IRISH. A popular Irish tune found in *A Collection of Hymns and Sacred Poems,* Dublin, 1749, with which John Wesley may have had some part. In present Irish use it is associated with the hymn, "O God, our help in ages past."
480   O Thou, in all Thy might so far.
331   Thy kingdom come! on bended knee.

Moravian

FAR OFF LANDS.
317   Remember all the people. Bohemian Brethren melody in the Swedish *Hemmets Koralbok,* 1921. Harmonized by Winfred Douglas.

Norwegian

BEHOLD A HOST.
599   Behold a host like mountains bright. Folk song of the early seven-

teenth century. Arranged by Edward Grieg, and popularized in America by the St. Olaf Choir.

HAUGE.
146   In heaven above, in heaven above.

CHRISTMAS EVE.
45   I am so glad each Christmas Eve.

OSLO.
586   The world is very evil.

Scottish

CAMERONIAN MIDNIGHT HYMN.
147   O wondrous type, O vision fair. A vigorous traditional Scottish hymn melody of unusually wide compass.

Swedish

VIGIL (Hof trones Lampa Fürdig).
14   Rejoice, all ye believers.

Welsh

AR HYD Y NOS.
230   God, that madest earth and heaven. A secular Welsh melody set to the words "All through the night." Reginald Heber heard it played by a harpist in a Welsh home and composed the first part of this hymn to fit the tune.

DOLGELLY.
268   Author of life divine.

ST. DENIO.
172   Immortal, invisible, God only wise. Welsh, *c.* 1810. Adapted by John Roberts, 1839, from Welsh folk tune known as *Joanna.*

THE GERMAN CHORALE

At the beginning of the Reformation the old ecclesiastical modes were still in general use, but were giving way to tonal concepts of the modern major and minor scale system. Melody was still supreme. Voice parts and harmony were little understood or employed.

Music in the pre-Reformation church was priestly and choral, though in German-speaking lands a limited number of Leisen (Kyrie eleison) hymns in the vernacular were permitted on festivals. The Hussites in Bohemia had published a hymnal at Prague in 1501 which contained 89 hymns in the vernacular, and Michael Weisse, a German, published a German hymnal in 1531 which contained 155 hymns.

Luther was the forceful leader in the movement which produced a vigorous vernacular hymnody in the regular services of the church. He translated hymns from the Latin, wrote original hymns himself, and set original and adapted tunes to texts in three notable collections in the year 1524, and in later collections for which he wrote four prefaces. All told, he wrote thirty-eight hymns. His work in the musical field, while containing some original tunes, was largely editorial. He adapted and arranged many melodies from earlier plainsong, popular hymn, and folk song melodies, contributing a few items of his own composition. The powerful impulse he gave to congregational song, however, is shown by the fact that no less than two hundred German hymnbooks by different editors were issued between 1525 and 1575.

These early chorales were virile melodies, quite in keeping with the sturdy character of their hymn texts, and possessing fine qualities of churchly dignity and propriety. In these qualities they have never been excelled, and rarely equaled. The period of the Thirty Years' War was a time of church disruption and musical decadence. Some excellent hymns, however, were born of the tribulations of the era. Johann Crüger's hymnal toward the end of the period (1644) ran through forty-three editions and contained many fine chorale melodies.

Pietism drenched the church with waves of subjectivity and cheap sentimentality. The old chorales were covered with silly ornamentation. Frivolous airs were composed for innumerable "spiritual songs." Hymnal editors vied with each other in producing hymns for every possible person and occasion. A Saxon clergyman edited a "universal hymnbook" in 1737 which contained hymns specially intended for "noblemen, ministers, officials, lawyers, barbers, bakers, fishermen, teamsters, merchants, apprentices and many other professions." Not satisfied with this array, the collection requested songs for "clowns, tightrope walkers, magicians, thieves and rogues." [1]

In the hubbub of all this the voice of the congregation became increasingly silent; the tones of the organ increasingly louder. Organists introduced flowerly interludes between stanzas of hymns, even as cantors had done before this. Hymnals flowed from the presses by the hundreds. Johann Freylinghausen's *Gesangbuch* of 1704, 1711, and 1741, contained more than sixteen hundred hymns and six hundred melodies. In these publications *Ein feste Burg* and other stately chorales were livened up with fancy rhythms.

Johann Sebastian Bach stepped upon the stage at this very moment. In the field of church music he had little to work with, but his genius made much out of little. He was occupied with greater projects than the composition of chorales, though apparently he did contribute twenty-nine "sacred arias" to a collection for home worship, among which *Komm, süsser Tod* is one of the few remembered. His profound religious nature, however, recognized the values in hymn texts and chorale melodies. He found pleasure in producing the incredible number of

---

[1] Paul Henry Lang, *Music in Western Civilization* (New York: W. W. Horton & Company, 1941), p. 470.

371 four-part harmonizations of several hundred chorale melodies which he had collected. Most of these are in his church cantatas. He also composed massive chorale preludes for organ, works which stand today supreme in the literature of that instrument.

By the time of Bach's death in 1750, Rationalism had reduced religion to the level of ethics and brought church music to ruin. The interest of the musical profession centered in the opera and the growing literature of the piano and the orchestra. The congregational chorale barely survived in a dreary monotony of even-noted and slow-moving melodies shorn of rhythm and devoid of relevance to the thought of their texts.

The churchly revival of the nineteenth and twentieth centuries produced monumental works of research by Winterfeld, Wackernagel, Zahn, and others. It witnessed the growth of the Church Choir Association with more than two thousand affiliated organizations, the establishment of the New Bach Society and similar groups holding annual church music festivals. New hymnals for the state churches were edited, continuing the debate between exponents of rhythmic and nonrhythmic forms of the chorale. But there has been little or no creative activity in the field. The peoples that forged one of Protestantism's mightiest weapons and fashioned an imperishable art form in the Reformation era seem satisfied to live upon their inheritance, resetting, rearranging the ancient jewels, but adding little, if anything, to the collection.

The *Hymnal* contains a representative selection of fine German and Scandinavian chorales suitable for use with English texts. We would have preferred to have more of them in fresher rhythmic form. But here, again, we enter the area of taste. New items, chiefly German, number forty-seven and are here listed, by composers and sources.

ABT, FRANZ (1819-95). Saxon *kapellmeister* in Zürich and in Brunswick. Composer of more than four hundred works, including many *Lieder* for male and mixed voices.
496 *Willingham.* Still, still with thee, when purple morning breaketh.
ALLGEMEINES KATHOLISCHES GESANGBUCH, Vienna, 1774.
167 *Te Deum (Grosser Gott).* Holy God, we praise thy Name. Both author and composer unknown. Original in eight stanzas. Frequently called the German Te Deum.
As HYMNODUS SACER, 1625. A small but important collection published in Leipsic, 1625.
286 *Ach Gott und Herr.* Strengthen for service, Lord, the hands. An anonymous chorale in the above collection.
BACH, JOHANN SEBASTIAN (1685-1750). Eminent organist and composer. Most distinguished member of the most famous family in all musical history. Organist at Weimar and several other cities before coming to Leipsic as choirmaster of St. Thomas' Church and director of its famous choir school. Here he composed his *B Minor Mass*, the Passions according to

St. Matthew and St. John, and other great choral works, as well as more than two hundred cantatas based upon the older chorale melodies associated with the Sundays and festivals of the church year. He wrote sixteen original tunes, none of which is in use today. He will ever be remembered for his more than four hundred chorale harmonizations based upon melodies not his own. Most of these are imbedded in his church cantatas. A "Bach chorale," therefore, is to be understood as meaning a chorale melody harmonized by Bach, and not a melody composed by him. Bach was a great Christian, and, because of the religious depth of his music and his profound interpretation of the moods and meanings of the Christian year, perhaps the greatest Lutheran preacher of his century. Seventeen of Bach's adaptations and harmonizations are included in the *Hymnal,* which were not previously included.

286 *Ach Gott und Herr.* Strengthen for service, Lord, the hands.
98 *Christ lag in Todesbanden.* Christ Jesus lay in death's strong bands.
460 *Darmstadt.* O God, eternal source.
171 *Darmstadt.* Our God, to whom we turn.
188 *Herr Jesu Christ, dich zu uns wend.* Lord Jesus Christ, be present now.
228 *Innsbruck.* The duteous day now closeth.
283 *Jesu, joy of man's desiring.* Come with us, O blessed Jesus.
53 *Liebster Immanuel.* Brightest and best of the sons of the morning.
501 *O Jesulein süss.* O Jesus so meek, O Jesus so kind.
88 *Passion Chorale.* O sacred Head, now wounded.
71 *Psalm 42 (Freu Dich Sehr).* Print thine image pure and holy.
194 *Psalm 42 (Freu Dich Sehr).* Praise to thee and adoration.
95 *Salzburg (Alle Menschen).* At the Lamb's high feast.
414 *Salzburg (Alle Menschen).* Let the whole creation cry.
29 *Schop.* Break forth, O beauteous heavenly light.
359 *Vater Unser.* Lord God of hosts.
34 *Von Himmel hoch.* The holy Son of God most high.
7 *Wachet auf.* Wake, awake, for night is flying.
67 *Werde Munter (Altered).* Jesus, Name all names above.
120 *Wie schön leuchtet.* O Holy Spirit, enter in.

BORTNIANSKI, DMITRI STEPANOVITCH (1752-1825). Russian composer of a favorite German chorale, was born in the Ukraine, educated in Italy. Director of the church choir of the Imperial Chapel in St. Petersburg. Composer of operas, concertos, and much music for the Russian Church, whose music he systematized.

399 *St. Petersburg (Cherubic hymn).* Jesus, Thy boundless love to me. Probably an adaptation of a Mass written in 1822, later set to a Russian hymn. The Prussian king, Frederick William III, heard this tune while attending Russian maneuvers and ordered Prussian military bands to use it.

COLOGNE, 1623.

Lasst uns erfreuen. Popular in Roman Catholic parts of southern Germany. First set to an English text in the *English Hymnal,* 1906.
103 Now let the vault of heaven resound.
173 All creatures of our God and King.

437   Ye watchers and ye holy ones.

CORNER'S GESANGBUCH, 1631. David Gregor Corner was abbot of a Benedictine monastery in Austria. Editor of two great collections of hymns and tunes.

282   *Omni Die.* For the bread which thou hast broken.

493   *Omni Die* (arr. by W. S. Rockstro). There's a wideness in God's mercy.

DECIUS, NIKOLAUS (d. 1541). Provost of a monastery who embraced the Reformation and became a pastor in Stettin.

70   *O Lamm Gottes.* O Lamb of God, most holy. Metrical version of the elaborated liturgical text, Agnus Dei. The tune is an adaptation of an earlier melody, probably by Decius.

EBELING, JOHANN GEORG (1637-76). German church musician, successor of Johann Crüger in important positions. Professor in Berlin and Stettin. Composed 113 tunes for two collections of Paul Gerhardt's hymns.

176   *Du meine Seele singe.* O God, the Rock of Ages.

203   *Voller Wunder.* At thy feet, O Christ, we lay.

FLEMMING, FRIEDRICH FERDINAND (1778-1813). A practicing physician in Berlin. Composer of musical setting to Horace's Ode beginning "Integer vitae." Also many part songs for male voices.

421   *Flemming* (*Integer vitae*). Praise ye the Father for his loving-kindness. Adapted from the setting mentioned above, and widely sung by male choruses.

FRANCK, JOHANN WOLFGANG (1641-88). German composer of fourteen operas (Hamburg) and of church music. Resident in London, 1690-95.

595   *Komm Seele.* Ten thousand times ten thousand. From *Geistliche Lieder,* Hamburg, 1681, which contained melodies by Franck for the hymns of M. Heinrich Elmenhorst, pastor of St. Catherine's Church.

FRITSCH, AHASUERUS (1629-1701). Chancellor of the University of Jena, Germany. Noted author, editor, educator.

Darmstadt (*O Gott, du frommer Gott*). From a collection edited by Fritsch and generally ascribed to him.

171   Our God, to whom we turn.

460   O God, eternal source.

GEISTLICHE LIEDER, Wittenberg, 1535. An important hymnal edited by Luther, published by Joseph Klug. Klug was one of four Wittenberg printers who published Reformation books, tracts, et cetera. The others were Lotter, Rhou, and Lufft.

113   *Nun freut euch.* Let all the multitudes of light. The third tune set to Luther's hymn, and later generally used for "Es ist gewisslich an der Zeit." A stately tune, ascribed to Luther by many editors.

GLÄSER, CARL GOTTHILF (1784-1829). A chorister of St. Thomas' Church, Leipsic, law student, and musician. Composed many songs and chorales.

428   *Azmon.* O for a thousand tongues to sing. Introduced into American hymnals by Lowell Mason in his *Modern Psalmist,* 1839.

GOUNOD, CHARLES FRANCOIS (1818-93). French composer of much church music and, later in life, of *Faust* and other operas.

Gounod (*Lux Prima*).

208   Christ, whose glory fills the sky.

229 Saviour, now the day is ending.

HANDEL, GEORGE FREDERICK (1685-1759). Born at Halle, Germany, lived forty-seven years in London. Spent nearly thirty years as composer and director of operas. Established the English oratorio form by his *Messiah* and other oratorios. Composer organ works, anthems, et cetera. His published works total ninety-seven volumes.

566 *Judas Maccabaeus.* Thine is the glory. Adapted from the oratorio of this name.

HAYDN, FRANZ JOSEPH (1732-1809). Viennese composer. *Kapellmeister* to Prince Esterhazy. Regarded as the inventor of the symphony and the string quartet. Composer of *The Creation* and other oratorios, 22 operas, 120 symphonies, 83 instrumental quartets.

442 *Creation.* The spacious firmament on high. Adapted from the chorus, "The heavens are telling," in the above oratorio.

HERMANN, NIKOLAUS (*c.* 1480-1561). Principal of a Latin school and cantor in Joachimsthal, Bohemia. Composed many chorales.

Lobt Gott, ihr Christen. Composed in 1554 for a children's hymn on St. John the Baptist.

197 O happy day, when we shall stand.

400 O Christ, our hope, our heart's desire.

HILLE, JOHANN GEORG (*c.* 1730). Cantor and teacher in Glaucha, near Halle, Germany. Composer of several well-known chorales, and probably contributor to Freylinghausen's hymnal.

319 *Einer ist könig.* Hail to the brightness of Zion's glad morning. An energetic chorale composed 1739.

HIMMEL, FRIEDRICH HEINRICH (1765-1814). Studied theology at Halle, but was sent by King Frederick Wilhelm, II, to study music in Italy. Later appointed composer and director of music at the Berlin court. Composed operas, oratorios, motets, songs, et cetera.

464 *Himmel.* Thou to whom the sick and dying. Tune from the Irish *Hymnal,* 1874, and attributed to F. H. Himmel.

HINTZE, JAKOB (1622-1702). Born in Bernau, near Berlin. Court musician to the elector of Brandenburg. After Crüger's death he edited the twelfth and later editions of *Praxis Pietatis Melica,* including sixty-five tunes of his own composition.

Salzburg (Alle Menschen). First published 1678.

95 At the Lamb's high feast we sing.

414 Let the whole creation cry.

LEISENTRIT, JOHANN L. (*c.* 1527-86). Born in Olmutz, Czechoslovakia. Ecclesiastical administrator in Meiszen and dean of the Catholic cathedral in Bautzen, Saxony. In an effort to offset the popular appeal of Lutheran hymnody he published the second German hymnbook of Catholic origin in 1567.

579 *Narenza.* Put thou thy trust in God. Adapted from a melody in a Catholic Hymnal of 1584, where it is set in triple time to the text "Ave Maria klare."

LÜNEBURG GESANGBUCH, 1686.

186 *Meinhold.* Light of light enlighten me. This tune first appeared, in slightly different form, in the Lüneburg *Gesangbuch.*

MAINZ, 1628.

87 *O traurigkeit.* O darkest woe.

MAINZ GESANGBUCH, 1661.

84 *Stabat Mater (Mainz).* At the Cross, her station keeping. Adapted from a setting of this poem in the Roman Catholic *Gesangbuch* of the Mainz diocese. Entered English use in J. Marmaduke's *The Evening Office of the Church,* London, 1748.

MENDELSSOHN-BARTHOLDY, FELIX (1809-47). Born in Hamburg, Germany, of a Christian-Jewish family. Distinguished composer and organist. A great favorite in England, which he visited nine times. Composer of the *Reformation Symphony,* 1830, and many other symphonies, oratorios, et cetera.

573 *Heavenly Love.* O blessed Sun whose splendor.

340 *Munich (Meiningen)* (arranged). From ocean unto ocean. Originally set to the text "O Gott, du frommer Gott," and arranged for the quartet, "Cast thy burden upon the Lord," in the oratorio *Elijah,* 1847.

MEYER, JOHANN DAVID. Prominent councilor in Ulm, where he published *Geistliche Seelen-Freud,* 1692. This contained fifty-four of his own melodies, including this one.

Meyer (Es ist kein Tag).

448 O Lord of heaven and earth and sea.

598 For those we love within the veil.

NAEGELI, HANS GEORG (1773-1836). A Swiss composer, teacher, writer, publisher. Founder, Swiss Association for Cultivation of Music.

543 *Dennis.* Blest be the tie that binds. Adapted by Lowell Mason from a manuscript tune which Mason had bought in Europe.

NEEFE, CHRISTIAN GOTTLOB (1748-98). German musician, teacher of Beethoven. Musical director and conductor at the court of the Elector. Composed operas and much church music.

540 *Meiringen.* Believing fathers oft have told.

NEUKOMM, SIGISMUND (1778-1858). Pupil of Joseph Haydn, director of the German theater in St. Petersburg. Lived in France, accompanied Mendelssohn to England. Wrote oratorios for English festivals.

277 *St. Vincent.* O Saving Victim, opening wide. An arrangement of a melody by Neukomm.

PRAETORIUS, MICHAEL (1571-1621). Composer and author. *Kapellmeister* at Lüneburg, and later for the duke of Brunswick. Author of *Syntagma Musicum,* an important theoretical-historical work. Edited *Musae Sioniae* (9 vols., 1605-16), a collection of twelve hundred choral works for Lutheran services.

94 *Puer nobis* (Adapted). That Easter Day with joy was bright. An adaptation of a fifteenth century carol.

PRAXIS PIETATIS MELICA, Frankfort, 1668.

68 *Gute Bäume bringen.* Christian, dost thou see them. By Peter Sohren, cantor at Elbing, West Prussia, and editor of Crüger's *Praxis Pietatis.* Composed 238 tunes.

REIMANN, JOHANN BALTHASAR (1702-49). Cantor in Neustadt, Breslau, and Hirschberg.

490   *O Jesu.* I look to thee in every need. A simple but appealing melody, with a distinctive fifth line.

ROSTOCKERHANDBOKEN, 1529.

174   *Ter Sanctus.* We worship thee, almighty Lord.

SCHEFFLER, JOHANN (Angelus Silesius) (1624-77). Physician of the duke of Württemberg and later of the Emperor Ferdinand, III. A mystic of the school of Boehme and Tauler. A Lutheran who became a Jesuit monk. Edited several hymn collections.

153   *Scheffler.* Jesus, with thy Church abide.

SCHEIN, JOHANN HERMANN (1586-1630). Distinguished musician, composer, and editor. Cantor, St. Thomas' Church, Leipsic. Eighty chorales attributed to him.

116   *Mach's mit mir, Gott* (Eisenach). To realms of glory in the skies. A particularly fine chorale in its original rhythmic form. Published in sheet form in 1628 to be added to Schein's Cantionale of 1627. Used by Bach in his *St. John Passion.*

SCHICHT, JOHANN GOTTFRIED (1753-1823). Organist, St. Thomas' Church, Leipsic. One of the ablest later composers of chorales, with three hundred to his credit.

156   *Ascendit Deus.* Fear not, thou faithful, Christian flock. A fine, free-moving melody. Popular in England.

SCHOP, JOHANN (*c.* 1600-65). Orchestral conductor at Wolfenbüttel, Copenhagen, and Hamburg. Famous violinist. Set many of Rist's hymns to music.

29   *Schop.* Break forth, O beauteous heavenly light. Composed for Rist's Christmas hymn. Harmonized by Bach in his Christmas Oratorio.

462   *Werde munter.* O my soul, on wings ascending. Composed for Rist's evening hymn.

283   *Jesu, joy of man's desiring.* Chorale composed by Schop, a popular variant of *Werde munter.* Harmonized by J. S. Bach in his Cantata No. 147 for the Feast of the Visitation.

SCHULZ, JOHANN ABRAHAM PETER (1747-1800). Director of theater in Berlin and royal *Kapellmeister* at Copenhagen. Composer, arranger of folk songs and of settings for original poems by contemporary authors.

49   *Paedia.* Thy little ones, dear Lord, are we.

SILCHER (PHILIPP), FRIEDRICH (1789-1860). A Württemberg musician. Conductor in Stuttgart. Director of music, University of Tübingen. Editor and composer.

292   *So nimm denn meine Hände.* O take my hand, dear Father.

STÖRL, JOHANN GEORG CHRISTIAN (1675-1719). *Kapellmeister* in Stuttgart, musical education in Austria and Italy.

13   *Störl.* Lo! He comes with clouds descending. Originally in triple time.

VULPIUS, MELCHIOR (*c.* 1560-1616). Editor and cantor at Weimar in Thuringia. Composed chorales, contrapuntal settings, a Passion according to St. Matthew, et cetera.

Vulpius (*Gelobt sei Gott*). Chorale dates from 1609, but the melody probably is an older traditional.

109   Good Christian men, rejoice and sing.

600   O Lord of Life, where'er they be.

274 *Das neugeborne Kindelein.* Victim divine, thy grace we claim. J. S. Bach used this chorale as the theme for a cantata.

546 *Weimar.* Let us now our voices raise. Composed in 1609 for a hymn by Petrus Herbert.

WEIMAR, GEORG PETER (1734-1800). Cantor in Erfurt and music director of the Gymnasium. Composed motets, cantatas, et cetera.

303 *Erfurt.* (*Allgütiger, mein Preisgesang.*) Lord of the Church, we humbly pray.

WEIMAR GESANGBUCH, 1681. Compiled by Conrad von der Lage, court preacher at Weimar. Printed in very large type, it had 1171 pages, but only 220 hymns. Of its 28 melodies, 5, including this one, were new.

582 *Was Gott tut.* Whate'er our God ordains is right. An adaptation of a melody by Severus Gastorius, 1675.

WITTENBERG GESANGBUCH, 1524. The so-called "Achtlieder-buch," the first little collection of Lutheran hymns.

259 *St. Paul* (*Es ist das Heil*). He that believes and is baptized. Tune probably with pre-Reformation background. Set to hymn by Paul Speratus in the 1524 pamphlet.

236 *Soldau.* The fading day adorns the west.

THE CHORALE IN SCANDINAVIA

The development of church music in Scandinavia followed the lines already sketched in Germany, with somewhat slower introduction of vernacular hymnody. Olavus Petri published a small collection of hymns in 1526, no copy of which is known to exist. His third edition of 1536 contained forty-four items, chiefly translations from the Low German hymnals of Speratus and Slüter. The year 1567 witnessed a Swedish hymnal by Laurentius Petri, with translations chiefly from the Danish and from Latin sequences and Graduals. Bishop Svedberg's hymnal of 1697, issued by royal authority, provided accompaniments for chorale melodies, the latter being a mixture of Gregorian and folk song types.

The early nineteenth century witnessed increasing conflict between foreign (chiefly German) musicians, who advocated the even-noted type of melody, and others who desired rhythmic forms drawn from the native folk song. J. C. F. Haeffner's chorale book of 1789 was one of the first with parts for four voices. Its tunes were, for the most part, in even-noted form. Bishop Svedberg's hymnal was superseded by Bishop Wallin's collections of 1819 and later.

German cultural influences penetrated Scandinavia first through Denmark. Musicologists, however, have found that some early Viking melodies passed south into Normandy, and thence into Germany, and finally returned to Sweden as German chorales.

There probably were a few Danish hymns before the Reformation. The first collection of consequence for Lutheran worship was Hans

Thomissön's *Psalmebog* of 1569. This contained 268 items, each with its own melody. This work was so highly regarded that for a century or more a copy was chained in each church for the use of the cantor. Jesperson's *Gradual* of the same year was an even larger work intended for city churches and schools. Bishop Kingo's hymnal, 1674 and later, was the first all-Danish book. It contained many tunes based upon folk song, some with triple rhythm. The hymnal of Pontoppidan, Bishop of Bergen, 1740, showed the strong influence of Freylinghausen's *Gesangbuch*. Later nineteenth century collections made approximately two thousand melodies available.

In Norway, favorite Danish hymns continued in general use, though German and Danish influence declined with the introduction of more and more hymns and melodies of native origin.

The work of the Lindemans, father and son, is especially to be noted. O. A. Lindeman's chorale book of 1838 was an outstanding work which largely replaced Zinck's earlier book, though it contained many even-noted melodies of the Haeffner type in Sweden. The general confusion was largely resolved in 1869 in a new hymnal by M. B. Landstad, a Lutheran clergyman in Telemark, a poet and collector of folk songs. Ludvig M. Lindeman, son of O. A. Lindeman, and organist of the principal church in Christiania (Oslo), published (1871) a chorale book to accompany Landstad's hymnal, including in this collection fifty-four chorales or tunes of his own composition. This work, which supported the rhythmic type of melody, is still influential today.

The excellent book, *The Chorale,* by Edwin Liemohn (Philadelphia: Muhlenberg Press, 1953), gives within the compass of 170 pages a very satisfactory account of the chorale in Germany and Scandinavia through four hundred years of its history.

AHLSTRÖM, OLOF (1756-1835). Swedish composer. Organist St. James' Church, Stockholm. Editor of a collection of folk songs.
   270 *St. James, Stockholm.* A voice, a heavenly voice I hear. Composed 1828.

BERGGREN, ANDREAS PETER (1801-80). Danish musician. Organist, Church of the Trinity, Copenhagen. Composer for church and opera. Editor eleven volumes of folk songs.
   128 *Berggren.* Lord, let thy Spirit, from earthly passion weaning.
   456 *Dana.* One there is above all others.

DÜBEN, GUSTAF (1624-90). Member of a Swedish family of musicians of German, and probably more remotely, of Bohemian origin. Organist in Stockholm and at the Swedish court.
   59 *Jesu.* Hark! the voice of Jesus crying.

GRIEG, EDWARD HAGERUP (1843-1907). Famous pianist and composer who created a new national art, quite as Chopin did for Poland and Liszt for Hungary.

599 *Behold a host.* Behold a host like mountains bright. A Norwegian folk song of the early seventeenth century. Arranged by Grieg, and set to Brorson's triumphant hymn of the saints of God. Now well-known in England and America.

HAGFORS, ERNEST AUGUST (1827-1913). Finnish teacher, director of choirs and music festivals.

536 *Pilgrim Song.* Lord, as a pilgrim on earth I roam.

HARTMANN, JOHAN PETER EMILIUS (1805-1900). Danish musician.

200 *Peace of God* (Fred Ti Bod). Peace to soothe our bitter woes.

HOFF, ERIK CHRISTIAN (1832-94). Organist in Oslo. Published a hymnal in 1878 in which he advocated use of the rhythmic form of chorale melodies "in so far as they can be used by the congregation."

423 *Hoff.* O sing, all ye lands, with a jubilant voice.

LAGI, RUDOLF THEODOR (1823-68). Finnish church musician. Organist St. Nicholas' Church, Helsingfors.

396 *I lift my eyes.* I lift my eyes unto heaven above.

LINDEMAN, LUDVIG MATTHIAS (1812-87). Born in Trondhjem, son of the organist of the Church of our Lady in that city. Organist of Our Saviour's Church and professor in the theological seminary in Oslo. Published a very influential *Koralbog*, 1871, which "taught the Norwegian people to sing." Many of his tunes have the rhythmic movement of the folk song.

82 *Holy Mountain.* Come to Calvary's holy mountain. Composed in 1871 for a hymn by Brorson.

100 *Easter Glory* (Fred Til Bod). Alleluia! Jesus lives. Composed for a hymn by Bishop Grundtvig.

106 *Spring of Souls.* Come, ye faithful, raise the strain.

151 *Kirken.* Built on a rock the church doth stand. Lindeman's first church tune. Composed for Bishop Grundtvig's hymn.

160 *Our Lady, Trondhjem.* Praise, my soul, the King of Heaven.

575 *Lindeman.* Jesus, priceless Treasure.

MAASALO, ARMAS TOIVO VALDEMAR (1885-). Organist St. John's Church, Helsinki, Finland. Instructor of voice in Teachers' Normal Training School and in the Helsinki School of Church Music. Director of the National Choir. Composer of orchestral suites, cantatas, and other church music.

383 *Jesus, hear.* Jesus, hear my humble pleading.

NYBERG, BERNDT MIKAEL (1871-1940). Finnish composer, teacher, editor of church music.

145 *Nyberg.* The saints of God! their conflict past. A Finnish hymn tune adapted by David Evans, distinguished Welsh musician.

OLSSON, OTTO EMANUEL (1879-). Swedish composer. Organist Gustavus Vasa Church, Stockholm. Professor in the conservatory. Composer of choral and organ works.

316 *Transfiguration.* O God of mercy, God of might.

SUOMEN KORAALIKIRJA, 1738. A Finnish hymnal.

191 *Finnish Song.* Lord, dismiss us with thy blessing.

SWEDISH KORALBOK, 1697.

81 *Swedish Litany.* Jesus, in thy dying woes.

104 *Riddarholm* (*Upp, min Tunga*). Praise the Saviour, now and ever.

146 *Laurinus.* In heaven above, in heaven above.

352 *Pax* (*Ack, bliv hos oss*). O God of love, O King of peace.

422 *Praise* (*Af himlens*). Sing praise to God who reigns above.

430 *St. Erik.* At the Name of Jesus.

449 *Blomstertid.* How marvellous God's greatness.

SWEDISH MELODY.

9 *Messiah* (Bereden väg för Herran). Prepare the way, O Zion. Seventeenth century.

302 *St. Lawrence, Lund* (Uppfaren är vår Herre). O pour thy Spirit from on high. Before 1697.

333 *Stockholm.* Full many shall come from the east and the west. 1694.

485 *Kalmar.* Jesus, Lord and precious Saviour. 1676.

572 *Sandell* (*Tryggare kan ingen vara*). Children of the heavenly Father.

THOMISSÖN, HANS, PSALMEBOG, 1569. An important Danish hymnal quite generally used in Sweden. It contained 268 items. Some of the melodies were adaptations from the German. Others were native Danish melodies.

253 *Island.* How blest are they who hear God's word.

Franzen.

264 Thine own, O loving Saviour.

288 My Lord, I hear thee pleading.

WENNERBERG, GUNNAR (1817-1901). Swedish poet and composer of oratorios and music for the church. Taught himself music.

378 *Wennerberg.* Search me, God, and know my heart.

WEYSE, CHRISTOPH ERNST FRIEDRICH (1774-1842). Danish musician. Organist at Vor Frue Kirke, Copenhagen. Composer of operas as well as church music.

46 *Christmas brings joy.* Christmas brings joy to every heart.

299 *Weyse* (Den Signede Dag). I know of a sleep in Jesus' Name. Composed in 1826 for Grundtvig's hymn commemorating the one thousandth anniversary of the introduction of Christianity into Denmark.

WIDEEN, KARL IVAR NATANAEL (1871-1951). Swedish teacher, composer, and editor. Organist of the cathedral in Skara. Composer of sacred and secular cantatas, hymn tunes, et cetera. Editor of the *Swedish Church Hymnal.*

218 *Skara.* Blest are the moments, doubly blest. One of the tunes found in the *Swedish Church Hymnal.* Arranged by Regina H. Fryxell and accepted in the Commission's tune competition.

WOLDER, DAVID (sixteenth century). Compiled a hymnal dedicated to King Charles IV of Denmark, 1598. This contained 178 new tunes.

251 *Wolder* (*Aus meines Herzens Grunde*). The Spirit of the Lord revealed. Probably a traditional melody, adapted.

ZINCK, HARTNACK OTTO KONRAD (1746-1832). Cantor and organist in Hamburg and later in Denmark. Associated with the Royal Theater in Copenhagen. Edited a book of chorales.

506 *Copenhagen* (*Jeg vil mig Herren love*). Let me be Thine forever. From Zinck's *Koral-Melodier* of 1801.

PSALM TUNES, CHIEFLY BRITISH

Luther introduced and developed the congregational hymn. Zwingli, a more accomplished musician than Luther, would not permit the congregation to sing in church. Calvin vigorously promoted congregational singing, but limited this to the singing of rhymed metrical versions of the Psalms. His rejection of hymnody in favor of Psalmody resulted in the appearance in various countries of metrical Psalters with Psalm tunes. Three of these are important, the French (Genevan), the English, and the Scottish.

Clement Marot, a poet and satirist attached to the French court, early published thirty Psalms in metrical form. These were sung to popular ballad tunes. When his work was condemned in the effort to suppress the Huguenots, Marot fled to Geneva where he published the first Genevan Psalter containing fifty Psalms in meter. Following his death in 1544, Calvin commissioned Theodore Beza to provide metrical translations or paraphrases of the remaining one hundred Psalms. The complete Genevan Psalter appeared in 1562. From 1542 to 1557 Louis Bourgeois had been the competent musical editor of this work. Lobwasser, a German Lutheran, published a German edition of it in 1573, with tunes harmonized by Claude Goudimel.

Calvin in his early ministry in Strassburg used a Lutheran Order of Service and Hymnal. The Genevan Psalter, which he later did so much to promote, was primarily a French work with traces of German influence. *Old Hundredth, Old 124th* (*St. Michael*), and *Commandments* are sturdy tunes from the Genevan Psalter. The new *Hymnal* adds *Old 130th* and *Nunc Dimittis* from this source.

In England Miles Coverdale, who like Luther had been an Augustinian friar, published thirteen Psalms in meter together with hymns on the Creed, Ten Commandments, Magnificat, and Nunc Dimittis. This work of 1539 was definitely based upon Luther's hymnals of 1524 and later. It received little attention as the spirit and practices of Calvinism were now prevailing over the earlier influences of Lutheranism. Ten years later, 1549, the year of the first Prayer Book, Thomas Sternhold published nineteen metrical Psalms without music. John Hopkins revised and enlarged this in 1551. This Sternhold and Hopkins collection was completed and supplied with sixty-five tunes and published by John Day in 1562. Nine new tunes in this book were by Thomas Tallis. The return of the Genevan refugees after the death of Queen Mary accelerated the process and the English people became, and remained for generations, Psalm singers and not hymn singers. The Sternhold and Hopkins text ran through six hundred editions. It was frequently bound in with copies of the Prayer Book or the Bible and came to have almost canonical authority. It was called the Old Version when superseded in many circles by the New Version of Tate and Brady, first issued in 1696.

All the early Psalters had the melody in the tenor part. The Psalter of Thomas Este in 1592 had four-part settings by ten prominent English composers and was the first to give names to tunes. This practice was carried much further by the important Psalter of Thomas Ravenscroft of 1621. The tunes *Cheshire* and *Winchester* first appeared in the 1592 edition of the Este Psalter.

Psalmody in Scotland received its greatest impulse from the Scotch and English refugees who returned to their native lands from Geneva after the death of Queen Mary. They had maintained a small but closely knit congregation, never more than two hundred, in Geneva, and they had there come under the strong personal influence of Calvin. The forceful leadership of John Knox fastened the tenets and the Psalm singing of Calvinism upon the Scottish people. The completed Scottish Psalter of 1564 shows stronger influence from Geneva than does the slightly earlier English Psalter of 1562. The tune *Dundee* (French) is from the Scottish Psalter. The new *Hymnal* adds from this source the tunes *Caithness, London New,* and *Wigtown.*

The Pilgrim Fathers brought with them from Holland copies of the Ainsworth Psalter, a collection prepared by their minister of this name in Amsterdam in 1612, eight years before the Mayflower sailed for the New World. As the colony grew the Sternhold Psalter was also introduced. In 1640 the *Bay Psalm Book* was published in Boston. This ran through more than seventy editions in the next century and a half. It contained the first music set from type in America.

The Historical Edition of *Hymns Ancient and Modern* (London, William Clowes and Sons, Ltd., 1909) gives an excellent account of these matters. The scholarly but coldly technical work by Maurice Frost, *English and Scottish Psalm and Hymn Tunes* (London: Oxford University Press, 1953) is an exhaustive study of the subject.

FRENCH PSALTER, STRASSBURG, 1539. The first French compilation by Clement Marot. Completed in 1562 by Theodore Beza. Louis Bourgeois arranged and composed many melodies for this work.
398 *Old 130th.* Mine eyes unto the mountains. Tune rarely found in modern hymnals.
BOURGEOIS, LOUIS (*c.* 1510-61). Born in Paris, resident in Geneva, close associate of Calvin. Composer and arranger of most of the settings in the Genevan Psalter, 1542-62, some tunes being of German source and others of secular origin. First to use a hymnboard.
220 *Nunc Dimittis.* O gladsome light, O grace. Tune set in the Genevan Psalter to a version of the liturgical Canticle.

GOUDIMEL, CLAUDE (d. 1572). Huguenot composer. His Psalm harmonizations appeared in Paris in 1564. Slain in Lyons during the St. Bartholomew's Day massacre. Harmonized the above tune, *Nunc Dimittis.*

SCOTTISH PSALTER, 1635. Published in Edinburgh, this was the musical climax of a series of Psalters, and the first Scottish Psalter to give tunes in four parts.

Caithness. The first phrase begins like *Dundee.* One of the thirty-one Common Tunes in this Psalter.

384 One who is all unfit to count.

466 O for a closer walk with God.

London New. First called Newtown. The name London dates from its use in Playford's *Psalmes,* 1671.

369 Approach, my soul, the mercy seat.

484 God moves in a mysterious way.

384 *Wigtown.* One who is all unfit to count. A melody of freer movement than many of the early Psalm tunes.

FRENCH CHURCH TUNES

This small but interesting group of melodies has a plainsong background. Its origin, however, is late and independent of the medieval musical modes.

The brilliant early years of the reign of Louis XIV developed an intense national character within the church of France. The Gallican Movement sought to restrict the authority of the papacy and increase the prestige of the local bishops. It led to preparation of neo-Gallican liturgies in the latter half of the seventeenth century. The Renaissance spirit, with its return to classical standards of Latin poetry, is evident in the work of the French poets who in this century composed new Latin hymns for the new breviary Offices.

The breviaries of Cluny and of Paris were particularly influential. By the end of the eighteenth century no fewer than eighty dioceses had abandoned the use of the Roman Breviary in favor of their own revised Offices. Jean-Baptiste de Santeüil (eighty-nine hymns) and Charles Coffin (eighty-three hymns) were among the most important scholars who wrote new Latin hymns.

In many instances new tunes were composed for the new Latin hymns. These tunes have a strong plainsong flavor, but it is plainsong modernized in clear recognition of modern measured rhythm and of the tonal system which was developing in all musical forms.

Among other features we recognize in these French church tunes a praiseworthy attempt to preserve unisonous and melodic singing of churchly character in an age infatuated with new-found scales, measured rhythm, and the freedom offered by concert and opera. Erik Routley of

Mansfield College, Oxford, regards these French church tunes as "the finest musical legacy of the post-Reformation Roman Catholic Church." [2]

The attention of the leaders of the Oxford Movement was early directed to these late Latin hymns and tunes of the French church. Isaac Williams, pupil of John Keble, published translations from the Paris Breviary as early as 1839. John Chandler published his volume of translations of early and late Latin hymns in 1841. From his collection we have "The advent of our God" and "On Jordan's banks the Baptist's cry" of Charles Coffin.

A few French church tunes were included in Thomas Helmore's *Hymnal Noted*, 1852, and in the important *Hymns Ancient and Modern*, 1861. It remained, however, for Canon Percy Dearmer and his musical editor Ralph Vaughan Williams to bring more than twenty of these interesting and beautiful tunes to popular recognition in their epoch-making *English Hymnal* of 1906. Many of these tunes are now found in standard hymnals of all Protestant communions.

A concise account of these matters will be found in *The French Diocesan Hymns and Their Melodies* by Cyril E. Pocknee (London: The Faith Press, Ltd., 1954).

ADORO TE, DEVOTE. A late (Paris Processional, 1697) form of an ancient plainsong melody associated with this hymn. Quite in a modern major scale.

272 Thee we adore, O hidden Saviour, thee.

AETERNA CHRISTI MUNERA. A late, semi-metrical form of the original plainsong melody as given by Guidetti, a priest and pupil of Palestrina, in 1582. This Rouen church melody became very popular in France.

133 O Trinity of blessed light.

CHRISTE SANCTORUM. Pocknee (French Diocesan Hymns) finds a form of this tune in the Paris Antiphoner, 1681.

137 Father, most holy, merciful and tender.

204 Father, we praise thee, now the night is over.

DEUS TUORUM MILITUM. A melody with quite modern tonality. From the Grenoble Antiphoner, 1753.

494 We sing the praise of him who died.

O QUANTA QUALIA (*Regnator orbis*). In the *Methode du Plain-chant*, 1808, and in *The Hymnal Noted*, 1852. Pocknee has located a slightly altered form in the Paris Antiphoner, 1681.

596 O what their joy and their glory must be.

PICARDY. A French carol, first located in modern times in Tiersot's *Melodies*, Paris, 1887. Must be sung slowly.

281 Let all mortal flesh keep silence.

343 Judge eternal, throned in splendor.

[2] K. L. Parry, *Companion to Congregational Praise* (London: Independent Press, 1953), p. 41. Notes on the music by Erik Routley.

HYMN TUNES

We have spoken of new Psalm Tunes, folk songs, carols, and traditionals and now turn to hymn tunes proper. It will be convenient to group composers in two English-speaking groups.

British

Remembering the early ascendancy of psalmody, and the late beginning of hymnody in England and Scotland, we cannot expect to find many British composers of hymn tunes in the sixteenth and seventeenth centuries. Some of the six new tunes we have from this period may have been set to Psalm versions at different times, but their later association has definitely been with hymns. Thomas Tallis represents the sixteenth century; Orlando Gibbons and Jeremiah Clarke the seventeenth.

Current Lutheran hymnals have a number of tunes by eighteenth century and early nineteenth century composers. Most of these fall within the time of the English glee (1700-1825). Their melodies are generally smooth-flowing, but less stately than those of the earlier period.

About the middle of the nineteenth century the volume of British hymn melodies swells from a gentle stream to a mighty flood. The early enthusiasm of the Methodists and Independents, and the later interest of the Church of England led to the appearance of many hymn collections and to incredible industry on the part of composers. Many of these are represented in our present hymnals—Goss, Reinagle, Stainer, Ouseley, Calkin, Cutler, Parry, and Elvey. Dr. Gauntlett confessed to having written several thousand tunes. Dr. Monk, musical editor of *Hymns Ancient and Modern,* contributed no less than fifty of his own tunes to that important collection. He secured thirty-one original tunes from John Bacchus Dykes for the same book.

Important composers represented by new items are Barnby, Sullivan, Dykes, Baker, Wesley, Smart, Monk, Hopkins, et cetera. Of the first three, Dykes has proven the most durable. Modern criticism of Victorian church musicians as a whole takes issue with the part-song character, the chromatic progressions of many of their tunes, the frequent sacrifice of melody to harmonic effects, and the too liberal use of dominant seventh chords. While recognizing the merit of these strictures, we know that our present day hymnals would be poorer without many of these tunes, rich in grace and harmonious beauty.

The more recent decades of the twentieth century have seen a group of distinguished British composers, many of whom are still living, lending their talents to tune compositions, the editing of hymnals, et cetera. Among these are John Hughes, Gustav Holst, Henry Walford Davies, David Evans, the brothers Geoffrey and Martin Shaw, Eric Thiman, and

Ralph Vaughan Williams. The finest modern hymnals in the English-speaking world have been edited by one or other of these men, such hymnals as the *Church Hymnary* of the Church of Scotland, the *English Hymnal, Songs of Praise, Congregational Praise,* British Broadcasting Corporation's *BBC Hymn Book,* and the *Hymnal for Scotland* (Church of England). While the original tunes of these composers and editors are varied in character, as a group these composers reflect the vigor, directness, and informality of our present time, with melodies quite in line with speech-rhythm principles and with harmonizations characterized by strength rather than grace.

ARNE, THOMAS AUGUSTINE (1710-78). Composer of oratorios, ballads, and popular music. Associate of Handel, composer for Drury Lane Theatre.
554 *Arlington.* Am I a soldier of the Cross. Adapted 1784 from a minuet in the opera *Artaxerxes,* 1762.

ATKINSON, FREDERICK COOK (1841-97). Organist at Mannington, Bradford, England.
129 *Morecambe.* Spirit of God, descend upon my heart. Composed 1870 for the hymn "Abide with me" and published in a leaflet.

ATTWOOD, THOMAS (1765-1838). A favorite pupil of Mozart. Organist of St. Paul's Cathedral and of the Chapel Royal. Prolific composer in the dramatic and the church fields.
124 *Attwood.* Creator Spirit, by whose aid. Composed as a brief anthem for four voices for an Ordination Service in St. Paul's.

BELL, JOHN MONTGOMERIE (1837-1910). A lawyer, botanist, and physician. Composer of fine tunes and anthems.
544 *St. Giles.* We give thee but thine own. First set to this hymn in the Scottish Hymnal, 1885.

BISHOP, JOHN (1665-1737). Organist of Winchester College, and later of Winchester Cathedral.
Illsley.
133 O Trinity of blessed light. Tune from *A Sett of New Psalm Tunes,* where it is set to Psalm 100.
217 O Son of Man, thou madest known.
175 *Leicester.* O King of kings, before whose throne. From the above collection, set to Psalm 112. An impressive chorale-like melody.

BOYD, WILLIAM (1847-1928). Anglican clergyman. Born in Jamaica. Vicar of All Saints, Norfolk Square.
557 *Pentecost.* Fight the good fight with all thy might. Tune composed 1864 for another hymn. At the request of Baring-Gould, set to the above hymn by Arthur Sullivan in his *Church Hymns.*

BUNNETT, EDWARD (1834-1923). Church organist and composer in Norwich, England.
Kirby Bedon. First published in the Congregational Hymnary.
179 Shepherd of tender youth.
311 Christ for the world we sing.

CAREY, HENRY (1692-1743). English poet, dramatist, and composer of songs, ballads, and cantatas.

359 *Surrey (Carey)*. Lord God of hosts, whose mighty hand. Set to Addison's Twenty-third Psalm in Church's *Introduction to Psalmody*, 1723.

CLARKE, JEREMIAH (*c.* 1669-1707). Organist St. Paul's Cathedral, London, and joint-organist with William Croft of the Chapel Royal. Composed for the theater as well as for the church. Cantatas, anthems, and hymn tunes.

476 *Bishopthorpe (St. Paul's)*. Immortal Love, forever full. Tune first published in 1790.

COBB, GERARD FRANCIS (1838-1904). Born in Kent, England. Studied music in Dresden. Composed choral music in Cambridge.

177 *Moultrie*. Round the Lord in glory seated.

COTTMAN, ARTHUR (1842-79). An English lawyer with special interest in church music. Composer of tunes.

593 *Dalehurst*. I know not what the future hath.

CROFT, WILLIAM (1678-1727). Organist of the Chapel Royal and later of Westminster Abbey. Remembered particularly for his fine anthems and tunes.

St. Matthew. Tune probably by Croft. One of eighteen tunes published in Philadelphia for the *Book of Common Prayer*, 1786.

254 Thy word, O Lord, like gentle dews.

324 Thine arm, O Lord, in days of old.

DAVIES, HENRY WALFORD (1869-1941). Professor of Music, University of Wales. Master of Music to the King. Conductor London Bach Choir. Author, and editor of hymnals.

27 *Christmas Carol*. O little town of Bethlehem. Composed 1905 for Bishop Brooks' hymn.

DEARLE, EDWARD (1806-91). English organist and composer of oratorios, services, and anthems.

275 *Penitentia*. Here, O my Lord, I see thee face to face. First published in Sullivan's *Church Hymns*, 1874.

DYKES, JOHN BACCHUS (1823-76). Anglican clergyman and outstanding Victorian composer. Precentor of Durham Cathedral. Composed more than three hundred hymn tunes. More widely represented in modern hymnals than any other composer. Twenty-five tunes in the *Hymnal*.

280 *Ecce Panis*. Very Bread, good Shepherd, tend us.

411 *Gerontius*. Praise to the Holiest in the height. A fine tune for the excerpt from John Henry Newman's poem, "The Dream of Gerontius."

523 *Lux Benigna*. Lead kindly Light. Composed by Dykes for Newman's hymn while walking through the Strand, London.

EDWARDS, JOHN DAVID (*c.* 1805-85). Anglican clergyman, Vicar of Rhosymedre, Ruabon.

65 *Rhosymedre*. My song is love unknown. A simple tune which fits the unusual rhythm of the text and thoughtfully repeats the last two lines.

EVANS, DAVID (1874-1948). Distinguished Welsh musician. Professor of music, University College of South Wales. Promoter of Welsh music festivals and of the National Eisteddfod. Many choral and orchestral works. Hymnal editor.

574 *Nyland* (Harmonized). In heavenly love abiding.

GIBBONS, ORLANDO (1583-1625). Distinguished Elizabethan church musician. Organist of Westminster Abbey. Composed some forty services and anthems and sixteen tunes. The latter appeared in 1623, in Wither's *Hymns and Songs of the Church*. Four of these tunes are in the *Hymnal*.

125 *Song 22*. Love of the Father, Love of God the Son. Set to a paraphrase of Hezekiah's prayer (Isa. 37:16-20).

130 *Song 13*. Holy Spirit, truth divine. One of four tunes set to sections of the Song of Solomon.

214. *Angel's Song (Song 34)*. Forth in thy Name, O Lord, I go. A setting of the Song of Angels (Luke 2:23).

350 *Song 1*. Eternal Ruler of the ceaseless round. Tune also known as *Canterbury, Norwich,* and *St. Irenaeus*.

GLADSTONE, WILLIAM HENRY (1840-91). Son of the Prime Minister, William Ewart Gladstone. Scholar, musician, hymnal editor. Member of Parliament.

118 *Ombersley*. Spirit of mercy, truth, and love. Name of a village in the constituency which Gladstone later represented in the House of Commons.

GOWER, JOHN HENRY (1855-1922). English organist who came to Denver, Colorado. Identified with mining interests. Organist in Denver and later in Chicago.

Meditation (Gower). Composed in 1890 for the hymn, "There is a land of pure delight."

77 There is a green hill far away.

263 O God, unseen, yet ever near.

HALLELUJAH, THE, 1849. Edited by J. J. White and H. J. Gauntlett.

121 *Malvern* (Arranged by John Roberts, 1822-77). Come, Holy Ghost, in love.

HARWOOD, BASIL (1859-1949). Organist of Ely Cathedral and of Christ Church Cathedral, Oxford. Composer of cantatas, anthems, and organ works.

159 *Thornbury*. Thy hand, O God, has guided. Composed for this hymn in Supplement of *Hymns Ancient and Modern*, 1916.

HAYNE, LEIGHTON GEORGE (1836-83). Church of England clergyman. Organist at Eton. Conductor Oxford University Chorus. Co-editor of *The Merton Tune Book*.

329 *St. Cecilia*. Thy kingdom come, O God. Composed for "Thy way, not mine, O Lord" in *The Merton Tune Book*.

HOLST, GUSTAV THEODORE (1874-1934). Prominent English composer, of Swedish ancestry. A student of Hindu literature. Many carols and vigorous tunes.

36 *Cranham*. In the bleak mid-winter. The first tune composed for this text. Published in the *English Hymnal*, 1906.

HOPKINS, EDWARD JOHN (1818-1901). English organist, author, editor, composer. Teacher of organ and eminent recitalist.

545 *Christmas Morn*. The wise may bring their learning.

HORSLEY, WILLIAM (1774-1858). English organist and editor. With George Smart and Thomas Attwood a founder of the London Philharmonic Society.

440 *Belgrave*. When all thy mercies, O my God.

225

HUGHES, JOHN (1873-1932). Welsh railroad man. Precentor in Baptist Church.

520 *Cwm Rhonda.* Guide me, O thou great Jehovah. Composed, 1905, for the annual Singing Festival, and sung during the next twenty-five years at five thousand such festivals.

HULLAH, JOHN PYKE (1812-84). Famous teacher of singing. London.

495 *Bentley.* Sometimes a light surprises. Composed, 1866, for this hymn.

IRVINE, JESSIE SEYMOUR (1836-87). Daughter of a minister in Crimond, Scotland.

522 *Crimond.* The Lord's my Shepherd, I'll not want. Arranged by David Grant, an Aberdeen tobacconist.

JACKSON, ROBERT (1842-1914). Organist, St. Peter's Church, Oldham, England, for forty-eight years, succeeding his father who had held the same position for forty-eight years.

470 *Trentham.* Breathe on me, Breath of God. Composed 1894 for Henry Williams Baker's hymn, "O perfect life of love."

JUDE, WILLIAM HERBERT (1851-1922). English organist in Liverpool and Manchester. Editor and composer.

553 *Galilee.* Jesus calls us; o'er the tumult. Composed for Alexander's hymn for St. Andrew's Day.

LE JEUNE, GEORGE FITZ-CURWOOD (1841-1904). Student of Barnby in London. Organist, St. Luke's Church, Philadelphia, and of St. John's Chapel of Trinity parish, New York, where he developed a famous boy choir.

Love Divine (Le Jeune).

397 Love divine, all loves excelling. Tune composed 1872 for this hymn, and dedicated to his pupil, George Edward Stubbs.

549 Saviour, thee my heart I tender.

LLOYD, JOHN AMBROSE (1815-74). Welsh musician. Founder of the Welsh Choral Union of Liverpool. Composer of two collections of hymn tunes.

Cromer. First published in the *Norwich Tune Book,* 1844.

62 O Christ, our King, Creator, Lord.

241 How blessed is this place, O Lord.

MACFARREN, WALTER CECIL (1826-1905). Principal of the Royal Academy of Music, and professor of music at Cambridge University.

203 *Barmouth.* At Thy feet, O Christ, we lay. Composed for this hymn at request of William Henry Monk for revised edition of *Hymns Ancient and Modern,* 1875. Macfarren and Monk had been lost for a day and a night in the Welsh mountains near the town of Barmouth.

MACLAGAN, WILLIAM DALRYMPLE (1826-1910). Born in Edinburgh. Archbishop of York, soldier in India in early life. Composed hymns and tunes.

377 *Bread of Heaven.* Sinners Jesus will receive. Composed for this text, 1875.

MAKER, FREDERICK CHARLES (1844-1927). Born in Bristol, England. Organist of Methodist and Congregational churches. Composer of anthems and hymn tunes.

332 *Ford Cottage.* O holy city, seen of John.

447 *Wentworth.* My God, I thank thee, who hast made.

MANN, ARTHUR HENRY (1850-1929). Born in Norwich, England. Organist, King's College, Cambridge, and of the University for fifty-three years. Edited Handel's manuscripts.
182 *Berno*. O day of rest and gladness.

MONK, WILLIAM HENRY (1823-89). Musical editor of *Hymns Ancient and Modern*, 1861, to which he contributed fifty tunes. Organist of London churches and Professor of Music, King's College, London.
111 *Ascension*. Hail the day that sees him rise. Composed 1861.
278 *Unde et memores*. And now, O Father, mindful of the love. Composed for the revised *Hymns Ancient and Modern*, 1875.

MORLEY, THOMAS (1842-91). Organist, St. Alban's, Holborn, London. Composed many tunes.
427 *David (St. Alban's)*. Praise the Lord of heaven. Written 1867 for the *St. Alban's Hymn Book*.

NAYLOR, EDWARD WOODALL (1867-1934). Organist, Emmanuel College, Cambridge, and lecturer at the university. Composer of operas and much church music.
564 *From Strength to Strength*. Soldiers of Christ, arise. Composed, 1902, for this hymn.

OWEN, WILLIAM (1814-93). Welsh composer, living at Caeathraw, Carnarvon.
114 *Bryn Calfaria*. Look, ye saints, the sight is glorious. The name is Welsh for "Mount Calvary." A typically rugged Welsh tune of "forbidding grandeur," well suited for texts of strength and character.

PRICHARD, ROWLAND HUGH (1811-87). Precentor in Bala and in Holywell, Wales. Employed in a flannel mill. Composed several fine tunes.
397 *Hyfrydol*. Love divine, all loves excelling. A tune whose striking rhythm gives life and movement, though, with the exception of a single note, limited in range to a fifth.

PURDAY, CHARLES HENRY (1799-1885). Precentor in the Scottish Church, Crown Court, Covent Garden, London. Author, publisher, and lecturer in the field of church music.
Sandon.
488 Unto the hills around do I lift up. A metrical version of Psalm 121, the "Traveler's Psalm."
523 Lead kindly Light. Perhaps the earliest setting to this hymn.

REDHEAD, RICHARD (1820-1901). Organist, St. Mary Magdalene Church, Paddington. A pioneer in the revival of plainsong. Editor of the first plainsong Psalter. Composer.
395 *Wolverhampton*. O for a faith that will not shrink. A simple, straightforward tune, typical of Redhead's style.

ROBERTS, JOHN (1822-77). Welsh musician, Methodist minister, and editor. Founder of the important national Welsh music festivals. Editor of a famous Methodist tune book, 1859.
121 *Malvern*. Come, Holy Ghost, in love. Roberts arranged this tune, which first appeared in triple rhythm in *Hallelujah*, 1849.

ROBERTS, ROBERT EDWIN (1879-). Editor, poet. On staffs of *Pall Mall Gazette, New Statesman, Time and Tide*, et cetera.
258 *Philippine*. O Lord, thy people gathered here.

ROCKSTRO, WILLIAM SMITH (1823-95). English musician. Studied at the Leipsic Conservatory. Concert pianist and authority on ancient church music. Author and composer.

493 *Omni die* (Arranged). **There's a wideness in God's mercy.** An arrangement of the tune in Corner's *Gesangbuch,* Nuremberg, 1631, set to the hymn, "Omni die dic Mariae." Appeared in the *English Hymnal,* 1906.

SCHOLEFIELD, CLEMENT COTTERILL (1839-1904). English clergyman. Curate at St. Peter's Church, South Kensington, where Arthur Sullivan was the organist. Sir Arthur included tunes by Scholefield in the S.P.C.K. (Society for Promoting Christian Knowledge) *Church Hymns,* 1874.

227 *St. Clement.* The day thou gavest, Lord, is ended.

SCHULTHES, WILHELM AUGUST FERDINAND (1816-79). Director of the choir at the Brompton Oratory, 1852-72.

Lambeth.

246 Thou, whose unmeasured temple stands.

457 Our God is love, and all his saints.

SCOTT-GATTY, ALFRED (1847-1918). Musician, authority on heraldry, composer of songs, musical plays, et cetera.

Welwyn.

382 Now once again, for help that never faileth. A nicely flowing tune, first published in the *Arundel Hymns,* 1902.

539 O brother man, fold to thy heart thy brother.

SHAW, GEOFFREY TURTON (1879-1943). Organist, composer, inspector of music in the London schools. Influential in the affairs of the British Broadcasting Company.

551 *Miles animosus.* Stand up, stand up for Jesus. A lusty modern English tune.

SHAW, MARTIN FALLAS (1875-). Elder brother of Geoffrey. Master of Music at St. Martin's-in-the-Fields. Associated with Percy Dearmer and Ralph Vaughan Williams in editing hymnals which introduced vigorous tunes and many folk songs.

168 *St. Anne.* O God, our help in ages past. Shaw has added a Faburden to this old tune by William Croft.

321 *Little Cornard.* Hills of the North, rejoice. A vigorous tune, composed in 1915 for this hymn.

413 *Cheerful.* Come, let us join our cheerful songs.

529 *Marching.* Through the night of doubt and sorrow. A strong bright tune with wide intervals.

SIMPSON, ROBERT (1790-1832). A weaver, by trade, in Glasgow. Precentor in a Congregational Church.

Ballerma.

289 O God, accept my heart this day. Tune arranged from a Spanish ballad and ascribed, not too certainly, to Simpson.

594 Give me the wings of faith to rise.

SMART, GEORGE THOMAS (1776-1867). (See p. 000.)

420 *Wiltshire.* Through all the changing scenes of life. Composed 1795. First associated with this hymn in the 1868 *Hymns Ancient and Modern.*

SMART, HENRY THOMAS (1813-79). Organist several churches in London.

Designer of great organs in Glasgow, Leeds, and Dublin. Composer of much church music.

148 *Trisagion.* Stars of the morning, so gloriously bright. Composed for Neale's translation.

362 *Gordon.* Lord, in thy Name thy servants plead.

498 *Pilgrims.* Hark! hark, my soul! angelic songs are swelling.

565 *Forward (Smart).* Forward! be our watchword.

SMITH, HENRY PERCY (1825-98). Anglican clergyman with parishes in England and in Cannes, France. A canon of the Cathedral of Gibraltar.

537 *Maryton.* O Master, let me walk with thee. Composed for "Sun of my soul." Dr. Gladden chose it for his hymn.

SULLIVAN, ARTHUR SEYMOUR (1824-1900). Professor of composition, the Royal Academy of Music, conductor of the Philharmonic Society, composer of anthems and hymn tunes, as well as many hymns. A master melodist, best known for his association with W. S. Gilbert.

Leominster.

66 Wide open are thy hands.

508 Make me a captive Lord. Tune arranged from *Pilgrim Song* by George William Martin, 1862.

534 *Homeland.* For thee, O dear, dear country. Sullivan's first hymn tune. Composed at the request of the editor of the magazine, *Good Words,* 1867.

TALLIS, THOMAS (c. 1510-85). The "Father of English Church Music." Organist of Waltham Abbey. Associate of William Byrd. Composed service music, anthems, et cetera for Latin and English texts. Also eight tunes for Archbishop Parker's Psalter, 1567.

499 *Third Mode Melody.* I heard the voice of Jesus say. Originally with melody in the tenor.

WALCH, JAMES (1837-1901). Student of Henry Smart. Organist and composer.

440 *Eagley.* When all thy mercies, O my God.

WALLACE, WILLIAM VINCENT (1814-65). Irish musician. A brilliant violinist, who lived an adventurous life in Australia, the South Sea Islands, South America, Mexico. Composer of operas and piano music.

476 *Serenity.* Immortal Love, for ever full. From his composition, "Ye Winds that Waft."

WESLEY, SAMUEL SEBASTIAN (1810-76). An eminent church musician. Composer of many fine tunes.

83 *Wigan.* Behold the Lamb of God. Composed especially for this text in 1872.

97 *Hawarden.* Sing, men and angels, sing. First published in the *European Psalmist,* 1872.

218 *Winscott.* Blest are the moments, doubly blest. First appeared in the *European Psalmist,* 1872.

318 *Ellingham.* Thy kingdom come! O Father, hear our prayer. Composed 1864. Published in a hymnal edited by Charles Kemble and S. S. Wesley.

WILLIAMS, RALPH VAUGHAN (1872-1958). Studied at Cambridge, Berlin, and Paris. Professor of composition at the Royal College of Music.

Collector of English folk songs, many of which he employed in his symphonies, hymn tunes, et cetera. Musical editor the *English Hymnal, Oxford Book of Carols, Songs of Praise.*

44   *Resonet in laudibus* (Harmonized). Long ago and far away.

123   *Down Ampney.* Come down, O Love divine. Composed for this text in the *English Hymnal.* Tune named for the composer's birthplace in Gloucestershire.

Christe sanctorum (Harmonized).

134   Father, most holy, merciful and tender.

204   Father, we praise thee, now the night is over.

144   *Sine Nomine.* For all the saints who from their labors rest. Composed in free form for Bishop How's hymn in the *English Hymnal,* 1906. A fine example of perfect coincidence of musical and verbal accents, as in speech-rhythm chanting.

344   *King's Lynn* (Arranged). O God of earth and altar. English traditional melody.

WILLIAMS, ROBERT (*c.* 1781-1821). Blind basket-maker living in northwest Wales. Able musician and composer of hymn tunes.

99   *Llanfair.* Christ the Lord is risen today. Composed 1817, and first called *Bethel.*

WILLIAMS, THOMAS JOHN (1869-1944). Welsh organist and choirmaster. Composer of anthems and hymns tunes.

547   *Ebenezer (Ton-y-Botel).* Once to every man and nation. From an anthem "Light in the Valley." First published as a hymn tune in 1890. Widely sung before this. A popular legend, without foundation, asserted that it had been washed ashore in a bottle. Hence the name, "Tune in a bottle." The entire tune consists of variations on the peculiar phrase in the first measure.

WOODWARD, GEORGE RATCLIFFE (1848-1935). Church of England clergyman. Translator from the Latin, Greek, and German. His *Songs of Syon,* 1904, was an important source book, providing 414 authentic versions of hymn tunes from many lands.

94   *Puer nobis* (Harmonized). That Easter Day with joy was bright. From *Songs of Syon,* 1904.

American

During the decades before the War of Independence and well into the nineteenth century the only hymn singers in America were the Lutheran, the Reformed, and the Moravians, and these chiefly in New York, Pennsylvania, Maryland, and Virginia. They sang chorales to German texts. All the other Protestants, including the Episcopalians, were Psalm singers. The only exceptions were in the relatively few areas where the hymns of Watts and Wesley were gradually introduced. The efforts of a few determined leaders finally shook off the shackles of Psalmody and introduced hymnody, first in New York and New England, and then more widely.

It would seem that hymnody, with its freedom of form and breadth of spirit, would have made a natural appeal to the people who had fought a war for independence and had broken all ties with Europe. In the end hymnody did triumph, but the conflict split the Presbyterians into Old and New Schools and kept controversy flaming in practically all other churches for nearly a century.

The three men who, above all others in those early days, served the cause of hymnody and better church music in general were Lowell Mason, William Bradbury, and Thomas Hastings. The three were born in Massachusetts, Maine, and Connecticut, respectively. Mason's sphere of influence was Boston and New England. The other two lived and labored chiefly in New York. All three were prodigious workers. All wrote hymns and composed hundreds of tunes. All issued dozens of collections for choirs, congregations, and schools, millions of copies of which were sold. All directed choirs and great choruses and organized musical conventions, institutes, children's festivals, et cetera. They taught tens of thousands to read music, secured the teaching of music in the public schools of Boston and New York, and fostered a love of choral music unknown before their time. They nobly served their day and laid foundations upon which later church musicians were able to build.

It was the fashion thirty or forty years ago to view the work of these pioneers with disdain. Editors of good church hymnals also scorned even the finest of the gospel songs that had swept the continent. It is now recognized that the simple tunes of these pioneers and the very finest gospel songs are an integral part of our religious heritage as a people. With all their naivety they are as American as pie and prairie schooners, as homespun as hominy. We respect the faith and fervor that produced them, and rather envy them for the simplicity and sincerity they express and which our more sophisticated society finds difficult to achieve.

The number of capable church musicians greatly increased in the latter part of the nineteenth century and the early years of the twentieth. The wider circle includes representative churchmen and really distinguished musicians, many now living or recently deceased, whose tunes are listed in the following pages.

In an effort to encourage original composition by our own church musicians, and to secure additional contemporary tunes, the Commission on the Hymnal in 1950 invited submission of original tunes for sixteen hymns listed in the church press. Nearly four hundred compositions were submitted anonymously. These were carefully screened by two separate sections of the Commission and finally passed upon by the entire Commission. Tunes by the following composers were finally accepted and are included in the *Hymnal*: Catherine Deisher Baxter, Regina Holmen Fryxell, Arnold Frederick Keller, Clive Harold Kilgore, Ralph P. Lewars, L. David Miller, Guiseppe Moschetti, Gordon C. Ruud, Ralph Alvin Strom, and Roger Charles Wilson. The following American Lutheran composers are also represented in the *Hymnal* by original tunes: Gerhard Theodore Alexis, John Victor Bergquist, John Dahle, George Christian Frederick Haas, Peter Johnson, Carl Wilfred Landahl, Jeremiah Franklin Ohl, Oscar Rudolph Overby, Rob Roy Peery, Luther Dotterer Reed, Leland Bernhard Sateren, and Winifred Jacobs Shearer.

ALEXIS, GERHARD THEODORE (1889-1927). Son of a pioneer minister of the Augustana Church. Studied organ in Stockholm. Teacher, composer, editor. Organist First Lutheran Church, St. Paul. Member of committee which edited the Augustana Hymnal.

301 *Ishpeming.* Lord, who at Cana's wedding feast. Tune named for the town in northern Michigan where he served as organist and met his future wife.

391 *St. Ingrid.* Thou hidden Love of God, whose height. Ingrid was the name of the composer's mother.

512 *Seraphim.* Jesus, I my cross have taken. Composed, like the tunes mentioned above, for the Augustana Hymnal.

BAXTER, CATHERINE DEISHER (1914-   ). Organist and choir director Trinity Church, Germantown, Philadelphia. Studied music at Lebanon Valley College; composition at Westminster Choir College, Princeton, New Jersey; advanced organ with Ernest White, New York City. Composer of six major church cantatas, a choral symphony with orchestral instrumentation, et cetera.

217 *Blest Moments.* O Son of Man, thou madest known. Tune composed, in competition, for the *Hymnal.*

BERGQUIST, JOHN VICTOR (1877-1935). Born in St. Peter, Minnesota, and graduate of Conservatory of Music of Gustavus Adolphus College in that city. Studied music in Berlin and Paris, in the latter city under Alexander Guilmant. Organist Augustana Church, and later of Central Lutheran Church, Minneapolis. Head Department of Music, Gustavus Adolphus College and, later, Augustana College. Composer of a Reformation cantata, an oratorio *Golgotha,* et cetera.

336 *Aline.* O happy home, where thou art loved the dearest.

BRADBURY, WILLIAM BATCHELDER (1816-68). Born in York, Maine. Studied in Leipsic. Organist Baptist Tabernacle, New York City. Associate of Lowell Mason and Thomas Hastings. Organized free singing classes in New York. Compiled and published fifty-nine singing books. Composer popular tunes and music for Sunday schools.

478 *Aughton (He leadeth me).* He leadeth me: O blessed thought. Composed for this text. Published in *The Golden Censer,* 1864.

497 *Sweet Story (Luke)* (Arranged). I think, when I read that sweet story of old. A Greek folk song, called *Salamis* or *Athens* in British hymnals.

524 *Bradbury.* Saviour, like a shepherd lead us. Composed 1859 for these words.

BRISTOL, LEE HASTINGS, JR. (1923-   ). Advertising man, church musician, and editor. Descendant of Thomas Hastings. Graduate of Trinity College of Music, London. Graduate studies in music, Geneva, Switzerland. Composer for organ and orchestra as well as composer and editor of hymn tunes, carols, et cetera.

515 *Sedgwick.* O Jesus, I have promised.

BROWN, RAY FRANCIS (1897-   ). Organist and teacher, Oberlin Conservatory and Fisk University. Since 1934 organist and professor of Church Music, General (Episcopal) Theological Seminary, New York. Editor *The Oxford American Psalter* (speech-rhythm pointing).

243 *Chelsea Square* (Harmonized). Put forth, O God, thy Spirit's might.

BUCHANAN, ANNABEL MORRIS (1888-   ). Teacher of music in Texas, Oklahoma, and Virginia. President, Virginia Federation of Music Clubs. Author, *Folk-Hymns of America,* 1938.

587 *Land of Rest.* Jerusalem, my happy home. (See American traditional melodies, p. 203.)

BURT, BATES GILBERT (1878-1948). Rector, All Saints' Episcopal Church, Pontiac, Michigan. Wrote this hymn and tune for a high school commencement.

548 *Lynne.* O God of youth, whose Spirit. Tune composed 1940, and named in honor of a grandchild.

CANTICA LAUDIS (Mason and Webb). A collection published by Lowell Mason and George J. Webb in 1850.

559 *Heath.* My soul, be on thy guard. Presumably "arranged from Schumann," and named in honor of George Heath, author of the hymn.

CHADWICK, GEORGE WHITEFIELD (1854-1931). Director of the New England Conservatory of Music, Boston. Organist, conductor, composer.

473 *Peace.* I sought the Lord, and afterward I knew. Written 1890.

CONVERSE, CHARLES CROZAT (1832-1918). Lawyer in Erie, Pennsylvania. Studied at the Leipsic Conservatory. Composed two symphonies, oratorios, much orchestral music, and many tunes.

459 *Erie (What a Friend).* What a friend we have in Jesus. Also called *Converse* in some collections. Published in *Silver Wings,* 1870.

DAHLE, JOHN (1853-1931). Born in Norway. Became one of the leading church musicians of the Norwegian Lutherans in the American Northwest. Composer of cantatas, anthems, hymn tunes. Edited many collections for male and mixed choruses. Organized the Choral Union of the Norwegian Synod. Co-editor, with F. Melius Christiansen, of the *Lutheran Hymnary.*

185 *Red Wing Seminary.* Safely through another week.

287 *Luther Seminary.* Lord of the everlasting light.

DALE, CHARLES J.

580 *Denby.* My Jesus, as thou wilt.

DAY, GARDINER M. (1883-   ). Organist and composer of cantatas, anthems, and hymn tunes. Active in the American Guild of Organists.

345 *Geneva.* Not alone for mighty empire. Named in honor of the city in New York State where Day was choirmaster of Trinity Episcopal Church.

DOANE, WILLIAM HOWARD (1832-1915). Inventor, manufacturer, compiler of forty song books. Composer of hundreds of songs, ballads, cantatas, et cetera. Won Mr. Sankey to the cause of evangelism.

392 *More love to thee.* More love to thee. Composed 1868 for the Moody and Sankey collections.

461 *Pass me not.* Pass me not, O gentle Saviour. Composed 1870 for Fannie Van Alstyne Crosby's hymn.

DOUGLAS, CHARLES WINFRED (1867-1944). (See p. 000.)

497 *Sweet Story (Luke)* (Harmonized). I think, when I read that sweet story of old. First published in longer form in 1841; in shorter form in Bradbury's *Oriola,* 1859. Harmonized, 1918.

563 *St. Dunstan's.* He who would valiant be. A vigorous tune in free ballad-like rhythm that well fits the text. Composed on the train, returning to his home in Peekskill, New York, from New York City, December 15, 1917.

FISCHER, WILLIAM GUSTAVUS (1835-1912). Born in Baltimore. A bookbinder, proprietor of a music house, and teacher of music in Girard College, Philadelphia. Influenced by Lowell Mason and Thomas Hastings. He composed two hundred gospel songs.

326 *Hankey.* I love to tell the story.

FRYXELL, REGINA HOLMEN (1899-   ). Organist and composer. Graduate of Augustana College and of the Julliard School of Music, New York City, subsequently teaching in both institutions. Studied composition with Leo Sowerby, Chicago. Presently organist St. John's Church, Davenport, Iowa. Composer of many fine published anthems.

218 *Skara* (Arranged). Blest are the moments, doubly blest.

GEORGE, GRAHAM (1912-   ). Born in Norwich, England. Came to Canada at the age of sixteen. Professor of music, Queen's University, Montreal. Organist, and composer for orchestra and for church services.

73 *The King's Majesty.* Ride on, ride on, in majesty. Tune composed for this text in the Episcopal Hymnal, 1940. A fine modern unison tune in free rhythm. Well befits the concept of majesty.

HALL, WALTER HENRY (1862-1935). Born in London. Organist, St. Luke's Church, Germantown, Philadelphia, and St. James' Church, New York. Founded the Brooklyn Oratorio Society. Professor of church and choral music, Columbia University after 1913.

535 *Oneonta.* Not always on the mount may we. Composed 1918 for the hymn, "Asleep in Jesus, blessed sleep."

HASTINGS, THOMAS (1784-1872). Early American musician. Associate of Lowell Mason and William Bradbury in endeavors to improve church music. Composed a thousand or more tunes and published fifty music books. Lived in New York City.

570 *Ortonville.* Majestic sweetness sits enthroned.

HODGES, JOHN SEBASTIAN BACH (1830-1915). Son of the organist of Bristol Cathedral. Came to this country at the age of fifteen. Graduated from

Columbia University and General Theological Seminary. Served Episcopal churches in Pittsburgh, Chicago, Newark, and Baltimore. Composed anthems and hymn tunes and edited tune collections. Founded the first choir school in the United States.

279 *Eucharistic Hymn.* Bread of the world in mercy broken.

JEFFERY, JOHN ALBERT (1855-1929). Born in Plymouth, England. Studied piano in Leipsic, Weimar, and Paris. Organist, All Saints' Cathedral, Albany, New York. Later taught piano at the New England Conservatory, Boston.

137 *Ancient of Days.* Ancient of Days, who sittest throned in glory. Written, 1886, for the bicentennial of the city of Albany and for the hymn by Bishop Doane.

581 *Ancient of Days.* Hope of the world, thou Christ.

JOHNSON, PETER (1870-   ). Organist, composer, editor. Born in Sweden, came to the United States when ten years old. Graduate Northwestern School of Music, Minneapolis. Organist Gustavus Adolphus Church, St. Paul, for many years. Contributed nine tunes to the Augustana Hymnal, 1925, of which he was an editor.

233 *Cecile.* The twilight shadows round me fall.

KELLER, ARNOLD FREDERICK (1890-   ). Pastor emeritus, Church of the Redeemer, Utica, New York. Composed many carols and hymn tunes. Two tunes here noted were chosen from nearly four hundred anonymous entries in the tune competition conducted by the Commission on the Hymnal.

43 *Holy Manger.* Under the feeble stable light. This carol is one of many "tributes to the Christ Child" composed by Dr. Keller. He writes: "A few years ago some harsh critic of my carols chilled my inspiration. A kind note of appreciation from Dr. Luther D. Reed gave me new heart. . . . I listened again to the music of the spheres and caught up some of the fragments."

362 *Springtime.* Lord, in thy Name thy servants plead. Composed in 1943 for the hymn, "In Christ there is no east or west."

480 *Redeemer.* O thou, in all thy might so far. Dr. Keller writes: "The opening line of Frederick Hosmer's poem, and the simple, eternal contrasts that follow, seized my imagination. But to carry such last lines required notes of simple assurance and light. I paused over the keyboard and waited. Then I heard the six notes of unaffected simplicity and truth."

KILGORE, CLIVE HAROLD (1889-   ). Accountant, musician. Studied piano, organ, theory, and composition in Pittsburgh, Pennsylvania. Organist-choirmaster, Zion Church, Coraopolis, Pennsylvania. Worked with the Mendelssohn Choir, Pittsburgh. Composer of anthems, choral works, including two Lenten cantatas.

349 *Pax* (Kilgore). God of peace, in peace preserve us. Tune composed 1946 for Dr. Olson's hymn which was occasioned by the distress of the Second World War. Tune chosen in the tune competition.

LANDAHL, CARL W. (1908-   ). Profesor of Music at Augsburg College, Minneapolis. Composer of anthems, choral preludes for organ, piano music, et cetera.

178 *Invocation.* Eternal God, before thy throne we bend. Composed for this text in the *Hymnal.*

LEUPOLD, ULRICH SIEGFRIED (1909-   ). Born in Berlin, Germany, son of a well-known organist and composer. Studied piano, organ, and composition with his father, musicology at the University of Berlin, theology at Berlin, Zurich, and the Seminary of the Confessing Church. Since 1945, professor of New Testament theology and director of music, Waterloo College and Seminary, Waterloo, Ontario, Canada. Dean of the Seminary. Edited collections of anthems, organ and choral music. Edited the German chorales in the *Hymnal*.

180 *Suomi* (Harmonized). Arise, my soul, arise.

LEWARS, RALPH P. (1883-   ). Organist Church of the Holy Communion, Philadelphia, Pennsylvania, since 1920. Teacher of piano, organ, and composition. Composer of anthems, hymn tunes, settings for the Introits and Graduals, and of antiphons for the Psalter.

249 *Festal Day*. Come, all ye people, come away. Composed for this text in tune competition.

LOWRY, ROBERT (1826-99). Baptist minister, composer of gospel songs. Born in Philadelphia, professor at Bucknell University. Co-editor of eighteen different collections. His musical activity began after his fortieth year.

463 *Something for Jesus*. Saviour, thy dying love. Composed for this hymn, and published in *Pure Gold*, 1871, a collection which sold more than one million copies.

479 *Lowry*. I need thee every hour.

MACMILLAN, ERNEST CAMPBELL (1893-   ). Canadian musician, educated in England, Scotland, and France. Principal of the Toronto Conservatory of Music and university dean. Orchestra conductor, organ recitalist, composer.

Vulpius (Gelobt sei Gott) (Harmonized).

109 Good Christian men, rejoice and sing.

600 O Lord of life, where'er they be.

MASON, LOWELL (1792-1872). Born in Massachusetts. Organist of the First Presbyterian Church, Savannah, Georgia, for seven years. Moved to Boston in 1827. President of the Handel and Haydn Society which had published his *Collection of Church Music* in 1822. Established the Boston Academy of Music and brought the teaching of music into the public schools. Very influential as a teacher, lecturer, composer, and editor.

152 *Harwell*. Glorious things of thee are spoken.

458 *Naomi*. Prayer is the soul's sincere desire.

525 *Watchman*. Watchman, tell us of the night.

543 *Dennis* (Adapted). Blest be the tie that binds.

McCARTNEY, ROBERT HYSLOP (1844-1905).

328 *Westwood*. Hail to the Lord's Anointed. From the American Lutheran Hymnal.

MESSITER, ARTHUR HENRY (1834-1916). Born in England, organist Trinity Episcopal Church, New York City, where he developed a famous boy choir. Composer, author, editor.

555 *Marion*. Rejoice, ye pure in heart. Tune composed in 1883, and set to Dean Plumptre's fine processional hymn in the Episcopal Hymnal, 1893, of which Messiter edited a musical edition.

MILLER, LESTER DAVID (1919-   ). Born Lenoir, North Carolina, son of a Lutheran minister. Graduate Southern Seminary, Master's degree, School of Music, Union Theological Seminary, New York. Since 1955 Director, School of Music, Wittenberg College. Lecturer on church music, Hamma Divinity School. Organist and choirmaster.

502 *Fortitudo.* The Lord our God alone is strong.

MOSCHETTI, GIUSEPPE (1908-   ). Born in Florence, Italy. Franciscan priest, excommunicated by the Pope and exiled by the Vatican and Mussolini. Organist and composer. Recitals in many cathedrals and music halls in Europe and America. Director of music, St. John's Church, Allentown, Pennsylvania.

276 *St. Francis.* Not worthy, Lord, to gather up the crumbs. Tune composed for this text in the tune competition conducted by the Commission.

NOBLE, THOMAS TERTIUS (1867-1953). Born in Bath, England. Organist Ely Cathedral and York Minster, and, after 1913, St. Thomas' Episcopal Church, New York City. Composer of notable anthems, services, and organ works, as well as many hymn tunes.

534 *Ely Cathedral.* For thee, O dear, dear country. Composed 1895 for the Ely Diocesan Festival.

542 *In Babilone* (Harmonized). Son of God, eternal Saviour. A Dutch traditional, introduced in the *English Hymnal,* 1906, by Vaughan Williams.

OVERBY, OSCAR RUDOLPH (1892-   ). Teacher, composer, music critic, columnist. Born Cooperstown, North Dakota. Studied music, New England Conservatory, Boston, Northwestern Conservatory of Music, Minneapolis, and St. Olaf College, Northfield, Minnesota (B.M.). Professor of Music at St. Olaf, 1921-50. Director National Choral Union since 1940. Author *Songs and Poems,* twenty choral works, et cetera.

593 *Our Christ.* I know not what the future hath.

PARKER, HORATIO WILLIAM (1863-1919). Born in Massachusetts. Musical education in Munich. Organist and choirmaster in New York and Boston Dean of the School of Music, Yale University. Distinguished composer and conductor. Musical editor of an edition of the Episcopal Hymnal, 1903.

75 *Parker.* The royal banners forward go. Composed for this hymn in Hutchin's *Church Hymnal,* 1894.

122 *Pixham.* Come Holy Spirit, God and Lord. Composed 1901, first published 1903.

436 *Jubilate.* Rejoice, the Lord is King. A jubilant tune, with effective use of unison passages. First published in Tucker's *Hymnal,* 1894.

PEERY, ROB ROY (1900-   ). Born in Saga, Japan, son of a Lutheran missionary. A.B. Midland College, B.M., Oberlin College, Mus.Doc., Midland College. Violinist and organist of churches in Kansas, Colorado, North Carolina, Brooklyn, and Philadelphia. Editor, Theodore Presser Company, editor Lorenz Publications, Dayton, Ohio. More than 250 published works for orchestra, chorus, piano, violin, and voice.

519 *Byrd.* O God of Bethel, by whose hand. Composed 1929 for the "Airmen's Hymn" of Harry Matt Farrington, Methodist minister, inspired by Charles Lindbergh's flight to Paris. Tune in many American hymnals.

REED, LUTHER DOTTERER (1873-   ). President emeritus, the Lutheran Theological Seminary at Philadelphia. Chairman of the two commissions that prepared the *Service Book and Hymnal.*

353   *Mount Airy.* O God of wondrous grace and glory. Melody composed at Lake Placid, New York, for this hymn which the author had written that same day. Harmonized by Leland Sateren, a member of the Commission on the *Hymnal.*

ROBBINS, HOWARD CHANDLER (1876-1952). Born in Philadelphia. Rector Episcopal Church of the Incarnation, New York City. Dean of the Cathedral of St. John the Divine. Professor at General Theological Seminary. Author and hymn writer.

243   *Chelsea Square.* Put forth, O God, thy spirit's might. Tune hummed by Dr. Robbins to Ray Francis Brown, who harmonized it for Dr. Robbin's hymn.

RUUD, GORDON C. (1920-   ). Evangelical Lutheran missionary in Madagascar.

494   *Madagascar.* We sing the praise of him who died. Tune submitted in the tune competition.

SATEREN, LELAND BERNHARD (1913-   ). Son of a Lutheran clergyman. Head of the Department of Music, Augsburg College, Minneapolis. Director of the college choir, which has made nation-wide tours. Choirmaster Messiah Church, Minneapolis. Composer and arranger of two hundred choral works for church choirs, high schools, and choral societies. Member Commission on the Hymnal, and editor of its Scandinavian chorales.

80   *Marlee.* Deep were his wounds, and red. A poignant, free moving melody for a poignant poem on the Passion.

342   *Eldora.* In Christ there is no east or west. Tune bears the name of Mrs. Sateren, wife of the composer.

353   *Mount Airy* (Harmonized). O God of wondrous grace and glory. Mount Airy is the suburb in which the Philadelphia Seminary is located, and the home address of the author of this hymn.

422   *Praise (Af Himlens)* (Arranged). Sing praise to God who reigns above. An arrangement of a late seventeenth century Swedish melody.

SHEARER, WINIFRED JACOBS (1882-   ). Daughter of Henry Eyster Jacobs, author of the hymn. Graduate of a Philadelphia Conservatory of Music. Studied piano with John Grolle, organ with Franklin Cresson, and theory with Hugh A. Clarke of the University of Pennsylvania. Organist, Church of the Ascension, Mount Airy, and St. Peters, North Wales.

265   *Filia.* Lord Jesus Christ, we humbly pray.

SHEPPARD, FRANKLIN LAWRENCE (1852-1930). A Baltimore businessman. Active in the Episcopal, and later, in the Presbyterian Church. Organist. Editor of *Alleluia,* 1915, a Sunday school hymnal which sold half a million copies. Intimate friend of Maltbie D. Babcock, author of this hymn.

487   *Terra Patris.* This is my Father's world. Dates from 1915, and probably originated with Sheppard, though he thought it might be reminiscent of an old English melody he had heard his mother sing.

SHERWIN, WILLIAM FISKE (1826-88). A Baptist. Teacher of voice, New

England Conservatory of Music, Boston. Organist and director of choruses at Chautauqua Assembly.

234 *Evening Praise.* Day is dying in the west. Composed for this hymn, and very popular in this country.

311 *Cutting.* Christ for the world we sing. Composed, in all probability, at Lake Chautauqua for Samuel Wolcott's hymn.

491 *Bread of Life.* Break thou the bread of life. Composed in 1877 for Miss Lathbury's hymn.

STEFFE, WILLIAM. A resident of Philadelphia.

356 *Battle Hymn.* Mine eyes have seen the glory. The original refrain of an old camp-meeting hymn, "Say, brothers, will you meet us?" was written in 1855 for a fire company. Five years later soldiers at Fort Warren in Boston Harbor improvised lines concerning "John Brown's Body" to fit this air, and it became a marching song of the Federal armies. Mrs. Howe lifted it to sublimity and immortality by writing her poem for the tune.

STROM, RALPH ALVIN (1909-). Organist and choir director Gustavus Adolphus Church, St. Paul, Minnesota. Teacher of choral music in high school, director nurses' choir, Bethesda Hospital. Composer of hymn tunes, piano and choral works.

67 *Name of Jesus.* Jesus, Name all names above. A successful entry in the tune competition conducted by the Commission on the Hymnal.

TAYLOR, VIRGIL CORYDON (1817-91). Born in Connecticut, descendant of the Mayflower Pilgrim William Brewster. Organist of Baptist, Dutch Reformed, and Episcopal churches in New York, Niagara Falls, and Des Moines, Iowa.

170 *Louvan.* Lord of all being, throned afar. First published in *The Sacred Minstrel,* 1846.

THOMPSON, WILL LAMARTINE (1847-1909). A resident of East Liverpool, Ohio. A graduate of Boston Conservatory of Music. Wrote the words and the music of many gospel songs and patriotic hymns.

578 *For you and for me.* Softly and tenderly Jesus is calling.

WALTER, WILLIAM HENRY (1825-93). Organist Episcopal churches and, after 1865, of Columbia University, New York City.

541 *Festal Song.* Rise up, O men of God. Beginning with a vigorous unison phrase, this tune flowers out in spirited, yet stately, four-part harmony.

WILSON, ROGER CHARLES (1912-). Musician, composer, conductor, associate editor of Lorenz Publishing Company since 1938. Educated University of Southern California, Dayton, Ohio, and Chicago. Composer of anthems, cantatas, et cetera.

243 *Spiritus Domini.* Put forth, O God, thy Spirit's might. A fine tune for Dean Robbins' hymn.

330 *Dayton.* City of God, how broad and far. Tune named by the composer in honor of his home city.

Chapter 14

MUSIC OF THE CHOIR

Choral organizations have assisted in liturgical worship from the days of the Hebrew temple to the present. Jewish choirs sang the Psalms. The medieval church cultivated choral music. After the Reformation the nonliturgical churches abandoned it except for the use of small, untrained groups to lead the Psalm singing. The Lutheran and the Anglican churches purified and preserved the liturgical system of worship, carried on the choral tradition, and enriched choral literature with notable compositions in new and significant forms—artistically harmonized chorales, vernacular motets, cantatas, Passions, services, anthems, and oratorios. The experience of the centuries has developed choir techniques and procedures which should be studied and mastered today.

Difficulties are encountered from time to time in maintaining good choirs. These may be technical problems or temperamental ones. They may relate to organization, administration, or financial support. Or they may have to do with the clash of personalities endowed with artistic sensibilities. But so valuable are the services of a good choir in affording leadership and support, in enriching corporate worship with forms of worth and beauty, and in developing the gifts of its people, that the church everywhere strives to maintain such organizations.

CHOIR ORGANIZATION AND MAINTENANCE

Local conditions will largely determine the kind of choir that may be developed. Important factors will be available material, character of the congregation and community, talents and experience of the choirmaster, et cetera. In the early church, and later under monastic influence choirs consisted of men and boys only. The Reformation introduced a wider recognition of personality and individual responsibility, and made possible the use of mixed choirs. The accompanying gain

240

in maturity, deepening of religious and emotional experience, and creation of more highly developed ensemble qualities greatly expanded the range and complexity of choral work.

Choirs of men and boys are still generally retained, where possible, in the Anglican communion. Their training and administration present peculiar problems demanding special knowledge and method. Apart from a few instances, notably such historic choirs as St. Thomas', Leipsic; and Holy Cross, Dresden, the Lutheran Church has generally maintained mixed choirs of men and women.

Maintenance of a good boy choir requires more than one rehearsal a week. The best results are obtained when a parish maintains a choir school in which a group of boys with good natural voices (from thirty to fifty of them in a large parish) is given private school education by teachers paid by the parish. In return for this, the boys give their services to the church, and a select division of the group constitutes the regular "service choir." Under this arrangement, one period of music study (voice, solfeggio, et cetera) and one rehearsal period may be worked into each school day. One or two additional full rehearsals with the men of the choir are also held every week. Some cathedrals, e.g., St. John the Divine, New York City, draw their boys from a wide territory, provide dormitories for them, and take complete charge of their physical welfare as well as of their secular, religious, and musical education. A few well-endowed parishes, such as St. Thomas' Episcopal, New York, and St. Peter's Episcopal, Philadelphia, maintain choir schools which provide full-time general education along with the musical instruction, with their boys living at home and not in a school dormitory.

The quartet choir, popular in many American churches a few decades ago, was concertistic rather than liturgical. Its very constitution as a small group of soloists definitely set it apart from the congregation. This led to the general development of a type of music which, drawn too frequently from oratorios, operatic transcriptions, or other secular sources, was characterized by the spirit of the concert hall rather than that of the church. With growing consciousness of congregational unity and responsibility in worship, and recognition of the fact that the devotional and liturgical spirit is the foundation of all worship, the present trend in all communions is definitely toward chorus choirs.

It is well to build upon a congregational basis. Choir members should be largely, if not entirely, from the congregation itself. From this as a foundation it will be possible to reach out into purely artistic areas. Every regular member of the choir should be a Christian, a member of some church body, if not of the local congregation.

The best type of organization includes a selected and balanced chorus of from sixteen to forty voices. Four soloists will each represent one of the different voice parts. If four are not available, one or two soloists in addition to the chorus are desirable. In good choir work the victory is not necessarily with numbers. A choir of twenty-four perfectly balanced and thoroughly trained singers can produce better effects and create deeper religious impressions than the cruder work of ten times this number.

Large congregations may well have a junior as well as a senior choir. Parishes which have large church schools and are able to command practically the entire time of the choirmaster may have additional choirs of different age groups. These auxiliary choirs under capable direction will discover and develop promising voices. They will form solid foundations for good music in the church school. Their members will receive valuable training which will equip them for later service in the senior choir. Upon festival or other occasions these junior choirs may be used in the regular services of the congregation, either in antiphonal singing or in the presentation of special numbers. The junior choir can also be used in the regular church services for a month or more in the summer when the senior choir is on vacation. Junior choirs, like boy choirs, introduce children at an early age to the services and music of the church, and awaken interests which, even if lost for a period, may be renewed later in life.

In cities and larger towns good volunteer choirs, with none of the chorus or the soloists paid, can be maintained only if able and magnetic direction is available. Usually it is necessary to pay at least one or more of the soloists. A small honorarium given to the other choir members is generally regarded a proper recognition of time and effort expended and a helpful means of assuring regularity at rehearsals and services.

Some congregations may secure good music with the expenditure of two thousand dollars a year, including two hundred dollars for the purchase of music and the care of the organ. Other parishes in the same city may maintain small artist-choirs of not more than a dozen selected voices, under the direction of able professional musicians, and spend as much as ten thousand dollars. There is no absolute standard or rule of procedure. Two general statements, however, may be made: first, that congregations as a rule do not appropriate as much as they might for choir work; secondly, that they do not understand how important the personality and work of the organist and the choirmaster are in the development of the musical resources of the congregation.

Congregations able to spend only a few thousand dollars a year for this part of their work will probably find one or another of the following plans suited to their needs:

1. A large congregation with plenty of volunteer personnel for soloists as well as chorus may do well to secure a very able organist and choirmaster and pay him as much as three thousand a year.

2. A congregation with ample material for soprano and alto chorus but with scarcity of male voices may engage a tenor or a baritone soloist for approximately seven hundred dollars.

3. In smaller congregations, where the choir is in the nature of an "augmented quartet," the first thought should not be of soloists. In most cases it will be well to spend nearly all the money available to secure a really good organist and choirmaster. He will be able to choose the best type of music for the particular requirements and abilities of the congregation and will be able by the force of his personality to maintain a good choir.

The congregation should do more than provide a liberal allowance in its budget for the organist-choirmaster's salary, choir maintenance, organ repair, the purchase of music, et cetera. It should recognize the choir as an important organization in the life and work of the church, quite as important in its own way as the auxiliaries. Choir members, in addition to usual human traits, generally possess a fair amount of artistic sensibility. This is chilled by an atmosphere of indifference. It flowers into fine purpose and performance under the warmth of appreciation and encouragement.

So far as local conditions permit, the choir should be provided with proper rooms for assembly and rehearsal, care of vestments, et cetera. Recognition of its corporate character may be expressed in annual dinners, outings, reunions. Such recognition is not pampering. It is the honest reward of a job well done and seldom recognized, and a spur to higher attainments.

MUSIC OF THE PROPERS

The *Service Book* provides the music of the responses of the Liturgy. Every effort should be made to render this music heartily and expressively. For this, careful study of the texts, as well as of the melodies, will be necessary. The liturgical choir numbers—Introits, Graduals, Responsories, et cetera—must receive particular attention. Musical settings for these Propers are available.

Archer and Reed's *Choral Service Book* supplies simple settings of the Introits to the Gregorian Psalm Tones. Another simple plainsong setting by Walter E. Buszin (St. Louis: Concordia Publication House) is available. *The Proper of the Service* by Albert O. Christensen and Harold E. Schuneman (New York: H. W. Gray Company) and Ernest White's *Introits and Graduals* (New York: St. Mary's Press) both provide Gregorian melodies more elaborate in character. Anthem-like settings are given in H. Alexander Matthew's two-volume work, and in the similar series by Ralph P. Lewars, both published by Muhlenberg Press, Philadelphia.

It should be noted that while an English translation of the historic Latin texts of the Introits and Graduals has been fully incorporated in our Liturgy, there has been no attempt to recover the historic plainsong melodies of these propers and to adapt them to the English texts.

This situation had its parallel more than forty years ago when the fine English texts of the Responsories in Matins and Vespers were without musical settings of any sort. Archer and Reed, in an effort to complete their series of settings for the Liturgy, arranged with the eminent German musician Max Reger to compose original musical settings in strict liturgical style for these texts. These remarkably fine compositions, twenty in number, were published in this country by the General Council Publication House, and also by the H. W. Gray Company, New York. Appearing from the press during the First World War (1914) they attracted little attention. The editions were finally cleared out, and there has been no reprinting of this distinguished work by one of the most famous composers in all musical history. It would be a matter of great value if the Reger Responsories were reprinted and if some church musician of equal eminence might be commissioned to compose comparably fine settings in strict liturgical style for the Introit and Gradual texts.

HYMNS

Where the hymnal offers alternate tunes, the better one, usually the first, should be used. It will not do to introduce too many new tunes at once. Unfamiliar melodies tend to upset the congregation. If the minister and the choirmaster co-operate, however, it will be quite possible to introduce new tunes gradually. Not more than one should be introduced at any particular service. They must be carefully rehearsed by the choir in advance. They should be repeated on successive Sundays, either as hymns for the congregation or as anthems, so that the people may become familiar with them. Careful, deliberate effort of this kind will gradually bring the average congregation to an appreciation of the dignity and devotional value of the best tunes, including plainsong, German chorales, French church tunes, and solid early English melodies. Once the people are familiar with these, there will be little desire for the catchy melodies and saccharin harmonies of poorer tunes.

ANTHEMS AND OTHER CHORAL FORMS

Some of the greatest monuments of religious art are in the realm of choral music. In grandeur of conception and perfected beauty of detail they compare favorably with the finest achievements in architecture, painting, and poetry. The choral music of the church also maintains a gratifying supremacy when compared with secular choral music. Secular compositions exploit history, folklore, legend, and imaginative poetry in operas, secular oratorios, and choral symphonies. Christian themes, however, have inspired the greatest works. Nothing in the secular field surpasses in nobility and beauty such compositions as Handel's *Messiah,* Bach's *B Minor Mass* or *St. Matthew's Passion,* Mendelssohn's *Elijah,* and the requiems of Mozart and Brahms. These have to do with the ultimate issues of life as viewed from the lofty plane of spiritual significance.

What is more to the point, however, is the significance of choral music in the worship of the congregation. Not only has a great literature developed in this field in the past, but choral music is an important field of endeavor in the life of the church today. All the activities of the choirmaster in liturgical and musical study, choir administration, voice production, et cetera find their ultimate justification and satisfaction in the rendition of choral music by voices under his command. Constant association with so many different personalities, and active co-operation with them in building up the musical structure of the church's services, make this feature of his work interesting and quickening.

The living quality of vocal art is one of its characteristic features. Music differs from architecture, painting, or sculpture chiefly in its vital and progressive qualities. Its effects are not gained by single fixed impressions, but by the constant movement of thematic and harmonic material, unfolding and developing its emotional content through manifold gradations, sequences, and climaxes. It is not static, but active. Choral music, as the product of many living personalities consciously adjusting themselves to each other, is a supreme manifestation of musical vitality. It is surprisingly alive. It challenges the best talents of the choirmaster at every point.

We have also seen that the choir is a gifted and trained segment of the congregation which leads and inspires the latter. But beyond this, as a group of worshipers, it proclaims and enforces spiritual truth and offers to God the highest expressions of worship in forms of artistic

245

worth. It serves God and not man. This is why choirs are admonished to face the altar or the chancel wall in singing, not the congregation as if giving a concert. The ideals of the choir must be churchly purity, liturgical unity, and artistic excellence. Conscious of its membership in the congregation and of fellowship with the church of all time, it brings to the temple its gifts of joyous service in all reverence. Nothing tainted with secular association, nothing irreverent, nothing irrelevant, trivial, showy, or merely sentimental is worthy of presentation.

With conceptions such as these the choirmaster is prepared to approach one of his most important tasks in the selection of choir music. The representative character of much of the choir's work suggests that its special music should not be too far beyond average comprehension. Two facts, however, should be remembered. First, congregational participation in the musical offerings of the choir will be greatly furthered if opportunity is afforded the congregation to follow the texts of choir numbers. The *Service Book* provides the texts for the strictly liturgical Introits, Graduals, Responsories, et cetera. The texts of anthems may be printed in the church bulletin, or on separate sheets. This makes possible an intelligent understanding of the subject matter which is emotionally expressed in the music, and encourages concentration and meditation. Secondly, congregational appreciation can be developed and popular taste educated by progressive use of better types of music. In recognizing and meeting this opportunity, the wise choirmaster, by his choice of choir music, will develop the congregation as well as the choir.

Simplicity is always desirable, but music merely pretty or showy must be ruled out. Music which exploits solo voices unduly, or is overloaded with elaborate organ accompaniments, should be avoided. Much of the finest choral music has been composed for voices alone. Choirmasters would do well to devote a good deal of their attention to *a cappella* (unaccompanied) singing. This, if well done, realizes devotional and churchly effects unapproached by other forms.

Good anthems may be repeated on the octaves of festivals or after a proper interval, rather than dropped in an attempt to supply new numbers for every service. It is not always possible to do a new work well each week, year in, year out. Good choir music is like good orchestral music, fine poetry, or the classics in drama, literature, or any other field. We love to hear and see the really beautiful things again and again, while we cannot welcome repetitions, or even first appearances, of the mediocre and the ugly.

It is needless to say that music of high liturgical and devotional character is not to be found in cheap monthly choir journals issued in connection with cheap hymnals. A wise choirmaster will build up his choir library by purchasing worthwhile octavo anthems published by responsible houses. In an effort to provide suggestions and guidance in this important field we have had the generous co-operation of professional friends, all composers and artists of repute in their own right in the special field of church music.

William Timmings, Mus.Doc., was born in England. He served as chorister and organist in St. Oswald's, Kidderminster, before coming to this country at the age of fifteen. A pupil of H. Alexander Matthews in organ and composition, and an active figure in the affairs of the American Guild of Organists, of which he is a Fellow, Dr. Timmings soon established himself as one of the ablest church musicians in Philadelphia. His original compositions include many fine anthems and organ works. For more than thirty-five years he has been the organist-choirmaster of St. Paul's Episcopal Church, Elkins Park, and the choirmaster of St. Michael's Lutheran Church, Germantown, both in the Philadelphia area. In addition he has directed many large choral groups. Dr. Timmings submits the following list of anthems, a list which practically represents the type of anthems regularly presented in the above-mentioned congregations by the choirs under his direction.

Anthems for Sundays and Festivals

I

Advent

1	Springs in the Desert	Arthur B. Jennings	Gray
2	The Bridegroom Cometh	Rimsky-Korsakoff	Fischer
3	How Beautiful Are Their Feet	C. Villiers Stanford	Novello
4	God Is with Us	Kastalsky	Fischer

Christmas

	Whence Is that Goodly Fragrance	Old French Carol	Summy-Birchard
	The Holy Boy	John Ireland	Boosey and Hawkes
	Let All Mortal Flesh Keep Silence	Davis	B. F. Wood

Epiphany

	Say, Where Is He Born There Shall Be a Star ("Christus")	Mendelssohn	Gray
1	Greater Love Hath No Man	John Ireland	Galaxy
2	God of Grace and God of Glory	William Timmings	Elkan-Vogel

247

3 Jesus Joy of Man's Desiring	J. S. Bach	E. C. Schirmer
4 Fierce Was the Wild Billow	T. Tertius Noble	Presser
5 Worship	Geoffrey Shaw	Novello
6 When God of Old Came Down	Maurice C. Whitney	Gray

Septuagesima

O Love Invisible	H. Alexander Matthews	Ditson
Thou Hidden Love of God	Timmings	Chappell-Harms

Sexagesima

King of Glory, King of Peace	Friedel	Gray

Quinquagesima

Though I Speak with the Tongues	Bairstow	Oxford

Lent

1 By the Waters of Babylon	Coleridge Taylor	Novello
2 Adoramus Te, Christe	Mozart	Ditson
3 Wash Me Throughly	S. S. Wesley	E. C. Schirmer
4 Like as the Hart	Palestrina	E. C. Schirmer
5 He Was Despised (*Messiah*)	Handel	all publishers
Surely He Has Borne (*Messiah*)	Handel	all publishers

Palm Sunday

The Royal Banners Forward Go	Candlyn	Ditson
Ride on in Majesty	Candlyn	Gray
The King's Welcome	Whitehead	Ditson

Easter

Come, Ye Faithful	Titcomb	B. F. Wood
That Easter Morn	J. Sebastian Matthews	G. Schirmer
Arise in Us	Shaw	Novello
1 Now Have We Peace with God ("City of God")	H. Alexander Matthews	G. Schirmer
2 Greater Love Hath No Man	John Ireland	Galaxy
3 Ye Who Now Sorrow	Brahms	Novello
4 All Ye Servants of the Lord	Elmore	Galaxy
5 In Every Corner Sing	Sateren	Paul Schmidt

Ascension

God Is Gone Up	Titcomb	Gray

Pentecost

Holy Spirit, Truth Divine	Robson	Patersons

Trinity

Trinity Sunday

Te Deum in B flat	Healey Willan	Gray
1 Praise	Rowley	Oxford
2 Father, Once More Within Thy Holy Place	H. Alexander Matthews	G. Schirmer
3 Psalm 150	Cesar Franck	Fischer
4 Benedictus es Domine	H. A. Matthews	Gray
5 O Love, How Deep	Titcomb	Gray
6 O God, Who Set the Seers Aflame	Baumgartner	Gray
7 Cherubim Song	Bortniansky	Kjos
8 With a Voice of Singing	Martin Shaw	G. Schirmer
9 Praise to the Lord	Arr. by Sanders	Ditson
10 Immortal, Invisible	Thiman	Novello
11 Lord, We Implore Thee	Cesar Franck	G. Schirmer
12 Fear Not, O Lord	Elgar	Novello
13 Brother James' Air	Arr. Gordon Jacob	Oxford
14 Let My Prayer Be Set Forth	MacPherson	Novello
15 I Am the Bread of Life	J. Sebastian Matthews	Ditson
16 Almighty God	Alfred Whitehead	Arthur P. Schmidt
17 Eternal God	Maurice C. Whitney	Gray
18 Turn Back O Man	Holst	Galaxy
19 Grieve Not the Holy Spirit	T. Tertius Noble	Gray
20 I Looked and Beheld a White Cloud	Healey Willan	Gray
21 Come, O Thou Traveller Unknown	T. Tertius Noble	Presser
22 My Soul, There Is a Country	C. Hubert H. Parry	Summy-Birchard
23 O Thou, the Central Orb	Charles Wood	Summy-Birchard
24 Lo, My Shepherd's Land Divine	Joseph Haydn	E. C. Schirmer
25 O Be Joyful in the Lord	Cesar Franck	all publishers
26 Send Out Thy Spirit	Schuetky	Gray

27 or Last Sunday after
    Trinity

How Lovely Is Thy Dwelling Place	Brahms	all publishers

Transfiguration

The Lord Is King	McCollin	Gray

Reformation

God Is Our Refuge	McCollin	Arthur P. Schmidt
Built on a Rock	Christensen	Augsburg

All Saints

Souls of the Righteous	T. Tertius Noble	Presser
There Shall Be No Night There	David Wood	Gray

A second list has been built up, with the valued assistance of friends. This list is intended, particularly, to bring to the attention of our choirmasters meritorious compositions, among other standard items, by Lutheran composers here and abroad, compositions available in American editions, but not too well known by church musicians generally.

Anthems for Sundays and Festivals

II

Advent

1 Lord, Hosanna	Schreck	Kjos
Hosanna to the Son of David	Willan	Concordia
2 Wake, Awake	Nicolai-Bach	Messenger Press
Lost in the Night	F. M. Christiansen	Augsburg
3 Three Chorales for Advent	Schütz	Concordia
4 Come, Thou Savior of Our Race	F. M. Christiansen	Augsburg

Christmas

O Rejoice Ye Christians Loudly	Bach	C. Fischer
Glory Be to God	Berger	Kjos
The Cradle	Arr. P. Christiansen	Augsburg
From Heaven Above	F. M. Christiansen	Augsburg
Let All Mortal Flesh	Arr. Holst	Galaxy
Lo, How a Rose	Praetorius-Sateren	Concordia
Born Today	Sweelinck	G. Schirmer

Epiphany

The Morning Star	Arr. P. Christiansen	Augsburg
1 Break Forth, O Beauteous	Bach	Augsburg

2 O Love, How Deep	Titcomb	Gray
3 He Is My Saviour	Bach	Kjos
4 Mountains of God	Pooler	Schmitt
5 But the Lord Is Mindful of His Own	Mendelssohn	Augsburg

Septuagesima

O Master, Let Me Walk with Thee	Moschetti	Augsburg

Sexagesima

Word of God	Grieg	Augsburg
O God, in Thy True Word	Walther-Lundquist	Concordia

Quinquagesima

Thou Goest to Jerusalem	Franck-Bunjes	Concordia

Lent

1 Lord, Keep Us Steadfast	(SAB) Arr. Malin	Summy-Birchard
2 Increase My Faith	Gibbons	Wood
3 Heavenly Light	Kopyloff	C. Fischer
4 Jesus, Let Our Souls Be Fed	Sateren	Messenger Press
5 O Spotless Lamb	Bach-Thoburn	Augsburg

Palm Sunday

Hosanna to the Son of David	Moe	Mercury
Hosanna, Son of David	Sateren	Augsburg

Maundy Thursday and Good Friday

O Christ, Thou Lamb of God	Kranz	Concordia
O Sacred Head	Hassler-Christiansen	Augsburg
Surely He Hath Borne Our Griefs	Graun	Concordia
Man of Sorrows	Pooler	Augsburg
Jesus, I Will Ponder	Schütz	Concordia

Easter

God's Son Has Made Me Free	Grieg	Augsburg
Easter Morning	P. Christiansen	Augsburg
Come Ye Faithful, Raise	Lindeman-Sateren	Augsburg
Easter Morning, Joyous Dawning	Lindeman-Sateren	Augsburg
Jesus Lives	Thiman	Gray

251

Christ, Our Passover	Willan	Concordia
Good Christian Men, Rejoice	Vulpius	Augsburg
1 Christ Is Arisen	Bach	Augsburg
2 Yes, Though I Wander	Georg Schumann	Augsburg
My Shepherd Will Supply	Arr. Thomson	Gray
3 In Heaven Above	Arr. F. M. Christiansen	Augsburg
4 I Will Not Leave You Comfortless	Titcomb	C. Fischer
5 The Name of Jesus	Des Pres	Concordia

Ascension

King of Glory	F. M. Christiansen	Augsburg
Lift High the Cross	Nicholson-Sateren	Kjos

Pentecost

If Ye Love Me	Tallis	Choral Art
Come, Thou Holy Spirit	Tchesnokoff	Kjos

Trinity

Trinity Sunday

Only Begotten Word of God Eternal	Lovelace	Augsburg
Glory Be to the Father	Schütz	Concordia
Lord of Hosts	Wennerberg	Kjos
1 God Is Love	Matthews	G. Schirmer
See What Love	Mendelssohn	Baltimore Music
2 What God Does, that Is Nobly Done	Arr. Luvaas	Kjos
I Heard the Voice of Jesus Say	Tallis-Sateren	Augsburg
3 Turn Ye	Ives	Mercury
4 Treasures in Heaven	Clokey	Summy-Birchard
5 Jesus, Grant Me This, I Pray	Kitson	Oxford
6 Be Thou Near Me, Lord	Morgan	Kjos
7 O Taste and See	Vaughan Williams	Oxford
8 Thou Knowest Lord	Purcell	Kjos
9 Grant Us to Do with Zeal	Bach	E. C. Schirmer
10 We Sat Down in Sorrow	Klaus Egge	Augsburg
11 Misereri Mei	Lotti	Boosey
12 Light Everlasting	O. C. Christiansen	Kjos
13 The Flower of Love	Christiansen-Sateren	Messenger Press

14	I Sing to Thee	Arr. Luvaas	Kjos
15	Treasures in Heaven	Clokey	Summy-Birchard
16	Still with Thee	Pooler	Augsburg
17	At Thy Feet	Bach	Wood
18	Jesus, Priceless Treasure	Bach	Any standard
	O Brother Man	O. C. Christiansen	Kjos
19	Grieve Not the Holy Spirit	Sateren	Wood
20	In Every Corner Sing	Malin	Summy-Birchard
	In Every Corner Sing	Sateren	Schmidt
21	Fight the Good Fight	Thiman	Gray
22	Have Mercy and Spare	F. M. Christiansen	Augsburg
23	Praise We God the Father's Name	Sateren	Concordia
24	Eye Hath Not Seen	Matthews	G. Schirmer
25	Wake, Awake	Nicolai-Bach	Messenger Press
26	E'en So, Lord Jesus, Come Quickly	Manz	Concordia
27	Day of Judgment	Archangelsky	J. Fisher

Transfiguration

| | Christ, Whose Glory Fills the Sky | Willan | Concordia |

The Presentation of our Lord

| | Presentation of Christ | Eccard | G. Schirmer |

St. Michael

| | To Such Belongeth the Kingdom | Sateren | Concordia |

All Saints

| | O How Glorious | Willan | Gray |
| | For All the Saints | Arr. Shaw | G. Schirmer |

Reformation

	Built on a Rock	Lindeman-Christiansen	Augsburg
	A Mighty Fortress (Rhythmic form)	Luther	Augsburg
	I Love the Church	Sateren	Messenger

253

Chapter 15

THE ORGAN: ITS HISTORY

The modern pipe organ is a marvel of craftsmanship and artistry. Mechanically complex, it contains a magnificent assembly of diapasons, flutes, strings, and reeds in many possible combinations. With musical tone at once powerful, brilliant, and rich in color, its emotional appeal covers the entire gamut of human feeling.

Crude mechanically and tonally before the Reformation, the organ was scarcely more than tolerated. It was not generally used in Luther's day. The Greek Church still forbids it. Yet in the corporate worship of all other communions today the organ is welcomed and given an important place.

The story of organ building and organ playing is interesting in itself. First of all, we shall trace this development. Then we shall describe the several parts of a modern instrument—the end result of ingenious triumphs over mechanical difficulties.

EARLY DEVELOPMENT

As early as the fourth century there is mention of a "hydraulic organ" in which there were both open and stopped pipes. It got its name from the fact that the weight of water regulated the wind supply. St. Jerome early in the fifth century speaks of an organ in Jerusalem which had twelve brazen pipes and was operated by fifteen bellows.

There were no organs in France before the middle of the eighth century. In 756, King Pepin, father of Charlemagne, requested the Byzantine emperor to send him one. An instrument of leaden pipes was forwarded by the emperor, who commissioned Bishop Stephanus to accompany the gift. Charlemagne received an organ from the Byzantine emperor Michael. In the year 812 he had another one built at Aix-la-Chapelle.

At this time Metz was the musical center of France. At Charlemagne's request, the pope sent two priests qualified in music to this city. One of them became ill and stopped enroute at the monastery of St. Gall in Switzerland, where he established the school of music which later became one of the most famous in Europe. The other priest went on to Metz, taking his copy of the Roman Antiphonary with him, and taught the Roman musical system in that city.

The early organs were instruments for the fist rather than for the fingers. The keyboards had only a dozen keys, each three or four inches in width, several feet in length, and separated by an inch or more from its nearest neighbor. A heavy blow was required to depress a single key. One man had charge of two bellows. By holding on with his hands to a bar above, and by alternately lifting each foot attached to one of the bellows beneath him, resting his weight on each of the bellows in turn, he was able to produce a constant supply of wind.

A thousand years ago the organ in the Winchester Cathedral had "twelve bellows above, fourteen below, seventy strong men as blowers, working like galley slaves in full swing, with toil and sweat and noise of shouting as they cheered one another, filled the wind chest, which was connected with no fewer than four hundred pipes." [1]

The first use of the organ was to attract people to the church. Small organs were used in cloisters to establish the tone for singing classes. The ability of the instrument to sound several notes simultaneously helped prepare the way for the introduction of harmony. Frequently there were two separate organs in the same building. The smaller was called the portative organ because it could be carried about; the larger was the positive and was stationary.

The use of flats and sharps developed slowly. By the fourteenth century the twelve notes of our scale were used. An organ installed in the Halberstadt Cathedral in 1361 incorporated the greatest improvements of that century. Its largest pipes were nearly thirty-two feet in length. It had twenty bellows operated by ten men. Variety and contrast of tone, hitherto largely impossible, were obtained by the use of three keyboards.

Pedals were used in German organs as early as the fifteenth century. They were unknown in England, however, for three hundred years. The first installation of them was in the Savoy German Lutheran Chapel in London, in an organ built by Johann Schnetzler of Passau. It remained for the later study of the organ works of Bach and Mendelssohn in the middle of the nineteenth century to bring the pedal keyboard into general use in England. Organ pipes were definitely

[1] E. G. Selwyn, *The Story of Winchester Cathedral* (London: Raphael Tuck and Sons, Ltd., 1934), p. 20-21.

classified as diapason, flute, string, and reed as early as the fifteenth century The introduction of "stops," by means of which certain sets of pipes could be silenced and others used, was a development of great significance.

The fundamental features of the pipe organ were well developed by the time of the Reformation. The finest organs of that date, however, were still exceedingly simple. Means of expression were not introduced until much later, and the instruments must often have been unpleasantly loud. We can understand why churchmen of the thirteenth century regarded the organ with disfavor. Fortunately, however, the church did not abandon it, but refined its character and developed its resources.

THE REFORMATION AND THE ORGAN

Luther certainly was not prejudiced against music of any kind. Yet there are only a few incidental references in his writings to the organ or to organ playing. It is also true that in his time the art of organ playing probably was less developed at Wittenberg than in other parts of Europe.

The earliest Protestant choir music carried on the churchly tradition of *a cappella* singing, which had been brought to perfection by centuries of high cultivation. The organ did not accompany the singing of chorales until quite late. Boy choirs and cantors were at first relied upon to lead congregational responses in the Liturgy and the singing of hymns. Thus the great developments of church music in the early period of the Reformation were accomplished independently of the organ. The instrument was chiefly used in alternation with vocal music and in preludes to the hymns.

The Interest of Italian musicians was centered in the opera. German musicians were the first to successfully adapt the organ and organ music to the requirements of liturgical use. Sweelinck, Praetorius, and Scheidt were among the pioneers. The placing of the congregational melody in the soprano instead of the tenor part made possible a new harmonic structure. It also enabled the organ to accompany and support the congregational chorale acceptably. This custom was not fully established until the eighteenth century.

Later composers like Theile, Alberti, Pachelbel, and Buxtehude paved the way for Bach. His genius developed the fullest powers of the instrument and gave a mighty impulse to its use in worship. He took the melodies of the congregational chorales and enriched them with solid, and often elaborate, harmonies. By using these same melodies as thematic material for his cantatas and chorale preludes, he extended the frontiers of church music in every direction and developed a style supremely devotional and artistically inspiring.

Zwinglian fanaticism in Switzerland and Puritan rage in Scotland and England destroyed many organs. Organists and organ builders were driven into exile. A glorious choral tradition was uprooted and left to perish from neglect on the desert plains of Dissent. Efforts were made to discourage the use of organs even in private homes. At a convention in Bridgewater in 1655 the question was proposed "whether a believing man or woman, being head of a family, in this day of the gospell, may keepe in his or her house an instrument of musicke playing on them or admitting others to play thereon?" The answer was, "It is the duty of the saintes to abstaine from all appearance of evil, and not to make provision for the flesh to fulfil ye lusts thereof."

After the Restoration, Charles II imported German builders to assist the newly-returned English builders in replacing and repairing wrecked organs. One of these, named Father Schmidt, built or rebuilt at least forty-five English organs, among which were those in Westminster Abbey, Durham Cathedral, and St. Paul's Cathedral. He introduced the first reed stops, the first mixtures, and the first echo organ in England.

Another famous builder was René (Renatus) Harris, whose grandfather had built the organ in Magdalen College, Oxford. His father had emigrated to France, returning with René in 1660 to England, a few months after Father Schmidt's arrival. Harris was a builder of great imagination and ability and became a formidable rival of Schmidt. He built the first four-manual organ in England at Salisbury Cathedral in 1710.

Shortly after the English deans had induced foreign builders like Schmidt and Harris to come from Germany and France to rebuild their ruined instruments in cathedrals, abbeys, and university chapels, German Moravians and Lutherans in Pennsylvania were building the first pipe organs in North America.

EARLY DEVELOPMENTS IN AMERICA

New England writers generally refer to the Brattle organ in Boston (1713) as the first organ known and used in America. But we can now carry the history of the instrument several decades further back. The first organ used in the New World was built in the Netherlands at a cost of a thousand thalers and brought on a Spanish vessel to Buenos Aires in 1670 for use in a college. The first organ built here was also in South America. It was built by Antonio Sepp, a German Jesuit who took part in the Spanish settlement of Paraguay. Being musically inclined, he taught the mission fathers sent to him both vocal and instru-

257

mental music. In 1690 he was commissioned by his superiors "to construct an organ in European style." In order to do this he retired to Ilapua, where the local priest, Franciscus Azbedo, had assembled a quantity of lead, pewter, and wire bought from the Spanish settlers. Father Sepp melted the pewter dishes for his metal pipes. As there was not sufficient material for casting the larger pipes, he hollowed out cedar trees and made wooden pipes. He also cut strips of cedar wood and joined and glued these together, making other pipes, and then "opened and loosened their tongues." His instrument had pedals and a simple form of stops, and when it was first played the astonishment of the Indians knew no bounds.

The minutes of the vestry of Trinity Episcopal Church, New York City, August 4, 1703, show that the rector and a committee were authorized to engage one **Henry Neering,** presumably a German, to build an organ for Trinity Church "on as easy terms as possible." John Klemm of Philadelphia, who had learned the trade of organ building in Dresden with **Silbermann, and** who came to America in 1736, built another organ of three manuals and twenty-six stops for Trinity Church in 1739.

John Gottlob Klemm was a Moravian who had been a teacher of organ at Herrnhut, Germany. After becoming estranged from **Zinzendorf,** he emigrated to Pennsylvania and settled in Philadelphia. Here he became foreman for Mons Gustaff Hesselius, a brother of the Rev. Andreas Hesselius of Gloria Dei Church. Hesselius was an organ builder and portrait painter of note. He arrived with his brother in Wilmington, Delaware, May of 1711. Later he moved to Philadelphia, where he painted the portraits of many notable men and women of the time. He also built spinets and organs. In 1746 he built an organ for the Moravian congregation at Bethlehem which was installed by his foreman John Klemm. He was paid twenty-five pounds for this instrument.

The organ was not generally used in New England until a much later period. The Scotch had called the instrument "a kist o' whistles," and the Puritans spoke of it as the "devil's bagpipes." The first organ known to have been used in that section of the colonies was brought from England by Thomas Brattle in 1710. Brattle was a businessman who had graduated from Harvard in 1676 in a class consisting of only three members. He later became treasurer of the college. For a New England Congregationalist he was an extreme liberal. When he died in 1713, he willed his organ, an instrument of six stops, to the Brattle Square Church in Boston. Though this church, too, was liberal in its outlook in many ways, it was still a Puritan congregation and did not approve of the use of organs. It declined the gift. Under the terms of the will the organ was then offered to King's Chapel, a congregation of the Church of England. Here it was accepted, though not without hesitation. After forty or more years in King's Chapel, the Brattle organ left Boston, being sold to St. Paul's Church, Newburyport, Massachusetts. Here it was used for another eighty years, and then sold to St. John's Church, Portsmouth, New Hampshire.

The Episcopalians were not averse to the use of organs. But they could not get them in New England. When they purchased instruments it was from the German-American builders or by importation from abroad. Edward Bromfield, Jr., was the first New England organ builder, and his earliest instrument dates from 1745. So far as is known, there were only five organs in Boston as late as 1814.

The ablest and best known American organ builder in the eighteenth century was David Tanneberger (Taneberg), who came to this country from Berthelsdorf, Saxony, in 1749. He became Klemm's assistant, and the two established a shop in Bethlehem, Pennsylvania. After Klemm's death in 1762, Tanneberger moved to Lititz, Pennsylvania. Here during the next forty years he built many organs, and a good number of pianos as well.

Tanneberger's largest instrument was for Zion German Lutheran Church, Philadelphia. The church, built in 1766, was one of the finest in the colonies and the organ was the largest in the country. It had three manuals and more than two thousand pipes. It was built at a cost of 3500 pounds, about $10,000 in our money. The organ was dedicated January 8, 1791, in a service attended by President and Mrs. Washington and members of Congress and the Pennsylvania Assembly. Unfortunately, both church and organ perished in a fire on the day after Christmas, 1794. The church was rebuilt two years later, and a large new organ was installed. This instrument was used at the funeral service of General Washington, held in this church December 26, 1799, and attended by the Senate, the House of Representatives, and the military. It was upon this occasion that General Henry Lee in his oration characterized Washington as "first in war, first in peace, and first in the hearts of his countrymen."

Tanneberger built his last instrument for Christ Lutheran Church, York, Pennsylvania. While superintending its erection, Tanneberger, then seventy-six years of age, fell from the scaffolding to his death.

Trinity Lutheran Church in Lancaster had an organ as early as 1744. In that year it secured a larger instrument of twenty stops. Trinity Church, Reading, contracted with Tanneberger to build an instrument in 1769, for which he was to receive 230 pounds, Pennsylvania currency. It is probable that the organ in the Moravian Church at Bethlehem at the time of the Revolutionary War was one of Tanneberger's. The Bethlehem Diary has this entry:

December 17, 1776, Generals Gates, Sullivan, Arnold, Sterling, Glover, and about 30 officers, came at dusk to attend our meeting, but owing to confusion in the town it was dropped. They were taken into the chapel to hear the organ and were pleased with the music.[2]

It is probable that there was no pipe organ west of the Alleghenies before 1837.

ORGAN PARTS

The organ, a wind instrument, consists of several instruments combined in one. Each stop may be thought of as an instrument in itself, comparable to the violin, the oboe, the trumpet, et cetera in an orchestra. Thus an organ of thirty speaking stops represents control over thirty individual instruments, with all manner of possible combinations.

Various stops comprise the major divisions of the organ. Each division in itself is called an "organ" and is played from its manual or keyboard. Most small organs have two manuals in addition to the pedal organ. One governs the great organ and the other the swell organ.

Of these the "great organ" is basic. It consists of stops which supply the fundamental organ tone. The Diapason chorus (composed of the Diapason stops of various pitches 8', 4', 2½', 2') provides the foundation. The great on a two-manual organ will have stops which normally are on the choir organ in a three-manual instrument—Dulciana, Melodia, a light 4' Flute, et cetera.

The "swell organ" derives its name from the arrangement of balanced shutters along the front of the box in which its pipes are enclosed. These are opened and closed by means of a foot pedal. This organ comprises stops of softer tone than the great organ. The basic stops of the swell ensemble will be the Trompette (a small-scale reed voiced with a wealth of natural harmonics), the strings—Viola, with its twin the Celeste, 8' and 4'—Flutes, and all of the secondary Diapason chorus that funds and space permit. It should be understood that the division suggested here between great and swell is not a hard and fast one. There are many possible arrangements, even in a small instrument. In organs of this size, there is often no real distinction between the two physically, since the whole set of pipes is within the shuttered swell box more often than not. However, two separate enclosures are desir-

[2] *Church Music and Musical Life in Pennsylvania in the Eighteenth Century* (Philadelphia: The Pennsylvania Society of the Colonial Dames of America, 1927), Vol. II, p. 206-207.

able. Swell organs must have all pipes under expression, that is, their volume controlled by the shutters. Still, the tonal distinction between the two groups of stops is sufficient to warrant division into great and swell.

Larger instruments have a third manual called the choir, and sometimes a fourth manual called the solo. The choir organ contains stops separately voiced and of smaller scale than stops of similar character in the great organ, and certain additional characteristic solo stops. Thus we find a Dulciana, a Melodia and a Diapason of smaller scale; a Lieblich Gedeckt, Flute D'Amour, Clarinet, Piccolo, et cetera. The choir organ is also generally under expression in a swell box of its own.

The solo organ is found only in large instruments. As its name indicates, it contains solo stops of distinctive quality—Philomela, Waldflöte, Tuba mirabilis, et cetera. Sometimes there is also an echo organ containing stops of soft but distinctive quality. This is built in a distant gallery or above the ceiling, and is usually controlled from the choir or the solo manual.

The pedal organ supplies the fundamental bass tone. It is controlled by a pedal keyboard, generally of thirty-two notes. The first pedal stop is a soft sixteen-foot Bourdon (generally called Lieblich Gedeckt). The second pedal stop should be a full-length sixteen-foot stop such as a Dulciana to give the necessary definite pitch to the lower tones. Instruments of moderate size usually have a sixteen-foot Diapason, a Bourdon, and possibly a Violincello, with couplers permitting pedal control of the lower octaves of the different manuals. Very large instruments have a thirty-two-foot open Diapason and additional stops of individual character.

The tonal range of the organ is thus very great. Its smallest pipes may be less than an inch in length and only as thick as a straw; its largest pipes may be thirty-two feet in length and as thick as an oak. The tone in all of these pipes, no matter what their size or shape, is produced by the vibration of air columns within their walls. "Stopped pipes" (called "gedeckt" by German builders) are so named because the pipe is covered, closed at the top. This mechanical feature so alters the vibration that a four-foot stopped pipe gives forth the pitch of an eight-foot open pipe.

Organ tone may be thought of in four classifications—diapasons, flutes, strings, and reeds. Not only fine craftsmanship, but artistry of the highest order is necessary to secure characteristic varieties of tone, or timbre, within these groups. The materials within the several pipes, their thickness and shape, their scale or relative proportion between diameter and length, the form of the side orifices and upper ends, et

261

cetera, are controlling factors manipulated by the "voicers," who thus secure proper tonal character and quality. This does not only mean that, to take an example, a violin pipe must be made to sound like a violin. Each pipe within a rank (a series of pipes) must be so matched with the rest as to make them sound not like separate pipes, but like the same pipe playing different notes. And, as if this were not enough, each rank in an organ must be so voiced as to blend perfectly with the others in any combination.

Strength of tone is supplied by "octaves" and "mixtures." The former are arrangements whereby a given rank is made to sound at an interval of an octave from the normal. The latter introduces overtones, such as the twelfth, fifteenth, and seventeenth, which add brilliance.

There are three types of action or transmission. Tracker-action transmits the movements of the keys to the valves of the pipes by a series of wooden levers and wooden strips or trackers. This is satisfactory in small instruments, and there are some very large trackers in Europe. Tubular-pneumatic action substitutes a small tube for the levers and trackers. Depression of a key opens a valve which releases compressed air and sends it through the tube to other valves which control the action in the wind chest. This type of action permits the console to be placed at quite a distance from the pipes themselves. It also makes possible a light and easy touch on the manual. Electropneumatic action substitutes electric wires for the tubes. The electric current lifts the armature of a magnet and thus controls the valves of the wind chest. Electrical action makes possible unified control over all parts of divided organs, some of which may be considerably distant from the console. Mechanical pistons which affect the entire series of stops give full control of all tonal resources of the instrument and permit prompt and varied registrations or changes in the combinations of stops to give variety and color in playing.

Many fine concert organs are now installed in auditoriums. For a time the instrument was also exploited and its tone coarsened and cheapened by movie theaters. But it still finds its most appropriate place in the church. In majesty and variety of musical tone it is equaled only by the orchestra. In devotional power and sustained serenity and dignity it exceeds the latter, particularly as a means of encouraging and supporting congregational song. It also has the advantage of being played by a single performer.

Modern developments in organ building have given increased flexibility to the instrument and greatly influenced organ music and organ playing. The multiplication of stops, and their marvelous imitation of practically all the instruments of the orchestra, led to an unfortunate amount of orchestral transcriptions and the loss thereby of a great deal that was peculiar to the organ itself and of high artistic value. Unfortunately too, partly in imitation of theater organs, a number of specialty stops have been introduced into some church organs. The inevitable result has been loss of fitness and dignity. We may be thankful, however, that the tendency today is toward fuller recognition of the limitations of the instrument and of the distinctive contribution which it is able to make to the liturgical service.

THE MODERN ORGAN

The development of the pipe organ into the instrument we know today, with magnificent tonal resources, fine action, and perfect control, has been achieved practically within the past seventy years. German, French, English, and American builders have all contributed features. The discovery of pneumatic action by Charles S. Barker, an Englishman, in 1832 led the way. The ancient tracker-action, with its use of slight strips of wood to convey motion, produced in large instruments a touch which was too heavy for either hands or feet to control without exhaustion. This limited the number of pipes and the strength of wind pressure that could be used. Barker employed a device which, upon the mere depression of a key, admitted compressed air into a small bellows, which in turn controlled the action of the pipes. The success of this invention ushered in a new era.

Dr. Gauntlett, an English organist and composer, was the first to develop electropneumatic action, which he introduced in 1852. Thus English builders, beginning with the introduction in 1712 of the swell box, first built by Jordan in St. Magnus Church, London, and later inaugurating both the pueumatic and the electropneumatic action, contributed to the developing organ three important features.

French and German builders took the lead in the production of new tone qualities. The French developed the reeds, using additional wind pressure; the Germans specialized in string tone stops. Stimulated by continental endeavor, as well as by the revival of liturgical life, the English builders in the nineteenth century produced instruments notable for size and for quality of tone. Germany, which in the early part of the century held leadership with the construction of such fine instruments as the Silbermann organ in Strasburg Cathedral, the Mooser organ in Freiburg, 1834, and the Walcker organ in Ulm Münster, 1853, fell somewhat behind.

"Father" Henry Willis was the first English builder to strike out into original lines in the development of organ tone. Other important English builders were Harrison and Harrison, John Compton, and W. Hill and Son. Father Willis was succeeded in the business by two sons and a grandson. The grandson, Henry Willis, III, is the builder of the organ in Liverpool Cathedral, the largest instrument in England.

In America the newness and extent of the field constantly stimulate endeavor and improvement. The installation of fine municipal organs and recital instruments in concert halls, et cetera, the use of the organ in private residences and, especially before 1930, in motion picture theaters, and the rapid increase of population and wealth have all been contributing factors. American builders have gathered the best workmen and the best ideas from European countries. American-built organs also combine ingenious native features and are better adapted to the climate and other local conditions than are foreign-built instruments.

The first American organ of importance, an instrument of four manuals and seventy stops installed in Tremont Temple, Boston, was built by Hook and Hastings in 1853. An important event was the installation of the fine organ in Boston Music Hall in 1863. This instrument was contracted for with the Walcker firm of Ludwigsburg by a committee which went to Europe to inspect famous organs and confer with prominent organists. The Civil War broke out before the organ could be shipped, and the final cost was nearly seventy thousand dollars. When the Boston Symphony Orchestra was founded, it was discovered that the organ interfered with the acoustic properties of the hall. After bitter controversy it was decided to remove the organ, and it was finally sold at auction for fifteen hundred dollars in 1884.

Hilbourne L. Roosevelt was the first great experimenter. He greatly improved the electropneumatic action in an instrument which he built for the Philadelphia Centennial in 1876, and in the large organ of 115 speaking stops which he erected in Garden City Cathedral, Long Island. In this instrument he employed three steam engines of ten horsepower each to operate the bellows, and used twenty-one miles of wire to establish connections between the separate divisions of the organ. Hope-Jones, an Englishman living in America, carried the principle of electropneumatic action to its greatest effectiveness.

John Turnell Austin of Hartford, Connecticut, contributed a significant feature in his invention, about 1890, of the universal airchest. This not only assures the maintenance of ample and equal wind pressure at all times, but permits necessary repairs to be made to the mechanism while the instrument is in use. Practically everything except the key action is installed within the wind chest. Mr. Austin's inventiveness, and that of his brother Basil, have also introduced original features in the mechanism of the console.

Among the names of the ablest and most original American builders is that of Ernest M. Skinner of Boston. Influenced at first by the work of Willis in England, his studies in acoustics and tonal production resulted in the creation of new stops of distinctive character and quality, and in new conceptions of the relation of differences in edifices and uses to organ building.

The best traditions of French organ builders have been perpetuated in America by the Cassavant brothers of St. Hyacinthe, Quebec. Many beautiful instruments of high artistic quality have been installed in the United States by this firm.

Mathias Peter Möller, a native of Denmark, came to America in 1872 and in 1881 established an organ building business in Hagerstown, Maryland, which has since grown to be the largest plant in the world devoted to the manufacture of pipe organs. The progressive policy of the founder's son, M. P. Möller, Jr., and the addition to its staff of expert authorities, have enabled this firm, long noted for its practical resources, steadily to advance to the highest standards of achievement.

Some of the largest and finest installations in America are the following:

Skinner organs in:
    Cleveland, Ohio, auditorium—five manuals, 143 stops;
    St. Bartholomew's Church, New York City—five manuals, 127 stops.
Austin organs in:
    Civic Auditorium, San Francisco—four manuals, 121 stops;
    First Presbyterian Church, Germantown, Philadelphia—four manuals, 127 stops;
    St. Matthew's Lutheran Church, Hanover, Pennsylvania—four manuals, 114 stops.
The Cassavant organ in:
    Emanuel Church, Boston—four manuals, 201 stops.
Möller organs in:
    United States Military Academy Chapel, West Point—213 stops. The largest pipe organ in a church building.
Kilgan organs in:
    St. Patrick's Cathedral, New York City;
    Carnegie Hall, New York City.

We should also mention the Grand Court Organ in the Wanamaker store, Philadelphia. Originally built for the St. Louis Exhibition of 1904, and consisting of 140 speaking stops, it was brought to Philadelphia in thirteen freight cars. In the Wanamaker shops it was entirely rebuilt in accordance with specifications prepared by Charles M. Courboin. Ninety-two new speaking stops were added. This instrument now contains more than eighteen thousand pipes in eight swell boxes and it is one of the largest organs in the world. The smallest pipe is three-quarters of an inch long, and largest thirty-eight feet. The longest pipe and the console weigh nearly one ton each.

265

There are no less than fifty-three reed stops of one kind or another. In richness and mellowness of tone, and in brilliance, this instrument in its best years was unexcelled.

In view of current heated discussions among organists and organ builders concerning designs and specifications, it may be well to devote a brief paragraph to the subject of so-called Baroque voicing and clarified ensemble. Many able recitalists criticize the average organ, particularly the extreme romantic type of thirty or more years ago, with its weakness in diapason tone and its profusion of orchestral stops. They believe that, particularly for the playing of Bach's music and similar contrapuntal compositions, independence of voices is indispensable if each voice part is not to be smothered in the "web of polyphony." They advocate a return to the type of instrument produced by the north European builders of Bach's era.

As a general observation, however, it may be stated that the Baroque organ is a relatively inflexible instrument. It has certain values for concert purposes. The church organ proper has requirements of its own. For liturgical use a well-designed instrument of conventional type, and under full expression is to be preferred.

Those who wish to pursue the subject of the organ and its construction further will find ample historical, theoretical, and practical material in two authoritative works of great compass: *The Art of Organ Building* (New York: Dodd, Mead and Company, 1905), a massive work in two volumes (1360 pages) by G. A. Audsley, an admirer of the "Romantic" organ; and later, *The Contemporary American Organ* (New York: J. Fischer and Brothers, 1930) by William Harrison Barnes, 341 pages, profusely illustrated. There is also a concise article on "The Organ" with bibliography in the Encyclopedia Britannica (1954 edition).

Chapter 16

THE ORGAN:
LITURGICAL REQUIREMENTS AND USE

Organists and organ builders have stimulated each other and have co-operated in the development of the instrument. The chorale introduced by the Reformation favorably affected organ playing. The Lutheran Church gave more opportunity to the organ than did the Roman Church, thus fostering its development. In Italy at this time the interest of musicians was centered in the opera. The result was loss of leadership to the Germans. Great seventeenth century organists were Scheidemann, Reinken, and Buxtehude in northern Germany, and Pachelbel, organist of St. Sebaldus Church, Nürnberg, in the south.

Bach, when only eighteen years of age, was appointed organist of the new church at Arnstadt. From here he set out on foot for Lübeck, a distance of over fifty miles, to study under Buxtehude, who presided over the organ at which Handel had played two years before. Returning to Arnstadt, he gained the displeasure of the authorities by embroidering the Service with organ enrichments. Removing to Weimar as court organist, he developed his mastery of the instrument.

In 1714 Bach declined the position of organist at Halle, where there was an instrument of sixty-three stops. Many of his fugues and other larger works for organ were composed during his stay at Weimar. After he removed to Leipsic in 1723, he devoted himself to composition and the direction of his choirs. His choral music, however, gained much of its peculiar distinction and power by being treated in organ style. In his compositions for organ he combined as never before tonal brilliance, intellectual mastery of form, and emotional expression of highest quality in original works of freshness and solid scholarship. His work was not fully appreciated by his contemporaries. It remained for Mendelssohn and Samuel Wesley to resurrect his music and establish his reputation.

Mendelssohn was a great organ virtuoso and composer. His sonatas, preludes, and fugues are classics for the instrument, and in other ways also he greatly influenced English musicians and English taste. Among modern German musicians, Max Reger and Karg-Elert have added new lustre to organ composition.

The English evolution of the organ and organ playing was relatively late. Puritan objection retarded both, and the English Service probably provided less opportunity for the organ than the services of either the Lutheran or the Roman churches. William Byrd, Orlando Gibbons, and John Bull were famous organists. Henry Purcell, born in 1658, was the greatest organist and composer of his period. Handel in his time was probably the greatest organist next to Bach. He exerted considerable influence upon organ playing and organ composition in England, his adopted country.

In the early nineteenth century, Samuel Wesley, son of Charles Wesley, established organ music on good foundations and was a brilliant extemporary performer. His son, Samuel Sebastian Wesley, achieved even greater renown.

French organ playing generally tended toward a light and sometimes trifling style. Lemmens, a Belgian, was the first to impress the French public with the character and quality of Bach's fugues. Later French organists, among whom may be mentioned Cesar Franck, Saint-Saëns, Widor, Guilmant, Dubois, and Lefébure-Wély, were musicians of ability and fundamental seriousness. Guilmant's fame was most definitely associated with the organ.

It is difficult to select names from the long list of able American organists. Among the older men are John Knowles Paine; George E. Whiting; Samuel B. Whitney; Clarence H. Eddy; David D. Wood, the blind organist of Philadelphia; John Frederick Wolle, another pupil of Wood and later of Rheinberger in Munich, whose work with the Bach choir of Bethlehem gained him an international reputation; and Lynwood Farnam, a native of the Province of Quebec, educated at the Royal College of Music in London, whose brilliant career in Montreal, Boston, and New York was recently ended by death.

Among many other eminent artists are Palmer Christian of the University of Michigan; Erich de Lamarter, a student of Widor and Guilmant; Charles H. Demarest, long associated with musical interests in Los Angeles and Seattle; Charles Heinroth, a student of Rheinberger, early identified with the Carnegie Institute in Pittsburgh and later working in New York City; William Charles Macfarlane, a London boy who came to this country when four years of age, organist in Portland, Maine, and New York City; Clarence Dickinson, a native of Indiana, organist of the Brick Presbyterian Church, New York, and head of the School of Sacred Music in Union Theological Seminary; Ernest White, renowned recitalist, former organist of the Church of St. Mary the Virgin, New York City; and Giuseppe Moschetti, acclaimed in Europe, as in America, director of music, St. John's Lutheran Church, Allentown, Pennsylvania.

ORGAN MUSIC

A good deal of the music which the average organist will be called upon to play will be in connection with the actual text of the Liturgy, or with the accompaniment of the choir or the congregation. It may be proper at this point, however, to call attention to the opportunities in the Service for organ music not strictly belonging to the Liturgy itself, but which should definitely be related to it. This includes all solo use of the organ before, during, or after the Service.

It is in this area that the organist probably feels most free to express himself and to display the resources of his instrument. This freedom, however, must be exercised within the limits of liturgical unity and propriety. The hour of public worship is not part Service and part concert. It must be all Service. Every part of it, from the very beginning to the very end, must contribute to the establishment and maintenance of a devotional mood. Silence is preferable to noisy or showy marches, preludes, interludes, or postludes, to crude extemporizations, or to transcriptions, however artistic, which introduce worldly suggestions. There may be a place for a recital of fine music of somewhat more general character immediately before the Service, but this must be strictly separated from the Service itself.

Organ music within the framework of the Service itself must be churchly in character and in full agreement with the feeling of the particular Service. Churchliness is difficult to define. Generally speaking it is to be found in organ music definitely devoid of secular associations and based upon melodic and modal forms associated with the church. Much of the best is founded upon the ancient Gregorian or plainsong system. The German chorale affords a second body of thematic material of equal interest and value. A number of modern English composers have employed Psalm tunes and early solid English hymn tunes in the same way in fine compositions for the organ, though most so-called hymn tune voluntaries are poor enough. There is also a fine body of freer but solid organ literature, comprising preludes, fugues, sonatas, improvisations, et cetera, by able and serious-minded composers which has churchly dignity and high artistic merit.

French organists, particularly, have composed organ works in the nature of chorale preludes, but based on plainsong tunes. Among these composers are Guilmant, Dubois, Vierne, Marcel Dupré, and Dallier. Latin melodies have been similarly treated by others, including Dr. Pearce, F. E. Gladstone, and Alfred Hollins.

Bach personally seems to have found more pleasure in his organ work than in other forms which involved vocal and instrumental co-operation, probably because the latter was frequently inferior. An earnest student of the scores of Corelli, Vivaldi, Frescobaldi, and others before him, Bach lifted the fugue and transformed it into an exceedingly expressive art form of high artistic quality. Parry, a Bach biographer, says the fugue is "the highest type of form based on a single thematic nucleus." Bach added genuine poetic inspiration to technical ingenuity and became master of the form. He composed forty-one fugues, nearly thirty of them while at Weimar.

After he left Weimar, Bach became a choirmaster. He frequently officiated, however, in opening new organs and similar concert occasions. His organ compositions at Leipsic were written chiefly as organ introductions to the seasonal hymns which were sung before the Gospel. Bach turned to the chorale for thematic material because this, next to the Bible itself, supplied the chief texts for the devotional life of the German people.

We have an indication of how closely Bach interpreted church doctrine when we see how he took six of Luther's hymns as thematic material for preludes in illustration of Luther's catechism. First of all he introduced two melodies to serve as an invocation of the Holy Trinity. Then he treated each of the six chorale melodies in two different ways, the one lengthy and elaborate and the other brief and simple. This was in recognition of the fact that Luther had prepared the *Large Catechism* for the clergy as well as the *Small Catechism* for the people. Three of the great preludes, the Vater Unser, Aus tiefer Noth, and Wir glauben all', rank among the greatest of his conceptions.

To understand Bach's chorale preludes we must, then, know not only the melodies he employed, but the text of the hymns as well. The Belgian organist Lemmens, who undertook to create a new style of organ music for the Roman Church, failed to appreciate the intensely religious spirit of Bach, whose music as such he highly estimated, because he did not understand how thoroughly Bach had penetrated into the meaning of the chorale texts. Widor also was unable to understand Bach until Schweitzer revealed his spirit and methods.

We must also know Bach's musical idiom. He used some twenty-five or thirty musical symbols, consistently employing a particular form of musical expression to indicate ascent or descent, distance, hurry, rest or fatigue, joy or sorrow, terror, the action of wind, waves, thunder. As

Wagner was to do later, though in different fashion, Bach employed a musical symbolism that was at once realistic and poetic. Professor Terry has supplied us fully with information on the text and melodies of the chorale preludes; Schweitzer and Pirro have discussed the musical ideas and logic which Bach employs. May deForest Payne (now Mrs. Reginald McAll) in her *Melodic Index to the Works of Johann Sebastian Bach* (New York: G. Schirmer, Incorporated, 1938) has given a complete tabulation of all the themes in Bach's works.

PRACTICAL CONSIDERATIONS

The average clergyman and his organ committee are, as a rule, inexperienced in matters having to do with organ tone, organ construction, and organ purchase, and are largely dependent upon the advice of others.

It is not generally appreciated that in the choice of an instrument quality and workmanship are more important than size. Organ committees are generally attracted by specifications which show the largest number of stops, even though many of these may be borrowed and not represent actual pipes, and others may have incomplete sets.

Some organ builders are purely commercially minded. With them organ building is a trade or industry. The best builders approach their work from the point of view of the artist. The making of a fine instrument, with distinctive quality of tone in each stop, perfect voicing, and durable construction throughout, calls for the highest craftsmanship and artistry.

It is unwise to reduce the matter of organ buying to competitive bidding. Great price variations are possible because of the ready opportunity of using inferior material, employing less able workmen, and giving only the most mechanical attention to the important work of voicing. Unscrupulous builders may substitute half-length stopped pipes for full-length open pipes, or wooden pipes for metal pipes in the lower notes. Cheap, soft woods, or woods that are too thin, and cheap metal, may be employed. These are points that only an expert can detect and prevent.

The poorest builders will offer what seems the largest number of stops and the most attractive mechanical features. The unprincipled among them will stop at nothing to get a contract. Many commercial builders who do good mechanical work do not have artists capable of producing the finest tone quality and of securing perfect voicing. Only the artistic builder is equipped with that proper combination of artistic, scientific, and mechanical information which can produce an instrument truly adapted to the type of service to be rendered. Good builders also have an advantage over medium-grade builders in their command of recent improvements by the control of patents, et cetera.

A cheap builder may offer an instrument for as little as five hundred dollars per set of pipes, while abler builders may ask a thousand or more. Quality should be sought rather than quantity. People of refinement and musical cultivation will be more pleased with a fine instrument of fifteen stops artistically voiced than with a commonplace organ of twice as many stops, though this can probably be secured for the same amount of money. The purchase of a larger instrument of cheaper construction may sometimes be justified where the size of the building and of the congregation demands a large instrument, and where financial resources are inadequate. But this should always be regarded as a matter of last resort, never an attempt to get something at bargain rates. Bargain organs do not exist.

It is well in any case to have specifications carefully drawn, covering a type of instrument to cost a budgeted amount, and submit this to builders of practically the same class. The specifications for this should be as carefully prepared as are the specifications for the church building itself. It will be well to secure the services of a capable organ architect. He will prepare specifications which he deems adequate for the building, and within the price limit which has been fixed. He will also supervise construction and installation. He will be able to detect any unwarranted substitution or borrowing, or other failure to live up to the terms of the contract. He will also generally play an opening recital. These facts, together with the fact that his supervision will have secured proper balance in the instrument, will more than justify the fee which will be required.

While this is the best plan in most cases, where there is a large amount of money to be spent—fifty thousand dollars or more—for an instrument of highest quality, it may be best to choose one of the ablest and most reliable builders in the country, and engage this particular firm without entering into negotiations with any other. There is no better way to secure the highest talent and the most careful attention to every phase of the problem.

The proper installation of an instrument is important. It must be well located with respect to the choir and the congregation. The organ chamber must be of ample size. The pipes must not be crowded, and there must be space above the highest pipes for free emission of sound. Sufficient room must be allowed inside the instrument for necessary repairs. Unfortunately, architects generally allow insufficient space.

It is essential that the organ tone be heard in balance. When the organ is placed on one or both sides of the chancel, it should speak out into the chancel only, and not directly into the transept or nave. If there be speaking pipes on both the nave and chancel walls, the congregation will hear the tone from part of the organ before hearing it from other parts, and will hear the sound of the instrument before the voices of the choir. It is better to have the organ tones come directly into the chancel, mix with the tones of the choir, and thus be heard as one tone by the congregation.

The console should be so placed as to secure for the organist control of the choir, while being as little visible to the congregation as possible. The organist must hear the organ and the choir equally well.

Acoustical engineers generally insist upon too liberal use of sound-absorbing tiles and similar material. Where employed at all, they should be used at a distance removed from the organ and not in immediate proximity to it.

It is foolish to install an expensive instrument and then give it little or no care. A pipe organ is a complicated and sensitive instrument. Dampness and lack of equable temperature will rust the metal parts, swell the wood, and decay the leather. Provision should be made when the instrument is installed for regular and frequent cleaning, and for maintenance of a fairly even temperature. It is inadvisable to have windows open into the organ chamber.

With reference to the practical matter of extra-liturgical use of the organ, it may be well to say that the organist should be given complete control. He should have the privilege of using it for his own practice and teaching. Members of the music committee or others should not extend the privilege of using the instrument to others. Those of the organist's pupils who are members of the congregation may have a reasonable amount of practice time allotted them. His other pupils may make arrangements to pay for the use of the organ, electric bills, et cetera. Some organists grant permission freely in order to encourage students, provide more organists, and keep the organ in good condition by regular use.

Weddings are played by the organist of the church in which the ceremony is performed. A definite fee for these services is usually fixed by the music committee when the organist is first engaged for the church. If the bride has a friend of the family who is an organist and desires his services, permission is obtained from, and the regular fee is paid to, the organist of the church. The fee in city churches for rehearsal and wedding is usually from fifteen to twenty dollars. This includes a thirty-minute recital before the ceremony. For an informal wedding with no rehearsal the fee is usually ten dollars or more. The organist's fee should be ascertained by the bride in advance.

The reasonableness of a fixed rule in the matter of organists' fees is obvious when one considers that the organist often loses teaching time or other remunerative work when called upon to play at times not regularly scheduled. This rule also sometimes saves the bride from embarrassment in declining the offer of a well-meaning but incompetent friend. A professional organist will not play a wedding in another organist's church unless the latter has received his fee.

The above rules represent the accepted practice of professional musicians in city churches. It will be recognized that modifications will be necessary to meet circumstances.

WEDDING MUSIC

There are frequent requests for suggestions of proper churchly music for weddings. Mrs. Regina Holmen Fryxell has gone into this question very extensively, in conjunction with the Blackhawk Chapter of the American Guild of Organists. With her kind permission, and the permission of her publishers, the Augustana Book Concern, we give selections from her extensive listings in the attractively printed booklet, *Wedding Music* (Rock Island, Illinois: Augustana Book Concern, 1956), 30 pp.

Organ music for Recital Preceding the Wedding Service

Bach, J. S.	Arioso	G. Schirmer
	Jesu, Joy of Man's Desiring (West)	Novello
	Like a Shepherd God Doth Guide Us (Sheep May Safely Graze)	H. W. Gray, Oxford
	Lord Jesus Christ, Be Present Now (*Little Organ Book*)	Oliver Ditson, Novello, Peters, G. Schirmer
	My Heart Ever Faithful (*Book of Airs*, E. S. Barnes)	Boston Music Co.
	Now Thank We All Our God (*Claude Means*)	H. W. Gray
	Prelude in G (*Wedding Music*, Vol. I)	Concordia
	Sinfonia to Wedding Cantata No. 196 (Porter)	H. W. Gray
Battishill, J.	Andante Quasi Allegretto (*Novelties for Organ*, Carl)	John Church

Boellemann, L.	Prelude, Suite Gothique (*Wedding Music,* Vol. I)	Concordia
Bossi, E.	Siciliana (*Historical Organ Recitals,* ed. Bonnet)	G. Schirmer
Clerambault, L. N.	Prelude in D (*Anthologia Antiqua,* Vol. I)	J. Fischer
	Dialogue, for upper and lower registers of the Trumpet from Suite (*Historical Organ Recitals,* Vol. I, Bonnet)	G. Schirmer
Dupré, M.	Prelude and Fugue in G Minor	Leduc
Edmundson, G.	Fairest Lord Jesus	J. Fischer
Franck, César	Pastorale (Vol. II)	
	Adagio (Chorale III)	G. Schirmer
	Fantasie in C (first movement, Vol. I)	Peters
Guilmant	Pastorale (First Sonata)	G. Schirmer
Handel, G. F.	Excerpts from "Water Music"	J. Fischer
Jongen, J.	Chant de Mai	Marks
Karg-Elert	Now Thank We All Our God (*Wedding Music,* Vol. 2)	Concordia
Mendelssohn, F.	Excerpts from Organ Sonatas	G. Schirmer, Peters
Milford, Robin	The King of Love (St. Columba, *Wedding Music,* Vol. 2)	Concordia
Oldroyd, G.	Three Liturgical Preludes (Nos. 2 and 3)	Oxford
Pachelbel, J.	Toccata and Pastorale (*Purcell to Handel,* ed. Nevins)	Gray
Peeters, Flor	Come, Holy Ghost (*Thirty Chorale Preludes,* Book II)	Peters
	Awake, My Heart, with Gladness (Easter, (*Thirty Chorale Preludes,* Book III)	Peters
Pierné, G.	Prélude, Cantilène, Scherzando	
Purcell, H.	Prelude in G (*Historical Organ Recitals,* Vol. I, Bonnet)	G. Schirmer

	Bell Symphony (Rejoice in the Lord)	Gray
Rheinberger, J.	Cantilena, Sonata XI (*Wedding Music*, Vol. I)	Concordia
Saint-Saens, C.	Fantasia in E flat	G. Schirmer
Sowerby, L.	Carillon	Gray
Vierne, L.	First Symphony: Pastorale, Allegro, Vivace, Finale	Marks
Walther, J. G.	Lord Jesus Christ, Be Present Now (*Wedding Music*, Vol. II)	Concordia
Whitlock, P.	Andante Tranquillo (*Five Short Pieces*)	Oxford
Widor, C. M.	Adagio (Symphony No. 5)	Marks
	Andante Cantabile, Scherzo (Symphony No. 4)	Marks
	Pastorale, Scherzo (Symphony No. 2)	Marks
Willan, H.	Prelude on Praised Be the Lord (Easter)	Concordia
Yon, P.	Pastorale, Fourth Sonata (*Modern Anthology*)	Gray

Processionals

Bach, J. S.	Sinfonia to Wedding Cantata, No. 196 (Porter)	Gray
	Sinfonia to Cantata; Thou Guide of Israel, No. 104	Gray
Bach-Fryxell	Sinfonia to "Praise, My Soul, the King of Heaven"	Augustana
Boellman, L.	Prelude: Suite Gothique (*Wedding Music*, Vol. I)	Concordia
Clokey	Processional (Wedding Suite)	J. Fischer
Couperin, F.	Offertoire (First section; *Mass for Parish Use*, Bingham)	J. Fischer
Franck, César	Fantasie in C (First Movement)	Peters

Handel, G. F.	Andante Maestoso (Concerto IV for Organ, *Wedding Music,* Vol. I)	Concordia
Processional Hymns (for choir and/or congregation)	Praise, My Soul, the King of Heaven	
	Praise to the Lord, the Almighty	
	All People That on Earth Do Dwell	
	Beautiful Saviour, King of Creation	

Recessionals

Bach, J. S.	In Thee Is Gladness (*Historical Organ Recitals,* Vol. 2, Bonnet)	G. Schirmer
	My Heart Ever Faithful (*Book of Airs,* Barnes)	Boston Music Co.
Boellmann, L.	Carillon (*The French Organist,* Vol. I, Bedell)	Marks
Clokey	Recessional (Wedding Suite)	J. Fischer
Karg-Elert	Now Thank We All Our God (*Wedding Music,* Vol. 2)	Concordia
Mendelssohn, F.	Maestoso excerpts from Organ Sonatas	G. Schirmer
Purcell, H.	Bell Symphony (Rejoice in the Lord)	Gray
Sowerby, L.	A Wedding Processional	Gray
Vierne, L.	Carillon (*Twenty-four Pieces in Free Style,* Vol. 2)	
Widor, C. M.	Toccata, Symphony 5	Marks
	Allegro, Symphony 6	Marks
Recessional Hymns (for choir and/or congregation)	Now Thank We All Our God	
	May the Grace of Christ, Our Saviour	
	Lead Us, Heavenly Father, Lead Us	

Vocal Music

Bach, J. S.	Jesus, Lead Our Footsteps Ever (Whittaker)	Oxford
	Jesu, Joy of Man's Desiring	Concordia, Galaxy
	My Heart Ever Faithful	G. Schirmer

Bach-Fryxell	Praise, My Soul, the King of Heaven	Augustana
Bairstow	The King of Love My Shepherd Is (S.A.T.B.)	Oxford
Bitgood, R.	The Greatest of These Is Love	Gray
Brahms	Though I Speak with the Tongues (*Four Serious Songs*)	

Bunjes, Paul (editor)

    Wedding Blessings (volume of twelve songs)   Concordia

        Jesus, Shepherd, Be Thou Near Me (Bach)

        O Love That Casts Out Fear (Bach)

        The Lord My Shepherd Is (Helder)

        O Jesus, Joy of Loving Hearts (Brahms)

        Jesu, Joy of Man's Desiring (Bach—2 arr.)

        Lord, Who at Cana's Wedding Feast (Buxtehude)

Clokey	O Perfect Love (*Wedding Suite*)	J. Fischer
	Set Me As a Seal Upon Thine Heart (*Wedding Suite*)	J. Fischer
Davies, Ivor	May the Grace of Christ, Our Saviour (Unison)	Novello
Dvorak	God Is My Shepherd (Vol. I)	Associated Music Publishers
	I Will Sing New Songs of Gladness (Vol. I)	Associated Music Publishers
	Sing Ye a Joyful Song (Vol. II)	Associated Music Publishers
Franck, César	O Lord Most Holy	G. Schirmer
Fryxell, Regina H.	Psalm 67 (Unison, two part, or solo)	Gray
	O Come, Creator Spirit, Come (S.A.T.B. or solo)	Augustana
	The Lord's Prayer (S.A.T.B., unison, or solo)	Augustana
James, Brother	Brother James' Air (Psalm 23) (S.A.T.B., Gordon Jacob; solo or unison, Trew)	Oxford
Lovelace, Austin	We Lift Our Hearts to Thee	Concordia
Mendelssohn, F.	The Voice That Breathed O'er Eden	Concordia
Rowley, A.	Here at Thine Altar, Lord (S.A.T.B. or solo)	Novello

Schuetz, H.	Wedding Song (high— Lenel)	Chantry Music Press
	Wedding Song (low— Leupold)	Chantry Music Press
Sowerby	O Perfect Love	Gray
Thiman	The God of Love My Shepherd Is	Galaxy
	Thou Wilt Keep Him in Perfect Peace	Gray
Willan, H.	O Perfect Love (high)	Gray
	Eternal Love (*Three Songs of Devotion*)	Summy-Birchard
Williams, Ralph Vaughan	O How Amiable (mixed voices, two parts, or solo; congregation optional on closing stanza)	Oxford

ELECTRONIC ORGANS

The aggressive methods of representatives of various electronic instruments make it necessary to say that fine qualities of tone, with the dignity, purity, and beauty appropriate for services of worship, can only be produced by real pipe organs. Electronic instruments, with their blatant, percussive tone—metallic and commonplace in quality—are not acceptable substitutes for real organs. One harsh critic says, "An electronic instrument is an unpredictable mongrel, neither pipes, nor strings, nor reeds." Real organs have many ranks of pipes with variety of pitches and tonal color, and with true harmonics. These can be blended in an ensemble which cannot successfully be imitated by the synthetic effects of electronic tone with its loudspeaker quality and untrue harmonics.

Volume is no compensation for quality. Not only is it impossible to play the great compositions of the masters satisfactorily on electronic tones, but the latter also lack the devotional and spiritual qualities essential in worship. They remind one rather of the dance floor, where they are in common use. Their dullness and impurity of tone unfit them for accompanying the human voice. Untrained ears, accustomed to similar commonplace qualities in radio reproduction, are often unable to recognize these deficiencies. But anyone who has come to know and love true pipe-organ music will be immediately repelled.

Apparent economy is an added inducement for selection of these substitute instruments. The economy is only apparent. Electronic instruments, however cheap to begin with, wear our rapidly, needing constant repair and frequent replacement. A good pipe organ, on the other hand, may last for centuries.

It may be that science will some day perfect an acceptable instrument of this kind. In their present state of development, electronic organs meet neither the musical nor the devotional requirements of the church. All who cherish artistic and devotional values in worship music should strive earnestly to keep electronic instruments out of the church.

Those interested in this subject should read the statement by the Council of the American Guild of Organists on "Organs and Electronic Instruments," June, 1936, and the articles incorporating the opinions of eminent organists and organ architects, published in *The American Organist* for January, 1936.

THE ORGANIST'S PRIVILEGE AND RESPONSIBILITY

It is to the credit of the musicians of the church that the art of organ playing has steadily advanced along lines of reverence and devotion rather than in the spirit of self-assertion. Under the influence of capable and spiritually-minded men and women, an organ technique has developed which makes the use of the instrument most acceptable in unifying the Service and preserving a devotional atmosphere. A noble literature of the instrument has been developed. Organists have been led to study the Liturgy, the church year, and all the elements of worship. As a result, the organist today is in a very real sense an extremely important factor in building up the fabric of each public Service, by his art establishing and maintaining the mood appropriate to the day or season and enhancing every part of the transaction.

The church organist who would realize the ideals of his art must not only master the organ itself, but also its literature. This includes, in addition to music especially associated with the Liturgy, hymns, and choir numbers, a large body of material suitable for solo work before, during, and after services. Here will be found preludes, fugues, sonatas, improvizations, and other substantial compositions by serious-minded composers who deliberately avoid secular suggestions and develop melodic and modal forms drawn from plainsong, German chorale, and Psalm tune sources. We have already mentioned Bach, Brahms, Reger, and Karg-Elert as the giants whose preludes and fugues tax the capabilities of the ablest modern organists. Similarly acceptable compositions by Merkel, Guilmant, Franck, Dupré, Stanford, Parry, West, Wood, and many others, some of whom we have also mentioned, are also worthy of note.

IDEALS OF SERVICE

Solo numbers of the sort mentioned must be mastered not only with respect to technical difficulties, but with regard to their liturgical significance. Every individual offering by the organist, like every sermon by the minister, must be an act of worship. The organist must approach his task not as an artist who is a churchman, but as a churchman who is an artist. His chief joy must come from recognition of the religious content and significance of his work rather than its aesthetic or emotional possibilities. Liturgical taste and judgment must enable him to view every Service as an offering to God and not a concert program. Operatic selections, sentimental serenades and romances, noisy marches and fantasias will be excluded. Musicians who realize this ideal regard their work in and for the church as a calling rather than a profession.

Such ideals can only be obtained by the fullest co-operation between the organist and the minister. The primary responsibility rests upon the minister. But he must look to the organist-choirmaster more than to anyone else for that intelligent assistance which will enable him to realize his ideals and the ideals of the church. Similarly, while the organist-choirmaster controls the musical resources of the parish, these can only be developed to the utmost and a real contribution made to the worship of the congregation by the active support and encouragement of the minister. In the few instances where these personalities fail to co-operate happily, the effectiveness of each is marred and the worship of the congregation impaired.

Occasionally the minister resents what he regards as an undue length of musical features arranged for festivals, Communion services, and special occasions. Quite as frequently an able organist is dissatisfied with the minister's low standards of musical taste and his preference for popular programs. Where there is mutual understanding and confidence, neither will crowd out the other, and the proper objectives of both will be furthered. Fortunately, high quality of personal character and religious consecration usually unite the minister and his organist-choirmaster in fullest understanding and endeavor.

ORGAN SPECIFICATIONS

Every church organ, like every church building, is an individual project. Stock plans and mass production cannot be depended upon to give the finest results in tone, color, transparency, timbre, and other artistic qualities which every good instrument should possess. Individual problems of the character of the building, location of the organ, space available, frequency of use, nature of musical programs, et cetera, must be studied and solved in every case. Nevertheless, with these facts clearly understood, it may be helpful to give several sets of specifications for relatively small church organs in different price ranges. This will indicate a properly balanced design in each category, and will also show approximately what may be secured from a reputable builder under present conditions (1958).

With these considerations in mind, we have requested Dr. William Timmings, who has professionally advised many congregations in these matters, to give us several sets of specifications for organs of moderate cost. With the co-operation of the Möller Organ Company, Hagerstown, Maryland, he has prepared the following.

Specification A — Cost $9,800

MANUALS: Compass CC to C4, 61 notes
PEDALS: Compass CCC to G, 32 notes
ACTION: Electropneumatic
CONSOLE: Detached. Stops to be controlled by tilting tablets
PITCH: A-440

Great Organ

Diapason	8'		73 pipes
Gedeckt	8'		85 pipes
Viole Dolce	8'		85 pipes
Octave	4'		61 notes
Flute	4'		61 notes
Fugara	4'		61 notes
Viole Twelfth	2 2/3'		61 notes
Viole Fifteenth	2'		61 notes
Trumpet	8'		61 notes

Swell Organ

Bourdon	16'	T.C.	49 notes
Gedeckt	8'		61 notes
Viole Dolce	8'		61 notes
Viole Celeste	8'	T.C.	49 pipes
Flute	4'		61 notes
Fugara	4'		61 notes
Flute Twelfth	2 2/3'		61 notes
Flautino	2'		61 notes
Trumpet	8'		73 pipes
Clarion	4'		61 notes
Tremulant			

Pedal Organ

Bourdon	16'	12 pipes
Viole Dolce	16'	12 pipes
Diapason	8'	32 notes
Gedeckt	8'	32 notes
Octave	4'	32 notes
Flute	4'	32 notes

Fully equipped with the usual couplers, adjustable combinations, pedal movements, and accessories.

Specification B — Cost $20,000
Two-manual Organ

MANUALS: Compass CC to C4, 61 notes
PEDALS: Compass CCC to G, 32 notes
ACTION: Möller's electropneumatic
CONSOLE: Detached. Stops and intramanual couplers to be controlled by draw knobs. Intermanual couplers to be controlled by tilting tablets.
PITCH: A-440

Great Organ

Diapason	8′	61	pipes
Bourdon	8′	61	pipes
Dulciana	8′	61	pipes
Octave	4′	61	pipes
Octave Quint	2 2/3′	61	pipes
Super Octave	2′	61	pipes
Chimes	Console only		
Tremulant			

Swell Organ

Rohrgedeckt	16′	12	pipes
Rohrflöte	8′	61	pipes
Viole de Gambe	8′	61	pipes
Viole Celeste	8′	49	pipes
Nachthorn	4′	61	pipes
Plein Jeu	III Rks.	183	pipes
Trompette	8′	61	pipes
Chimes	Console only		
Tremulant			

Pedal Organ

Bourdon	16′		32	pipes
Rohrgedeckt	16′	from Swell		
Principal	8′		32	pipes
Bourdon	8′		12	pipes
Rohrflöte	8′	from Swell		
Octave	4′		12	pipes
Bourdon	4′		12	pipes
Octavin	2′		12	pipes

Fully equipped with couplers, adjustable combinations, pedal movements, and accessories.

Specification C — Cost $30,000
Three-manual Organ

MANUALS: Compass CC to C4, 61 notes
PEDALS: Compass CCC to G, 32 notes
ACTION: Möller's Pitman electropneumatic
CONSOLE: Detached, tracker touch, electropneumatic operation, drawknob type.
PITCH: A-440

Great Organ (Unenclosed)

Gemshorn	16′		61 pipes
Principal	8′		61 pipes
Bourdon	8′		61 pipes
Octave	4′		61 pipes
Octavin	2′		61 pipes
Fourniture	III Rks.		183 pipes
Chimes (console only)			
Tremolo			

Swell Organ

Rohrflöte	8′		61 pipes
Salicional	8′		61 pipes
Voix Celeste	8′		49 pipes
Spitzprinzipal	4′		61 pipes
Plein Jeu	III Rks.		183 pipes
Trompette	8′		61 pipes
Clarinet	4′		61 pipes
Tremolo			

Choir Organ

Lochgedeckt	8′		73 pipes
Erzahler	8′		73 pipes
Erzahler Celeste (TC)	8′		61 pipes
Harmonic Flute	4′		73 pipes
Nasard	2 2/3′		61 pipes
Piccolo	2′		61 notes
Tierce	1 3/5′		61 pipes
Tremolo			

Pedal Organ

Sub Bass	16′		32 pipes
Gemshorn	16′	from Great	32 notes
Quintade	16′	from Swell	12 notes
Principal	8′		32 pipes
Gemshorn	8′	from Great	32 notes
Rohrflöte	8′	from Swell	32 notes
Quinte	5 1/3′		32 pipes
Oktav	4′		12 pipes
Double Trumpet	16′	from Swell	12 notes
Clarion	4′	from Swell	32 notes

Couplers

Great to Pedal 8′	Swell to Pedal 8′	Choir to Pedal 8′
Great to Pedal 4′	Swell to Pedal 4′	Choir to Pedal 4′
Great 16′	Choir to Great 16′	Swell to Choir 16′
Great Unison Off	Choir to Great 8′	Swell to Choir 8′
Great 4′	Choir to Great 4′	Swell to Choir 4′
Swell to Great 16′	Swell 16′	Choir 16′
Swell to Great 8′	Swell Unison Off	Choir Unison Off
Swell to Great 4′	Swell 4′	Choir 4′

Adjustable Combinations

Pistons No. 1-2-3-4-5-6   Affecting Great Organ
Pistons No. 1-2-3-4-5-6-7   Affecting Swell Organ
Pistons No. 1-2-3-4-5-6   Affecting Choir Organ
Toe Studs No. 1-2-3-4-5   Affecting Pedal Organ, at right General, affecting entire organ

No. 4-5-6-7 duplicated to pedal, at left

General cancel piston

Pedal Movements

Swell Expression Pedal
Choir Expression Pedal
Crescendo Pedal, with indicator lights
Great to Pedal Reversible Piston, duplicated to pedal, affecting Great to Pedal 4' in off movement only
Swell to Pedal Reversible Piston, duplicated to Pedal, affecting Swell to Pedal 4' in off movement only
Choir to Pedal Reversible Piston, duplicated to Pedal, affecting Choir to Pedal 4' in off movement only
Tutti Reversible Piston, duplicated to pedal, with indicator light

Accessories

Starter buttons mounted in console
Tremolo-celeste-percussion cut-out for Tutti and Crescendo
Organ bench with music shelf and backrest
Concave, radiating pedal clavier
Electric motor, steel slow-speed Kinetic blower, and Orgelectra action current rectifier of ample capacity

Chapter 17

THE MINISTER'S PART

The church itself has a large responsibility in the matter of public worship. It determines the Liturgy, the hymnal, the Christian year, the plan and appointments of the church building, et cetera. Ecclesiastical authority, however, cannot be relied upon to sustain the spirit or the form of worship indefinitely. Personal leadership is necessary; and foremost among the leaders must be the minister.

PERSONAL ATTITUDE

Worship must be for the pastor more than a duty. He must himself have a right attitude toward all things connected with it, or the worship of his people will suffer. In a nonliturgical church the minister has great freedom. He may prepare many different forms as effective settings for his sermons. In a liturgical church the minister's leadership includes a responsibility to the whole church as well as to the local congregation. He must respect the Order of his church as well as edify his people. This means that he must master a body of liturgical principles and practices, and maintain standards of churchly purity in all official acts.

The minister's attainments in these matters should more than equal those of intelligent members of his congregation. He must know the Liturgy and the music of the church; the history and theory of worship, with their doctrinal implications; the classical expressions of church architecture and the minor arts; the significance of the great festivals and seasons; et cetera. Such an intelligent grasp of the whole field is as essential for leadership in worship as a liberal education in science, philosophy, history, and literature is in preparation for social contacts and effective pulpit ministrations.

The genius of Lutheranism reacts against externality and insincerity. The simplicity and forthrightness of its Liturgy requires corresponding qualities in its setting and performance. Overelaboration, fussy decoration in the church building, excessive ceremonial, or other spectacular features, are all out of harmony with our understanding of worship. On the other hand, a strong sense of historic values and of what is inherently proper, distinctive, and beautiful, best expresses the Lutheran spirit. Indifference and individualistic practices are equally bad. Appreciation of historic continuity and churchly values in traditional liturgical usages will seek to conserve the best and employ them in the services of the contemporary church.

The literature of worship should form a fair part of the minister's reading. Identification with the life of the church as a whole will enable him to free himself from personal crudities and lead his people to a realization of the dignity and beauty of common forms and ceremonies. Once convinced that the minister has a proper understanding of these matters and that he is a man of judgment and taste, congregations which have not been accustomed to full liturgical uses will follow where their pastor leads.

The wise pastor will seek the co-operation of others, among whom none is more important than the organist-choirmaster. Upon the basis of mutual respect and friendship, in which the minister will fully recognize the responsibility and authority of the leader of his musical forces, a fine program of co-operative endeavor can be carried out.

The special gifts of the organist-choirmaster, and indeed of the choir members as well, are usually developed upon the background of spiritual sensitiveness. This makes these groups peculiarly responsive to ideals. Their gifts and training make them impatient with ignorance, indifference, slovenliness, and lack of standards. They will follow leadership they respect, and follow it unstintingly. Their co-operation can be readily secured if the minister is careful not to entangle himself with petty details, or to ignore the authority of others in their special fields.

As opportunity affords he can make his influence felt in the choice of an organist and/or choirmaster, in the development of certain types and forms of music, et cetera. He can help improve congregational singing with the use of the full round of the church's *Hymnal* with its rich provision not only of English and American hymn tunes, but of German and Scandinavian chorales, French church tunes, Psalm tunes, plainsong, et cetera. He can aid his choirmaster in improving the caliber of his choir by his personal interest and an occasional reference to the work of the choir; he can knit his forces together and give support and encouragement to all who give their time and service in this important activity.

THE FIELD OF EDUCATION

A second important sphere of influence is in the field of education. All historic institutions have a body of usages and traditions, a spirit and a form of life. The church is no exception. Appreciation of the church's standards, and loyalty to them, can best be secured by processes of education. As personal character develops by active work under definite convictions, so churchly character grows from church consciousness which seeks to develop a worthy and distinctive church life. Apart from this, congregational existence is almost purposeless. We must give our people foundations, backgrounds, and models of liturgical beauty if we would lift their worship above flabby emotionalism and establish it upon planes of intelligence and spirituality.

Such instruction can be given in the public services by occasional references to parts of the Liturgy, the *Hymnal,* or the usages of the church. Special lectures on the hymns and the music of the church, the church year, the Liturgy, the church building, church history, et cetera, may be given, particularly in Advent and Lent, after the mid-week services. Or one Sunday evening a month might be devoted to such themes. Brief notes in the parish paper will be informative and helpful. The Sunday school and the catechetical class afford opportunity for acquainting the youth with essential facts. One might, for example, use in the Sunday school some of the great hymns of the church instead of sentimental items "on a child's level." Such masterpieces of religious expression are not too difficult for the minds of youth; and how better acquaint the congregation with good new hymns than by means of the clear, hearty voices of the younger generation?

It is not sufficient to instruct catechumens in the five parts of the catechism. With the extension of the time of preparation for Confirmation to two or three years, opportunity will be found for acquainting children with the distinctive and meaningful features of the Liturgy, the church year, the chancel and its appointments, the most common Christian symbols, et cetera, all of which will enrich their understanding of Christian worship. General direction and supervision should also be given to the work of the altar guild, the duties of the acolytes, et cetera. While time consuming, personal and sympathetic attention to all these matters will reveal its worth in the quickened interest of members of these groups, and in the improved character of congregational services.

Solid churchmanship will be built up, not by petty and superficial tinkering with externals, nor by focusing attention on trifling details, but by careful and constant instruction along broad and fundamental lines. People will follow intelligent and inspiring direction, but the minister must lead the way.

PERSONAL PREPARATION

We may believe with the Apostle that some matters should not even be once mentioned among saints. Experience, however, proves that it is often necessary to refer to details of even the most elementary character.

The minister's preparation for his public ministrations must include matters of the most common sort. He must be sure to give attention to personal appearance, neatness of clothing, cleanliness of linen. He may not lag behind his people in these matters. Clerical attire is generally appreciated and respected. "The cloth," like the uniform of a policeman or an army officer, is an indication that the wearer is "on duty." A minister, for very good reasons, may decide not to wear clerical dress at all times. Propriety and decency, however, demand conventional clerical attire when conducting public worship. There is little point in having an edifice of churchly character, correct chancel appointments, an altar properly vested and furnished with cross and candles, a pulpit and lectern of ecclesiastical design—and then have the minister appear in the chancel in attire which suggests the prosperous businessman, the sportsman, or the entertainer. The clergyman's dress as he ministers at the altar is not a matter of personal preference. The congregation and the church have a right to expect what is proper.

The ministry is a calling. It is also a profession whose practice demands proficiency. The minister should be as expert in his work as is the surgeon, the lawyer, or the engineer. There is a body of technical detail which he must master. If he does not, it will master him. He must have exact knowledge about liturgical details and matters of procedure, and must develop a feel for churchly things. His technical mastery of these matters must be such that he will have confidence in strange surroundings and be able to conduct the Order of the church under the most exacting circumstances.

The minister's sacristy should be a citadel for his spirit. It should be a place reserved, where he may be uninterrupted and give himself, if only for a few moments, to spiritual and intellectual preparation before every service. No matter how great his gifts, he cannot hope to pass instantly from the hurly-burly and strain of other duties or social intercourse and enter the chancel fully poised and spiritually prepared. He must have quiet and solitude, if only for a brief moment, or he will fail to do what his people and his Lord expect of him.

Every minister should insist upon having such a place and such a time for preparation. Nothing should be allowed to interfere with this. If people are informed, they will understand and respect this provision.

LITURGICAL PROPRIETIES

Form is something more than forms, just as manner is something more than manners. Good form in the conduct of worship is essentially an expression of right attitude toward God and the congregation. The minister in the chancel must be conscious of the presence of God and of the presence of the people. Consciousness of self should fall away before these greater realizations. A high spiritual concentration should pervade every part of the Service.

Leadership in worship involves not only proper interpretation but good example. In all his public ministrations the minister occupies a conspicuous position. His conduct profoundly affects the worshipers. His attitude throughout should be one of devotion and spiritual concentration. Inattention, fussy rearrangement of notes or announcements, conversation, careless crossing of legs, adjustments of vestments, or too evident scrutiny of the congregation—these are false notes which produce liturgical discord.

Personal devotions at the beginning of the Service, before preaching, before the Preface, or before the administration of Baptism, Confirmation, and at the close of the Service, should be characterized by dignity and reverence.

Service books should not be carried by the minister as he enters or leaves the chancel; or from one part of the chancel to another. They should be placed upon the altar and in the stalls beforehand.

The spirit of devotion and concentration suggests that the minister join his hands as he moves about the chancel or officiates at the altar. Loose hands and swinging arms belong on the platform and not in the chancel.

The minister should not face the congregation unless he is speaking to it directly, in the sacramental parts of the Service, or in making announcements. At other times he should face the altar or the chancel wall.

The altar should be approached and left in dignified fashion from the center and not by diagonal short cuts.

The minister should remain in position until each response is completed and then move promptly, though with dignity, to the next liturgical station. Thus he will remain until the Amen at the end of every prayer has been said or sung; until the Gloria Patri at the end of the Psalm has been completed, et cetera.

Hymns should not be mutilated by the omission of stanzas, unless for some important reason. A hymn is a poem which usually progresses to a climax of thought. The entire point is often missed by the congregation when the development of the thought has been broken

290

Lutheran Church of the Redeemer, Atlanta, Georgia

Architect: Harold E. Wagoner, Philadelphia. Rugged expression of modern Gothic. Built of native stone. Excellently detailed trim contrasts well with massive masonry. Clerestory windows. Main entrance is easily approached by a series of steps rather than by a single long run.

University Lutheran Church, Cambridge, Massachusetts
Architect: Arlan A. Dirlam, Boston. Contemporary. Good proportion and simple detail, window
nicely composed and grouped. Easy approach to doorway, which has sufficient detail to give interest.

Memorial Presbyterian Church, Montgomery, Alabama

chitects: Pearson, Tittle, and Narrows, Montgomery. Consulting architect: Harold E. Wagoner, iladelphia. Churchly contemporary design. Local stone. Planted areas form base of structure.

Christ Evangelical Lutheran Church, Minneapolis, Minnesota
Architect: Eliel Saarinen. Bold contemporary design, depending on mass shapes and the use of contrasting materials and colors. Façade ornamented with carved bosses. Glass door and connecting wa

Interior

teral natural lighting focuses attention on altar. The stark simplicity of table altar with unimpressive
aments immediately in front of massive stone wall gives impression of studied austerity.

Weaver Memorial Chapel, Wittenberg College, Springfield, Ohio
Architect: T. Norman Mansell, Philadelphia. Rugged expression of contemporary architecture w
concrete arches and laminated wood trusses. Gothic feeling of height. Especially fine craftsmanship.

Immanuel Evangelical Lutheran Church, Chicago

all contemporary church with strong Gothic feeling. Carvings in wood and stone, stained-glass, metal
rk are Swedish in character. Stone interior with pleasing proportions. Fine craftsmanship.

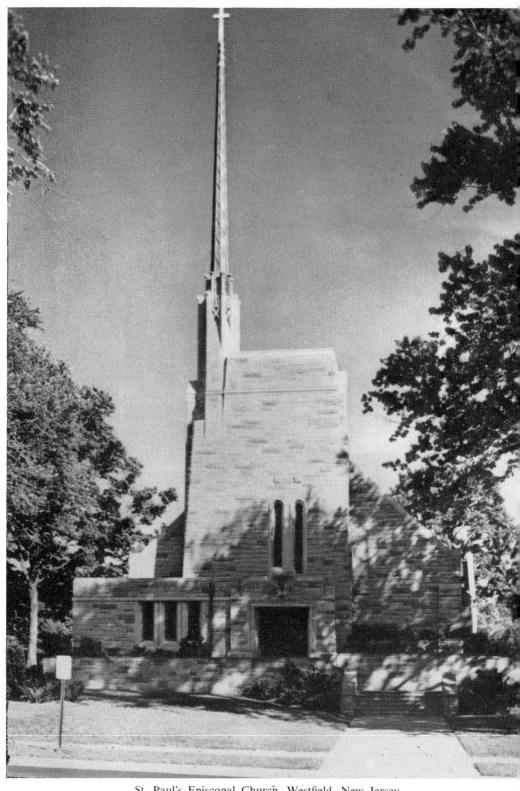

St. Paul's Episcopal Church, Westfield, New Jersey
Architect: Harold E. Wagoner, Philadelphia. Contemporary design with simple masses and sparse det.
Gothic influence. Tower and spire interesting by combined, imaginative detail well placed.

by thoughtless omissions. Nor should the hymn be broken by the congregation rising before it is ended to prepare for the next liturgical act. The congregation should either sit or stand throughout the entire hymn.

When several ministers officiate, all details should be arranged beforehand in the sacristy. There should be no confusion, conversation or belated planning or management in the chancel itself. No effort should be made to parcel out the Service to all the clergymen who may happen to be in the chancel. One minister should be the officiant, and conduct the entire Liturgy. Another may preach, and it would be proper for him also to read the Lessons.

At the celebration of the Holy Communion, the officiant and his assistant should not alternate in the distribution of the elements. Historic use suggests that the officiant administer the wafer and pronounce the blessing. The assistant should administer the wine. The Reformation emphasis upon the restoration of the cup to the laity attached unusual importance to the administration of the wine, and is probably responsible for the unhistoric custom, frequently found, of administration of the cup by the officiant.

LITURGICAL READING

Good liturgical reading develops from an appreciation of the meaning of the Liturgy and an understanding of liturgical principles, as well as from a knowledge of what is on the printed page.

If the Liturgy is thought of as a mere form and used as such, it will be cold and lifeless. It cannot be otherwise. Spiritual perception and purpose can make it warm and vital. Personal faith and earnestness can express themselves in fixed and formal language with such sincerity and strength that they will be immediately recognized.

Good liturgical reading is impersonal, but never indifferent. The Liturgy belongs to the congregation as well as to the minister, and to the church as truly as to the congregation.

There must be no attempt to interpret the text dramatically with strongly accented words or vocal tricks. Neither should the reading be casual or conversational in tone. Every word and phrase should be given distinct enunciation which will carry to the back pew.

In order that the congregation may interpret the reading intelligently, the latter must be deliberate and clear, with brief pauses between the larger divisions of the Service. There should, however, be no hesitation, dawdling, or awkward breaks. These immediately raise suspicions concerning the reader's ability or preparation. A halting or inaccurate reading is an affront to the congregation and to the church, which has a right to expect better things of its trained ministry.

It follows that the reader must thoroughly know the fundamental structure of the Liturgy, the text of Holy Scripture and the Collects, as well as every detail of the Service.

He should not read every syllable from the book—particularly brief sentences like the Salutation, the Oremus, the Versicles—nor follow every word of the printed page in the Confession, the Declaration of Grace, and similar longer parts. The *Service Book* should be left on the missal stand on the altar when the reader turns to the congregation for the Salutation, the Oremus, the Benediction, et cetera. These brief forms which the church has employed for centuries should be committed to memory and used accurately and forcefully. Awkwardness and ignorance in the use of the Liturgy kill devotion and bring discredit upon the Service itself.

THE SERMON: AS WITNESS AND WORSHIP

In every period of vigor the church has recognized the power and the importance of preaching. The Apostles preached the gospel before the Gospels were written. When the world "by wisdom knew not God, it pleased God by the foolishness of preaching to save them that believed." Every age of the church produced great preachers. And instruction in the art of preaching has a large place in our training of men for the ministry today.

The sermon has no value in itself. It is important as an effective means of proclaiming the Word of God. Such proclamation, of course, is accomplished not only through the sermon but also by the reading of the Scriptures, by public worship as a whole, by the administration of the sacraments and other rites of the church. But it remains for the sermon to do most effectively certain things which Bibles, liturgies, and hymnals alone cannot do.

To the Christian all life is worship. "Whether ye eat or drink, or whatsoever ye do, do all to the glory of God." But particularly in public worship do we need the complete and harmonious adjustment of all parts which gives strength and beauty to the whole. The altar, the pulpit, and the organ are not separate and unrelated pieces of furniture such as we might find in a salesroom or a drawing-room. They fit definitely into the plan and purpose of an organic structure. Similarly, neither the sermon nor the music may be independent or self-assertive. In the liturgical churches, the Service cannot be thought of as a program, with the sermon as the central and dominant feature. The Liturgy is a living unity, a body with related members, each complementing the rest.

In the history of the church, two great periods stand out: the formative period of the early church and the reformative period of the six-teenth century. In both the sermon assumed great importance; in neither did it have independence.

In the early centuries, the sermon was more than the testimony of the individual, or an unrelated utterance. The thought of believers was concentrated on definite themes. Whatever the occasion, hymns and homilies and other available material contributed to the devotional unfolding of the common theme.

The Service was divided into two parts. First, there was a general Service for instruction and edification. Here all were welcome. The second part was restricted to those who were baptized. This Service centered around the celebration of the Holy Communion. The sermon held an important place in the first or general Service, and the preaching was intended for believers and unbelievers alike.

Likewise, in the Reformation, the preaching of the Reformers was most important. It aroused and inspired the people, gave them new conceptions of faith, of worship, of life. It made effective the reform of the church. But it was never regarded as a merely personal or independent function. As we study the published sermons and homilies of Luther, Bugenhagen, Melanchthon, Veit Dietrich, Spangenberg, and others, we find them fitting into the fabric of the Liturgy and the church year as part of a comprehensive act. Luther's sermons contain strong speech—fearless arraignment of error and abuse combined with tender assurances and consolations of the gospel. But they are never mere assertions of self. Essentially they breathe a spirit of reverence and humility, a spirit of love for Christ, of subjection to God's Word, of appreciation of the magnitude of human need and of the riches of divine grace—all of which, too, are expressed in worship.

The theology of the church is expressed not only in Creeds and Confessions, or in published systems of doctrine, but more popularly and not less powerfully in its forms and acts of corporate devotion. A normal service will provide adequately for both worship and witness, not in separate sections, but intertwined in a common transaction. We may think of the Liturgy as primarily worshipful. The church service, however, like the church building, is a witness to the faith, a testimony to the world. In similar fashion, the sermon, if kept within the frame-work of the Liturgy, definitely becomes an act of worship. The Liturgy requires the sermon to relate the faith of its forms to the contemporary thought and needs of the people. The sermon needs the Liturgy to guard it against secularism, eccentricity, narrowness, and self-exploi-tation. The personal talent and testimony of the preacher must be geared into the common worship of the congregation and into the full round of the church's faith.

The formal Liturgy includes many elements—confession; adoration; praise and thanksgiving; prayer and intercession; the celebration and administration of the Holy Communion; the instruction, exhortation, edification, and challenging and quickening power of the sermon. The latter, to realize its fullest power, must breathe the spirit of worship. Otherwise, no matter what its intellectual or moral strength, it differs little from the platform utterances of secular speakers on serious matters. The Word of God becomes the voice of God in a sermon. Whether it be the word of prophecy or the word of testimony, it meets the need of believer and agnostic alike. It is most effective when in fullest harmony with all other features.

The sermons of the great preachers of the early church—Gregory, John Chrysostom, Augustine, Ambrose—were powerful in large part because they were delivered in the setting of the Mass. The later increase of priestly functions at the altar, with resulting decline in the relative importance of the sermon, weakened the structure of corporate worship. Preaching of a sort continued throughout the medieval centuries, with many priests continuing to give vernacular expositions of the Gospel after the Latin text had been read in the Mass. The great revival of preaching, however, came independently of the Mass in the zealous activities of the mendicant friars who preached to great crowds in hall-like churches, at wayside "crosses," and similar stations in the open air. This severance of the sermon from the Liturgy marked the beginning of a cleavage which persists in Protestantism to this day. For while the Lutheran and the Anglican Reformations purified and simplified the Liturgy and restored the sermon to its rightful place, the Reformed churches, of every branch, abandoned or mutilated the historic structure of worship, together with the church year, choral music, and other liturgical features. They exalted the sermon to a position of unique importance, surrounding it with simple, and often individualistic, forms of devotion which served as preliminaries and conclusions.

The preacher in a nonliturgical church, in lonely independence, must create and sustain an intellectual and spiritual mood appropriate to the theme he has chosen. Tremendous responsibility is thrown upon him. He has only the uncertain aid which the miscellaneous features of a devotional program may contribute. His themes are more or less arbitrarily chosen. Suggestions may very well come from all sources, some worthy and others trifling. Events of more or less secular and ephemeral character become the basis for discussion.

There have been times when portions of the Protestant Church set themselves defiantly against the deepest currents of Christian thought, and preached upon the death of Christ at Christmas time, or upon his birth in the Lententide. The weakness inherent in this flaunting of universal thought and feeling is evident. The liturgical churches, with greater wisdom and psychological insight, study the tides rather than the weather, knowing that "the tide lifts all ships." Fortunately this fact is now generally recognized in all communions. The annual recurrence of great festivals establishes moods and sets in motion currents of thought.

Some may not realize that this principle applies not only to the great festivals, but to the season, and indeed to each individual service. Church people live in the mood and spirit of the church year. They instinctively know when they are in the Adventtide, the Lententide, or the Eastertide. They expect to have the themes of the church seasons unfolded in Lessons, hymns, and prayers. They likewise expect to have the sermon enforce and apply at least the general thought of the season in its relation to the full round of Christian truth and life.

The sermon is one element in the Service. It gains effectiveness because it is *in* the Service, and not apart from it. It is the pointed spearhead which focuses thought and penetrates. And the spearhead gains direction, weight, and power by reason of the shaft to which it is affixed. The Liturgy with its varied but harmonious structure supports and strengthens the sermon. Ultimate power comes from the Spirit of God working through the minister spiritually attuned to his environment and wholly consecrated to his calling. Without this worshipful quality, his sermon may be a mere physical and intellectual effort. With it, the sermon gains the spiritual dynamic which convinces, enkindles imagination, and appeals to conscience and will. Professor Herbert Henry Farmer in his Warrack Lectures says, "Preaching is not merely telling me something. It is God, actively probing me, challenging my will, calling on me for decision, offering me His succour." [1]

The Word of God, in the sense of the full sweep of the gospel, has supreme significance in worship. It must speak in every part of our worship. All that we should know of the nature and the will of God, of the mind that was in Christ Jesus, of the quickening power of the Holy Spirit as he deals with human sin and need, of the full range of Christian duties and opportunities, of the mission of the church as the communion of saints and the custodian of the Word and sacraments—

[1] Farmer, *The Servant of the Word* (New York: Charles Scribner's Sons, 1942).

all these aspects of our holy religion provide proper sermon material.

Nor is the influence of the sermon limited to personal edification and parochial interests. It can, and often it must, reach out widely in its application of the Christian gospel to the contemporary situation. We are increasingly aware of the fact that not only individuals as such, but communities and nations as well, live and act in accordance with their beliefs concerning God, themselves, and their fellow-men.

Luther was a great preacher, and he had a high estimate of preaching. He believed that the Word of God must not only be written but spoken. He said: "The ministry of the New Testament is not inscribed in dead tablets of stone, but is entrusted to the sound of the living voice." In his *German Mass* (1526), he said, "Everything in worship is to be done for the sake of the Word and the sacraments." The sacraments provide personal applications and individualizations of the Word. Thus Word and sacraments together become proclamations of the gospel and Means of Grace. This fundamental principle, later developed in the Lutheran Confessions, effected a complete reform of Christian worship.

Archbishop Brilioth in an article on "Preaching as Worship" says: "The preacher should not talk or lecture. He should preach, that is, he should proclaim the Word of God. . . . For this eloquence is valuable, but spiritual insight is more important. The preacher's aim should be . . . to make the law and the gospel present realities, to place his hearers before the Cross of Christ. The sermon should be truly an act of worship that gives to the liturgical Service its full depth, and receives from it solemnity and strength." [2]

It is in this sense that we think of the sermon as an act of worship. Unfaithfulness to the Word impairs its worshipful character. Devoid of the spirit of worship, the sermon is an affront to man and God, and a help to no one. Secular themes, political discussions, entertaining novelties, and sensational deliverances are cheap and tawdry substitutes for the gold of the gospel. The whole range of human experience may be explored. History, science, philosophy, literature, and art may be drawn upon to illustrate and enforce Christian truth. But the gospel must be proclaimed in it all, and proclaimed in the spirit of a holy communion with God and with men. The church in arranging for common worship provides a pulpit, not a platform.

One of the welcome accomplishments of the broad liturgical movement of the last century in all churches is the general recognition of the fact that each great division of Christianity has made a contribution,

[2] *Christendom*, Vol. VI, 1941.

and that each can learn something from the others in the solution of the problems of preaching. The liturgical churches, in some measure at least, have been influenced by the freedom, the greater range, and the popular appeal of the type of preaching developed within the Free Churches. The latter, in many quarters, are growing in appreciation of devotional and spiritual values in historic liturgical material, and of liturgical form in general as a proper setting for the sermon.

Chapter 18

VESTMENTS

The subject of vestments is at once important and unimportant. In every period of liturgical activity it becomes a matter of controversy, with intense preferences and prejudices in evidence. It deserves, however, broad and objective consideration. Extreme positions are bad, for extremes meet. By stressing his point of view to the utmost the ritualist becomes an individualist, the individualist a ritualist.

The fact that the subject is difficult will not justify us in evading it. Rather, it challenges us to supply, so far as possible, accurate information and constructive suggestions.

Vestments are in themselves not essential. The efficacy of the gospel and the sacraments is not dependent upon them. We must also remember that the traditional ecclesiastical vestments approved in the Middle Ages, and continued to the present in the Roman and in some parts of the Lutheran Church, are not ecclesiastical in origin. They are survivals of the usual street dress of men in the Roman Empire during the early Christian centuries. Customs changed in the secular world, the style of male attire changing with the rest. The church, with its usual conservatism, retained the customary vestments for its clergy, eventually establishing them as a uniform and universal use. Similarly, less than half a century ago, the clergy of certain Protestant groups in America continued wearing the frock coat ("Prince Albert") as a sort of liturgical garment long after it was no longer used as street dress.

The alb, from *alba*, Latin for "white," is simply a conventionalized form of the ancient Roman tunic. The surplice, from the Latin *superpellicum*, developed in the cold climate of northern Europe as a vestment that could readily be put on over a fur coat, which was often required in unheated church buildings. The maniple and stole are derivatives of the Roman gentleman's handkerchief and napkin which he wore because he had no pockets. The maniple, as a handkerchief, was originally worn in special forms by consuls and other officials. The stole developed in much lengthened form and became a distinctive vestment for any sacrament. The chasuble and the cope have developed from the cloak of which St. Paul speaks in his letter to Timothy. Thus the ordinary lay attire of classic times has persisted in the church and become the "ornaments of the ministers." Back of this development has been a strong aesthetic feeling, and an even stronger appreciation of scriptural symbolism which associates white garments and clean linen with our Lord's Transfiguration.

VESTMENTS BEFORE THE REFORMATION

Let us, if we may, reconstruct pre-Reformation procedure. The priest, in preparing to celebrate Mass, first placed the amice over his neck and shoulders. This was an oblong linen cloth which served as a protection for the other vestments. Then he put on the alb, a wide white linen robe with full folds and close-fitting sleeves. This covered the body down to the ankles. The cincture, or girdle, next fitted the alb to the body. Then the maniple, a narrow strip of material originally a linen handkerchief, was placed on the left forearm. Then the stole, a narrow scarf of silk in the liturgical colors, was drawn over the shoulders and held by the cincture in the form of a cross over the breast. Finally the chasuble, a garment of precious material in the liturgical colors, and large enough to cover all the other apparel down to the knees, was put on.

At services other than the Holy Communion, such as baptisms and confessions, the priest wore the surplice and stole. The surplice, a three-quarter length vestment with flowing sleeves, was developed by shortening and widening the alb. It was first introduced, as we said, in northern Europe, where it was sometimes worn instead of the alb at the Eucharist.

For processions, litanies, et cetera, and on Sundays and feast days at Vespers, the cope was worn. This resembled the chasuble except that it was open in front, being held together by a clasp over the breast, and was generally somewhat longer. The cope was sometimes called the Vesper mantle.

In addition to these vestments of the priest, the bishop wore the tunic, the dalmatic, sandals, buskins, gloves, mitre, and a pectoral cross. Some archbishops, in addition to these, wore the pallium.

Besides these definitely liturgical vestments, two other garments should be mentioned. These were rather of the nature of private clerical attire or habit. The first is the cassock, an under-robe of cloth or stuff, usually black in color, with upright collar, and reaching to the ankles. This was worn in the house and even out-of-doors on ordinary occasions. It served as a foundation garment for choristers and priests in church. The so-called clerical coat has developed from the cassock with shortened skirt.

The second is the priest's gown. This black garment was originally worn by the clergy over their cassocks in going to and from the church. The preacher frequently wore it in the pulpit, while the celebrant at the altar wore the vestments proper.

Only prelates and clergy holding high academic degrees were entitled to use silk for cassock and gown and for the biretta, which was worn as a head covering.

THE REFORMERS AND THE CHURCH ORDERS

The Reformers had to face this question of vestments. And they did it in characteristic fashion. Zwingli declared that vestments, crosses, et cetera, were not only nonessential, but absolutely impermissible. Luther's conception of liberty made him stand equally against those who insisted that all the vestments of the church must be worn and those who demanded their discontinuance. In his *Formula Missae* he says concerning vestments, "We think about these as we do about other uses; we permit them to be used without restraint, only let pomp and the excess of splendor be absent. For neither are you the more acceptable if you should consecrate without vestments. For vestments do not commend us to God." [1] Bugenhagen's views were similar, and in this spirit he reorganized the church life in Brunswick, Hamburg, Pomerania, Schleswig-Holstein, Denmark, et cetera. In a letter to M. Görlitz, September 27, 1530, Bugenhagen defends the use of chasubles with surprising vigor. He says: "There is a twofold doctrine on chasubles . . . one is the truth, namely, that chasubles can be used . . . the other is a Satanic lie out of the doctrines of devils, namely, that it is never lawful to use chasubles." [2]

Luther himself laid aside his monk's habit in his own home, though he continued to wear it for church services. On October 9, 1524, he appeared at the morning service in this fashion, but in the afternoon he went into the pulpit in his doctor's gown (*Schaube*), a custom which he appears to have continued. This does not mean, however, that he read the altar service in this garb. We know from the account of his travels given by the Augsburg preacher Wolfgang Musculus that the

---

[1] *Works of Martin Luther* (Philadelphia: Muhlenberg Press, 1932), Philadelphia Edition, Vol. VI, p. 93.

[2] O. Vogt, *Dr. Johannes Bugenhagen's Briefwechsel* (Stettin: Leon Saunier, 1883).

alb and chasuble were regularly in use in the Wittenberg services in the year 1536. As late as 1732, Gerber, in his discussion of church ceremonies in Saxony, declares that these same vestments were still used at the altar "in most places." Frequently the minister wore only the alb or the black gown until he finished the sermon, after which he put on the chasuble and began the Communion Office.

December 4, 1539, Luther wrote a letter to Provost Buchholzer, who was concerned about the request of the Elector Joachim of Brandenburg, that copes and surplices might be used in processions on festival days and Sundays. In this he said, "If your Lord, the Margrave and Elector, allows you to preach the Gospel of Christ purely, without man's additions, and permits the sacraments of Baptism and the Lord's Supper according to Christ's appointment . . . then in God's Name go through with them carrying a silver or a gold cross, and a cowl or surplice of velvet, silk or linen. And if one of these be not enough, put on three as did Aaron the High Priest. . . . For such things if not abused, neither add to nor take from the Gospel, but they must never be regarded as necessary." [3]

Many of the Lutheran Church Orders, probably the majority of them, specifically retained or permitted the "customary vestments," at least the surplice and chasuble and, less frequently, the stole. Occasionally, in districts where Reformed influence was felt and had to be met (as in the Ostfriesland Order, 1529, near the Holland border), white or elaborate vestments were explicitly required at the Holy Communion as honoring the Sacrament and expressing belief in the real presence. The cope was also used for processions. In general the Lutheran view, which respected historic development and continuity, and believed that Christian liberty permitted retention of usages which did not conflict with Scripture, was given characteristic expression in Article XV of the Augsburg Confession and chapter IV of the Apology.

THE PROCEDURE IN SCANDINAVIA

The Reformation in Scandinavia was carried out in a conservative manner. The opposition of radical Reformers was not seriously felt. The historic vestments were generally retained. The cope was extensively used by bishops, apart from celebration of the Holy Communion, and for state and ecclesiastical occasions, such as coronations and royal weddings.

Archbishop Laurentius Petri's Swedish Church Order of 1571 defends the use of the historic Mass vestments, altars, and altar paraments. Dr.

---

[3] Condensation of letter. The original text is in *D. Martin Luthers Werke Briefwechsel* (1938), Weimar Edition, Vol. 8, p. 625.

Oscar Quensel, commenting upon this, says that in this defense the archbishop "turns upon the enthusiasts, Anabaptists, profaners of the Sacrament, Zwinglians, and Calvinists with no less sharpness and violence than just previously against the Papists." [4]

Though the influence of Rationalism was later felt in the mutilation and abolition of historic observances, the Scandinavian churches generally returned to the use of the principal vestments of the ancient church, though with local variations. The cassock or another black undergarment, the surplice, the alb, and the chasuble are regularly in use today, particularly in cathedrals and city churches. The Danish and Norwegian churches still retain the ruff around the neck, as is also done in a number of cities in northern Germany. The Swedish clergy wear linen bands as a neckpiece. The stole has not always been worn, but its use is increasing. In Finland and Czechoslovakia the Lutheran congregations also generally retained the historic vestments.

LATER DEVELOPMENTS IN GERMANY

Notwithstanding Luther's practice of wearing his doctor's gown, the historic vestments were continued in many parts of the church in Germany for centuries. In Paul Gerhardt's time, 1650, the vestments were in use in his church (St. Nicholas', Berlin). The chasuble was worn well into the nineteenth century in Hamburg, Luebeck, et cetera, in northern Germany. Sometimes only the black gown was worn during the first part of the Service and in the pulpit, the other vestments being reserved for the Communion Office proper, as had been done for centuries. Frequently, however, the surplice was worn in the pulpit. We know from the inventory of Bach's effects that he wore the surplice as organist in Leipsic. The surplice and other vestments were only discontinued in Nuernberg in southern Germany in 1810, by which time Rationalism had disastrously affected all church attendance.

In many sections the Thirty Years' War occasioned the loss, destruction, or abandonment of vestments. This tendency was increased by the indifference to historic and churchly observances shown by the church leaders of the time of Pietism and Rationalism. The latter period witnessed the widespread adoption of the black gown, with the biretta as a head covering. French influence in northern Germany as in Sweden led to local use of a small black mantle, but this disappeared after 1811, when the Prussian Ordinance required the use of the talar, or black gown, similar to the one worn in the Reformed churches in Switzerland. In fact, the modern universal use of the black gown by

[4] *Bidrag till svenska liturgiens historia* (Upsala, 1890), Vol. II, pp. 74-75.

Lutheran clergymen in Germany has come about rather as a result of Calvinistic influence than because of the earlier use of it in the pulpit by Luther. We must also remember that Luther occupied an academic post, which made it natural for him to use a black gown. There are steel engravings of Luther celebrating the Sacrament in Mass vestments.

In Brandenburg, Prussia, while the populace was largely Lutheran, the royal house was Reformed. King Frederick William I in 1733 prohibited Communion vestments, as well as copes, candles, chants, the sign of the cross, et cetera, in all churches of his realm. The Lutherans protested in Koenigsberg, Magdeburg, Halle, and Pomerania. The royal decree was repeated in stronger form in 1737, and some Lutheran ministers were dismissed. Though the king's son, Frederick III, a few years later rescinded his father's injunction and allowed full liberty in matters of worship, the historic vestments were not restored except in a few churches as Rationalistic indifference was increasingly felt. Thus the black gown did not become universal in German churches until less than a century and a half ago, and then only after the official decrees of a Reformed ruler and religious indifference in general had combined to bring all churchly observances to the lowest level ever attained in Lutheran history.

The association of the bands (*Beffchen*) with the black gown was also quite late. These originally had no ecclesiastical significance. They represented the survival of social and academic class distinctions. During the sixteenth and seventeenth centuries, the nobility and the educated professional classes—lawyers, judges, and physicians, as well as clergymen—came to wear a white neckpiece, which either stood out stiffly, as in the case of the Danish ruffs and the Elizabethan ruffs in England, or else covered the neck and shoulders in a "falling band" such as we see worn by physicians and others in the paintings of Rembrandt. When the wig or peruke was introduced, the long queue interfered with the ruff or collar. The latter was reduced in size and modified until it consisted of two broad bands over the chest. The nobility and the other professions finally discarded these bands entirely. The clergy, with characteristic conservatism, retained them, particularly in Switzerland and Germany, as well as England and Scotland.

The latest, and the most complete, survey of this subject is the thoroughly documented study of Professor Arthur Carl Piepkorn of Concordia Seminary, St. Louis, published in 1956 by the School for Graduate Studies of the seminary under the title, *The Survival of the Historic Vestments in the Lutheran Church after 1555.* In his summary Dr. Piepkorn states:

The alb, the cincture, the surplice and the chasuble have never passed wholly out of use in the Church of the Augsburg Confession. . . . The cope has survived as an episcopal vestment in Scandinavia. . . . The maniple disappeared from use in the seventeenth century, the dalmatic in the late eighteenth or early nineteenth century. The stole passed out of general use by the seventeenth century, although here or there it may have survived into the eighteenth. Where these vestments are currently in use, they are restorations, not survivals.

THE PRESENT SITUATION

And what of the present? There is still no uniform practice in Europe. The churches in Denmark, Norway, Sweden, Finland, Czechoslovakia generally use the principal historic vestments—at least the cassock and surplice, and frequently the stole—with the alb and the chasuble for Holy Communion.

The black gown, which was the ordinary street attire of clergymen and public officials in the sixteenth century, is universal in Germany. The liturgical revival in the nineteenth century under the leadership of Loehe, Kliefoth, Schoeberlein, and others restored the historic Liturgy and led to a great development in church music, hymnology, et cetera. It did not concern itself with such matters as vestments and ceremonial. The bands are generally worn with the black gown, though in some northern cities, as already stated, the ruff is still used, as it is in Denmark and Norway. The alb, in modified form, is regularly used in Leipsic, Weimar, Koenigsberg, and other northern cities, as well as throughout Woerttemberg in the south, for the administration of Holy Communion.

In America the confusion noted in Europe has been perpetuated. Erik Björck, pastor of the Swedish Lutheran colonists at Wilmington, Delaware, records in his diary that when Holy Trinity Church was dedicated, July 4, 1699, he and Pastor Rudman wore surplices without chasubles, "since we could not obtain them here." When Justus Falckner was ordained, Wednesday, November 24, 1703, in Gloria Dei Church, Philadelphia, by Andreas Rudman, assisted by Erik Björck and Andrew Sandel, he was invested with surplice and possibly, but not certainly, a stole. His was the first Lutheran ordination, and probably the first regular ordination of a Protestant clergyman in America. There are varying accounts of this service. We know that Andreas Rudman, the senior clergyman, acting as suffragan or vice-bishop under authority from the Archbishop of Upsala, used the Swedish ritual. It is generally agreed that he was vested in an alb with girdle, over which was a white lace garment. It is not certain that he wore a stole. His two clerical assistants wore black gowns. Falckner wore his black university gown, and over this was later placed the surplice or linen chasuble (*Messhemd*) and possibly, stole.

The Muhlenbergs had black gowns made for them in London, and their example eventually established this use in the American churches. Pioneer conditions, however, and the influence of nonchurchly and sectarian groups led to great laxity and informality for a time. In some parts of the church no vestments at all were worn. The use of the black gown gradually spread. Early in the present century it was in use in most congregations.

The bands are rarely worn in English services. The stole in the liturgical colors is common. Some Scandinavian and Slovak congregations use the alb and chasuble for the Holy Communion, as do also a few English and German congregations. In recent years, however, the trend has not been to either extreme, but to a middle position—the use of cassock, surplice, and stole.

The Lutherans in America, like their brethren in Europe, regard the subject of vestments as a nonessential (*adiaphoron*). While contesting earnestly for points of doctrine, they have been willing to yield in nonessentials. This principle explains the ease with which the black gown, more expressive of the gloomy theology of Calvinism than of the reverent joy of Lutheran worship, became fastened upon the Lutheran Church in Germany. It also explains how some "union churches," and others in America as well—even after pioneer conditions had passed—fell into the practice of neighboring Protestant communions and discarded all vestments, a custom not justified by Lutheran precedent anywhere in Europe.

PRESENT-DAY TRENDS

The desire is now evident, in all parts of the church, to arrive at a more uniform and satisfactory practice. The Common Liturgy affords a basis for liturgical solidarity. This Service represents generic Lutheranism rather than any one national or provincial type. Its use in English-speaking congregations in all bodies and synods will lay the foundation for substantial uniformity and eventual unity. Conscious of solidarity in faith and of their evident destiny as one of the largest and most important Protestant churches in the country, the different groups, no matter how diverse their European backgrounds, are being drawn more and more closely together in conferences, co-operative endeavor, education, missions, et cetera. The general use of a common Liturgy, common types of church architecture, with similar chancel appointments, and similar forms of church music, naturally leads to a desire for greater uniformity in the matter of vestments and church usage.

What is desired is the establishment of a normal and distinctive use in agreement with the principles which produced the Common Liturgy.

Its framers have made no declaration on the subject of vestments. Theirs was a literary and musical work, a matter of text and tune. Any effort to establish agreement on external matters now must rest, first of all, upon the procedure of the church in the sixteenth century, and beneath this upon the broad foundations of the pre-Reformation church which, with all its errors, yet preserved and transmitted to succeeding generations the great Christian traditions. The use we choose must not only be historically correct. It must be appropriate and adequate for the requirements of American church life today.

The composite character of American Lutheranism and its varied backgrounds must also be borne in mind. In this connection the suggestion of Dr. J. A. O. Stub challenges thought, at least as a long-range program. He says, "The American Lutherans, largely of German extraction, have preserved for us, and have acclimated for us, the beautiful Liturgy of the universal Christian Church. Perhaps under God, American Lutherans, largely of Scandinavian extraction, shall bring in their contribution, the hallowed and beautiful vestments of the same Church Universal." [5]

SUGGESTIONS FOR A NORMAL USE

So far as present conditions are concerned we stand with Luther against extremists who would wear no vestments at all, and others who would have us reinstate the entire historic series. In the middle ground we place the cassock, surplice, and stole. The bands drop from consideration, though historically definitely associated with the black gown. There is no point in perpetuating in America a mark of class distinction which, generally speaking, no longer obtains in Europe and never was important in this country. The stole has none but ecclesiastical associations. It brings the vestments of the minister into harmony with the vestments of the altar and pulpit, and emphasizes the thought of the church year. If the stole is not worn, the bands may be used with the cassock and gown as affording some contrast and relief from the depressing gloom of an all-black attire. The use of the colored stole with the black gown cannot be justified by historic precedent or liturgical logic. The best that can be said for the custom is that it is a faint-hearted compromise which seeks to brighten the gloomy effect of the black gown and bring the vestment of the minister into harmony with the vestments of the altar and the thought of the season or festival.

The black gown, while having its own proper dignity, and better than no vestment at all, is meeting dissatisfaction on various grounds. Its

[5] "Vestments and Liturgies" (printed privately), p. 44.

306

origin is academic or domestic rather than ecclesiastical. This is true whether we think of the doctor's gown, which Luther wore in his home and in the classroom; the pre-Reformation priest's gown, worn over the cassock on the way to and from church; or the cloak or mantle which the learned and middle classes in Germany in the eighteenth century generally wore. When the modern doctor's gown is worn in the chancel, its velvet facings and chevrons are as suggestive of class distinctions as were the bands of old. There may be some justification for its use by ordained teachers in seminaries and colleges of the church. But even here it should not be worn by officiants at Holy Communion, and it should not be worn by teachers or pastors in the regular services of a congregation.

From every point of view, the black gown suggests associations which are personal and private rather than common and churchly. Cassock and gown anciently comprised the private full-dress of the clergy in the home and on the street. When several ministers are in the chancel, their black gowns are oppressively suggestive of a Calvinistic conception of worship. The services of the church gain no festival or joyous character whatever from the funereal gown which Geneva adopted and Puritanism found convenient and appropriate to continue and transplant.

If the black gown is not used, the alternative must be the surplice. This has only ecclesiastical association; it possesses dignity and beauty; it expresses the joy of Christian service; and there is ample justification for its use in Lutheran as well as ancient church history. Its reintroduction presents little difficulty, particularly in congregations where choirs are already using the cassock and cotta, the latter an abbreviated surplice.

The movement toward liturgical unity in the Lutheran Church in America is definitely in the direction of the universal use of the Common Liturgy, and an increasing use of the cassock, surplice, and stole. These vestments are now used in many congregations by ministers who, with few exceptions, have no thought of introducing any other vestments. Rare even fifty years ago, they are now worn by the majority of pastors in many synods.

A WORD TO EXTREMISTS

Thus far we are on solid ground. For the peace and welfare of the church we might well wish that all of our ministers and congregations would be satisfied with this and strive to unify the present practice of the church along these lines.

The Common Liturgy is as representative an expression of Lutheranism in the field of worship as are the Augsburg Confession and the

Small Catechism in the field of doctrine. Yet there are congregations which do not know or use either it or the Common Service which preceded it. A few ministers do not use any vestments at all. The two omissions are parallel phenomena. The unity of the church, under these circumstances, will best be obtained by a process of moderation and development which will encourage the use of the Liturgy with simple vestments as the normal and universal practice of the church. The zeal of a few who urge more than this makes the universal attainment of such a normal use more difficult.

Liberty may be allowed in individual cases for a program of liturgical enrichment in matters not officially prescribed. Certain practical considerations, however, cannot be ignored. While the alb and chasuble have been in unbroken use in parts of the Lutheran Church, they have so dropped out of general use that the attempt to reintroduce them is likely to occasion surprise and controversy. In large centers, those who desire the most complete expression of the church's liturgical forms may be attracted to a particular congregation and attend its services. Here something may be said for a fuller use if the membership generally approves. But attempts to reintroduce these vestments generally will not strengthen the appeal of the church in the average community. We may believe that "all things are ours." We also know that not all things are "expedient" or even desirable under normal conditions.

A few extremists on the other side persist in wearing no vestments at all. They misrepresent their church, which has ever been a liturgical church. They should remember Bugenhagen's rebuke of the ministers in Brunswick who sought to give up all vestments, and also the plain words of the Coethen Church Order of 1534, which expressly follows the Wittenberg use, and which characterizes as irreverence the celebration of the holy sacraments "in the dress in which the minister goes about daily or sits in the tavern with the farmers."

Those who insist on the reintroduction of all the ancient vestments should ask themselves whether they are not laying undue emphasis upon externals and nonessentials, and inciting needless controversy and division. They should remember Luther's admonition to the pastors in Livonia concerning worship and the spirit of unity: "It is unchristian to be disunited over such things and thereby confuse and unsettle the people. . . . For even if the external uses are free, and, taking the faith into consideration, may with good conscience be changed at all places, at all hours, by all persons; still, taking love into consideration, you are not free to use such liberty. . . . It does not help you any when you are wont to assert: 'Yea, the external thing is free; here in my own place I am going to do as pleases me.' You are in duty bound to consider

308

what the effect will be on others . . . for we should not please ourselves, since Christ also did not please Himself, but us all." [6]

The mission of the church and the need of the times should determine our course. The world is in as great confusion and distress as it was in Luther's day. Its sins call for rebuke; its sorrows need the consolations of the gospel; its doubts need the assurance of Christian certainty; its life needs to be purified and elevated by the power of the Holy Spirit. Men and women everywhere need the strongest elements of religion. Anything less is inadequate. The gospel can shine as clearly through the wearer of a chasuble as through the man in the black gown. But discussions and controversies over either or any of these unimportant externals are deplorable. Vestments have their proper value in securing dignity, uniformity, and a sense of historic continuity. But other things are more important.

The church must maintain communion with God in reverent and beautiful services of distinctive character. It must provide vigorous and effective preaching. It must be zealous in missionary, educational, and social service endeavors. Services, sermons, and activities must be characterized by spirituality, intelligence, and moral earnestness. All who seek the sanctuary must be refreshed and inspired. The attainment of these objectives requires balanced comprehension and churchmanship. Real effectiveness may only be expected from a normal functioning of all parts without undue emphasis upon a few.

IN SUMMARY

Some form of liturgical vestment must be worn in formal liturgical worship.

Whatever other vestment is used, the cassock should be worn as a foundation garment. The minister's body should be entirely covered with silk or silk and linen. Cloth vests with bone buttons, watch guards, pockets filled with lead pencils, fountain pens and notebooks are unpleasantly informal and improper.

Over the cassock may be worn the surplice and stole.

The surplice and stole are to be preferred to the black gown because of their distinctly ecclesiastical character, because of their continuous use in our own church and universally, because their general effect is in agreement with the Lutheran conception of worship, and because their use brings the vestments of the minister into harmony with the vestments of the altar and the choir.

[6] "Exhortation to the Christians in Livonia Concerning Public Worship and Unity," *Works of Martin Luther* (Philadelphia: Muhlenberg Press, 1932), Philadelphia Edition, Vol. VI, p. 147-148.

The black gown is permissible, in spite of its drawbacks, because of extensive but relatively late use in Germany and America.

The academic gown (the usual "doctor's gown") should not be worn in the regular services of the congregation or by officiants at the Holy Communion. This is not so much because it marks a distinction between some ministers and others—for there will ever be such distinction—but because it is an academic and not an ecclesiastical vestment. The use of an academic hood with the surplice and stole is an even greater violation of propriety.

The stole is traditionally associated with the surplice. It should not be worn with the black gown. The bands may be used with cassock and gown, but not with cassock and surplice.

It is not necessary that the same vestments be worn at all services. Surplice and stole may be used for the Holy Communion and on festivals, and the gown and bands at other times.

Like most compromises this will not satisfy everyone. The purist believes that the alb and chasuble are the only proper vestments for Holy Communion. Those of opposite opinion may hold out for their right to wear no vestments. In the absence of law and in the exercise of liberty, however, custom frequently accepts and establishes compromises. It can be said with certainty that surplice and stole for all services is gaining wide acceptance in the Lutheran Church in America as it has been widely accepted in the Anglican communion everywhere.

The right of individual ministers to wear the alb and a simple linen chasuble for the Holy Communion, if their congregations approve, is recognized. Pastors and congregations, however, should not be involved in discord over such nonessentials. They should also consider the effect of their practice upon others, and particularly as concerns the influence and appeal of the congregation in the community.

In addition to Professor Piepkorn's study already mentioned, attention may be called to the following: the approval by the United Lutheran Church in America in its convention at Omaha, 1940, of a Report on Vestments by the Common Service Book Committee (ULCA Minutes, 1940, p. 570 ff.). A convenient Roman Catholic authority is Dom E. Roulin, *Vestments and Vesture* (St. Louis: B. Herder, 1931). An Anglican work is Percy Dearmer, *The Ornaments of the Ministers* (London: A. R. Mowbray and Company, 1920). On the usages of the Church of Sweden: Linderoth and Norbrink, *Den svenska Kyrkan* (Stockholm, 1943), second edition.

310

Chapter 19

CEREMONIAL

Corporate worship requires the use of some commonly accepted form. This rite in turn involves the use of ceremonial. This includes postures, gestures, and other visible movements and features accompanying the Liturgy. The rite determines the what or matter of worship; the ceremonial determines the how or mode of worship. The rite has to do with words; the ceremonial with actions designed to express or illustrate those words.

A broader definition identifies ceremonial with ritual. Thus "rites and ceremonies" are combined in a phrase which includes everything connected with the appointed order of worship—not only the Liturgy and all outward actions connected with its use, but also the appointments of worship, such as the altar, font, pulpit, vestments, lights, and colors. It is in this wider sense of the term that the word "ceremonies" is frequently employed by the Reformers and the Confessions.

IN EARLY AND MEDIEVAL TIMES

Ceremonial, like the Liturgy, developed naturally with the life of the church. Our Lord gave his Disciples no fully developed form of worship. By precept and example he taught them to pray, and he gave them a form of prayer; he observed days and hours and frequented the synagogue and the temple; he read the Old Testament Scriptures; he sang the Psalms; he submitted to the baptism of John; he commissioned his followers to preach, teach, and baptize, and to observe the Holy Supper.

From these principles and examples the church elaborated fuller forms and ceremonies, as it developed systems of theology, principles of organization, and methods of work. Advancing beyond the simplicity of Apostolic times, the church invested the sacraments of Baptism and the Holy Communion with a dignity and beauty which impressed the

311

pagan world and helped to win consideration for the claims of Christianity.

The medieval church carried the use of ceremonial to great excess, perhaps partly from necessity, in view of the fact that the great majority of the people were unable to understand the Latin of the Mass. Allegory and symbolism ruled in worship, as in everything else. Indescribable richness characterized the church building and the church service. Winged altars, massive reredoses, rood screens, and choir stalls; paintings on stone, wood, and canvas; fonts, holy water basins, chalices, and ciboriums; reliquaries, altar crosses, crucifixes, croziers, censers, and incense boats crowded the structure. The Liturgy became complicated and the ceremonial vast in its proportions. The impure doctrines of the time called for the importation of fresh ceremonial to illustrate their meaning. Additional lights and reverences acknowledged the bishop's presence. Multiplied crossings, genuflections, elevations, reservations, and adorations attested belief in transubstantiation. The medieval Liturgy carried as heavy a weight of ornament as did the medieval cathedral. The curiosity of the unintelligent was stimulated. Spiritual values suffered.

Rome removed some of these extravagances as she met the protests of the Reformation. The modern Missal, however, which is essentially the same as that of the Council of Trent, 1570, provides an elaborate ceremonial which perfectly expresses the Roman doctrine of the Mass and the Roman emphasis upon externals. Minute rubrical directions are given for the celebrant, deacon, sub-deacon, thurifer, acolytes, and torchbearers. The official decrees of the church contain forty-three hundred rubrical decisions which are supposed to cover more than twenty thousand possible questions as to procedure. Reverences are classified into prostrations, genuflections, inclinations, and bows. Genuflections may be double or single. Inclinations are either of the body or the head. Those of the head may be profound, moderate, or slight, according to situations which are specifically described. Gestures of the hands include acts of extension, folding, imposition, washing, and making the sign of the cross. This last occurs no less than forty times during the course of a single Mass. The instructions for episcopal services are so complicated that each bishop is supposed to have two masters of ceremony, whose duty it is to know the functions to be performed.

THE REFORMERS' ATTITUDE

The Reformers reacted strongly against externalism. The Zwinglians, Anabaptists, and other radical groups carried their opposition to the point of destroying the Liturgy, along with its ceremonies. The conservative Reformers in Germany and England were concerned primarily with purifying the services and revising liturgical texts. Ceremonies and usages not positively repugnant to the gospel were continued, at least for a time.

A large part of the correspondence and other writings of the Reformers was occupied with discussion of these matters. A few extracts may be interesting. It should be noted that the word "ceremonies" is generally used here in its broadest meaning .

In *A Treatise on the New Testament That Is the Holy Mass* (1520), Luther refers to the simplicity of Christ's institution of the Supper and to the later additions made by man, such as vestments, ornaments, postures, singing, organ-playing, and bell-ringing.

When Christ Himself first instituted this sacrament and held the first mass, there were no patens, no chasuble, no singing, no pageantry, but only thanksgiving to God, and the use of the sacrament. . . . External additions and differences may by their dissimilarity make sects and dissensions, but they can never make the mass better. Although I neither wish nor am able to displace or discard all such additions, still, because such pompous forms are perilous, we must never permit ourselves to be led away by them from the simple institution by Christ and from the right use of the mass.[1]

In the *Formula Missae* (1523), Luther said, "External rites, even if we are not able to do without them—just as we cannot do without food and drink—nevertheless, do not commend us to God, just as food does not commend us to God." Similarly, he permitted Eucharistic vestments "to be used without restraint, only let the excess of pomp and the excess of splendor be absent." [2]

Writing in 1545, a year before his death, to Prince George of Anhalt, Luther said:

I am an opponent even of necessary ceremonies, but utterly hostile to those which are not necessary. Experience not only of the papal church but the example of the ancient church, too, infuriates me. For it is easy for ceremonies to grow into laws, and laws once being fixed, quickly become snares to the conscience and the pure doctrine is obscured and buried.[3]

In general, we may say that Luther throughout his life consistently upheld the principle of Christian liberty which he so characteristically expressed as early as 1524 in his tract, "Against the Heavenly Prophets in the Matter of Images and Sacraments":

We however take the middle course and say: There is to be neither commanding nor forbidding, neither to the right nor to the left. We are neither

[1] *Works of Martin Luther* (Philadelphia: A. J. Holman Company, 1915), Philadelphia Edition, Vol. I, p. 296.
[2] *Works of Martin Luther* (Philadelphia: Muhlenberg Press, 1932), Philadelphia Edition, Vol. VI, pp. 92-93.
[3] Original text in *D. Martin Luthers Werke Briefwechsel* (1948), Weimar Edition, Vol. XI, p. 132.

papistic nor Karlstadtian, but free and Christian, in that we elevate or do not elevate the sacrament, how, where, when, as long as it pleases us, as God has given us the liberty to do. Just as we are free to remain outside of marriage or to enter into marriage, to eat meat or not, to wear the chasuble or not, to have the cowl and tonsure or not. In this respect we are lords and will put up with no commandment, teaching, or prohibition. We have also done both here in Wittenberg. For in the cloister we observed mass without chasuble, without elevation, in the most plain and simple way which Karlstadt extols [as following] Christ's example. On the other hand, in the parish church we still have the chasuble, alb, altar, and elevate [the host] as long as it pleases us. . . . The pope and Dr. Karlstadt are true cousins in teaching, for they both teach, one the doing, the other the refraining. We, however, teach neither, and do both.[4]

THE CHURCH ORDERS

The Church Orders of the sixteenth century reflect the confusion of the period and illustrate the principles enunciated by the Reformers. The first of these was that accustomed uses should be retained except where positively unevangelical, in order that the people not be disturbed by radical changes. The second was that in these external and unessential matters Christian freedom must be recognized, and that rigid uniformity was neither necessary nor desirable.

The Orders were concerned first of all with providing a pure text of the Liturgy, including the Propers. The program of reform thus made its greatest changes in the text of the services, particularly in the parts said by the minister. As these had previously been in Latin, the people were unfamiliar with them and were not in a position to understand how much change was really made. Alterations in ceremonies, on the other hand, would be noticed at once.

The Reformers did not edit the mass of detail in the rubrics of the old service books, and the Church Orders give very few rubrics. This does not mean that the ancient rubrics were abrogated. We could not attempt a reconstruction of sixteenth century services on the basis of the rubrics given in the Orders. The ministers were supposed to know the ceremonial tradition of the church. Almost without exception they had been trained in the old order and knew the rubrics as well as the texts. Most of the ceremonial usages had been observed for centuries. These ancient customs had practically the force of law. They were taken for granted. The force of tradition carried a fuller ceremonial for a longer period in post-Reformation Germany than in England. In conservative districts such as Saxony, Hamburg, Nürnberg, and Mecklenburg, where we have earlier noted the general retention of the more complete liturgical texts, many of the usual ceremonies were retained

---

[4] *Luther's Works* (Philadelphia: Muhlenberg Press, 1958), American Edition, Vol. 40, pp. 130-131.

throughout the sixteenth century, and in some instances very much later. Such practices as orientation (eastward position in prayer), the use of lights, simple vestments, and altar cloths were universal. The use of plainsong and the intoning of the services by the minister were also continued, as we have seen.

In sections where Zwinglian or Calvinistic influences were strong, most of these ancient ceremonies were discontinued. Everywhere a slow but definite process of simplification took place, and unnecessary or doubtful ceremonies were gradually dropped. The Formula of Concord (I:10:7) toward the end of the century (1580) expressed the general Lutheran position: ". . . no Church should condemn another because one has less or more external ceremonies not commanded by God than the other, if otherwise there is agreement among them in doctrine and all its articles, as also in the right use of the holy sacraments. . . ."

DECLINE AND REVIVAL

Other factors contributed to the eventual abandonment of many ancient ceremonies. The older ministers who had been trained in historic observances died. Their places were taken by men who were not familiar with the ancient tradition. The Thirty Years' War in the beginning of the seventeenth century brought devastation and confusion. Ministers were scattered, church services interrupted, and service books lost or destroyed. Pietism, with its emphasis upon the individual and upon subjectiveness in general, made worship a private and domestic affair. Rationalism shifted all attention to the sermon, and definitely destroyed forms and ceremonies. And the Prussian Union in the early nineteenth century, while tending toward general historical appreciation in the matter of the Liturgy, had a Reformed rather than a Lutheran approach. In each case, as the liturgical form disappeared, the ceremonial intended to interpret that form also vanished.

The Lutheran Church was planted in America during the weakest period of its life in Europe. We have seen that here it faced pioneer conditions and a climate of thought most uncongenial to its liturgical heritage. Not only the Quakers and the German sects in the early period, but later practices of nonliturgical communions retarded the growth of churchly consciousness among the rapidly and self-consciously Anglicizing Lutherans.

A revival of churchly attitude and practice was inevitable. It came in the nineteenth century. The leaders of the liturgical movement in Germany—most prominently Loehe, Kliefoth, Schoeberlein, Daniel, Hoefling, et cetera—were concerned chiefly with restoring the historic Liturgy and the liturgical music of the church. Details of ceremonial were scarcely mentioned in their writings. In 1888 the liturgical revival in America produced the *Common Service*. Its rubrics and ceremonial directions, however, were of the simplest character. The general introduction of this Liturgy into the life of the church was not accompanied by efforts to reintroduce ceremonial practices which had dropped from usage.

The *Common Service Book* of the United Lutheran Church gave more complete rubrical provisions, particularly in its General Rubrics. But even these, while specifically providing for orientation, altar vestments, the use of colors, et cetera, did not go much beyond recognized practices which had never entirely died out, at least in parts of the church. Recent decades have witnessed increasing appreciation of historical and beautiful ceremonies and accompaniments of worship, many of which invest the services with dignity, and properly belong to the distinctive life of the church. This slow advance has been natural and unforced. In consequence it has quite generally been accepted without controversy or bitterness.

Recently small but vocal groups in Germany, Scandinavia, and our own country have adopted some of the objectives of the Oxford Movement in England and press aggressively for recovery of the "lost ceremonies." They make it clear that they are not borrowing things Anglican or Roman but seeking to reintroduce what was customary in Lutheran worship in many areas in the sixteenth century and later. In their writings and in elaborate liturgical services at retreats, conferences, et cetera, they attempt to reintroduce practically the entire system of ritual acts and ceremonies found in the early Lutheran Orders of the most conservative type. The result is that in certain areas of Europe and America the question of ceremony has again become a burning one.

What people hear does not impress them as quickly or as vividly as what they see. The Reformers could and did make immense changes in the text of the Liturgy without disturbing the people. They refrained from making changes in innocent ceremonies because they knew that these would be instantly noticed and discussed. The Common Service and the *Common Service Book* won general acceptance because of the purity and perfection of their texts and the simplicity of their ceremonial detail. If the latter features had been elaborated as fully as the textual provisions, the Liturgy would have itself failed of general acceptance. The liturgical Reformers of the sixteenth and the nineteenth centuries were to this extent wiser in their generation than are some in the twentieth.

This, however, does not completely dispose of a matter which cannot be permanently settled by considerations of expediency. The reforms which concentrated upon texts and for the time ignored ceremonial simply postponed matters which now appear in present discussions in the nature of unfinished business.

It is only fair to those who give especial attention to ceremonial at this time to state their case. Some, very likely, are interested chiefly because this sort of thing appeals to them personally. Others are interested because they believe that the church is seriously endeavoring to master the contents of the Common Liturgy and to use its forms correctly; that intelligence and loyalty are here protesting against carelessness and individualism; and that broadly speaking, we should have refinements in these matters not universally found in our churches.

There is also a definite desire for completeness and consistency. The movement which produced the Common Service was an intellectual, literary, and theological effort. It involved no study of proper music, vestments, ceremonial, or of the liturgical requirements of the church building. Preparation of the new Common Liturgy included study of some of these matters. Other secondary subjects are now being given attention with the realization of their psychological and practical necessity. Man is more than pure mind or spirit, just as he is more than mere body or senses. He is all of these. Similarly, worship is more than a purely intellectual exercise. Sound, line, color, and action are among its component parts just as surely as are words. Ceremonial particularly represents the element of action. Our Lord "took bread, and when he had given thanks, he brake it, and gave it." In the scriptural account the action is as important as the words.

We are also beginning to realize, as never before, how greatly Calvinism and Zwinglianism have unhappily modified Lutheran worship, particularly in this country. Many who see these influences are not pleased by them. They wish to restore Lutheran worship, with its associated usages, to a level approximating that of the early sixteenth century, where the church was still free from the influence of radical movements. They believe that the church's confessional position gives a freedom in this matter equal to that enjoyed by those who pay little or no attention to historic liturgical procedure and conduct services in an individualistic manner.

CEREMONIAL PRESCRIBED BY THE CHURCH

Discussion may begin with an attempt to see what is officially prescribed by the church. Our rubrics provide the most necessary ceremonial. The congregation is directed to rise, to stand, to kneel, or to be seated at different times, to sing or to say certain parts of the Service —practically nothing else. Orientation and the use of the liturgical

317

colors are expressly permitted. The minister is directed to remain in the outer or choir section of the chancel for the Confession, and to go to the altar for the Introit; to face the altar at certain times and the congregation at other times; to uncover the sacramental vessels before the consecration; to take the paten and the cup in his hand as he recites the Words of Institution; to cover the elements after the administration.

Similarly in the Occasional Services the minister is directed to lay his hand on the head of the child in Baptism and in Confirmation; to apply water three times in Baptism; to place the right hand of the woman in the right hand of the man in Marriage, and to lay his hand upon their joined hands; to lay his hands upon the candidates in Ordination; to strike the cornerstone of a church thrice with a trowel or hammer; to receive the keys of the church building at the time of dedication, and to place the Bible and sacramental vessels upon the altar.

In addition, certain features are implied or permitted as belonging to the pure and generally accepted tradition of the church. Among these may be mentioned the use of the cross and Eucharistic lights upon the altar; the extension of hands in benediction and in the Salutation; the reverence to the altar during private devotions before and after the Service; bowing at the Gloria Patri, the limited use of the sign of the cross in benedictions, et cetera.

UNDERLYING PRINCIPLES

This practically represents our prescribed or commonly accepted ceremonial. It may help us to understand the ceremonies we have and to pass judgment on others if we indicate the principles which underlie our present use. Four may be mentioned: the historical, the functional or utilitarian, the interpretative, and the symbolical.

With reference to the first we may say that the rites and ceremonies of the church, like other conventions of cultivated society, represent the fruits of experience and refinement. In worship, as in social contacts, there is a right and a wrong way, or at least a better and a poorer way of doing things. By the constantly repeated method of "trial and error" the right or better way has been ascertained. General recognition of this has established conventions, ceremonies, and usages. Only the boor will ignore these canons of taste and experience.

The functional principle is the most obvious. It explains, on a primary, practical basis, many rubrical directions. Common forms and procedure are required in order to ensure common worship with all things done "decently and in order." Thus, as a matter of practical necessity, we have detailed directions for standing, kneeling, singing or saying, facing the congregation or the altar, the ordering of the elements, the application of water in Baptism, et cetera.

The interpretative principle is another obvious one. Actions of genuine and proper nature make ideas inherently present in the spoken word effective. The very use of common forms, moreover, expresses the ideas of the communion of saints, the unity of the faith, the universality of the church. The minister's reading of the Service, though impersonal, and not in any sense dramatic, should be interpretative of its real meaning. By his position at the altar, now facing the congregation and again facing away from them, the minister interprets the objective and the subjective elements in worship respectively. Kneeling for the Confession is expressive of humility and penitence. Standing for the Gospel, in prayer, or at the entrance of the clergy, is expressive of ideas which it is important to understand. The folding of the hands and the closing of the eyes in prayer affirm that we are occupied with nothing else, and that we would shut out the sights and distractions of the world. The extension of the hands in benediction, or the imposition of the hands in Ordination, Marriage, et cetera, are visible expressions of the idea of blessing.

The symbolical principle involves the importation of fresh ideas not necessarily inherent in the actions of the minister. For example, the church building, by its substantial and permanent character, expresses the sincerity and honesty of our purpose. The cruciform design in the ground plan suggests the faith of the church in the central doctrine of the Atonement. The openness of the nave and the freedom of approach to the chancel express the congregational idea of worship. The elevation of the altar is a mark of honor as well as a practical requirement. Altar lights, provided they are natural candles and not artificial electric devices, suggest the Light of the World, and convey the emotional suggestion of a living Presence.

OTHER DETERMINATIVE FACTORS

It will not always be proper, however, to introduce into our services additional ceremonies simply because they are either historical, utilitarian, interpretative, or symbolical. Regard must be had not only for Reformation and pre-Reformation backgrounds, but also for present conditions. Edification and spiritual helpfulness must be afforded worshipers today by every form and ceremony.

Many ancient observances found in some sixteenth century Orders—genuflections, osculations, repeated use of the sign of the cross, observances of obscure feasts of Mary and of the saints—were hangovers from pre-Reformation days. Generally speaking, they were traditions merely tolerated and finally dropped when it was realized that they did not truly interpret the spirit of Lutheran worship. We cannot appeal to occasional instances of delayed change as if these were marks of orthodoxy. Thus many minor matters, important to extremists today, are meaningless now, or are filled with a meaning which we cannot accept. Fussy and meaningless practices will not satisfy men who are seeking reality. The mechanics of worship must be unobtrusive. Details must not attract attention to themselves. They must never introduce a false focus or deaden the devotional spirit by the weight of machinery.

This same judgment must be brought to bear upon the extent to which individual practices may be used, once allowed. A single bow or reverence to the altar is appropriate. Twenty bows or reverences during the Service—one every time the minister passes the altar—are objectionable. The sign of the cross, if desired, may be edifying and permissible at the beginning of the Service or at the Benediction. Employed repeatedly throughout the Service, it becomes formalistic, childish, and highly objectionable. It is proper for the minister to keep his hands joined and his arms from swinging while officiating in the chancel. But hands continually and ostentatiously held at a precise angle constitute an example of silly formalism.

The best ceremonial is that which expresses the rite clearly and naturally. The simplicity and clarity of the Lutheran Liturgy require a correspondingly simple, clear, and consistent ceremonial. This dare not exist for itself. It must not in any way suggest the theatrical or the spectacular. This makes elaborate processions with copes, acolytes, crucifers, torch bearers, thurifers, and incense undesirable. Features, too, which are merely decorative or aesthetically emotional are questionable. In this category some will include the sanctuary lamp with its long association with the objectionable practice of adoration of the reserved Host, though, in fairness, it should be stated that canonically the veiled tabernacle, and not the lighted sanctuary lamp, is the sign of the reserved Sacrament. Other considerations also may enter here, such as the even longer use in Jewish worship and the general evangelical understanding of the practice in Protestant circles as suggesting a living Presence in the sanctuary.

Four factors—purity, significance, simplicity, and restraint—are important. They must be taken into account together with purely historical, utilitarian, interpretative, or symbolical considerations.

We would not conclude this chapter on a negative note. We may have unduly magnified dangers, urged moderation, and needlessly repeated positions previously stated in the Foreword. Now having painted this side of the shield, let us look once more at the other side and say that the picture is not good. If conditions there were perfect, there would be no need for this present volume, or for any like it. The simple facts are that corporate worship requires a large amount of good and proper ceremonial. The beauty and effectiveness of an otherwise satisfactory service are often marred by deficiencies in necessary ceremonial quite as much as by overelaboration. There is still much to be learned by many whose liturgical technique falls below even average standards of professional proficiency, not to mention the highest form or finesse.

Every part of our liturgical procedure, every bit of ceremonial we do have, should be correctly performed. This is particularly necessary today because of the emphasis upon visual features in education and life. It is necessary in adding solemnity and stateliness to our worship; in accenting its reality; in showing that we do not come before Almighty God carelessly or casually, but with reverence and the spirit of adoration and praise. We have too many pastors who are blissfully ignorant of the fact that their disregard of rubrics, inaccurate reading of texts, inept interpolations, awkward gestures, and similar personal peculiarities are simply bad spelling and poor grammar in a language they have never really learned—the language of liturgical refinement and propriety. We need to improve the bad spelling and poor grammar of the Sloppy Joes quite as much as to curb the zeal of the Sweet Williams!

The early Christian liturgies, and the liturgies of the present Orthodox churches, seek to portray the entire drama of salvation. We have no such purpose. Our common forms and ceremonies, however, do celebrate events, proclaim facts and truths, express doctrinal distinctions, inspire reverence, make possible the reception of divine gifts of grace, and promote the good life. As such, these rites and ceremonies are important. We may not use them thoughtlessly or mechanically. Our constant concern must be: What do we really wish them to express?

We have indicated a limited number of things that must, or should, be done. Students who wish to explore the voluminous detail of ceremonial in its broadest aspects will find ample material—which must be evaluated in accordance with principles stated above—in such works as Adrian Fortescue's *Ceremonies of the Roman Rite Described;* Percy Dearmer's *The Parson's Handbook,* eleventh edition (London: Milford, 1928); *Ritual Notes,* ninth edition (London: W. Knott and Son, 1946), an Anglo-Catholic authority; *A Directory of Ceremonial,* third edition (London: Oxford University Press, 1931); *The Chichester Customary* (London: The Society for Promoting Christian Knowledge, 1948). Such study might even include the appropriate use of the minister's hands, as this is discussed in the illustrated volume on *Hands at Mass,* by Walter Nurnberg (New York: Sheed and Ward, 1951).

Chapter 20

CELEBRATION AND ADMINISTRATION
OF HOLY COMMUNION

The importance of the subject suggests discussion of details at this point, even though this may involve repetition of some earlier statements.

Two guiding principles must be kept in mind. The first is the effort to promote reverence and devotion and to secure for the people the highest possible edification and spiritual blessing. The second is to recognize that centuries of experience have established usages which must be understood and respected. Departures from these and innovations of any kind, even though they may not invalidate the efficacy of the Sacrament itself, are confusing and should not be made except for the weightiest reasons.

PREPARATION

Preparation for the celebration should be made with care, and in ample time before the Service, so that all may be in order before the congregation begins to arrive. The Altar Guild, which should have among its membership mature women who will take these responsibilities seriously, should see that the altar is properly vested, with the seasonal vestments (for description see Chapter 3, pp. 34-49) in place. They must also place the altar linens, which should be immaculately clean and freshly laundered before each Communion. The sacramental vessels and linens, which are described in the General Rubrics of the *Service Book*, are also the responsibility of this group.

In most of our churches, the sacramental vessels are placed beforehand upon the altar, and are left there, veiled, throughout the first part of the Service. In that case, the guild will place the corporal in the center of the mensa or top of the altar, its forward edge even with the edge of the altar. The sacramental vessels—paten, chalice, ciborium, flagon or cruet, and perforated spoon—should be properly placed on the corporal. The chalice goes foremost, the flagon and ciborium

322

behind it, and the spoon at its right. The paten, if of proper size, will fit over the mouth of the chalice and over it will be placed the pall. Otherwise, the paten must be placed beside the chalice, and the pall will rest on the chalice. The purificators are small linen napkins for sacramental use, folded in thirds lengthwise. One of these will be placed over the chalice and under the paten to prevent scratching. The rest, as many as may be needed, will be placed outside of the corporal. The veil will then be placed over the vessels, but not over the purificators. Also outside the veil, if desired, may be a silver lavabo, a dish of pure water, used by the minister in cleansing his fingers and the rim of the chalice.

In a number of churches, the sacramental vessels are placed by the altar guild on a credence table in the sanctuary, and not on the altar. There they remain until the hymn before the Communion, when the minister brings them to the altar himself. If this is the case, another linen, not the corporal, will be placed under the vessels. The arrangement will then be as before, with one exception—the corporal and purificators will be placed in the burse, which lies on top of the veil and over the pall. The lavabo, if used, and generally also the flagon, will be left outside of the veil. An additional purificator, for use with the lavabo, may be placed beside it.

When local conditions permit, the preparation and care of the elements and the sacramental vessels may properly be entrusted to "a deacon or other officer," as the General Rubrics suggest.

The minister should assure himself before the Service that everything is in order. Broken altar breads, or altar breads stuck together, or even cardboard circles inadvertently placed on the paten, may become embarrassing at the time of distribution and disturb the devotions of communicants.

During the singing of the Offertory the minister goes to the altar and prepares for the administration. This preparation should be reverent and unhurried. After silent prayer he uncovers the vessels, first of all removing the veil and folding it, if it be not too large to be handled easily. If its size is prohibitive, it should be dropped in easy folds behind the sacramental vessels.

Further preparation suggests the removal of the lids from the ciborium and the flagon, and the pall, paten, and purificator from the chalice. If the elements have been placed on the credence table, they are now brought to the altar. Some prefer to do this earlier in the Service as part of the symbolism of the threefold Offertory—gifts, selves, prayer. If the vessels are brought from the credence, it will of course be necessary first to place the corporal on the mensa, so that the vessels may be placed upon it, and not upon the fair linen. The proper places should be found in the Altar Book on the missal stand. The latter should be drawn near enough for convenient reading.

These preparations are to be made by the officiant. If there is an assistant minister (the "deacon"), he should come to the altar with the officiant, but remain standing in a subordinate position and in a devotional posture facing the altar until his services are required.

THE SERVICE OF COMMUNION

The minister begins the Communion Office by turning to the people and reciting from memory the Salutation. Here the minister may extend his parted hands, with his elbows close to his body. He joins his hands and may slightly incline his head in recognition of the response. Hands joined, or (often in poor taste) with a rising gesture, he continues with the Sursum Corda, "Lift up your hearts," also from memory. The *Service Book* should be left on the missal stand, and both hands kept free for the manual acts to follow.

The minister turns to the altar again at the Vere Dignum, "It is truly meet," which is addressed to God, and remains facing the altar until after the Prayer of Thanksgiving (or the Verba) and the Lord's Prayer, when he turns to the people again for the Pax. During this time he may keep his hands joined, or, as a mark of special solemnity, he may raise his separated hands to shoulder height, the palms facing each other, and extend them straight forward a few inches from his body. This was the ancient attitude of prayer in both the Jewish and the early Christian Church. The practice has been traditionally associated with the Eucharistic Prayer in the liturgical churches ever since.

The Proper Preface for a festival is used throughout the festival season, except that the Proper Preface for the Festival of the Holy Trinity is used only on Trinity Sunday and its Octave.

In the consecration, as in the administration, it is possible to use either the ciborium, with its larger quantity of wafers, or the paten. Historically, the paten is to be preferred for the consecration, and the ciborium, because of its obvious capacity and handiness, for the distribution to the communicants. In neither case is it necessary that all the altar breads be handled at the consecration. In the consecration the paten (or ciborium) should be held firmly in both hands and lifted in ceremonial dignity to a point between shoulder and eye level. The chalice should be held in similar manner during the recitation of the words which apply to it. Again, the flagon need not be touched. Nor, need we mention, should the minister turn to the congregation during the consecration. The use of the Verba is more than a recitation of an historic account, or a citation of authority for the Communion. It is a solemn, corporate act of prayer, part of the whole thanksgiving. Dr. Edward Traill Horn said many years ago: "The Words of Institution are addressed to God. They are the warrant of the act in which we are engaged, and of the faith nourished by the sacrament, and they ask and receive from the Risen Lord the grace by which the bread and wine become to those who receive them his Body and his Blood." [1] Details of this character are not mere personal preferences, but usages sanctioned by centuries of devotion and development in liturgical procedure.

THE ADMINISTRATION

The approach of the congregation to the altar should be conducted by the recognized officials of the church and not left to youthful ushers. The deacons, or others who direct this, should permit only as many communicants to come to the first table as may comfortably find a place before the altar. A second group of equal size may be brought forward to stand before, or in, the chancel, awaiting their turn. This reduces the awkward and noisy pauses which otherwise lengthen the time required for the administration. The deacons remain standing, facing the altar, until each group has been communed and another table is to be sent forward. If more communicants come forward than can be accommodated, the additional ones should stand reverently in or before the chancel, facing the altar, while those at the rail receive the Sacrament. After communing the people should leave the chancel by side exits, or by an open lane in the center, and return to their pews, while the next group comes forward promptly.

Another method, common in Lutheran churches in Europe, and in Anglican churches everywhere, maintains a constant line in the chancel. The first table kneels or stands as usual, and receives the elements. After a communicant has received both elements and made a brief devotion, he rises and returns to his seat, and another takes the vacant spot at the rail. In this manner, by the time the minister has finished administering the cup, the communicants at the other end of the altar rail are ready for the host. If this plan is used, the blessing and dismissal are given at the end of the entire administration instead of after each table.

It should be unnecessary to state that the communicants kneel or stand at one place along the communion rail while the minister moves from one to the other administering the elements. Any method which makes the minister stationary, and requires the communicants to pass

[1] H. E. Jacobs and J. A. W. Haas, *The Lutheran Cyclopedia* (New York: Charles Scribner's Sons, 1899), p. 282.

before him and receive the elements in cafeteria fashion, is destructive of personal devotion and churchly propriety.

The administration is a personal act. The Formula of Distribution repeated by the minister is intended for the individual communicant. The Common Service provided quite a long formula for this distribution, and most pastors found it necessary to divide it among three communicants in order to expedite the Service. The Common Liturgy provides the briefer form of the early Greek liturgies, and the present Church of Sweden, "The Body of Christ, given for thee," and "The Blood of Christ, shed for thee." These words, it will be seen, may easily be used with a single communicant, and the personal element be given proper emphasis.

The entire distribution should be conducted in clear but low tones which will not interfere with the devotions of communicants in the pew. Nor should the devotion of individual communicants at the altar be disturbed by the use on the part of the minister of unusual formulas or Scripture passages, which in particular cases may be thought of by the communicant or by others as having a personal application.

The altar bread is to be received directly in the mouth, but may also be placed in the bare hands. The traditional manner of reception in the hand requires the placing of the open right hand upon the left, thus forming a "throne." The minister places the altar bread in the uppermost hand. This is the earliest form of reception, to which Tertullian and Cyril of Jerusalem both testify. Its use is general in the Anglican communion, though in places this seems to be declining in favor of oral reception, which the Lutheran Church has generally retained from medieval usage. This latter use developed because the people frequently carried the altar breads home as amulets. To prevent this, the wafer form and direct oral reception were introduced. Whatever the manner, the minister begins the administration at the south (Epistle) end of the rail and works toward the north (Gospel) end. This practice should be maintained if for no other reason than that it is generally easier to move to the right while passing along the rail.

In administering the wine, the minister should be certain that each communicant receives a portion. Not that the Sacrament would be invalid for one who happened to miss the wine, but in recognition of the fact that administration "in both kinds" was a valued recovery of the Reformation era which became a mark of Protestant practice. We must also remember that missing one element is likely to disturb the equilibrium of all but the best informed layman. To insure that each individual receives the wine, and only a proper portion of it, the communicant may tip the base of the chalice with his hand in receiving. The people will, of course, need instruction in this matter if they are to feel that touching the chalice is proper.

The ministers at the altar make their communion first. When there is an assistant minister, he may administer to the officant, whose reception of the elements is necessary for the formal, if not for the actual, completion of the ceremony. After his own reception, the officant administers to the assistant minister. Both then take part in the administration, the officiant giving the bread and the deacon the wine. The officiant says the dismissal.

OF INDIVIDUAL CUPS

The foregoing remarks presuppose the normal administration of the Sacrament in accordance with the historical use of the church. This use includes unleavened bread in the form of wafers, and real fermented wine administered to each communicant from a common chalice. Departures from the traditional method, of whatever nature, involve difficulties and break the ancient order of the church. One of these departures is the use, now frequent, of the individual cup. Because of its widespread introduction, it is necessary to suggest a manner of distribution which will preserve so far as possible important features of the traditional liturgical use of and retain the significant symbolism associated with the common chalice.

The Sacrament is a divine institution. It unites, strengthens, and uplifts believers. It occupies a place in the thought of the church far above all considerations of method. But confusion is deplorable, and unworthy methods must be rejected.

The individual cup is the direct result of agitation against the common drinking cup with its possibility of conveying germs. This agitation has doubtless been valuable in a general way in conserving public health; but popular feeling, once aroused on this subject, has magnified possible dangers in the Sacrament to an absurd degree. The Anglican clergy apparently suffer no more in proportion from communicable disease than the clergy of other communions, though they are required to consume wine which remains in the chalice after every administration of the Sacrament. Strong prejudices exist, however, which cannot be satisfied even when the utmost care and cleanliness are exercised in the use of the common cup. In view of these facts, as well as of the further fact that the validity of the Sacrament is not impaired by the use of the individual cup, we should provide for a reverent administration which will maintain as fully as possible the traditional usage of the church even though the individual cup is employed.

The introduction of the individual cup is generally ascribed to a minister who was also a physician. In 1893, in a country church in Ohio, he first employed such cups, for which he later invented a filler. The idea met with ready response in certain circles, and the practice spread rapidly throughout the nonliturgical churches. In the communions which regard the Sacrament primarily as a memorial and an evidence of Christian piety and fellowship, there were no particular scruples concerning historical and churchly usages. Manufacturers and commercial dealers were quick to develop the novelty, and to place all manner of cups, trays, and filling devices on the market. Thus the pressure for the introduction of the individual cup or glass soon became largely a commercial one. These accessories have been thoughtlessly accepted by many without comprehension of how entirely they have developed from local conceptions of the Sacrament itself. The important thing to know now, however, is that it is possible to use the individual cup without employing the machinery of trays and filling apparatus so frequently found. The filling of cups in the sacristy before the Service by the use of syringes or aluminum fillers, the placing of trays on the altar, and the assistance rendered the minister at the altar by deacons and choir boys in picking up the empties are all unnecessary and destructive of liturgical order.

Where individual cups are used, they should be of crystal glass or silver, and never of paper or plastic. The communicants may secure the empty cups as they come to the altar, taking them from the top of a cabinet or chest of drawers in front of the first pews, or at the foot of the chancel steps. The used cups may be deposited in other open drawers in the cabinet as the people return from the altar, or if they return through side exits, the used cups may be left in the sacristy through which they pass. A deacon should have charge of the cabinets.

Another arrangement, possibly not as good, provides small and inconspicuous racks in each pew, with their material and finish the same as the pews. Communicants secure the cups in their own pews and take them to the altar. After communing, they return the cups to the same racks from which they were taken, and the cups are collected and cleansed after the Service.

The common chalice should be retained and provided with a pouring lip, so that the minister can administer the wine from the chalice directly into the empty cup which each communicant holds in his hand at the altar. Any ordinary chalice can be converted in this fashion by a good silversmith, who will place a protecting shield over the pouring lip, which thus has but a small orifice through which the wine can flow. A purificator in the hands of the minister will guard against possible dripping.

These recommendations are not theoretical suggestions, but practical plans in successful use in many congregations. They meet popular feeling by providing an individual cup for each communicant. They retain the impressive symbolism of the common chalice for the consecration and administration. The entire sacramental action is located at the altar within view of the congregation. Personal and direct administration by the minister to each communicant is assured. The arrangement is simple and practical and requires no extra assistants and no cumbersome machinery.

Various synods of the church, desiring to unify the practice of their congregations, have approved the foregoing plan as a possible alternative to direct chalice administration. Thus the Ministerium of Pennsylvania and the Synod of New York and New England have officially recommended "that in case a congregation formally decides to abandon the historic method of administration, the communicants shall receive the wine at the altar, poured by the minister from a common cup into the individual receptacle held by the communicant." [2]

It is greatly to be desired that this method, or one comprising its fundamental features, be employed by all congregations which use the individual cup. Only in this way can unchurchly practices drawn from nonliturgical sources be eliminated, harmful confusion minimized, and desirable uniformity established throughout the church.

THE POST-COMMUNION

After the conclusion of the administration, a suitable period of time should be allowed for the congregation to commune in spirit with the Lord whose Presence they have experienced in the Sacrament. During this time, the officiant will close the flagon and the ciborium, replace the purificator, paten, and pall upon the chalice, and replace the veil. It is probably better not to return the vessels to the credence at this time, but to leave them upon the altar until after the Service. When the minister has finished replacing the veil and has made a brief devotion, the organist will begin the Nunc Dimittis, and the congregation will rise.

The Nunc Dimittis at this place is a Lutheran peculiarity, though it has been found in liturgies no longer in common use. It is peculiarly fitting for a moment such as this, but in case of necessity it may be omitted. The minister remains facing the altar.

Then follows the brief but essential thanksgiving. In the Common Service, only one form was provided. More latitude is allowed in the Common Liturgy, but the Collect may not be omitted.

[2] Pennsylvania Ministerium *Minutes,* 1917. See also minutes of the Pennsylvania Ministerium and New York Synod for 1915, 1916.

The minister then turns to the congregation and, extending his hands with his elbows to his sides, gives the Salutation. Then he joins his hands, and perhaps inclines his head, for the Response. The Benedicamus is said in a hearty tone, but not a shout, the hands joined. Finally, but not simply as a conclusion, comes the last sacramental element of the Service, the Benediction. In the Common Liturgy the trinitarian formula has been added to the Aaronic form found in the Common Service. This is a blessing, not a prayer, and should be delivered with calm assurance. The sign of the cross is in order here, if desired.

After the Service, the minister will see that the sacramental vessels are properly cleaned and stored again. The remaining altar breads may be placed in a safe place against the next Communion. The wine remaining in the chalice may be poured upon the ground whence it came, consumed, or otherwise decorously disposed of (not poured down the sink).

ON FREQUENCY

The Reformation shifted the emphasis of the Holy Communion from the consecration and elevation to the distribution and reception. In comparison with medieval custom, it enormously increased the number of those who communed. The Lutheran Reformers, like Augustine of old, celebrated and administered the Sacrament every Lord's day and on festivals, at least in the larger city congregations. Calvin to the end of his life desired a weekly celebration. Concerning the Roman custom whereby the laity generally received the Sacrament but once a year, usually at Easter, he said this was "quite certainly an invention of the devil." At Strassburg he was able to have a monthly Communion, but at Geneva the city council would permit only a quarterly Communion. Knox and the Scottish Church had monthly Communions, a practice which continues to this day in the cities.

Drs. Huxtable, Marsh, Micklem, and Todd give this interesting statement:

Calvin has left us the clearest indication of his own conviction and desire, both in his *Institutes* and in his correspondence. He could not have his full way in Geneva, but he writes: "I have taken care to record publicly that our custom (in not having the Lord's Supper fully celebrated every Sunday) is defective so that those who come after me may be able to correct it the more freely and easily" (Calvin, *Opera* XL, p. 213).

To this they add:

The Reformers intended to reinstate what the medieval church had lost— the full service of sermon and Supper—as the normal act of worship on the Lord's day.[3]

[3] *A Book of Public Worship Compiled for the Use of Congregationalists* (in Britain), p. x ff.

Leo Jude and Zwingli in Zurich were responsible for the complete separation of the Communion from the preaching service and for the quarterly Communion idea. Due to the decline of church life in Germany and England during the period of Rationalism, and to later pioneer conditions in America, the quarterly Communion became general throughout Protestantism. The Oxford Movement led the Church of England back to a high appreciation and more frequent celebration of the Sacrament. The Lutheran Church in Europe and America during the past century has also reintroduced more frequent Communions in line with the normal practice of the Church of the Reformation and of the early church.

Even in the smallest congregations an opportunity to receive the Holy Communion should be afforded not less than once or twice a month. Large city congregations may well follow the example of Lutheran churches in Europe today which administer the Lord's Supper every Lord's day, even though at times the number of communicants is small. Christian people may receive comfort from the Scriptures and pray to God at home. They are dependent upon the provisions of their congregations with respect to the Sacrament. The church should not withhold from the people the gift which has been entrusted to it, but give it freely and gladly.

There are exceptions to the normal procedure. Parishes with small membership, in rural communities, or under other unfavorable conditions, will not find it possible or necessary to provide weekly Communions. Large city congregations may find it desirable, under modern conditions of life and work, to provide two celebrations every Sunday, or an early service on a weekday as well as a Sunday celebration. The point is that it is the church's responsibility to provide Communion services at frequent and convenient times. It is the people's responsibility to recognize the Sacrament as a Means of Grace and to make their Communion more frequently. Whether many or few present themselves at any particular celebration is not the most important consideration in building a program. With people constantly on the move, with employment, in the cities, at least, continuing around the clock, it is unrealistic and unreasonable to expect the laity to serve the convenience of the clergy and come to the Sacrament precisely at eleven o'clock on four or six Sundays, and at no other time during the entire year. Railroads, department stores, hotels, and commercial centers provide schedules to meet popular convenience. Why should the church, the only institution in the world entrusted by God with the proclamation of the gospel and the use of divinely appointed Means of Grace, arbitrarily limit its public services to one Sunday morning hour a week, and its provision of the Sacrament to a single hour every three months?

UNIQUENESS OF THE SACRAMENT

Holy Communion is not of human invention, but of divine appointment. No government on earth, no prince or president, or other ruler of men, inaugurated or decreed it. None less than He who is King of kings and Lord of lords established it by his almighty word, "This do." It is thus uniquely Christian in origin and use. No other religion celebrates it. No other human society, social group, or fraternal organization would ever use the Liturgy of the church and administer the Lord's Supper. None but a Christian minister may celebrate it, and none but Christian believers should ever receive it. Nowhere but in the Christian Church may this gift be obtained. To others it is an empty form, a meaningless ceremony. To the believer it is a Means of Grace, an individualization of the gospel. Should we not give this unique institution of our Lord deeper thought and more frequent observance than we often accord it? Our theology in general, and our Confessions in particular, would certainly strongly support this endeavor.

Fortunately, the liturgical movement of the past hundred years has stimulated thought and promoted better practice, particularly in the liturgical churches, but also quite generally throughout Protestantism. Some pastors, and others, still stand upon positions of half a century ago, without realizing how far the church as a whole has moved forward in appreciation of the historic sacramental character of corporate worship, and in recognition of Holy Communion as truly a Means of Grace, and not merely a pious memorial or an opportunity for "table fellowship."

Higher appreciation of sacramental worship in the Reformed section of Protestantism stems from the growing conviction of leaders in these groups that the Reformed churches at the time of the Reformation were too radical and broke too sharply with the Liturgy, the church year, and established church practice in general. They have come to believe that the conservative position and practice of the Lutheran and the Anglican churches preserved values which they would like to recapture. In our own country, the establishment of the Federal Council's Commission on Worship more than twenty years ago and of the recent Department of Worship and the Arts of the National Council of Churches is very significant in this regard.

Within the Lutheran Church the liturgical revival and the higher appreciation of the sacraments as Means of Grace have been a natural corollary of the Confessional Movement with its historical perspective and its doctrinal emphases. The foundations and the fabric of historic

Lutheranism in its primal vigor have been uncovered. It has become evident that, with respect to the Sacrament, the normal practice of our church was higher, stronger, and finer than the shriveled types we still find in many areas today.

It is contrary to the facts of history to believe that the custom of four or even fewer Communions a year is the normal and proper procedure, and that those who advocate more frequent Communions are proposing something novel and foreign to Lutheran principles. As noted previously, Luther in his *Von Ordnung Gottesdienst* (1523) had said "On Sunday . . . if anyone desires to receive the Sacrament at this time, it is to be administered to him. . . . But should some desire the Sacrament on a day other than a Sunday, Mass is to be held, as devotion and time permit; for in this connection one cannot lay down either a law or a limit." [4] Our Confessions expressly state: "Among us masses are performed every Lord's Day and on the other festivals in which the sacrament is offered to those who wish to use it, after they have been examined and absolved. And the usual public ceremonies are observed; the series of lessons, of prayers, vestments, and other like things." [5] Such, we know, was also the practice of the early Christian Church.

The Lutheran conception of Holy Communion is sacramental, not sacrificial. The Sacrament is first and foremost a divine gift, an assurance of forgiveness for Christ's sake, and a promise of our Lord's Presence with his believers. Only as a response to this divine institution is it a thanksgiving, a solemn memorial, and an expression of Christian fellowship. This high ground was tenaciously held in the classic period of our history. In agreement with it, the practice of weekly Communion services was the normal procedure. Those who today advocate weekly celebrations, or at least more frequent Communions, are simply urging a return to the normal historic practice of the Lutheran Church and of the early Christian Church.

VALUES FOR CLERGY AND LAITY

A narrow and unwarranted theory of the Sacrament as a purely congregational function would forbid celebrations at conferences and synodical conventions, at ordinations, quiet days, and retreats. These are occasions which primarily concern the clergy, men whose minds are confused by ever-shifting and conflicting theologies such as the Neo-Orthodoxy of Karl Barth and, to a lesser degree, of Emil Brunner; the

[4] *Works of Martin Luther* (Philadelphia: Muhlenberg Press, 1932), Philadelphia Edition, Vol. VI, p. 63.

[5] Henry E. Jacobs, *Book of Concord* (Philadelphia: G. W. Frederick, 1882), Vol. I, p. 259.

bold, if not reckless, "demythologizing" of Rudolph Bultmann; the "New Being" and the subtle philosophical propositions of Paul Tillich which seem to skirt the borders of Kierkegaard's existentialism; the philosophical attitudes of disciples of Alfred N. Whitehead; and the reactions from extreme dogmatism by Archbishop Temple in England or Reinhold Niebuhr in our own country.

These are earnest men whose lives are dedicated to the search for ultimate truth. We respect them and their endeavors. We need theologians. They stimulate and systematize our thinking. We profit by studying their works. But, obviously, none of them has the full and final answer. Which, then, of these brilliant but finite intellectuals shall we follow, at least until revised editions of their books reveal quite different trends? In addition to all this, the faithful pastor bears upon his heart and mind the sins and griefs of a whole parish, the burden of which at times seems intolerable. Is it not good that perturbed parsons, amid the clamor and conflict of these affirmations, and under the weight of his people's distresses, should occasionally hear a Voice saying, "Come ye yourselves apart . . . and rest awhile," and, coming, remember his command, "This do," and his promise, "Lo, I am with you, even unto the end of the world"?

And what of our thoughtful laity? They, too, share the confusion and distress of our times. They sense the magnitude of the problems confronting the church, the state, and society in general in this our one world. They are conscious of the might of materialism, the brutality of godless autocracy and the police state, the paralyzing fear of nuclear warfare, the deviltry of juvenile delinquency, of vice and crime rings, the bestial debauchery of our manhood and womanhood. Many of them, too, in this our machine age, feel themselves but cogs in a wheel, grinding out a humdrum and meaningless existence, day by day. Amid all of this they hunger and thirst for the things of the Spirit. Those who turn hopefully to the church often find that what they hear from the pulpit differs but little from the editorials they read in the press, the moralizations of columnists, and the conflicting discussions by contemporary authors in the magazines. Men and women everywhere are weary of words of men like themselves. They want to hear God speak. And they, too, do hear the simple words of Christ, "Come unto me, all ye that are weary and heavy laden, and I will refresh you," and his further word, "This do, in remembrance of me." In the quiet and the mystery of the Sacrament they find a reassuring Presence, a peace and a power that passeth understanding. They find that the Holy Communion is just what Christ meant it to be—a Means of Grace.

Whatever the factors that contribute to a higher appreciation of the

Sacrament and its more frequent celebration, we should be grateful for them all and not quench the spirit. Naturally there will be problems, and there will be abuses that must be corrected. Some open questions may not be settled categorically by dogmatic pronouncement and legalistic regulation, but must remain, for the time at least, in the area of individual liberty and pastoral counsel.

Many debated topics are primarily questions of good order and the welfare of the whole church, rather than matters of extreme doctrinal importance, though doctrinal implications may be evident. In every case the primary source of authority, the *locus* of final appeal, is not the theoretical assumptions and ever-changing opinions of theologians as such. Higher than these are the official Confessions and pronouncements of the church, and high above these the positive statements of Scripture.

Luther as a theologian floundered about in an attempt to put strictly theological and philosophical foundations under the practice of infant Baptism. As a simple believer he finally came to rest upon the firm ground of the Word of Christ. What our Lord commands, as recorded in the Gospels, and what St. Paul says in his Epistles, are the ultimates to which we bow. Christ's command to remember him and to "Do this" is as broad and unconditional as his command to preach the gospel. His omission of minute instructions and petty prohibitions concerning the where and when, the how and the how often, are as significant as are his positive commands. In his divine wisdom he left these particulars within the sphere of liberty. The church, at various times and places, and in the interest of good order and the common welfare, has given guidance and instruction. The Lutheran Church, however, has ever been sparing of dogmatic pronouncements on points not specifically mentioned by our Lord or his Disciples.

The limitations of the benefits of the Sacrament to "the forgiveness of sins, life and salvation" is too narrow. Lutheran doctrine stresses this strongly, but other ideas are also important. Among these are remembrance and fellowship. Our Lord's words, "in remembrance of me," may not be overlooked. Forgiveness of sins is but one article of the Creed. Our whole belief is involved when we receive the Holy Communion in common with our fellow-Christians and realize at that moment a unique gift of grace from a Presence we can recognize, the awareness of peace and power we sense though we cannot explain.

Such is the grace and virtue of the Sacrament committed to the church, and to no other institution on earth, that it should be available to Christian men and women whenever it is needed or may be helpful—which is what our Confessions clearly affirm.

Those who would summarily prohibit corporate Communions should reverently recall the happenings at the Last Supper in the Upper Room. This was precisely such a Communion with a special group, and not with the Seventy or the whole company of believers in Jerusalem.

The denial of privilege and power to chaplains in theological seminaries and other institutions to hold Communion services for students or others under their spiritual care would result in a half-ministry for chaplains and spiritual impoverishment for students and others concerned. Such restrictions not only limit the responsibility and power of decision of every ordained minister, but obstruct the progress of the gospel itself. Chaplains, no less than other ministers, have a pastoral responsibility which includes both Word and Sacrament. If we believe that our Lord comes to his people in the Sacrament, who are we to bar his entrance? Or why should any of us wish to close the door in his face? The church must be free to adapt its ministry to ever-changing conditions. Where there are grave errors of judgment or real abuses on the part of individuals, it must employ a patient pastoral approach to each problem and each offender.

Chapter 21

THE ORGANIST-CHOIRMASTER

It is impossible to estimate the service which music has rendered religion. As an art it is a child of the church. Without the church's fostering care it would have developed much differently. On its part, music has fully repaid the debt by giving impressive and beautiful utterances to the text of the Liturgy, enabling the people to voice religious emotion in congregational song, developing the talents of gifted groups, and enriching the musical literature of the church. In choral motets, anthems, and cantatas, and in compositions for the organ, we have some of the most exalted expressions of the human spirit.

Entering this tradition of service, organists and choirmasters should have a sense of both privilege and responsibility. Conscious of the high heritage with which creative artists before them have endowed the church, their first endeavor should be to appreciate that heritage and to understand the formal fabric of the church's services. Then, disdaining unworthy, personal, or purely artistic ambitions, they should seek close co-operation with their respective ministers in the attainment of the church's devotional objectives.

ATTITUDE AND APPROACH

Natural gifts and technical training are both necessary for effective leadership in the church's musical program. Personality is indispensable. Character, essential manliness (or womanliness), intelligence, refinement, the power of discipline, and the ability to co-operate are fundamental requirements. Upon these must be grafted Christian conviction, love of the church and its services, adequate technical equipment, and willingness to work—to study, or to practice, as the need may be.

The ideals of the organist and choirmaster must be guided by churchly propriety. This will enable him to resist secular and sentimental influences and any inordinate desire for self-expression. Technical equipment

337

alone, however adequate, cannot attain the highest artistic standards in playing or conducting. Not clever performance, but sincere and spiritually-minded contributions to corporate worship must be the aim of all who minister, in whatever capacity.

This spirit is particularly incumbent upon the organist and choirmaster. It must come to the fore particularly in the accompaniment and interpretation of the Liturgy and the hymns. This is perhaps the most important, and in some respects the most difficult, phase of leadership which the choirmaster is called upon to exercise. He has three elements with which to work—the Liturgy, the congregation, and the musical resources under his control. He must master all of these. He must so thoroughly understand the structure of the Liturgy and the meaning of all its parts that, with the aid of the organ and the choir, he shall be able to convey these ideas to the congregation and encourage it to follow him in an expressive musical exposition of the liturgical texts. As the minister must read the Liturgy intelligently and clearly, and also express by spirit and manner, no less than by voice, a proper interpretation of the very soul of the Service, so the choirmaster must unite technical powers and spiritual perceptions in his direction of the music. He must grasp the significance of every part of the responses and hymns, and be able to convey his understanding of these elements to others.

The church year, with its festivals and seasons, is not of his making. The Liturgy appointed for a particular day is not his personal composition. But like the conductor of a symphony orchestra, he must master these compositions of the church and by his own perception, feeling, and gifts of organization and leadership give them significant interpretation. While subordinate in one sense, in another his work is creative. It is determinative and practically final with respect to mood, atmosphere, and popular understanding of the Service as a whole and of its separate parts.

PRINCIPLES AFFECTING THE SERVICE ITSELF

Two considerations make it important that the music of the Liturgy be given the first thought rather than the anthems or other special music. The Lutheran Church is a liturgical church. It provides complete liturgical services with historical texts for each day or festival. It does not expect its ministers and organists to build up "worship programs." Lutheran worship also is fundamentally congregational rather than choral in character. The special music of the choir is important and has its place in the whole scheme. But the first consideration in every service must be the presentation of the Liturgy for the day with all its appointments.

Because of these facts, the Lutheran choirmaster must constantly hold his organist and choir to the highest point of effectiveness in the rendition of every part of the Liturgy. The choir must be made to feel that in singing the Service it is a part of the congregation which has been called upon to exercise its own peculiar gifts of leadership. Every part must be sung clearly and intelligently without mumbling, dragging, or undue haste. Variety in method will add interest and effectiveness, although this must not be overdone, as, for example, in the Gloria in Excelsis, where choirs sometimes produce violent contrasts of volume between the middle section and the first and third parts. Most of the responses in the chorale type, and a good number in Anglican chant, but none in the plainsong, may be sung in four parts. Congregational participation, however, will gain if portions usually sung in harmony are occasionally sung in unison.

The organist (if he is not himself both choirmaster and organist) must do more than follow the choirmaster and accompany the choir and the congregation. He, too, is an interpreter of the liturgical texts. The choirmaster and the minister can indicate what is desired, but in the last analysis it is the organist who must bring out the contrasts in mood between such elements as the Kyrie and the Gloria, and even between the different sections of the Gloria in Excelsis, the Sanctus, et cetera. Similarly in his playing of hymns he must teach the congregation to sing the words as well as the tunes. Nothing is more unintelligent and uninteresting than to have every stanza of every hymn sung precisely alike, with monotonous equality of expressionless tone from beginning to end. This is singing with lungs and throat, but not with head and heart. The organist should study the text before playing the hymn over. He should then follow its mood closely as the congregation sings it, and by changes in registration, very slight modification of tempo, the building up of climaxes, et cetera, make the thought clear and effective, while definitely avoiding theatrical effects.

Considerations such as these place before the conscientious organist an opportunity and a privilege demanding study, spiritual insight, and real leadership. Frequently it will be found that adequate accompaniment and interpretation, the mastery of principles and methods of chanting, and similar churchly requirements are more difficult, and more important, accomplishments than brilliant solo playing.

THE SPECIAL MUSIC OF THE CHOIR

The preparation of special choir music is an important feature of the work. This calls for scholarship, gifts of administration, technical proficiency in voice production, conducting, and the less brilliant but equally important gift of being able to work successfully with others. The effort to unite the powers of the many personalities under the choirmaster's direction in the finest possible production of a common work week after week challenges his best talents at many points.

First consideration will be given to the Introits and Graduals. These are "liturgical anthems," specific choir elements which vary with each service. Additional choir numbers of freer character may be chosen from the great body of harmonized chorales, motets, anthems, and cantatas. In each of these groupings there is so much that is worshipful, noble, and beautiful, in all grades of difficulty, that only ignorance or poor taste can explain the use of unworthy material. Composers, editors, and publishers have made available, with English texts, a vast store of choir music from all lands and communions.

Particular attention should be given to unaccompanied compositions. These provide, as we noted in an earlier chapter, a peculiarly churchly and beautiful type of music which represents the Lutheran rather than the Anglican tradition. Selection will be influenced largely by the ability of local choirs and the preference of local congregations and communities. Popular taste and appreciation, however, as well as the ability of choral groups, can be greatly developed, we have said, by a progressive use of different and better types of music.

If a recital of choral music or the rendition of an oratorio, is given after Vespers, or any devotional service, it is proper for the choirmaster to direct the choir publicly as in a concert. But during the Service itself the personality of the director should never be forced upon the attention of the congregation. He must get his effects by thorough work in rehearsals and by such inconspicuous directing as he may be able to give from a point not in view of the congregation. In order to meet these requirements and still secure able control over the choir, the organ console may be recessed or otherwise screened from public view.

The church bulletin should be utilized to present whatever notices may be desired concerning organ numbers, choir music, or new hymns. Every service, however, must be regarded as an offering to God and not as a concertistic program.

High qualities of personal character and religious consecration should unite the minister and his organist and choirmaster in happy understanding and endeavor. The details of all services should be discussed in conferences weeks in advance in a united effort to present the church's message effectively and artistically. The organist-choirmaster may expect respect from the minister for those talents and endowments which nature and training have given him. At the same time, he will remember that in the last analysis it is the minister who is in charge of the services. The minister's decisions should be graciously accepted by all who assist him in creating the public worship of the congregation.

There is no limit, except that of endowment and training, to the qualities which a competent choirmaster may exercise in his work. All his powers of insight and imagination, of sensibility to mood and meaning, of magnetic leadership and mastery of method will be brought into play. The finest artistic and devotional effects can only be attained by painstaking and intelligent work. This will cover details of voice production, intonation, enunciation, phrasing, rhythm, and ensemble qualities. A choirmaster who grasps the essential significance of the church's services and the finest values in the church's music, and who has the ability to lead others in mastering technical difficulties and expressing musical thought, will be able to attract and hold capable singers and maintain high standards of excellence.

The choirmaster should have charge of all the music in the different departments of the church. If he directs the music of the Sunday school, trains the junior choir, and assists the societies and organizations of the church in their musical undertakings, unity of purpose and uniformity of method can be attained, to the great benefit of the congregation. This involves adequate remuneration. Even if the choirmaster cannot personally attend to all of these matters, he should be consulted. The actual work may be cared for by capable amateur assistants who are members of the different organizations.

A SCHOOL OF CHURCH MUSIC

This listing of standards and qualifications inevitably leads to certain important questions. Where shall we find men and women equipped to meet these requirements? Can we expect self-made musicians or musical amateurs, or even serious music students under private instruction by competent general musicians, to acquire the knowledge and skills requisite for leadership in this special field? Must we in our congregations and institutions be forever satisfied with organists and choirmasters who have had only a general musical education—and perhaps not a very good one at that—but no special study or training in church music as such? Must pastors and congregations who desire and can support competent musicians depend entirely upon graduates of schools of church music maintained by communions or institutions other than our own? If we really have high regard for the personality and the work of our organists and choirmasters why does not our church establish and maintain schools of church music in connection with one or other of our colleges or seminaries? We would never depend entirely upon nonchurch-related institutions, or upon seminaries of other communions, to educate our clergy. We say that next to the minister, the organist-choirmaster occupies the most important position and exercises the greatest influence upon corporate worship and in the development of the talents of our youth. And yet, as a church, we do nothing to prepare qualified men and women for this ministry. We pick and pay our church musicians as we do our sextons—taking them as we find them.

The marvel is that the church gets as satisfactory results as it does. All credit must go to others and not to ourselves. We are indebted, first of all, to the zeal and earnestness of the organists and choirmasters themselves who seek to improve their skills as best they can; and, in the second place, to the encouragement and aid afforded individual students by teachers specially interested, or by schools of church music conducted by communions or institutions other than our own.

The Lutheran Church in this country has excellent departments of general music in connection with some of its colleges. It has no fully-equipped and functioning school of church music that will compare with the best institutions of the kind maintained by others. The Roman Church has a number of special schools for the training in church music of priests, organists, choirmasters, and the members of their sisterhoods. The Gregorian Institute at Toledo, Ohio, regularly conducts summer schools in many cities, alternating their location from year to year, and providing as many as thirty in a single summer. Similar courses are offered at the Catholic University in Washington, D.C., and at the Pius X School of Liturgical Music in New York City. Serious work of more fundamental and extended character is done at the latter institution in courses covering years of study. Here the Liturgy of the church receives almost as much attention as the music of the church. It is recognized that not all the music in the world will make a priest, an organist, or a sister, liturgically competent; and that not all the Liturgy in the world will make these leaders of worship musically competent. Only balanced and combined instruction in both fields will give the competence required.

Union Theological Seminary in New York established a School of Sacred Music in 1928. This school operates on the highest level and renders distinguished service to all Protestant churches. It is a graduate school, and a college degree, or its equivalent, is required for admission to its classes. It equips organists and choirmasters for service in the churches and trains others for the teaching of sacred music in schools and universities. It has a faculty of eighteen specialists in organ, voice, choral music, musicology and theory, composition, conducting, improvization, et cetera. Among these are some of the most distinguished musicians and churchmen in the metropolitan area. In 1956 this school enrolled one hundred students from many states and foreign countries. In its courses and in its community life it seriously enters the fields of theology, church history, and religious education. Its professional and technical equipment is of the highest order—organ, piano, and recording facilities, sixteen practice rooms, library recitals, et cetera. Its graduates receive the Bachelor's degree in Sacred Music. Its advanced courses, with required residence, lead to the higher degrees of Master and Doctor of Sacred Music. Students of exceptional ability, but without a college degree, are admitted to its classes but cannot receive a degree.

The Westminster Choir College at Princeton, New Jersey, founded and directed by Dr. John Finley Williamson, is another institution of high rank which provides specialized training in organ, voice, choral work, et cetera, for church organists, choirmasters, and professional musicians in general. Its own choirs, which have toured several continents, have attained remarkable brilliance. In its service to the churches it has been particularly helpful to the Free churches, though organists in many Episcopalian and Lutheran churches have also benefitted by its courses and discipline.

The Roman Catholic schools, of course, will not meet our special requirements. The excellent, but very brief, summer schools conducted by the Rev. Frederick M. Otto, Dr. Ulrich S. Leupold, Dr. Paul Ensrud, and others are limited in scope and results. Recognizing the resources and quality of schools like the institutions at Union Seminary and at Princeton someone may ask whether we really need a specifically Lutheran school, and if so, why? We do definitely need such a school, for two principal reasons. Considerations of distance, cost, and exceptionally high entrance requirements means that only a few of our students can hope to take advantage of the instruction offered at the above-mentioned schools. Also, the musical traditions of these fine schools are closely identified with the life and work of the Free Churches. The lack of definite liturgical structure and consciousness in these communions gives to the work of these schools, with all their ecumenical sympathies and professional standards, something of an eclectic character.

The Lutheran Church, with its liturgical system and atmosphere, and its own rich musical inheritances, should have well-equipped schools of church music that will rank with the best in the land. Only in schools of this sort under its own direction, can the church in this country hope to provide the best and fullest training for its organists and choirmasters and, at the same time, promote original composition and other creative work expressive of its own genius. In this particular field the Lutheran inheritance is as great and as distinctive as are the traditions of the Roman or the Anglican churches. It is very much greater in quantity and quality than are the achievements in any of the Free Churches.

We are deeply indebted to musicians in other communions, particularly the Anglican, for much of the music we regularly employ in our services—chants, anthems, and larger works. We in this country at least have scarcely begun to appreciate and use the resources that are our own birthright. These should be our own cherished possession and our contribution to the church universal. Much of this liturgical, choral, and congregational music, because of foreign language texts, is still unknown and unavailable even to our own musicians. An institution such as we are suggesting would discover these hidden treasures, as well as make fullest use of currently available material and methods from other communions.

In this whole matter there are striking similarities even in widely differing communions. Paul Hume, in his recent book on *Catholic Church Music,* in discussing possible improvements in his church says: "There is at least an obvious starting point." He then makes the further statement, which arrests our attention from several points of view:

As of 1956, there are seventy-eight diocesan seminaries in the United States, in which about ten thousand prospective priests are being educated. Over six thousand diocesan students are distributed around other seminaries. . . . Three hundred and eighty-five religious seminaries and scholasticates are preparing over sixteen thousand future members of religious orders, many of whom will be teachers. Think what it would mean to the future of Church Music in this country if in every seminary there were one real church musician—one man of impeccable taste, thoroughly trained in all types of church music, able to produce convincing results with the choir, able to communicate a healthy respect for the principles of the art.[1]

Apart from the astonishing figures presented, the above statement is perfectly applicable to the situation in our own and other communions. When can we hope that our church will learn the facts and act to improve the situation?

If what has been written in the last few paragraphs should reach the eye of a man or woman of wealth, desirous of doing something worthwhile for his church, let this person be assured that no finer or far-reaching project could be found than the establishment or support of a first-class school of church music for the training of organists and

[1] *Catholic Church Music* (New York: Dodd, Mead and Company, 1956) pp. 14-15, 94.

choirmasters for Lutheran churches and institutions in America. We note with thanksgiving a first step in providing the church with church music schools in the establishment of a Department of Church Music at Wittenberg College, Springfield, Ohio, under the direction of Dr. L. David Miller, a Lutheran clergyman and a graduate of the School of Sacred Music of Union Theological Seminary. This is most welcome news.

Chapter 22

ACCOMPANIMENT AND INTERPRETATION

THE ORGANIST AND THE LITURGY
Proper interpretation of the Liturgy and the hymns is exceedingly important. In the Roman Church the Service is conducted by the priest and the choir. The congregation assists by its presence at Mass, but sings no responses or hymns. The movement to introduce vernacular responses, at least in the Ordinary of the Mass, is recent and limited. In the Anglican Church, while the congregation has a larger part in the Service and joins in the hymns, the musical emphasis, again, is primarily upon choral excellence, with perfectly trained voices, artistic balance of parts, and careful preparation of changing musical material. Other Protestant communions are also inclined to regard the special numbers of the choir as the central musical feature of their services.

In contrast to all this, the Lutheran emphasis is very definitely upon congregational participation in the responses of the Liturgy and the hymns. The artistic music of the choir is highly appreciated and has its proper place in the Service, but congregational participation in the Liturgy and hymns is fundamental. Congregational singing may not attain the aesthetic standards possible for the choir, but it has its own peculiar importance. Furthermore, under intelligent direction, it has the power to attract and hold people generally in a way that even the best choral work cannot do. Its promotion requires intelligent skill and patient persistence on the part of the pastor, the organist-choir-master, and choir members. It is well worth the effort it requires. It should be their first concern as musical leaders of the congregation.

In accordance with this point of view the *Service Book* provides three relatively simple musical settings for the Liturgy. These chants and melodies have been chosen not only on the basis of historic connections with the text, exclusive church association, and wide usage, but also because of simple breadth, strength, and objectivity. These

346

qualities satisfy the requirements alike of liturgical taste and congregational ability.

The importance of hearty congregational participation in the Liturgy is not always fully appreciated. One of the signal gifts of the Lutheran Reformation particularly was the right and ability given the people to assist in divine Service not only by their presence but by actual participation. They become a real part of the worshiping body of Christ, rather than simple bystanders giving occasional nods of approval. The Liturgy in turn becomes part of them, molding their thoughts and their lives. This congregational participation has been so developed, particularly in English Lutheran services in this country, that it is one of the glories of the church. The Anglican churches, because of the choral emphasis in their worship, and the Reformed churches, because of their loss of the Liturgy, have both restricted the development of congregational singing. There is a definite movement in the Episcopal Church which seeks earnestly to promote congregational singing of the responses, Canticles, et cetera.

The organist-choirmaster should give most careful attention to the musical settings of the Liturgy, and by frequent rehearsals bring the choir to perfect familiarity with all their parts. Most thoroughly rehearsed each week will be the Propers (Introit, Gradual, et cetera), which change every Sunday and which are the choir's own responsibility. The rest of the Service, however, must be gone over occasionally to smooth out rough spots, and to forestall mechanical rendition, racing, or dragging.

Certain responses may be sung by the choir in four parts. But as we have suggested earlier, it may occasionally be effective to have portions in unison, thus encouraging and strengthening the congregational participation. It should not be necessary to repeat that no plainsong will ever be sung in parts.

The director, then, should constantly work with the choir, so that every part of the Service is chanted or sung intelligently, without dragging, confused mumbling, or senseless haste. Full explanation should be given of the unbarred responses, which, as in the opening Versicles, the Gloria, and the Sanctus give opportunity for the music to accommodate itself to the natural rhythm of the text, the length and type of the notes having no significance whatever. The chants should be frequently rehearsed so that the rendition may be kept at the highest level of intelligence, dignity, and devotional power. Promptness of attack, with resulting confidence on the part of the congregation, can only be maintained by constant effort. In all of this work the choir should be made to realize that it is a part of the congregation, worshiping along with the rest, but exercising its own peculiar gifts of leadership.

The matter of accompaniment and interpretation concerns the organist particularly. A broad rhythmical accompaniment of good volume is required for most congregational singing. Promptness is essential in binding the Service together as well as in evoking confident participation by the people. The pace, however, should never be forced, in a nervous manner. The thought uppermost in the organist's mind should be the interpretation of the text, the giving of leadership and support, and not the display of the organ or of his own skill.

Even with this understood, there is ample scope for the player and for his instrument in the accompaniment. This should be expressive, beautiful, and varied without attracting too much attention to itself or losing the spirit of devotion. Generally speaking, the diapason chorus should be used as the foundation, with solo stops reserved for particular effects. Variety should be gained rather by broad contrasts of tone than by over-refinement and elaboration of detail. An unvarying, monotonous accompaniment is deadly; a brilliant exhibition of personal skill or of the instrument's resources is distracting. The organist must steer between these extremes.

The different manuals should often be used independently, and the tonal quality often changed, though not violently. The general sentiment expressed in the text will suggest the appropriate atmosphere or mood which the organist should seek to create and maintain. The fault of choking an accompaniment with thick chords should be avoided. The pedal should be used with discretion, and its occasional omission will be found effective, e.g., omission in the next to the last stanza of a hymn. Its re-entry in the final stanza—provided this is the climax of the poem—will be emotionally suggestive.

The essential meaning of each part of the Service should be grasped and expressed. The Gloria Patri and the Kyrie are essentially different; the Gloria in Excelsis and the Sanctus each have contrasting portions within themselves. These facts should be made evident without employing violent contrasts. A pianissimo in close juxtaposition to a fortissimo is too startling. Regard must be had for the total unity of the Liturgy and its devotional purpose. The limits of congregational participation must also be considered, and excessive retards, diminuendos, et cetera, avoided.

It should be unnecessary to remind organists that accompaniment is desired only in connection with sung parts. Organists who insist upon covering the Confession, the Creeds, or the prayers in sentimental fashion by soft organ accompaniment are guilty of sentimental nonsense and liturgical impropriety.

Conscientious organists will often find that brilliant solo playing is an easier accomplishment than the apparently simpler task of accompanying and interpreting the Liturgy. This is not a matter of manual dexterity but of study, of spiritual insight, and of regard for the unity and the corporate character of liturgical worship. A liturgical Service is not a "worship program," with separate, unrelated numbers.

One other important qualification should be mentioned—the ability to modulate from one key to another, and, when necessary, to improvise. It is no longer deemed essential that every part of the music of the Liturgy should be in one key, or even in closely related keys. The Lessons, the sermon, the prayer of the church, to say nothing of the hymns, all provide breaks in the musical tonality. When the break between numbers is brief, and the change in key quite noticeable, the capable organist can ease this situation by a quiet and simple modulation from the final chord of the first number to the key of the next number, thus establishing the latter tonality before actually entering upon it. Again, many situations arise in which it is helpful to have a bit of unobtrusive improvisation in just the right mood of the moment to cover some action of the minister, or of the congregation as it settles into its seats after the hymns, the Collect, the sermon, et cetera.

THE ORGANIST AND THE HYMN TUNE

The hymn and the hymn tune are small art forms. Their size is no indication of their value. Like cut and polished jewels, they give light and color to the entire fabric of the Service, and make their own peculiar and popular appeal. Not many of the mighty—few of the really great poets or great composers—have interested themselves in this small art form. But men and women of high spiritual perception and excellent gifts have drawn upon their deepest religious experiences and created tunes of surpassing beauty which edify and inspire.

When we consider the great number of good hymns and tunes available, it seems incredible that many Protestant services should be disgraced by the constant use of gospel hymns and similar unworthy material. A few of the best of these are worthy of inclusion in representative collections, but the overwhelming majority are cheap and sentimental productions, pitiful poetically and musically. Their use in divine worship is degrading. The church everywhere should resist the persistent efforts of purely commercial concerns which publish them.

The minister can do a great deal to awaken interest and promote good hymn singing by occasional references to hymns and tunes. These references may have to do with the content and value of the hymn, or with interesting historical and musical associations of particular hymns or tunes. One Sunday evening a month for a limited period may be devoted to hymn services, with such comments interwoven. During Lent, or possibly during Advent, a period of informal explanation of hymns, and rehearsal of them, may be held before or after the regular midweek services. Occasionally Sunday afternoons may be devoted to musical services in which the singing of new hymns, or those of particular variety or association, may be featured. Musical instruction in public schools and interest in good music generally may be counted upon to strengthen popular interest in hymns and tunes.

Given such sympathetic co-operation on the part of the minister, the final success or failure of these efforts rests largely with the organist and choirmaster. He can make hymn singing dull and uninteresting, or he can fill it with joy and inspiration. It is not sufficient for him to play the tunes correctly and provide tonal support for the congregation. He must add to this personal interest, enthusiasm, and artistic quality.

The following brief suggestions may be helpful, not only in introducing new tunes, but also in general accompaniment of congregational singing:

1. Master new tunes first of all in the choir. They may be introduced to the congregation before the latter is asked to sing them by having the choir sing the hymn in question in place of an anthem.

2. When first using a new tune in the congregation, have the choir sing the melody in unison, at least for the first stanza or two. It is also wise, no matter how well-known the hymn, to have the choir sing in unison when processing or recessing, so that members of the congregation are not disturbed by hearing first one part and then another as the choir passes.

3. Do not use the full organ to play over a hymn tune, but give it out on a separate manual in the tempo in which it is to be sung.

4. Prompt and full attack must be secured by the choir, not only in anthems and other choral numbers, but particularly in the congregational responses of the Liturgy and in hymns. Uncertainty or weakness at this point destroys the confidence of the congregation. The choir, and the congregation, will attack and will sing better if no note or chord is given beforehand. There is always doubt as to how long the note or the chord is to be held, or how long a rest there will be between that and the actual singing. An alert choir can begin out of a clear sky within a fraction of a second after the attack on the organ. It is not necessary to complicate matters.

5. In beginning the different stanzas do not sound the first note of the melody alone. The pedal, or the entire final chord, may be held in reduced volume between stanzas, being released exactly one beat before the next stanza is begun. The re-entry of the solid organ part *on the beat* will enable the congregation to feel the point of attack and participate without hesitation. Usually an interval of one complete measure between the final beat of one stanza and the attack on the following stanza is the right allowance. Similarly in the Liturgy, after the loss of key between parts, the fundamental note may be sounded on the pedal board with exactly one beat rest prior to the entrance of choir and congregation.

6. Give sufficient support and exercise leadership in holding the congregation to tempo without dragging.

7. Avoid thoughtless rush. The dignity, beauty, and power of German chorales are sacrificed if they are treated like Anglican hymn tunes. On the other hand they must not be sung in the heavy manner commonly found in European churches. Never play introductions to hymns faster (or slower) than the tempo which the congregation is expected to maintain.

8. As a rule use the first tune given in the *Hymnal* if there are alternates. In most cases the second tune is inferior musically. In the matter of hymn tunes, as in every other form of music, popular taste can be educated and improved. Do not always keep the congregation on the lowest level.

9. In playing the hymns, interpret the mood and the thought by suggestive and varied organ accompaniment. Do not strive to express the meaning and spirit of each particular line by differences in volume and tonal quality. This would be fussy and distracting. Deal thoughtfully and broadly with the text as a whole, or at least with stanzas as a whole.

10. The organist must lead, and not follow, unless the choir is really trained to assume leadership. When the latter is the case and the choir can be depended upon to lead, the organist may be rather free in his accompaniments. While, generally speaking, a good deal of organ is better than too little, when the singing is going well the organist may employ a light, transparent organ tone with good effect.

11. A poor organist will make of hymn playing a commonplace thing. A good organist will challenge the intelligent interest of the congregation and charge its hymn singing with thought and feeling.

12. The organist may check his own volume and registration by having a friend play parts of the Liturgy and the hymns according to his

351

own combinations. Listening to this, he can get the effect, and make changes that seem desirable.

The rich variety and quality of tunes in the *Hymnal* will be appreciated only if the minister and the organist together endeavor to use them freely and fully. It is natural for the minister particularly to fall into a rut and to choose only a limited number of hymns. Ministers often overestimate the difficulty of singing certain hymns with which they are not themselves familiar. Consultation and sympathetic cooperation will generally clear the way and permit a development which will expand the congregation's interest and ability, and enrich its devotional life by an acquaintance with the full range of the church's hymns and tunes.

The type of instrument at command necessarily affects the style of accompaniment. Frequently, the diapasons are too thick, heavy, and opaque. Those built from 1900 to 1930 are generally too fundamental, and without natural overtones to blend with the upper work. Eight-foot stops, being at the same pitch level as the choir and congregation, must be loud in order to lead. Light 8' Geigens, reeds, et cetera, well-furnished with 4', 2 2/3', and 2' stops give a transparent ensemble which, being at a different pitch level from that of the voices, is easily heard and followed. Many organists regard a tonal scheme based around good 4' stops as the best. The better builders today make diapasons of smaller scale, lower wind pressure, and with enough upper harmonic development to blend with the light upper work. What is desired is energy without weight.

Chapter 23

CHANTING

In considering choir music as such, we think not only of parts of the Liturgy such as the Introit and the Gradual, of anthems, motets, and larger forms like the cantatas, but also of chanting. The congregation is expected to join in the responses of the Liturgy, the Psalms, and the Canticles, and the chant forms to which these texts are set require particular study. In order to give definite leadership, it will be necessary for the choir to give particular attention to the principles and practices of chanting in general.

Chanting is a feature of corporate worship. It has developed from the conception of the worshiping church, the Christian community unitedly adoring, praising, and beseeching the God and Father of all in common acts of prayer, praise, and thanksgiving. The individual loses himself in the group; he becomes a part of the church at worship. All that he does, he does in common with others, and when he sings hymns or other metrical verse, he joins in a common melody. When he says the responses in the Liturgy, or recites the Psalter, the lyrical and poetic quality in both lead naturally to a common recitation in monotone—the earliest form of chanting.

Broadly speaking, chanting covers all forms of liturgical music in which there is recitation of the text on sustained notes, concluding with melodic inflections. Gregorian chants and Anglican chants are specific forms, but other settings, freer in form, may also contain chants, and principles of chanting must apply to their rendition. In fact, one of the chief differences between traditional liturgical music and modern metrical music is this freedom of form which characterizes the music of the Liturgy. Liturgical music generally accommodates itself to the rhythmic flow of the text and does not confine and artificially limit the words between bars, as does measured music.

The chant forms in the Service have developed from the ancient unisonous liturgical chant which, beginning in the Orient, received definite development at the hands of the Greeks, and reached its modal (scale) character in the Middle Ages. The ancient Office books of the church—the Missal, Gradual, Antiphonary, et cetera—contained an enormous number of chant melodies of this kind, some simple and some elaborate. The daily recitation of the Psalter and Canticles in the monasteries eventually lead to the adoption of a limited number of different chant forms clearly related to the musical idioms of the time for these parts of the Service, one for each mode or scale of the ancient system. Nine of these finally came to be known as the Gregorian Tones (Tones I-VIII, and the Tonus Peregrinus). Others of similar structure were locally used and named (Parisian Tone, Cologne Tone, et cetera).

The Gregorian Tones consist of the following parts:

1. *The Intonation,* an introduction of two notes or groups of notes.
2. *The Reciting Note,* on the dominant of the mode or scale. The greater part of the text in each half of the Psalm verse is recited on this note.
3. *The Mediation,* a musical inflection closing the first half of the Psalm verse. This is found in festival and ferial forms.
4. *Reciting Note or Dominant,* repeated for the second half of the Psalm verse without introduction.
5. *The Cadence or Termination,* a melodic inflection concluding the chant. Variety is given by the choice of several "final" inflections.

These chants are without bars or measures. While this assures flexibility and permits the melody to accommodate itself to the rhythm of the words, it increases the difficulties of smooth recitation and the holding of a body of singers together in a precise enunciation of the text.

The Anglican chant, a much later development, is a modification of the Gregorian Psalm Tones. The intonation has been eliminated. The mediation and the cadence are generally given with fixed bars and measures. The new form expressed the spirit of its period and the richer resources of modern music, particularly in its harmonizations. Once adopted, it permitted the composition of an incredible number of melodies which were harmonized and sung in four parts instead of in unison. Originally the melodies themselves were in the tenor, but the Restoration in the seventeenth century, following years of disuse of the Prayer Book and the disruption of cathedral choirs with their groups of men, gradually developed the "treble chant" with melodies in the soprano. Desire for variety of form led to the use of double chants with four reciting notes instead of two. Some of these are remarkable for their interesting melodies and ingenious harmonizations. Lighter taste eventually produced triple and quadruple chants, often with "pretty" melodies and weak chromatic harmonies.

The simple chants in themselves, repeated over and over again without words, would not long hold interest. In association with the text, they become a flexible instrument for the corporate musical recitation of unmetrical poetry, and as such they are both practical and pleasing.

Taking the widest use of the term "chanting" to include not only the Psalms and Canticles, but also the rendition of all unmetrical responses, the following explanations and suggestions may be of value in the use of the settings for the Common Liturgy.

In responses such as the opening Versicles, the Gloria, the Gloria Tibi ("Glory be to thee, O Lord"), and the Preface melodies, no bars or other metrical restrictions are given. The notes do not have equal value, and strict time must not be observed.

The text is of primary importance. The music is the servant of the words and must adapt itself to the changing requirements of the latter.

The words must be chanted deliberately with the natural rhythm and accent of dignified speech. Each syllable must be enunciated distinctly and sung to a pure tone. While chanting is a declamation of the text, it is a musical declamation and musical standards must also be maintained.

Chant each response or Psalm at a pace appropriate to the words, and preserve the same pace throughout all parts, including the recitation as well as the inflection.

Give all attacks a pure intonation. Make pauses and breathing strictly uniform, and only at commas or other punctuation marks. It may not be necessary to observe every one of these. The choirmaster must decide doubtful cases and give clear instructions.

Dragging and undue haste are equally bad. Avoid both.

Varied and expressive accompaniment may be provided by careful registration. The effort should be to interpret the spirit and mood of the text and its emotional content in general rather than to heighten the effect of particular words and phrases. The accompaniment should support and interpret without being assertive or dramatic.

Good chanting requires complete familiarity with words and music and constant practice. There is value in rehearsing chants first in unison, and then in harmony, without accompaniment. There is much greater value in having the choir read the text of responses, Psalms, et cetera, aloud together before singing. In especially difficult passages, this should be done several times to get a common expression of the meaning and the rhythm of the words before beginning the chant itself.

Volumes have been written concerning early plainsong notation and

355

the proper manner of plainsong rendition. Broadly speaking, there are two schools of theorists. The older, represented among others by F. X. Haberl and his institution at Regensburg, believes that the ancient chants were composed and sung in notes of different duration. That is, that some were of longer value and others of shorter, without having the exact relationship of modern whole notes, half notes, and quarter notes. The other school, under the leadership of the scholars of Solesmes, believes that all the notes originally were intended to have practically the same duration. It regards accent as dynamic rather than rhythmic, being derived either from the text exclusively, or from the accent inherent in certain groupings of notes in the music. These discussions are important not because of archaeological considerations, but because they have led to two major systems of interpretation in chanting, both of Gregorian Tones and Anglican chants.

THE FIRST SETTING

In its best estate the Anglican chant, a child of the English cathedral system and practically unknown outside of English-speaking countries, is a useful addition to liturgical music. When it departs too greatly from the strong melodies and solid diatonic harmonies of the old system, it becomes flippant and weak. Many Anglican chants of dignity and churchly feeling enrich the services of all English-speaking churches in America and elsewhere. The First Setting in the *Service Book* contains such chants. The Continental Setting and the Plainsong Setting represent a different type of music, with historical associations more intimately connected with the history of the Lutheran Church in European lands. The association of language, however, the appeal of modern tonality, and increased attention to the text and its meaning will in all probability attract many congregations to the First Setting. Fundamentally the difference between the First and Second Settings is the difference between chanting and singing. Chanting gives first attention to the text, singing emphasizes the music.

Dr. Harold W. Gilbert, who edited the First Setting of the Liturgy, has kindly furnished us with extended notes, and upon the basis of these and of the excellent Introduction and Appendix in Professor Ray F. Brown's *The Oxford American Psalter* (New York: Oxford University Press, 1949) and some other sources, we sketch the later history of the Anglican chant, with mention of notable systems of pointing and, particularly, with discussion of the principles and methods of speech-rhythm pointing as given in the *Service Book* of the Lutheran Church.

The Anglican chant had its development in the English cathedrals, where the Psalms are sung daily, and in thousands of parish churches in England and in other parts of the Anglican communion, where the Psalter is commonly sung, at least at Evensong on Sundays. Many church musicians have at different times set the text of the Psalms (in the Prayer Book version which differs from the Authorized Version) to a great variety of Anglican chants. This setting of the text to music is called pointing. It is obvious that the editing of such a musical Psalter involves not only the choice of chant melodies and harmonizations, but also problems of interpretation in the meaning of the text and smoothness of musical flow in the chant. Both of these are determined by the relation of verbal and musical accents.

One of the greatest difficulties in applying historic principles to Anglican chants arises from the different speech stresses and accents in Latin and English respectively. Latin also has few monosyllables; English has many. Latin never accents the final syllable of a polysyllabic word. Efforts to overcome these and other difficulties, as well as to preserve strict time in the inflections of the chant, have frequently led to mechanical results with such infelicities as the "double knock" or the "Anglican thump."

Details on the early history and development of the Anglican chant may be found in "Anglican Chant and Chanting," *The Oxford Companion to Music* (London: 1947) by Percy Scholes; Sydney H. Nicholson, *Quires and Places Where They Sing* (London: G. Bell and Sons, 1932); and E. H. Fellowes, *English Cathedral Music* (London: Nethnen and Company, 1941).

In the earlier period (before 1913) editors gave prime consideration to the melody and its inflections. The latter became stereotyped in metrical form, with bars separating the measures and accents falling in every case upon the first chord in each measure. Pointing in this period consisted in fitting the text as smoothly as possible into this fixed pattern of the chant melody and its inflections. As Dr. Ray Brown says, "The unmetrical poetry of the Psalms was forced into the metrical mold of the music. The chant was always repeated with exactly the same inflexible rhythm, and with a consequent distortion of the accentuation and duration of many words and syllables." [1] The outstanding and most influential example of this type of pointing was *The Cathedral Psalter* (London: Novello and Company, 1874).

Rules were laid down which insured the preservation of the metrical rhythm of the tune. For the guidance of the singer, the printed words of the text were interspersed with dots, dashes, vertical bars, and

[1] *The Oxford American Psalter* (New York: Oxford University Press, 1949), p. 232.

specially devised accent marks. The virtue of this system was that the singers succeeded in keeping together, for an inflexible mold was prescribed for the latter part of each half-verse of the text. The great failure was that very little regard was had for the interpretation of the words. Consequently, much abuse and stiffness characterized chanting under this system.

Early in this century, and appreciably influenced by the mounting interest in plainsong, church musicians began to give increased attention to the free and natural recitation of the texts. This involved changing the inflexible metrical character and the musical accents of the chant inflections to agree with the rhythmic flow and verbal accents of the text—chanting in speech-rhythm.

Several simple illustrations may help to make clear the primary difference between cathedral pointing, with its fixed metrical accent of the chant, and speech-rhythm pointing, with its natural accent of the words and flexible accent of the chant.

In the beginning of the Benedictus, the cathedral pointing reads:
> Blessed be the Lord God of ′ Is-ra ′ el.

In speech-rhythm the line would read:
> Blessed be the Lord ′ God of ′ Israel

Here the final strong accent in words and music properly falls upon the first and not the last syllable of the word "Israel."

In the Magnificat, the cathedral pointing reads:
> My soul doth magni ′ fy the ′ Lord.

This brings an unnatural accent upon "fy." In speech-rhythm the pointing would be:
> My soul doth ′magni -fy the ′ Lord.

The Barless Psalter (London: Novello, 1913) was the first attempt at improvement. One of its features, as its name indicates, was the removal of all bars in the chant inflections. A marked advance was made by *The Psalter Newly Pointed* (London: Society for Promoting Christian knowledge, 1925), edited by Robert Bridges, late poet-laureate of England, Walter Marshall, and others. Other Psalters later appeared in England, all devoted to the principle of subordinating the music to the text, and providing a system of pointing and chanting in speech-rhythm. Among these were *The English Psalter* (London: Novello, 1925), *The St. Paul's Cathedral Psalter* (London: Novello, 1934), *The Parish Psalter* (London: Faith Press, 1932), and *The Oxford Psalter* (New York: Oxford University Press, 1929). Canon Louis E. Daniels of Trinity Cathedral, Cleveland, in his *Songs of Praise for America* (New

York: Oxford University Press, 1938) used the speech-rhythm system for his pointing of his *Short Psalter with Canticles.*

The most important American work employing this system is the *Oxford American Psalter* by Ray F. Brown, Mus.Doc., a former pupil of Sir Sydney Nicholson and now professor of church music in the General Theological Seminary (Episcopal), Chelsea Square, New York City. This gives the complete Psalter and all the Canticles of the Prayer Book, with a rich collection of chants. The pointing in the *Common Service Book* of the United Lutheran Church is that of the *Cathedral Psalter,* 1874; that of the Canticles in *The Hymnal,* 1940, of the Episcopal Church, is a modification of the *Barless Psalter* style, 1913.

From the above, it will be evident that the speech-rhythm system of pointing is not an unproven novelty. It has been in use for many years in cathedrals and parish churches in England, where chanting has received deeper study and much wider practice than in America. The system has been successfully introduced in quite a few cathedrals and parish churches of the Episcopal communion in this country. It is taught in important church music schools, and is coming into general recognition.

At this point the observation of the late Sir Sydney H. Nicholson, one of England's most distinguished church musicians, is pertinent. He says:

The older, stiff system still lingers on in many places, for Church people and Church choirs are conservative and take slowly to new ideas; but it is certainly doomed, for it is founded on false principles. Unless the music can add to the meaning of the words it is worse than useless. . . . When it comes to a choice between the claims of the words and of the music, the words are bound in the end to prevail, for it is for them that the chant exists.[2]

At all events, it is a significant and important fact that both the Anglican chant and the chorale, as found in modern hymnals and service books, are also moving out of strict metrical form into the freedom of the plainsong from which both originally were derived. Further discussion of this topic may be found in *Music and Worship* (especially chapter x) (London: Eyre and Spottiswoode, 1935) by Walford Davies and Harvey Grace and a much fuller study in Nicholson's *Quires and Places Where They Sing.*

Editors frequently differ in details of pointing, such as the number of syllables assigned the inflections, the matter of permitting secondary accents in the text to be set to the first notes of inflections, the division of syllables between the two notes of a measure, and, of course, the kind of type and devices employed in the printing. They practically all agree in setting a syllable of primary accent to the final note of every

[2] *Quires and Places Where They Sing* (London: G. Bell and Sons, 1932), p. 122.

inflection, and in determining the pointing of every verse backward from this point.

The *Service Book* of the Lutheran Church is the first official service book of any American church to employ this system of pointing. Its proper use is a bit more difficult to acquire than the pointings to which we have been accustomed. Its principles, however, are sound, and it is believed that our church musicians will meet the challenge, master it, and be plentifully rewarded by an unusually clear, natural, and meaningful recitation of the text and an interesting and varied flow of melody and harmony in the chants.

No system in itself is perfect, which does not mean that all are equally good. Some are hopelessly bad, and good results cannot be secured by their use. But even with a good system of pointing, painstaking care is necessary. The choirmaster must thoroughly understand the system in use, and he must make its principles clear to the members of his choir. Difficult places must be worked over patiently to secure good readings. A keen ear must be kept open to detect roughness or slovenliness, which must be corrected at once.

No method has been contrived that entirely does away with signs to guide the singer. It has been proved practicable, however, to reduce the number of these signs to a minimum. In restoring the printed text to a more normal appearance, the singer is encouraged and enabled to concentrate upon the words and their meaning, rather than upon the interpretation of the various signs.

With respect to the text, two simple devices are used: a short vertical line at the top (') divides the text in agreement with the measures of the music; a dot (.) divides the text between the notes of a single measure. The placing of these lines and dots expresses the judgment of the musical editor as to how text and music should be rendered. These indications must be followed scrupulously even though other interpretations may be as good or even better. Strict observance of every detail of the pointing is the only possible guarantee of good results.

In chanting the important thing is observance of the natural accent and rhythm, as well as the meaning of the text. The next is to realize that, though the chant is measured, the notes have no time values except the time required for speaking the words or syllables assigned to them. The notes only indicate changes in pitch and nothing else. The chant must be thought of as something flexible and elastic, whose accents may vary with the accents of the words.

If one will read aloud a given phrase of prose, giving to his reading a natural rhythm suited to the interpretation he wishes to express, he need only apply the singing voice to exactly the same phrase and the same rhythm, and he will find himself chanting in speech-rhythm. The pointing shows him when to move from measure to measure in the tune, or in some cases from note to note.

More than one interpretation is possible, and more than one rhythm may seem good when several singers are performing together. But experience has proved that an interpretation having been agreed upon, a group of singers will readily keep together, and unity will be achieved under intelligent direction.

Good pointing requires more than clear exposition and occasional interpretation of the text. The inflections of the chant may be freed from their metrical mold, but certain other features of the music may not be ignored. Among these are the form of the chant itself, the shape of the melody, and the character of the harmony. These all tend to produce primary and secondary musical accents which, so far as possible, must be accommodated to the primary and secondary verbal accents of the words. High notes in the melody and organ bass in the accompaniment, moving downward by a skip, both tend to receive a natural accent, which must, so far as possible, be accommodated to the verbal accents. It will be seen that good pointing, which has to consider all these factors, involves not only study and interpretation of the text, but sensitivity and discriminating taste with respect to the music. So far as possible, the normal accents of the text must be brought upon the normal accents of the chant.

_____

The Continental or Second Setting differs in origin, character, and manner of use from the First Setting. Most numbers in the First Setting are chant forms—to be *chanted* and not sung. In the Second Setting a few of the shorter responses have reciting notes and simple inflections. The rest of the music consists of adaptations from plainsong and chorale melodies, presented for the most part in free chorale style, to be *sung* and not chanted. The observations on chanting (pp. 353-361) may, however, be of some value in using this setting.

THE THIRD SETTING

The melodies in this Plainsong Setting are free, expansive, and unmetrical forms, and speech-rhythm, as we have discussed it in connection with the Anglican chant and its inflections, does not determine the pointing of the these Gregorian chants.

Space limitations, the size and weight of the *Service Book,* and contractual agreements with the publishers, made it necessary, to the deep regret of the Commission on the Liturgy, to omit the Plainsong Setting from the *Service Book.* This setting has been prepared, at the request of the Commission, by Ernest White, until recently musical director of the Church of St. Mary the Virgin (Episcopal) in New York City, a distinguished organ recitalist, music editor, and recognized authority on Gregorian music. It has been issued separately, with recordings, as a part of the Commission's complete program.

Mr. White, with the approval of the Commission, chose to set the Liturgy in the *Service Book* to an adaptation of the plainsong melodies of the well-known Mass XI (*Orbis factor*). He has given the author the following notes upon this setting and its proper rendition. It will be evident from these notes that plainsong, particularly in its fuller forms, is a unique art form with sutble refinement, mastery of which requires special training, unending study, and constant attention to detail.

The notation is "natural," viz., on a key of C basis. This in no way determines the pitch at which the music is to be sung but merely easily and clearly sets forth the pattern of tones and half-tones involved. This obviates the key signature difficulty. The melodies should be sung at the level comfortable to the singers involved.

As for rhythm and time, eighth notes are the basis of the notation and of time-counting. Quarter notes are then cadence points. When properly sung, the chant exhibits a regular counting flow, which is kept from being mechanical by the varying weights of the notes and syllables, but always the eighths flow evenly. The space sideways of notes is constant though the weight varies.

The time group of a series of single eighth notes is indicated by a small line above or below the note. This is named the "ictus point." At that spot a one count starts. The ictus and its attendant one count have nothing whatever to do with accent or stress. Groups of notes under one tail or flag, and quarter notes as well, are always subject to one count. The whole of the chant is grouped in twos or threes. There is never a single note. If there seems to be, an eighth rest is understood to go with it, because only groups of twos and threes are able to produce a rhythmic flow.

The ictus points are necessary as a means of dividing notes into groups of twos and threes. Word accents have nothing to do with this flow of twos and threes. The light and shade of the word accents is carried on top of this rhythmic flow.

The performance is valid only on the equality of the eighth notes. The stress and lightness with which they are performed will make the correct accommodation to the text. This again has nothing to do with rhythmic flow. Any colloquial word accentuation or undue stress at any point will damage the result.

The usual accentuation of the English text must never interfere with the progress of the eighth notes. The music has its own rhythm, and the text in its own way has its rhythm. They may or may not coincide, but as long as they flow on evenly, the effect is heightened rather than diminished if the rhythm of the music and that of the text do not coincide. Also, the chant takes into account the light and the strong syllable idea of the text. Many times strong syllables are treated casually by the music, while weak syllables are given a series of notes so that they will not drop out of hearing, or be slighted in any way.

The singers should strive to sing the vowel sounds out their full length and let the consonant sounds control the start or stop of that particular vowel. Nowadays it has become popular to turn many consonants into vowel sounds, and this seems to be the basis of popular singing delivery. This is ruinous to the true melodic style of chant singing. This interrupting of the line by vocalized consonants both breaks the melody and adds other rhythms. These remarks are not to be interpreted as a permission to omit consonant sounds; they are extremely important.

The Credo and Gloria are generally to be sung at a faster pace than the Sanctus or Agnus Dei. The Kyrie is generally at a pace that is a mean between the fast and slow movement.

If accompaniment is to be used, the tone chosen should be light and clear. A light pedal bass is effective, but weight here is a detriment. Manual tone should include all the normal harmonics of the eight-foot register.

It is customary to have two voices (cantors) start a phrase, or part of a phrase, of each movement; the choir then joins in.

Chapter 24

CHOIR ADMINISTRATION

Ministers, architects, and congregations seldom appreciate the importance of providing adequate rooms in the church building or the parish house for choir rehearsals, care of the choir library and vestments, et cetera. The result is that many choirs are without any real place of their own. They are frequently crowded into dimly lighted and poorly ventilated quarters which they must share with other organizations. They need a commodious practice room, a good piano, comfortable seating arrangements, and ample closet space.

A good choir library, built up with care over a period of years, is a valuable possession, involving the expenditure of hundreds of dollars. It provides a collection of standard choir music which should be carefully indexed. Each anthem should be purchased in sufficient quantities to allow for expansion of the personnel of the choir over the years. It should be kept in its own folder or heavy envelope and properly labeled and filed. Every copy of every anthem should be marked with breathing marks and other penciled notations representing the choirmaster's decisions as to interpretation and rendition. A librarian should assist him by entering these notations in all new music. The librarian should also care for the collection in general, trace missing pages, repair torn copies, distribute and collect the anthems at rehearsals, and keep a record of copies borrowed for practice at home.

The library may also contain a selection of books covering the general fields of the Liturgy, church music, et cetera. These may be loaned to choir members under proper regulations.

The choir vestments should be placed in the charge of a responsible woman, a member of the congregation. It will be her duty to see that they are properly cared for, cleaned and ironed when necessary, and in the proper order for quick identification by the choir members when they come to vest before the services.

REHEARSALS

Choir rehearsals are important. They afford each choir member the opportunity of contributing his best in preparation for the church services, as well as realizing a measure of self-improvement. The success or failure of a choir may generally be forecast by the attitude of its members toward rehearsals. Social considerations, though sometimes important among maturer groups, are a minor matter here. Everyone should feel that the rehearsals are worth while because of the dignity and responsibility of worship, the satisfaction of contributing one's best to a common cause, and the thought of self-improvement. Rehearsals should be interesting. A capable director will have his music programmed for a month or more in advance. Many anthems will have to be worked on for a much longer time than this before the choir can present them.

Voice production and the securing of good individual and ensemble tone should be a primary consideration. Some excellent directors begin their rehearsals with soft singing of scales and the production of vocal sounds without words. Helpful exercises are given in Dr. F. Melius Christiansen's *School of Choir Singing* (Minneapolis: Augsburg Publishing House, 1916). Other valuable suggestions are to be found in Sydney H. Nicholson's *Quires and Places Where They Sing* (London: Bell, 1932) and in Sir Henry Coward's *Choral Techniques and Interpretation* (New York: H. W. Gray). A good choirmaster will have at his command several types of exercises to meet various problems of voice production, breath control, phrasing, et cetera.

Other very capable musicians doubt the wisdom of spending time and effort on vocal exercises, believing that better results will be attained by careful study of specific situations as they arise, and patient effort to improve tonal quality, smoothness, attack, and release whenever needed. A recent issue of *The Diapason* (August, 1956) carried an interesting discussion of this question. Dr. Seth Bingham of Columbia University contributed an article on "Vocal Exercises for Choristers Can Pay Rich Dividends." On another page of the same issue, Professor Philip Treggor, choral director at the University of Connecticut, takes two lengthy columns to develop this thesis: "I believe it to be quite debatable whether vocal exercises are necessary, or, indeed, contribute any real and lasting good to the singing of choral groups in general." In a later issue of this professional journal for organists, Mr. Harry Wilkinson of Philadelphia writes: "We should be grateful to Mr. Treggor for saying something that has been needed for a long time. With amateur church choirs and other groups, in which the voices are often beyond hope or repair, the time would be better spent on learning the music and applying correct principles of enunciation and vocal production directly thereto as problems arise. The law of diminishing returns sets in quite early, almost immediately, in the case where the choral conductor spends much time on exercises, per se."

Every new anthem or other number should be analyzed, the thought of the text mastered, and the general structure of the composition explained. The work will then be sung through in a preliminary way to give a general impression. The parts should be rehearsed separately, at least sopranos and altos alone, and basses and tenors alone, difficult details being given particular attention. For this the aid of a piano, rather than the organ, will be necessary. The piano is more responsive than the organ, which is mechanically unsuited to the expression of rhythm. Moreover, choirs are generally more sensitive to the pitch of a piano. For these reasons better results in the rougher work of rehearsal are obtained from it than from the organ. This is particularly true in studying soft passages and effects. Accuracy of reading and sureness in pitch will be furthered even more by practicing a great deal without instrumental accompaniment except at the very beginning.

Every anthem should have at least four rehearsals, even when the singers are professionals and learn the notes at home. New cantatas and works of similar scale need proportionately more work, and are best prepared after the heavy Lent and Easter schedule has been completed. They can be repolished before presentation the following season.

Never sing anything publicly which has not been mastered in rehearsal, or at least brought to the point of the choir's best ability. The choirmaster will see that the material chosen is well within those limits, though a constant effort will be made to raise the general level. It is far better to present a simple work well done than to stumble through something too complicated.

A wise choirmaster will have everything prepared so that not a moment's time will be lost in conversation or confusion between numbers. Desultory rehearsal is dreary and ineffective. An able director will accustom his singers to almost instant stopping and starting. Hard and uninterrupted drill of this kind for half an hour may be followed by a brief period of relaxation and another period of intensive work. Sustained concentration is one of the keys to success. One type of interruption, however, should be permitted. Individuals in the choir should be encouraged to ask questions. This is not really an interruption, but part of the work, and the answers sought by one member are frequently valuable to all. Questions should be answered promptly and the rehearsal continued immediately. It is needless to say that remarks among the choir members themselves should not be permitted during any of the working periods.

366

A thorough understanding of the meaning of the text is fundamental to proper vocal expression. The voice should express the thought. If vocal expression is unsatisfactory it may well be that the fault lies in a wrong or inadequate thought as much as in any deficiency of musical attainment. The text lies at the foundation of any musical number. The choirmaster should make the text perfectly clear as the first step in working up every piece.

If the choir members are not receiving private instruction in voice culture and interpretation, something of this sort should form a part of the regular rehearsals. Proper breath control should be taught all singers. This is fundamental to tone production. Breath should be largely controlled by the abdomen and back, which by contracting and expanding fill the lungs. Lung capacity may be developed greatly by daily exercises in deep breathing which expand the lower part of the chest. Proper breath control produces adequate tone with the smallest amount of breath possible passing through the throat, just as a good violinist secures a fine tone by a very small movement of his bow.

Tone production depends largely upon keeping the throat free and loose and upon training the ear to appreciate tonal values. A deaf person cannot produce a pure musical tone, because he is unable to hear it, and thus correct and develop it. Some voices are naturally clear and musical. Others must be cultivated, that is, worked with unceasingly to keep them free from nasal, throaty, or muffled tone. The vowel sounds offer the best exercises. The "ah" sound particularly holds the tongue flat and enables the tone to have a free outlet.

Good enunciation is an art in itself. This involves the combination of full, unimpeded vowel tones with distinct pronunciation of consonants, which are produced by impeding the tone. A clear pronunciation of final consonants is particularly important. A common fault is the tendency to distort the vowel shape upon approaching the final consonant. For example, "great" becomes *grayeet* instead of *gray't;* "my" becomes *m-ah-ee,* with the *ee* prolonged instead of barely touched. It is often well to recite the text of a difficult passage first, and then to sing it. He who cannot recite a phrase properly cannot sing it effectively. Care must be taken not to run words together. In similar manner, individual notes must be attacked directly without sliding from one to the other.

Much of the effectiveness of good choir work results from proper phrasing. As there are phrases in speech, so there are in music. These should be clearly separated from each other by breathing at the end of each phrase, and only there. Usually the phrases in the text and the music coincide, and the breath can be taken at the commas and other punctuation points. In elaborate compositions, however, this does not

367

hold, and there may be several musical phrases within the same textual phrase. The phrasing of a composition should be clearly marked. If this is not already done in the printed copies, breathing marks should be indicated in pencil in the director's copy and entered in the other copies by the librarian and his assistants. Or the director may call, "Breath," at the various points in one of the first readings of the composition, and the singers, always provided with pencils, may indicate the breath marks in their own copies. The best mark is a slur drawn from the beginning of the phrase to the next breathing point. This shows by its length how much breath will be needed, and is thus a more suggestive notation than the check or diagonal line frequently employed. Careful observance of these marked phrases by the entire group results in clean cut expression of text and music. Even in the singing of hymns this principle can be observed. Choirs can be trained not to take a breath at the end of a line of text where the sense carries over to the next line.

Dynamics, that is control of the volume of tone by crescendo, diminuendo, accent, and similar details of expression, may well be practiced by the entire choir. They may either sing in unison or take a chord, and follow the choirmaster's direction so as to secure perfect gradations of tone. This is worth while as an exercise apart from any particular musical example in an anthem or other number.

Ensemble singing is like ensemble playing. Choir members, like the members of an orchestra, must "feel after" the tones of others and unite with them to secure a good effect. The singer who sings independently is the one who ruins the effect. The individual must not be lost, but absorbed, in the group. His strength and quality of tone must contribute to the total effect, but not be individually recognizable.

Unaccompanied singing is one of the best means of developing appreciation of tone, pitch, and balance. Singers long accustomed to this type of singing develop marvelous accuracy, and by long working together secure that bell-like quality which is only found with pure intonation.

Effectiveness and sustained interest in rehearsal will be realized largely in proportion to the intelligence, enthusiasm, imagination, and magnetic leadership displayed by the conductor. He must be more than a good drillmaster. He should be able to light up the text and focus attention upon characteristic musical details, such as melodic forms, rhythm, unusual intervals, modulations, and contrasts by brief and challenging comments.

Power of discernment and capable direction should be accompanied by good discipline. Artistic temperaments are frequently deficient in the ability to hold large groups in order and to command continuous attention and effort. Here again, personality is more important than knowledge. Fairness and firmness will be respected. Tact and a sense of humor will add the remaining essentials.

The first attention at rehearsals should be given to the strictly liturgical music for the following Sunday: the Introit and Gradual for the Service; the Psalmody, Responsory, et cetera, for Vespers. Some of the regular responses (opening Versicles, Kyrie, Gloria) may well be rehearsed occasionally, so as to be held to a point of effective interpretation and not allowed to drag or droop into lifeless routine. Inclusion of the hymns for the following Sunday is also desirable, especially if tunes new to the congregation are on the list.

After this, effort should concentrate upon anthems or other numbers. The wise choirmaster will keep his work progressive, not only in the sense of gradually introducing more difficult numbers for study, but in working toward important objectives over a relatively long period of time. Several anthems may well be under way and the more difficult portions of them rehearsed for weeks before they are used. They will be perfected gradually, and the final result will be better than if hurried preparation is made.

Regularity of attendance is essential. Men are more difficult to hold to regularity of attendance than women. In the case of choirs having very young members, it may be necessary to have a certain number of rules, but the fewer and simpler these are the better. Sometimes it may be necessary to insist that only those who have been to the last rehearsal may sing on any given Sunday, though choir members ought of their own accord to withdraw if they have not been present for the final polishing of the day's music. The best way to guarantee attendance is to make the rehearsals worth while. This, in maturer groups, together with a tradition built upon the basis of broad and fundamental ideas thoroughly understood and accepted by all, should practically eliminate such difficulties as may arise concerning attendance.

CHOIR VESTMENTS

The historic choir vestments are the black cassock and the shortened white surplice, or cotta. Black academic gowns are not ecclesiastical and should be confined to colleges and high schools. Especially when adorned with broad white collars of various shapes, their effect is domestic and secular rather than churchly. Nonliturgical communions without established traditions frequently use academic costumes of various shapes and colors. There is no excuse for these in liturgical churches.

Colored cassocks with elaborate rope cinctures are affected by art choirs with concertistic tendencies. Such artistic costuming belongs to the platform rather than to the chancel. Cassocks of church choirs should always be plain and black.

Stoles belong to the clergy, and whether long or short, should never be used on choir vestments.

The women in the choir should wear black toques or soft velvet caps rather than stiff mortarboards. The latter are objectionable because of academic associations, and the restless motion of their tassels.

Commercial manufacturers, without liturgical or even Christian traditions to guide them, frequently urge the purchase of choir vestments of all sorts. Since the cassock was originally a man's vestment, they offer "Priscilla" types of gowns and other novelties for women. They also offer a variety of red and blue gowns with assorted capes or collars for junior choirs. Secular schools and societies may take their choice of these ever-changing styles. The church, however, should not encourage this commercial trifling, which breeds confusion and suggests the possibility of new styles in choir vestments—and perhaps just as logically in clerical vestments—every few years. No matter what others may do, the historic liturgical churches should use the historic liturgical vestments and nothing else.

To be certain of securing proper styles and good materials it is necessary to purchase choir vestments only from the best church supply houses. One must beware of the products of cheap commercial manufacturers.

OTHER FORMAL DETAILS

Formal vestments necessitate a formal entrance into the church. The group, however, should not keep precise step, swaying like a platoon of soldiers. The artificial and silly "bridal step" is entirely out of place. Each pair should keep step and be in general agreement with the pair ahead. The pairs should keep well apart and be evenly spaced. An arm's length plus twelve inches is about the proper distance. If there is an uneven number at any particular service, a pair of women and a pair of men should always be the last in their respective groups, preceded in each case by a woman or a man walking alone.

Upon festivals and other special occasions the choir may enter the church singing a processional hymn. On ordinary Sundays the choir should enter in quiet dignity without singing or looking about. After reaching its location, it should stand quietly in the stalls until the organist leads into the opening hymn, in which all join. After the Service the choir should retire in the same manner. This procedure is more devotional and impressive for general use than the noisier, showier processional and recessional hymns, which may well be reserved for festivals and special occasions.

The responsibilities of leadership extend beyond the purely musical work of the choir. By attitude and personal demeanor, with entire absence of conversation and restlessness, the members must help establish and maintain a devotional atmosphere throughout the entire Service.

Soloists should never turn to face the congregation, nor should the choir. They should maintain their regular position in the stalls, singing either toward the altar or, to be better heard, straight toward the opposite chancel wall.

As soon as the organist begins to give out the hymn, the choir, if seated, should rise as one person. It will also rise in similar fashion at the very beginning of anthems and other choral numbers. At the end it will remain standing formally without movement of music sheets et cetera until the final chord is played.

In accordance with ancient liturgical usage, the choir may turn and face the altar during the Creed. In some congregations this custom, though with much lighter weight of tradition behind it, is extended to the Gloria Patri.

All choir music for a particular service should be placed in black bound covers of uniform size for use in the stalls. Loose music sheets of varied size, color, and form introduce a disturbing note.

Before the choir enters the church, a Collect or other brief prayer should be used in the choir sacristy or vestibule. After the recessional another Collect or blessing should be used. The following are suggested forms.

Before the Service

O LORD, open thou our lips and let our mouths show forth thy praise: through Jesus Christ thy Son, our Redeemer. Amen.

LET the words of our mouths and the meditations of our hearts be acceptable in thy sight, O Lord, our Strength, and our Redeemer. Amen.

ALMIGHTY GOD, in whose Presence we stand; sanctify our hearts by thy Holy Spirit; open our lips to sing thy praise; and give us grace to worship thee in spirit and in truth; through Jesus Christ, our Lord. Amen.

After the Service

DISMISS us now, O Lord, with thy blessing, and accompany us ever with thy grace, that we may henceforth live in peace, love and holiness; through Jesus Christ, our Lord. Amen.

GRANT, O God, that what we have said and sung with our lips we may believe in our hearts, and that what we believe in our hearts we may show forth in our lives; through Jesus Christ, our Lord. Amen.

Chapter 25

THE LITURGICAL MOVEMENT

It would be difficult to find a broader term than this to describe the revival of interest in the theory and practice of corporate worship over the past century and a half. Yet, as broad as this phrase is, the full dimensions of the phenomenon are seldom recognized. It cannot be restricted to specific forms and ceremonies. It is not merely a matter of aesthetics. It is something as deep and as broad as Christian history and life.

We give first and particular attention to the broad liturgical movement which has developed within the Lutheran Church and which has been in part a stimulus for the preparation of this particular volume.

IN THE LUTHERAN CHURCH

The development of the liturgical movement as a quiet, persistent force in American Lutheranism has been treated in chapter 5, at least to the extent of showing its results in the developing Liturgy. At the risk of some repetition, we may say here that American Lutheranism began just before the full tide of Rationalism set in. The earliest groups in this country were thus able to produce the acceptable Muhlenberg German manuscript Liturgy of 1748 and the first printed Liturgy and Hymnal of 1786. Then Rationalism struck. One has but to examine the long-winded, didactic, and anemic forms of the "liturgy" issued by Dr. John A. Quitman in 1814 under authority of the New York Ministerium to see how thoroughly unevangelical and antiliturgical this was. The Liturgy of 1835 was equally poor.

Now, however, two forces intervened. One was the reawakened interest in the Lutheran Confessions. The other was the infant liturgical movement. Twenty years later, in 1855, a partial recovery of responsive services was effected. Increasing use of English, and the influence of English-speaking scholars, produced the *Church Book* of the General

Council in 1868. This revealed full acquaintance with liturgical and hymnological developments in England as well as Germany. An era of wider outlook and broader scholarship had begun.

This flowered into the Common Service of 1888, framed upon the "consensus of the pure Lutheran liturgies of the sixteenth century." A purely literary work, it was, after the manner described in chapter 5, greatly extended in 1918 in the *Common Service Book* of the United Lutheran Church in America.

Meanwhile, other churches—The Joint Synod of Ohio, Augustana, the Norwegian synods, the Danish and Finnish groups, Lutheran Church —Missouri Synod, et cetera—continued to use forms based upon the liturgies of the state churches in Europe from which they had sprung. As they began to hold English services, they made English translations of these same European liturgies. The excellence of the Common Service and the principles of its preparation eventually led to its general introduction among all groups. Each church, however, continued to use its own particular hymnal, musical settings, Occasional Services, et cetera.

The movement for a complete, common *Service Book and Hymnal* got under way at a meeting of the United Lutheran Church in Minneapolis in 1944. Representatives were appointed by all the co-operating churches, and Joint Commissions on the Liturgy and the Hymnal were organized. Earnest labors of more than a decade produced the new *Service Book and Hymnal* whose forms we have been discussing.

The liturgical movement which has helped to produce these books represents in its broader aspects a return to things of universal and permanent value, as well as a desire to share in the cultural developments of the time. Several contributing factors should be noted: the complete Americanization and Anglicization of the Lutheran people in America; their strengthened church consciousness and sense of spiritual unity; the emergence of strong theological and liturgical leadership among the English-speaking groups; the desire for completeness in liturgical, hymnological, and musical forms; and the strong desire for consistency and positive Lutheran character in common forms entirely free from the modifications made by Calvinism and Zwinglianism in the early period of the church's English development. It is important to note that none of the leaders in the liturgical movement in the American church have been mere ceremonialists. Where ceremonialism has appeared at all, this has been an individualistic outcropping by small groups on the fringes of the movement.

The church has been conditioned for this major effort by informative books and articles. This literary output has not been as extensive as similar work in Germany and England, but it has had its own importance. A few authors may well be mentioned.

From the United Lutheran Church: Henry E. Jacobs (*The Lutheran Movement in England*); Edward T. Horn (*Outlines of Liturgics, The Christian Year,* many articles); Paul Z. Strodach (*Oremus, A Manual on Worship, The Collect for the Day, The Church Year*); Luther D. Reed (*The Lutheran Liturgy,* early works with Harry G. Archer—*Psalter and Canticles, Choral Service Book, Season Vespers*—many articles); J. F. Ohl (*The Parish School Hymnal,* articles); Clarence B. Lund (editor *Sursum Corda*).

From the Augustana Church: Conrad Bergendoff (*Olavus Petri and the Ecclesiastical Transformation in Sweden,* articles); E. E. Ryden (*The Story of Our Hymns,* co-editor of the Augustana Hymnal, articles).

From the Danish and Norwegian churches: J. Madsen and J. A. O. Stub, respectively (treatises on vestments, et cetera).

From the Lutheran Church—Missouri Synod: Frederick R. Webber (*Church Symbolism, The Small Church*); W. G. Polack (*Handbook to the Lutheran Hymnal*); Arthur Carl Piepkorn (*Survival of the Historic Vestments,* many articles in *The American Lutheran, Una Sancta*).

Liturgical societies of different kinds stimulated interest. As early as 1900, the Lutheran Liturgical Association of Pittsburgh enrolled members in twenty-two states and four provinces of Canada. Its president, the author of this volume, edited its *Memoirs* in seven small volumes in 1907, and some of its articles are of interest today. The Liturgical Society of St. James was organized in Hoboken, New Jersey, in 1925, by the Rev. Dr. Berthold von Schenk and others. The St. Ambrose Society was organized seven years later in Philadelphia by the Rev. Arthur G. Marcell, Dr. Lloyd M. Wallick, and others. These societies and the somewhat later Liturgical Institute at Valparaiso University, gave special attention to the relationship between doctrine and the liturgy and the "lost ceremonies" of the Lutheran Church, and conducted practical demonstrations of liturgical procedures, plainsong, et cetera, besides holding convocations, retreats, quiet days, and similar affairs. Other leaders in the Missouri Synod are Dr. A. Wismar, Professor Theodore Hoelty-Nickel, and the Rev. Carl Bergen.

The fine work in the field of church music by the St. Olaf Choir under the direction of F. Melius Christiansen, as well as later choral organizations at Gettysburg, Wittenberg, Wagner, Capital University, Augustana, Augsburg, Thiel, Concordia, and other colleges must be mentioned. Also the editorial work in the field of Lutheran church music by Carl F. Pfatteicher, Ulrich S. Leupold, Frederick M. Otto, Walter E. Buszin, et cetera. The recent establishment by the United Lutheran Church of a Department of Worship and of a Department of Architecture, each with a full-time director and the opening of a School of

Church Music at Wittenberg College promise good things for the future.

Increased attention is being given to liturgics and church art in our seminaries, though the importance of this is not yet fully realized. Worship is the stepchild in most theological seminary curricula, receiving less consideration than the other two great activities of the church—missions and education. These subjects generally have departmental status, which they deserve. Worship, in its larger aspects of Liturgy, architecture, music, hymnology, and art, is also a permanent and very important institution and activity of the church. Expenditures on worship, in terms of time, effort, and money, probably exceed similar expenditures of missions and education combined. Its topics, however, if they are discussed at all, generally receive sketchy treatment from different instructors, and worship as a whole is not given the broad scientific treatment it deserves. The Lutheran Liturgy is one of the three great liturgies of the Western church. This fact, and its significance, seem at times to be better appreciated by others than by ourselves. An Episcopalian said, "The Lutheran Church has as rich a liturgical heritage as any branch of the Catholic Church, and to many of us it may seem to have an ever richer one because of its purity." [1]

From every point of view—historical, theological, and practical—the subject deserves departmental status. The activities of such a department should reach far beyond the classroom to include organization of daily services of dignity, reverence, and beauty in the seminary itself, practical training of students in the conduct of all services, as well as stimulating the writing of books and articles. The Lutheran Theological Seminary at Philadelphia is to be noted as the one institution which has established, and maintained for more than forty years, such a full department of worship.

Among other things, the liturgical movement seeks to restore the historic Lutheran equation of Word and sacraments as "marks of the church." Higher appreciation of Holy Communion and more frequent opportunities for celebration and reception are urged. Particular issues are seen in their relation to the social and cultural problems of our time, and the church is encouraged to adapt its ministry and extend its service to meet changing conditions in our modern world. This involves adaptations in normal parish life, and also the meeting of special situations in colleges, seminaries, social missions, hospitals, military installations, and institutions of various kinds.

Modern liturgical students are exploring vestments, ceremonial, and other matters historically associated with sixteenth century Lutheran

[1] E. Sinclair Hertell, in an article in *The Living Church* (July 7, 1934).

worship in Scandinavia and parts of Germany where the church had a normal development free from Calvinistic and Zwinglian influences. Those interested believe that in this, and in advanced liturgical practice in general, the church's confessional position accords them a freedom equal to that enjoyed by others who are ignorant of, or indifferent to, the church's historic liturgical life.

As with any movement, there are some within this one who, through ignorance or impatience, do more harm than good. The good name of groups of honestly interested men has been ruined more than once by the excesses of a single individual. Yet the constructive and unifying power of the liturgical movement cannot be denied.

Thus, perhaps more than any other single factor, the movement has repaired the appalling damage inflicted by Pietism, Rationalism, and the cultural deficiencies of an immigrant church; has helped in recent years to keep intelligent and sensitive people within the Lutheran Church; and has made it possible to attract and hold similar groups from other sources. The promise of still greater influence is one of its great assets.

THE PERSPECTIVE OF HISTORY

The liturgical movement in the Lutheran Church in America is a blood relative of the liturgical revival which began with Lutheranism in Europe in the sixteenth century and which developed a spirit at once critical and constructive. The Reformers who restated the doctrine of the church were equally concerned with its worship. They participated in the preparation of official national, provincial, and local Church Orders many years before the reform movement in the Church of England produced the *Book of Common Prayer* of 1549. The movement on the Continent was characterized by a freedom and flexibility which led to the production of a large number of liturgies of local or provincial character. Strong historical consciousness and inner doctrinal unity, however, secured a harmonious development except where Zwinglianism and Calvinism were powerful. Rich forms and usages from the past, if evangelical, were retained. Important new features were created. Tremendous activity in hymnody and church music also characterized this early revival.

Luther himself sparked the activity. In 1523 he published his *Formula Missae,* and in 1526 his *German Mass.* The latter stressed the importance of the sermon and opened an era in provisions for the use of German hymns. He also wrote many Collects and prayers, composed thirty-eight hymns, revised the Litany and the Orders of Baptism, Marriage, Ordination, et cetera. His translation of the Bible must also be thought of as related to his other liturgical reforms.

Luther's close colleagues and associates were similarly engaged. Melanchthon, Bugenhagen, Jonas, Brenz, Osiander, Bucer, Cruciger, and others helped commissions of theologians and jurists prepare many of the one hundred and thirty-five Church Orders which appeared in Germany before 1555. Great collections of choir music (Cantionales) were edited and issued by Spangenberg, Lossius, Eler, Keuchenthal, Ludecus, and other musicians. Luther himself requested Spangenberg to prepare his superb folio volume of seven hundred and fifty pages. Melanchthon wrote the preface to the eight hundred page *Psalmodia* of Lucas Lossius. Other musicians composed hundreds of chorales and choral works. Heinrich Schütz led the movement which produced a wealth of church cantatas and oratorios and culminated in the mighty achievements of Johann Sebastian Bach.

Only brief reference can be made to parallel developments in Scandinavia. Bugenhagen prepared the Church Order of Denmark in 1537. Olavus Petri and his younger brother Laurentius were the leaders of liturgical reform in Sweden. Bishop Wordsworth refers to the latter as "the Cranmer of Sweden as Olavus was its Luther." Olavus translated the New Testament into Swedish in 1526, and followed it with his important *Manual* in 1529 and his *Swedish Mass* in 1531. This followed the general outline of Luther's Latin Service, but contained original material of penitential character. The bishops generally supported the national movement and accepted the Reformation. They retained the historic episcopate and many features of pre-Reformation worship, including vestments. In contrast to Germany, Zwinglianism and Calvinism exerted little influence.

The Thirty Years' War (1618-48), with its destructions, the exile and murder of ministers, its famine and disease, was the first important destroyer of church life and worship in Germany. After the restoration of peace, Orthodoxy gave a mechanical and legalistic character to worship. The spirit and life of the Reformation century were not recaptured.

Pietism was a reaction which emphasized "vital godliness," personal morality, and a subjective view of religious experience. Its substitution of private devotional assemblies for regular church services weakened the church and led to a multiplication of sects and religious societies.

Rationalism was a late-born child of the Renaissance. It glorified human nature, denied the necessity of revelation, and asserted the supremacy of reason over faith. Theologically it ran out into Unitarianism. Politically it spawned the French Revolution. The Liturgy, the hymnal, and the Scriptures were mutilated. A flood of private agendas offered sentimental phrases and moralizing soliloquies as a substitute for the historic Liturgy. The fact that the Lutheran Church was transplanted into American soil during this period of desolate spiritual and liturgical poverty in Europe helps to explain a number of phenomena in American Lutheranism which could not otherwise be understood.

A revival in the Lutheran Church began with the tercentenary of the Reformation (1817), thus anticipating by a few years the Oxford Movement in England (1833). Klaus Harms and others lifted their voices in behalf of historic faith and worship. Frederick William III of Prussia led the movement "back to Father Luther," and himself prepared the Liturgy of 1817 (and 1822) for the Garrison Church and the court at Berlin. In Bavaria a revised Liturgy was in use as early as 1823.

The ablest leader in northern Germany was Theodor Kliefoth of Mecklenburg. His *Theorie des Kultus der evangelischen Kirche* (1844) and *Die ursprüngliche Gottesdienst Ordnung* (1847) were works of great erudition. A south German leader of great practical gifts was Wilhelm Loehe. He founded the deaconess motherhouse at Neuendettelsau, Bavaria, and wrote important doctrinal and liturgical works, among others *Drei Bücher von der Kirche* (1845) and *Agende für christliche Gemeinden des lutherischen Bekentnisses* (1844). This *Agende,* brought to America by missionaries trained in his institution at Neuendettelsau, was used in the German Iowa Synod which his students founded, and also strongly influenced the liturgical studies of Drs. C. P. Krauth, H. E. Jacobs, B. M. Schmucker, and others who prepared the *Church Book* of the General Council and also the later Common Service.

Closely following Loehe and Kliefoth were Heinrich Alt, J. W. F. Höfling, H. A. Köstlin, H. A. Daniel, Theodosius Harnack, Philipp Wackernagel, J. W. Lyra, R. von Liliencron, and others, who wrote exhaustively upon the church year, the Liturgy, and Latin and German hymnody. Ludwig Schoeberlein, in his monumental *Schatz des liturgischen Chor- und Gemeindegesangs* (1865-72), explored the musical as well as the liturgical treasures of the sixteenth century. Zahn's six volume *Die Melodien der deutschen evangelischen Kirchenlieder* discussed nearly eight thousand chorale melodies and their variant forms. Bach societies and church music associations were organized everywhere. Revised liturgies and hymnals appeared in the state churches of Saxony, Bavaria, Hannover, Württemberg, Mecklenburg, et cetera, the sumptuously printed *Cantionale* of this last duchy being a four-volume folio work of great merit.

This liturgical movement of the latter half of the nineteenth century was, of course, influenced by other developments such as the revival of historical research and the new scientific approach to scholarly endeavor. Its significant affiliation, however, was with the Confessional movement which swept through the entire Lutheran Church at this time. This, in a sense, paralleled developments in England, where the Oxford Movement was definitely related to the broader Romantic movement.

The early twentieth century produced other important writings: Rietschel's *Lehrbuch der Liturgik;* Richter's, and later Sehling's, collections of the Church Orders; studies in Collect literature and the Canon by Althaus and Drews respectively; Lietzmann's critical editions of liturgical texts; Fendt's illuminating explanation of the relationship between the Roman Office books and the Church Orders; and many others. Lietzmann's later material and the important works of Friedrich Heiler and Rudolf Otto must also be mentioned. *Siona* and the *Monatschrift für Gottesdienst und kirchliche Kunst* were influential periodicals which supported the movement from different angles. The Eisenach Conference of the state churches adopted an important series of Lessons, regulations concerning the church building, et cetera.

The past three decades have witnessed efforts to restore worship to a place of central importance in theological thinking. The conviction has deepened that in spite of the earlier labors of Loehe, Kliefoth, Harms, Schoeberlein, and others, the recoveries of worship in the late nineteenth century were partial and confusing, reflecting too closely the diverse character of the church itself under its historic territorial development. Romantic restoration of historic forms has been succeeded by reconsideration of worship itself, with witness recognized as an important factor. Barth, Gogarten, Jeremias, Sasse, and other scholars, like the framers of the *Common Service* in America seventy years ago, have leaped over provincial forms of impoverished centuries to find guidance and inspiration in the doctrinal and liturgical writings of the Reformers and the witness of the Church Orders of the classic period of the sixteenth century. Luther research has reinforced this effort. Nor have they stopped at the sixteenth century. In recent years more and more attention has been turned to the question of worship in the New Testament and the early church. The Brotherhood of St. Michael, particularly, has stressed the point that creative activity in the preparation of new forms appropriate for our day should be encouraged, rather than mere repristination. Complete breviaries of evangelical character by Oskar Johannes Mehl and by Hans Christian Asmussen have enriched the devotional life of the clergy and the laity.

In more practical areas, and involving marked lay activity, youth movements have stressed personal consecration, strict ordering of the spiritual life, and increased corporate devotion and reception of the Sacrament. Among these groups are the Evangelical Brotherhood of St. Michael, the Berneuchener Circle, the High Church Union, and the Alpirsbach Circle. The leadership of Karl Bernhard Ritter and of Bishop Wilhelm Staehlin has been strongly felt, particularly in and through the Brotherhood. Other leaders are Hans Asmussen, Peter Brunner, Joachim Beckmann, Theodor Knolle, and Karl Ferdinand Mueller. The experiences of the Confessional Church during and after the Hitler regime have had something to do with these developments.

After 1945, these studies and efforts resulted in the appearance of new Orders of worship, hymnals, et cetera, of official or semi-official character. A significant feature is the fact that the movement has pushed beyond private publications, and produced authoritative and officially authorized works. The church in Bavaria has published a great Cantionale. Saxony is committed to the ideal of a complete Service with Holy Communion as the normal procedure every Sunday. Rhineland-Westphalia has issued an important Agende of quite progressive type.

A high point of the movement was reached in the establishment of the Lutheran Liturgical Conference of Germany. Under the leadership of Christhard Mahrenholz, the scholars and church administrators who make up this conference hope to reconstruct the historic Liturgy and produce a fully developed common Service for all the Lutheran churches in Germany, and possibly for other German Protestants as well. They seek to restore the full and undivided form of the Holy Communion, the observance of Matins, Vespers, and Compline, the full round of liturgical Lessons, collects, et cetera. Quite as in the case of the Joint Commissions which prepared the new *Service Book* of the Lutheran Church in America, the conference in Germany is giving careful study to the worship services of the early Christian Church.

This special concern of scholars in Germany, and elsewhere, with worship and the Liturgy is an earnest effort to uncover the biblical and theological foundations that underlie historic liturgical forms and to study their relevance for the church today. The author is indebted to his colleague, Professor John H. P. Reumann of the Philadelphia Seminary, for fresh insights into this particular field. Recent scholarship suggests that the New Testament includes more material concerning the worship of the primitive church than has been recognized. Community needs that existed from the very start were met by accepting materials from both Judaism and the pagan world. These were adapted in the spirit of the new faith. In addition new forms were created which, together with the old, served to express the experience of the church in the Resurrection and exaltation of her Lord. Thus many creed-like formulas and statements in the New Testament are now definitely regarded as liturgical fragments.

Perhaps the earliest discussion of liturgical quotations in the New Testament was by John Mason Neale in his *Essays on Liturgiology and Church History,* chapter XV, (London, 1863). The more recent discipline of form criticism (*Formgeschichte*) recognized the role which the primitive Christian community played in transmitting and shaping materials during the period from the Resurrection to the appearance of the letters of St. Paul and the earliest written Gospels. The importance of the subject, and current interest in it, may justify additional references. See Hans Lietzmann, *Messe und Herrenmahl* (Bonn: Marcus, 1926). English translation of this important work has been begun by Dorothea H. C. Reeve under the title *Mass and Lord's Supper* (Leiden, 1953-). See also Joachim Jeremias, *The Eucharistic Words of Jesus* (Oxford: Basil Blackwell and Mott, Ltd., 1955); Oscar Cullmann, *Early Christian Worship,* Studies in Biblical Theology, No. 10 (London: SCM Press, 1953); also his *Earliest Christian Confessions* (London: Lutterworth Press, 1949). For the earliest forms of particular parts of the Liturgy, e.g., of the Kyrie, see Franz Joseph Dölger, *Sol Salutis* (Münster, 1930). For examples of scholarly analysis of particular liturgical fragments in the New Testament see James M. Robinson's article, "A Formal Analysis of Col. 1:15-20," in *Journal of Biblical Literature* (Philadelphia) Vol. LXXVI, Part. IV (December, 1957). Also E. Lohmeyer, *Die Briefe an die Philipper* (Göttingen, 1920), who regards Phil. 2:5-11 as a pre-Pauline "Christ-Psalm," probably originating in the Aramaic-speaking church.

It is generally accepted that theology determines and informs Liturgy. What men in the early church believed about God and Christ they confessed in worship and life. This, in perhaps not quite so direct a fashion, is still the case today. It is not so generally recognized that worship practice over the years colors the theology of the church. In the medieval period particularly, liturgical practices, some of which had come into Christian use from outside sources, reshaped the formal Confessions of the church. In the beginning, however, the experience of the risen Lord overshadowed all else, and theology and worship were both reflections of the living fellowship men enjoyed with God through Christ. The New Testament contains passages which show what men believed about God and the response of their hearts to him in praise and adoration. Belief led to worship and worship forms aided in formulation of later creedal expressions of belief. This set a pattern for all future worship of the church.

In general, we may say that biblical scholars and theologians are rendering a valuable service in their study of historical and theological foundations underlying liturgical forms. Architects of the Liturgy, however, in constructing or reconstructing liturgies, must also recognize, and respect, as Luther did, the "art-principle" of the Liturgy, to use Abbot Herwegen's familiar phrase. Doctrine gives corporate worship a body; history gives it continuity; art gives it wings to soar in the heights. Students particularly interested will find interesting discussions in Liemar Hennig, *Theologie und Liturgie* (Kassel: Johann Stauda Verlag, 1952), in *Leiturgia, Handbuch des evangelischen Gottesdienstes* edited by Karl Ferdinand Mueller and Walter Blankenburg (Kassel: Stauda Verlag, 1952-   ) and in the important study of *Luther on Worship* by Vilmos Vajta.

This work by a Hungarian scholar was written in German (*Die Theologie des Gottesdienstes bei Luther*), published in Sweden in 1952 and is now available in an English translation and condensation by Ulrich S. Leupold under the title *Luther on Worship* (Philadelphia: Muhlenberg Press, 1958). In its English dress the book suffers because of omissions of much important material. The German work is a volume of 375 large pages. This has been compressed into 200 much smaller pages in English.

The book's important constructive contribution is its support and expansion of an opinion originally expressed by Professor Georg Rietschel of Leipsic, namely that Luther regarded worship primarily as an institution of God, and only secondarily as a work of man. As a divine institution worship provides a medium for the use of God's gifts of the Word and the sacraments, gifts which are appropriated by the faith of believers in common acts of praise and thanksgiving. Worship is thus, in Luther's view, strongly sacramental with sacrificial accompaniments. This makes it possible to harmonize the antitheses between pedagogical and representative conceptions of worship frequently ascribed to Luther.

If, however, from a different point of view, we are to regard Vajta's book as an attempt to fit liturgics narrowly into a Procrustean bed of theology, we must demur. Theology as such is but one of many formative factors in the development of worship and the Liturgy. Liturgical communions, especially, submit their worship forms to the final arbitrament of doctrine, but fashion them freely to give full expression to their faith and devotion. These forms soar in poetic flights high above mere dogmatic definition. We recite the creed, but our Te Deum is a song of praise. From this point of view Vajta's work overshoots its mark and makes of Luther a much smaller man than he really was. He was a theologian, though not a particularly systematic one. His ruling thought stressed the greatness and the givenness of the gospel and the central importance of justification by faith. But he also was a poet, a musician, a lover of beauty, a master of language, a scholar who respected the common man and the traditions and limitations of the uneducated. His passion for freedom was as strong as his passion for truth. All of these things reveal themselves at one place or another in his liturgical pronouncements. In the heat of controversy he often ignored consistency and defended extreme positions. It is impossible to bypass these facts in the effort to prove that every single item in Luther's liturgical practices and pronouncements was consistently fashioned and theologically inspired.

DEVELOPMENTS IN SCANDINAVIA

There were revisions in the Liturgy of the Church of Sweden, with recovery of historic features, in 1811, 1894, and 1917. The present Service of 1942 retains the rhetorical Allocution ("Holy, Holy, Holy, Lord God Almighty") of 1811 in abbreviated form, with special Introits for major festivals. Proper Prefaces are reintroduced. The Sanctus is restored to its proper place at the end of the Preface. A brief Eucharistic Prayer, with an Epiclesis, or invocation of the Holy Spirit, is a noteworthy feature. The note of thanksgiving is more definitely expressed than formerly.

The mid-nineteenth century movement in Germany sparked a similar movement in Sweden, with members of the Lund faculty and others exercising leadership. The unity of the Swedish state and of the Swedish Church, in contrast to the territorial developments in Germany, together with the retention of the episcopate, produced certain resemblances to liturgical reform in the Church of England. Bishops Aulen and Rodhe, Gunnar Rosendahl, Quensel, Linderholm, and Archbishop Yngve Brilioth are specially to be noted as leaders. Brilioth's *Eucharistic Faith and Practice, Evangelical and Catholic* is a discriminating and scholarly work which, in translation, has been widely read in other countries.

The Young Church Movement developed the Sigtuna Foundation and other efforts to "bring the church to the people" and to "proclaim the catholicity of the Swedish Church." Greatly increased attention to church music is a marked feature. The Liturgy of 1942 has complete musical settings of objective churchly character, based upon traditional plainsong with melodies drawn from sixteenth century Swedish manuscripts. The Brotherhood of the Apostolic Confession has been organized among the parish clergy.

In Norway, Michael Hertzberg, who declined the bishopric of Stavanger unless his consecration would reintroduce the historic episcopate, published, until his death, the periodical *Pro Ecclesia.* In Denmark there is the monthly *Kirken,* edited by Dr. Scharling, Dean of Riebe, and a university student society known as the Oratorio of the Holy Trinity.

One final observation may be made. In many instances the attitude and activities of Lutheran liturgical scholars in Europe today were anticipated by the framers of the Common Service in America in 1888, and by the Joint Commission which has prepared the new Common Liturgy of 1958 for the church in America. For the architects of the Common Service built their reconstruction of the Liturgy upon thorough study of the Church Orders of the sixteenth century; and the Common Service and the *Common Service Book* first of all Lutheran liturgies restored a complete series of historic Propers, including the Introit and the

Gradual for the Service, and antiphons and Responsories for Matins and Vespers.

Similarly, the Joint Commission on the Common Liturgy of 1958 has anticipated our Lutheran brethren in studying the worship of the early church; in reintroducing a series of Old Testament Lessons to be read before the Epistle; in clarifying the structure of the Liturgy with the Office of Confession as introductory and preparatory; and with the Offertory beginning a new section after the sermon; and with the encouragement of more frequent Communions and the promotion of the ideal that the normal Service on Sundays and festivals includes an opportunity for the reception of the Sacrament. One further accomplishment must be noted, namely, that the American churches have succeeded in fashioning and approving a Eucharistic Prayer of significant proportions and evangelical character, while our churches in Europe are still wrestling with this problem. It is not too important to discover who is first in these matters. The gratifying fact is the common purpose and progress of the church in Europe and America in the liturgical field.

Details of life and work in the Anglican and the Roman communions, and in the Free churches, are not within the particular province of this volume. However, in the interest of a fairly complete review of the liturgical movement as such, we may attempt a very brief sketch of the forms the movement has taken in these churches.

IN THE ANGLICAN COMMUNION

The Anglican communion, including the Protestant Episcopal Church in the United States, lacks the doctrinal definiteness and cohesion of Lutheranism or Calvinism. Because of its emphasis on episcopacy and the use of the Prayer Book, however, it possesses stronger institutional and liturgical unity than either of these groups. Diversity in doctrine, with High and Broad Church distinctions popularly recognized, finds expression in diverse liturgical practice.

Official revisions of the Prayer Book represent a compromise in forms, with common emphasis upon primitive tradition, orders, and sacramental worship. Efforts are made to restore the Sunday Eucharist as the principal parish Service. This Service, either at nine or at eleven o'clock, is often followed by the "parish breakfast," reminiscent of the ancient Agape. Father A. G. Hebert of England is a leading exponent of this idea.

In England the Proposed Book of Common Prayer of 1928 failed by a few votes to gain parliamentary approval. Material from this book, however, is used locally in many places with the sanction of individual bishops. The American book was revised in 1928, and the hymnal in

1940. The *Book of Common Prayer* is used throughout the world, in whole or in part, in more than one hundred and fifty translations.

Changes in the English and in the American books represent two tendencies: desire for liturgical "enrichment," chiefly in the interest of Anglo-Catholic theory and practice; and "Broad Church" desire for greater freedom, flexibility, and simplicity. The American book includes new invitatories, a new Canticle, a table of Psalms, new prayers and thanksgivings, et cetera, with permissions to shorten Morning Prayer and Evening Prayer under certain conditions. Helpful introductions and commentaries on the Prayer Book may be easily obtained. Among them are scholarly works by Walter Lowry, Bishop Parsons and Bayard Jones, Dean William Palmer Ladd, Massey H. Shepherd, Jr., Leonard Ellinwood, Ray F. Brown, and others.

The Oxford Movement restored and revitalized the church as an institution. Its earliest leaders protested against Erastianism or state control of the church. Later they directed their studies into doctrinal and historical fields. Keble and his early associates were not particularly interested in ritualistic practice. John Henry Newman did not even have a cross upon his altar as late as 1845. But their successors eventually restored to the English Church the general type of worship which the Lutheran as well as the Anglican communion had known immediately after the Reformation.

The close relation, through Wordsworth and others, with the broad movement of Romanticism awakened interest in the medieval backgrounds of the Liturgy, hymnody, church music, Gothic architecture, stained glass, wood carving, embroidery, and other arts and crafts. Incredible wealth and endeavor were expended in the restoration of cathedrals, abbeys, and churches; the installation of beautifully designed altars, church furniture, organs, et cetera; the establishment of choirs and choir schools upon solid foundations; and the publication of an extensive literature. All of this exerted an undeniable influence upon all other Christian groups in the English-speaking world. It also exhibited a broader and more intelligent lay interest and activity than was evident in the Lutheran liturgical revival on the Continent in corresponding decades.

IN THE NONLITURGICAL CHURCHES

Protestant communions which until recently gave but scant attention to liturgical worship are now deeply concerned about their lack.

The liturgical movement in these groups is a reaction from the extremes and vagaries of individualism, with its uncertainty and mediocrity, and a recognition that overemphasis upon the sermon has generally left worship itself void and without form. It seeks to recover lost or impaired qualities of dignity, reverence, and beauty, and an "awareness of the presence of God." There is an assertion of refinement and taste, and an appreciation of the service art may render religion. The platform and auditorium type of church building has been superseded by churches of traditional design, with roomy chancels, pulpits on one side, and communion tables, if not actual altars, centrally placed.

More important is the increasing volume of substantial literature on aspects of worship; the adoption, for voluntary use, of officially prepared orders of worship; the introduction of courses in liturgics and hymnology in the curricula of theological seminaries; and the establishment of thoroughly organized schools of church music at Princeton, Union Theological Seminary, Northwestern University, and other institutions.

The Presbyterian Church has revised and reissued the *Book of Common Worship,* originally prepared by Drs. Henry Van Dyke and Louis F. Benson. Its Commission on Worship and Church Music has conducted conferences in many parts of the country. The Methodist Episcopal Church has issued the *Book of Worship,* in which a return has been made to many of the forms used by John Wesley.

Some of the more important works by Free Church authors in America are: *Reality in Worship,* by Willard L. Sperry, late dean of the Harvard Divinity School; *The Quest for Experience in Worship,* by Edwin H. Byington; *The Way of Worship,* by Scott Francis Brenner; *The English Hymn,* by Louis F. Benson; *Art and Religion,* by Von Ogden Vogt; *The Arts and Religion,* edited by Albert E. Bailey; *Music in the History of the Western Church,* by Edward Dickinson; *Music in the Church,* by Peter Christian Lutkin; *Protestant Church Music in America,* by Archibald T. Davison; and the elaborate collection of historic liturgical forms in *The Book of Common Worship,* done by Bishop Wilbur P. Thirkield and Oliver Huckel.

An important agency for promoting and unifying this liturgical effort was the Commission on Worship of the Federal Council of the Churches, which was established in 1932. It consisted of sixty-two members from many different Protestant communions. The Commission published a hymnal, a *Pamphlet Library on Worship,* a study of the Christian year, et cetera. With the aid of members, its executive secretary, the Rev. Deane Edwards, conducted seminars on the subject of worship in many parts of the country.

With the organization of the National Council of Churches in 1950, the work of this commission was continued and extended by the establishment under the council of a Department of Worship and the Arts, with six separate but related commissions on architecture, art, drama, literature, music, and ways of worship. The Rev. Marvin Halverson is executive director of the department, and the commissions are headed by eminent professional authorities whose voluntary contribution of time and effort will certainly produce important results in this wide field.

An unofficial, but nonetheless important, organization is the Hymn Society of America, the Rev. Deane Edwards, president, with members in every state of the Union and eighteen foreign countries. The American Guild of Organists and the Church Architectural Guild are national organizations of professional musicians and architects which work in closest co-operation with the churches.

The Free Churches in Britain are equally active, Nathaniel Micklem, principal of Mansfield College, edited an important work on Christian worship. Dr. William Delbert Maxwell, a leader in the movement, published *An Outline of Christian Worship, John Knox's Genevan Service Book,* and *A History of Worship in the Church of Scotland.* Earlier works were written by G. W. Sprott, T. Leishman, W. McMillan, and J. Kerr. The Church of Scotland's official standard of worship is its *Book of Common Order* of 1940, an admirable work which reveals mastery of liturgical literary form.

In America an early interest expressed itself in the fields of hymnology and church music. Professor Waldo Selden Pratt, in his *Musical Ministries in the Church,* 1901, and Professor Edward Dickinson in his discriminating *Music in the History of the Western Church,* 1902, which we mentioned previously, took high ground at Hartford Theological Seminary and Oberlin College, respectively. Dr. Louis F. Benson of Philadelphia soon after began publication of his important hymnological works. The trumpet blast by Dr. C. E. Clarke, founder of the Christian Endeavor Society, in his article on "The Menace of the Sermon" in the *Yale Review,* 1922, was heard in Free Church communities around the world. His closing paragraph expressed the growing conviction of many: "There is but one way to fill our churches with men and women and to keep them filled. They must be filled with the spirit of worship. 'This is none other than the house of God' must be written over the lintel."

It may be questioned whether a liturgical movement as such can develop strength and character where there is no actual Liturgy. The enterprise, in these communions, lacks the historic and theological foundations which give significance to the movement in the liturgical churches. Without doctrinal definiteness and historical consciousness the movement too often grounds itself on general devotional feeling and builds its superstructure according to individual taste in so-called "worship programs." Use is made of historical material from many sources. These selections, however, almost always lack unity, logical progression, and permanence, being intended usually only for one service quite unrelated to other services. The movement in these areas is at present definitely worshipful. It may lead to results of great and permanent value. If it should become purely psychological, experimental, and programmatic, it will run out in new manifestations of individualism, and will eventually be supplanted by new enthusiasms for something different.

IN THE ROMAN CHURCH

The shock of the Reformation produced a movement within the Roman Church itself, which, as a result of the reforms of the Council of Trent and the establishment of the Congregation of Sacred Rites in 1588, unified and partially purified liturgical rites and ceremonies. This however, was a matter of simplification rather than material revision.

Today there is a widespread effort within the church to have liturgical practices more clearly understood and to encourage lay participation. The Benedictines have been zealous in scholarly research and in maintaining services of liturgical and musical quality. The Jesuits, conscious of the tides of democratic thought sweeping through all peoples, are leading the laity into intelligent and active participation in the services of the church. In this they stress, as never before, the idea that all baptized persons share with the clergy in the Christian priesthood. The basis for this concept they find in the doctrine of the Mystical Body of Christ.

Liturgical retreats have been conducted continuously in many areas, and scholarly liturgical publications have appeared. The Catholic laity, particularly in academic circles, has been drawn into the movement, and the youth in certain countries have been reached to a remarkable degree. Every effort has been made to give concrete expression to the idea of the communion of saints in the congregational celebration of the Mass. Translations and explanations of the Liturgy are everywhere disseminated.

In America the movement has gained considerable momentum. The Pius X Institute of Liturgical Music was established in New York City in 1918. Here, under the direction of Mrs. Justine B. Ward and Mother G. Stevens, thorough courses have been established in the Gregorian chant. The Liturgical Art Society and the quarterly *Liturgical Arts* have enlisted the co-operation of leading scholars, architects, and craftsmen, most of whom vigorously promote the cause of modern art.

St. John's Abbey, the Benedictine community at Collegeville, Minnesota, publishes the excellent monthly, *Worship* (formerly *Orate Fratres*), and also a "Popular Liturgical Library," chiefly pamphlets, but including translations of larger works by German scholars. Other leaders here are Father Gerald Ellard, a Jesuit, professor of liturgical theology at the St. Louis University School of Divinity, and Monsignor Hellriegel, also of St. Louis, whose Holy Cross Parish has been the testing ground for a number of the movement's ideas.

Some churches provide Mass books in Latin and English for worshipers. Among the more popular of these are *The Daily Missal with Vespers for Sundays and Feasts* and the *Saint Andrew Daily Missal* by Dom Gaspar Lefebvre. The people are also encouraged at Low Mass to say the responses in Latin, the location of the Propers being indicated by placards placed near the high altar. Or, as in Corpus Christi Church in New York under Father Ford, they may be taught to say the responses in English, while the celebrant and server use Latin at the altar.

Other features of the current movement in the Roman Church include the holding of liturgical conferences, chief among which is the National Liturgical Week, begun in 1940; the introduction of the "Basilican posture" at the altar; encouragement of the people to have a representative bring bread and wine to the altar at the Offertory; and the reading by the priest of vernacular Epistles and Gospels after the Lessons have been read in Latin. Nor should we forget the publications for choir and organist produced by the publishing houses, e.g., the excellent work being done by the Gregorian Institute of America in Toledo.

But even though much progress has been made, the movement has not taken the American Roman Catholic Church by storm. It has influenced common practices here far less than in Germany, Austria, Holland, and Belgium. In Germany it has reached the educated groups. In Austria the center is at Klosterneuburg, where the late Dr. Pius Parsch was the leading spirit. The late Middle Ages are still the model in France and Italy, and perhaps especially in England, where the liturgical movement has had the least success.

The Missal of Pius V, 1570, was the first attempt to impose an absolutely uniform Liturgy upon the entire church, an attempt stubbornly resisted for centuries, especially in France. Dom Prosper Louis Pascal Guéranger first of all raised his voice in an effort to force the dioceses of France to use the Roman Missal instead of their local liturgies. He became the restorer of Benedictine life and of liturgical unity. With three companions he began a monastic community in an abandoned abbey at Solesmes in 1833. The author of many liturgical and polemical treatises, he is perhaps best known by his *Liturgical Year* and his *Institutions*. His efforts resulted in the general abandonment of local breviaries and missals and a return to the authorized Roman use, all within his lifetime. His community at Solesmes became the center for the study of the Liturgy and its music, and from it powerful influences spread through many lands. Of his successors, Dom André Mocquereau became the greatest modern exponent of the Gregorian chant, and Dom Pothier was appointed head of the papal commission which prepared the official Vatican edition of the chant. Important also in the late nineteenth and early twentieth centuries were Duchesne and Fernand Cabrol, both of whom were connected with Solesmes.

In Germany, Dr. Francis Xavier Haberl founded a famous school for church musicians at Regensberg. In addition to directing this and editing much church music, he became the president of the St. Cecilia Society, which soon had daughter societies in many countries. Other liturgical scholars, Professor Valentin Thalhofer and Dr. Nicholas Gihr, contributed scholarly works, such as the comprehensive *Handbuch der katholischen Liturgik* by Thalhofer and *The Holy Sacrifice of the Mass* by Gihr. The Jesuit, Professor Joseph M. Braun, published a number of authoritative works, among which may be mentioned *Der christliche Altar* and *Die liturgische Gewandung.* Another Jesuit, Professor Joseph A. Jungmann of the University of Innsbruck, is the author of a very important study entitled *Missarum Sollemnia,* first published in Vienna in 1948. This authoritative and comprehensive work has been translated from the second German edition by Francis A. Brunner, and published in two massive volumes by Benziger Brothers (1951) with the title *The Mass of the Roman Rite: Its Origins and Development.*

It was Abbot Illdefons Herwegen (d. 1946) of the Benedictine monastery at Maria Laach, however, who really took the lead in the movement away from the French. In 1918 he began publishing his series of booklets entitled *Ecclesia Orans.* In 1921 he inaugurated the important series of *Jahrbücher für Liturgiewissenschaft.* After that date the writings of Dom Odo Casel (d. 1948), also of Maria Laach, attracted great attention. The parent Benedictine congregation (monastic community) at Beuron, founded 1863, as well as the daughter community at Maria Laach, has cultivated liturgical music along with painting, sculpture, and the plastic arts with remarkable success.

The strength and scope of this movement in the Roman Church is not generally recognized. Its theological foundations are deeply laid. Its belated appreciation of the priesthood of believers gives it popular support. Jesus Christ is the Vine, the Head of the body, the Life of the church. The spirit of Jesus penetrates mystically his body which is the church. The church at worship is Christ communing with the Father. The sacraments are channels through which the fruits of redemption flow into the individual and perfect the soul in the life of grace.

There have been popes, notably Pius X in the early years of this century, who have heartily favored the work of the Liturgical Apostolate, but the conservative attitude of the Congregation of Sacred Rites, which reflects the feeling of many in the hierarchy, holds the movement in check. Pius X, in his encyclical *Motu proprio* of 1903, laid the foundation for thorough reforms in church music. Pius XI encouraged the movement when he established the Feast of the Kingship of Christ in 1925 and said, "It is most necessary that the faithful, not as outsiders, or as mute spectators, but as understanding truly and as penetrated by the beauty of the Liturgy, should so assist at the sacred functions that their voices alternate with those of the priest and the choir." There have been developments during the reign of Pius XII. The continuing efforts to woo the Eastern churches into the Roman fold (*Sempiternus Rex*, 1951) have turned the eyes of the West upon the practices of the Orthodox. The famous *Mystici corporis* (1943) and *Mediator Dei* (1947) have given the Liturgical Apostolate a much freer hand in a number of items, and indicated to its supporters that the See of Peter is behind them. Perhaps most important is the recent change in the Breviary and in the Liturgy of Holy Week. Here is definite evidence that the hierarchy is taking notice of the work which the scholars have done.

Other things go on apace. Mass books and pamphlets are increasing in popularity; vernacular hymn selections and tracts are appearing; cards announcing the pages of the Propers are more frequent; and responsive worship, in Latin or in the vernacular, continues to gain popularity. There have even been occasions when the whole Mass has been said in the vernacular by special permission. The obvious effort is to encourage the laity "not to pray *in* the Mass, but to *pray* the Mass."

Thus the movement in the Roman Church is at once dogmatic and democratic; theological, yet popular. With stronger support from the hierarchy it could become a great force.

Considerable literature has appeared in recent years. The most readily available study—and by a Lutheran author—is the recent *The Liturgical Renaissance in the Roman Catholic Church* by Professor Ernest B. Koenker of Valparaiso University (University of Chicago Press, 1954). A comprehensive, though concise, survey of the movement is given in *Liturgische Erneuerung in aller Welt,* by P. Theodor Bogler, Order of St. Benedict (Maria Laach: Verlag Ars Liturgica, 1950). This work interestingly includes, as an important feature of the movement in the Lutheran Church in America, an early version of the Eucharist Prayer, as printed in *The Lutheran,* July 28, 1948. A good article by Professor Gerald Ellard entitled "The Liturgical Movement in Catholic Circles" is printed in *Religion in Life,* summer number,

1948, p. 370 ff. An important full-scale volume by Professor Ellard is *The Mass in Transition* (Milwaukee, Wisconsin: Bruce Publishing Company, 1956), 387 pp.

So far as the Lutheran Church in America is concerned, we may accept as our own the statement by Evelyn Underhill about the significance of the Oxford Movement in the Church of England. In a paper read before the Newcastle Theological Society in 1933 she wrote:

We may allow that the Oxford Movement has meant for English religion the restoration of two great essentials of religious life. It has given a renewed contact with history and tradition, bringing new access to the common treasury of the Church, and a new appreciation of all we have to learn from those who have gone before. It has revived that rich liturgic and sacramental worship in which, as in some living work of art, the Church's corporate life of adoration and sacrifice is expressed. All this has meant—or rather is meaning, for there is much work yet to be done—a gradual penetration of the Anglican mind by the profound truth that God works through history, and that a great religious tradition gathering the insights and experiences of countless souls is one of the chief instruments through which He feeds and moulds the spirit of man.[2]

Also in 1933, the centenary of the Oxford Movement, this gifted student of worship and the spiritual life wrote in a letter to "F. H.," "If all the Tractarians had imitated Newman's spiritual selfishness, English religion today (unless God had raised up other reformers) would be as dead as mutton." [3]

If the Lutheran Church in America had had no part in the liturgical movement, and if its liturgical and musical practice had remained on the low cultural level of aesthetic inappreciation, naive simplicity, and dreary dullness with strong "foreign flavor" that prevailed generally when Luther Reed entered the ministry, it, too, would now be "as dead as mutton." Education and improved economic conditions have greatly helped our people. But the culture and the refinements that result from education and economic welfare led many to revolt against the crudity and uninformed individualism that then prevailed. This colorless, unhistorical, and unimpressive atmosphere caused thousands of our brightest youth to seek refuge within the sanctuaries of other communions. The liturgical movement, building upon the rich but long-neglected liturgical forms and practices of our own faith, and developing them, has held others within the church. By lifting the cultural and intellectual life of the church to higher levels, the movement has enabled the church to nourish and educate its own children in the beauty of holiness and the joy of common worship. Once upon these higher liturgical, musical,

[2] Margaret Cropper, *Evelyn Underhill* (New York: Harper and Brothers, 1958), p. 156.
[3] *Ibid.*, p. 157.

and cultural levels, and only then, could the Lutheran Church in America successfully appeal to men and women of education and sensitivity in our cities and towns. Now, with vital preaching and teaching of Christian truth, and with the full order and beauty of its liturgical and musical life come to expression in the language of the land—now the church may be expected to command attention and win respect in our contemporary American society and thus fulfil its mission.

As these final lines are written, we note encouraging items in the contemporary scene. The prompt absorption, with generally favorable comment, of a million and a half copies of the new *Service Book and Hymnal* testifies to the interest and the ability of our congregations in all parts of the country. What may prove very significant is the launching in 1958 of The Lutheran Society for Worship, Music and the Arts.

Thus we see that the liturgical movement is something bigger, broader, and deeper than any one of its manifestations. No one group, no one section of the church, no one decade or generation represents it in its fulness. It is something more than the fancy of a few for trivia. It has helped our people understand that the genius of the Lutheran Church requires the Liturgy; that the Lutheran Reformation did not despise or destroy the Liturgy, but purified and preserved it; that it was Zwinglianism and Calvinism and the later forces of Pietism, Rationalism, and Agnostic Rationalism within the Lutheran Church itself, that neglected, mutilated, and destroyed the Liturgy and the liturgical system; that recovery of positive faith and confessional consciousness required the recovery and re-establishment of the Liturgy, and of churchliness in all its forms; and that while doctrine determines the form of the Liturgy, and of corporate worship in general, the Liturgy in turn is the vigilant guardian of the faith, and a very effective teacher of the church's doctrine.

The dimensions of this phenomenon entitle it to be called a movement —something as deep as Christian thought, as lofty as Christian aspiration and revelation. Its principles are more important than its forms. Its foundations are embedded in the Scriptures and the doctrines of the church. The fabric of its edifices, its services and ceremonies, its music and the poetry of its hymnody are fashioned by art and the culture of every age. Its towers and spires pierce the heavens and keep open the channels of the spirit, fostering intercourse between God and man. In every vigorous period of the church's history—especially in the early Christian centuries, the great Gothic era, the Reformation, and the modern development of the past one hundred years—movements such as this have been factors of universal significance. Wherever and whenever found, they have sought to restrain individualism, subjectivism, and emotionalism—the trio nurtured by Pietism and Rationalism—and to lift corporate worship to lofty levels. Of special significance is the fact that the movement most certainly has a future, as well as a present and a past. For this we can be profoundly grateful.

INDEXES

GENERAL INDEX

415

INDEX OF HYMNS AND TUNES

I. FIRST LINES

II. TUNES

III. ORIGINALS OF TRANSLATED HYMNS

426

INDEX OF PROPER NAMES

428

437

Type used in this book
Body, 10 on 12, 9 on 9 and 9 on 10 Times Roman, 8 on 9 Garamond Bold
Display, Times Roman
Paper: Standard White Antique